Governance and Investment of Public Pension Assets

Governance and Investment of Public Pension Assets

Practitioners' Perspectives

Editors

Sudhir Rajkumar
Mark C. Dorfman

THE WORLD BANK
Washington, D.C.

©2011 The International Bank for Reconstruction and Development / The World Bank
1818 H Street NW
Washington DC 20433
Telephone: 202-473-1000
Internet: www.worldbank.org
E-mail: feedback@worldbank.org

ISBN: 978-0-8213-8470-1
e-ISBN: 978-0-8213-8471-8
DOI:10.1596/978-0-8213-8470-1

Library of Congress Cataloging-in-Publication Data
Governance and investment of public pension assets : practitioners' perspectives / Sudhir
Rajkumar and Mark C. Dorfman, editors.
    p. cm.
Includes bibliographical references.
ISBN 978-0-8213-8470-1 (alk. paper) — ISBN 978-0-8213-8471-8

1. Pension trusts. 2. Pension trusts—Investments. 3. Financial crises—21st century.
I. Rajkumar, Sudhir. II. Dorfman, Mark C.
HD7105.4.G68 2011
332.67'254—dc22
                          2010044312

Dollar figures in this book are U.S. dollars unless otherwise specified.

Contents

Part Four: Investment of Public Pension Assets

Figures

Tables

Foreword

The global financial crisis of 2008–09 hit pension funds hard, reducing the value of their assets dramatically. Together with increased fiscal pressures and the longer-term aging trend in populations, it has brought the pension funding challenge to the top of the policy agenda in many countries. Much of the solution to this challenge, of course, lies in addressing the scale and structure of promised benefits and burden sharing among different stakeholders. But governance and investment policy—the subjects covered in this volume—also play a crucial role.

Public pension funds are among the largest pools of assets in many countries, and therefore are an important category of long-term institutional investors. At the same time, investment returns on public pension funds in many countries have been below the inflation rate or lagged growth in per capita income, undermining the financial sustainability of these pension systems. Weak governance, susceptibility to political interference, and a low level of transparency and public accountability to often contribute to this troubling outcome, as does the public sector's unwillingness or inability to invest adequately in the human capital and physical infrastructure essential to achieve adequate risk-adjusted returns.

In an effort to address some of these weaknesses in governance and investment capabilities, and contribute to the World Bank's broader development mission, the World Bank Treasury partners with pension funds and other public sector asset managers in our member countries as they build the capacity to address these issues. These partnerships are grounded in the essential cooperative nature of our institution, and build on the Treasury's 60 years of experience in managing assets in global markets across a broad spectrum of asset classes.

Governance and Investment of Public Pension Assets: Practitioners' Perspectives brings together contributions from more than 30 pension fund practitioners, policy makers, regulators, and experts from around the world. It illuminates key issues related to the governance and investment management of pension funds using real-world examples. The editors designed the volume as an accessible guidebook for senior policy makers seeking practical ways to tackle the issues they face in governance and investment of public pension assets.

I believe this book meets a widely acknowledged need for more practitioner-oriented information on these issues, and should catalyze further work in this important field.

Kenneth G. Lay
Vice President and Treasurer
World Bank

Acknowledgments

This book could not have been possible without the contribution and collaboration of a large group of individuals inside and outside the World Bank. More than 30 practitioners who hold leadership positions in public pension funds, and pension policy making and regulatory agencies in different parts of the world, as well as experts in various global and multilateral organizations, took the time from their busy schedules to contribute papers for this book. Their knowledge and experience in the practical aspects of the governance and investment of public pension assets, coupled with their professional insights, will without a doubt be highly useful for governing board members and other officials of public pension funds, as well as government officials responsible for pension policy and regulation.

We are grateful for the insights offered by Jeffrey Carmichael, Chief Executive Officer of Promontory Financial Group Australasia, and Jai Parihar, retired Chief Investment Officer of Alberta Investment Management Corporation, both of whom provided objective and constructive comments as external reviewers on earlier drafts of the book. Jeffrey and Jai's efforts allowed us to fashion the structure, clarify the content, and improve the overall utility of the book.

Within the World Bank, we are indebted to Kenneth G. Lay, Vice President and Treasurer, and Jennifer Johnson-Calari, Director, Sovereign Investment Partnerships, for their institutional leadership and support for this project. Robert Holzmann, Senior Policy Advisor, supported the global pensions symposium held in Bali, Indonesia, in June 2009, where many of the themes addressed in this book were first discussed, in addition to jointly contributing a paper on risk mitigation in national pension systems.

Dana Vorisek rendered excellent professional editing services, providing much-needed clarity to the body of writing and advising on the organization of the book. Nita Congress provided exceptional design services, and proved adept at copyediting and typesetting and in providing insights on the aesthetics of the book, all under a tight deadline. Tomoko Hirata of the World Bank successfully designed the cover under a rigorous deadline. Our sincere gratitude goes to Dana, Nita, and Tomoko; we were privileged to have them as part of our team.

We would like to express particular thanks to Paola Scalabrin and Mayya Revzina at the World Bank's Office of the Publisher. Paola not only patiently provided expert guidance throughout the process, but also offered invaluable contributions at every stage and helped us bring this project to a satisfying culmination. Mayya guided us through the maze of legal requirements and handled all issues related to the transfer of copyrights.

This book would not have seen the light of day without the outstanding project management leadership provided by Beata D. Debek of the World Bank Treasury. No words can describe the deep appreciation we feel toward Beata, who skillfully managed the myriad interactions with contributors, lawyers, the production team, and the publishers, and who gently reminded us, the editors, of the many deadlines we needed to meet. All of this was done with good humor. In addition, Beata enthusiastically contributed creativity, knowledge, and long hours, to every aspect of this book's conception, editing, and production. Thank you, Beata, for your many contributions!

PART ONE

Summary and Key Messages

Governance: Summary Findings

Investment Management: Key Messages

Governance: Summary Findings

Mark C. Dorfman, Senior Economist, World Bank

The impact of good governance on investment management and performance is immense. Several key factors contribute to good governance within pension funds—appropriate governance structures; well-defined accountabilities, policies, and procedures; and suitable processes for the selection and operation of governing bodies and managing institutions. Not surprisingly, good governance requires leadership by individuals with the expertise, professionalism, and integrity to navigate a fund's direction and withstand pressures from multiple constituencies. In the current context of aging populations in many countries, fiscal burdens on pension funds are increasing. At the same time, the necessity of delivering on pension commitments in contributory schemes means that governance, transparency, and accountability should be of utmost importance to pension fund managers.

In addition to increasing pressure from demographic shifts, the financial crisis of 2008–09 has had serious impacts on public pension funds, intensifying fiscal and management challenges and acting as a catalyst for policy and institutional reforms to support adherence to pension funds' statutory mandates. Not only will policies and institutional reforms adopted in response to the crisis be important for fiscal sustainability, they will also affect the adequacy and affordability of pensions for workers and retirees worldwide.

With these concerns in mind, part three of this book provides useful perspectives from senior managers of public pension funds, international pension authorities, and multilateral institution representatives on the structures, policies, and processes that aim to support good governance. Principally reflecting on the characteristics that have been conducive to good governance, including reform measures undertaken, they also consider policy and investment management measures taken to effectively manage fiscal risks, including those that emerged from the financial crisis.

Governance structures and accountabilities

Governance structures establish the architecture for decision-making processes within pension funds, while the accountabilities of pension funds' governing bodies and management strongly influence the incentives for sound, judicious decision making. The experiences of the New Zealand Superannuation Fund and the Queensland Superannuation Fund illustrate substantial changes and refinements in their governance processes and accountabilities. Similar insights can be drawn from the process of pension governance reform being considered in the Republic of Korea. Although the World Bank Staff Retirement Plan and Trust has not undertaken a similar reform program, its experience illustrates significant delegation of decision-making authority to staff, thereby encouraging ownership, accountability, and role clarity.

As detailed by Tim Mitchell of the New Zealand Superannuation Fund, the Guardians of New Zealand Superannuation have established an appointment process for its governing board, clearly defined the responsibilities and accountabilities of the board, and delineated the difference between the governance responsibilities of its board and the management responsibilities of its executive. The role of the board has evolved, however, as the organization has grown, and board committees have been established and disestablished in response to ongoing assessments of their utility. The Guardians support their vision by integrating key inputs to the governance and management process with a series of activities to produce an output that delivers on their intended outcome to reduce the tax burden on future taxpayers. Finally, the Guardians have sought to achieve a high degree of transparency and accountability through documenting the board's decisions and shifts in investment policies in a series of formal annual reports and on their Web site.

John Carpendale of the Queensland Superannuation Fund (QSuper) discusses how QSuper reformed its governance structure in response to changes in the Australian regulatory environment and investment management governance requirements. The arrangements were modeled on Gordon Clark and Roger Urwin's best-practice exemplar to provide a high level of protection for member interests. Under the revised governance structure, the decision-making authority of the trustee board is now restricted to high-level strategic issues, while the investment committee has been delegated accountability for investment policy setting, policy implementation, and performance monitoring. The internal investment team now has decision-making accountability for asset management and investment operations. External partners have no direct governance accountability and are responsible only for the implementation of some parts of asset management and administration of investments. The reforms within QSuper also set out to change practices and procedures to aid accountability.

The case of the Republic of Korea's National Pension Service (NPS), writes Seuran Lee of the Ministry of Health, Welfare, and Family Affairs, illustrates a deliberate program to establish a stronger governance structure and processes. Reforms proposed in 2009 focus on increasing the expertise and qualification requirements of committee members with the objective of achieving higher investment returns and securing the long-term financial stability of pension assets of NPS (referred to here as "the Fund"). Five principles are incorporated in the proposed reform: expertise, securing the government's role, increased representation of the Fund members, transparency, and decision-making processes independent from political interventions. The reform aims to separate the Fund Management Center from NPS, as the two bodies have different functions and therefore operate differently and require staff with different skills. It would also establish a dotted-line reporting between a slimmed-down National Pension Fund Management Committee—of 7 investment professionals compared with 20 members representing different stakeholders at present—and the Ministry of Health, Welfare, and Family Affairs. The legislation provides for modifications in the selection process and would obligate the Fund Management Committee to comply with the prudent investor principle and to act honestly and in good faith, to not reveal information obtained from the position to others, and for members to inform the minister of their securities ownership within a month after their appointment and to abstain from voting on resolutions or participating in discussions when they have a conflict of interest.

Though the World Bank Staff Retirement Plan and Trust has not engaged in any particular reform of the roles and accountabilities of participants in the investment management process, writes John Gandolfo of the World Bank, the plan's management process represents significant delegation of decision-making authority to staff, which encourages ownership, accountability, and role clarity. Staff develop, recommend, and implement asset allocation, investment management, and other policies for pension assets. The Bank has also designed and implemented an effective governance structure to mitigate potential risks associated with hiring external managers. Periodic, relevant, and reliable reporting is key to the World Bank's pension governance processes. Policies and procedures supporting the World Bank Staff Retirement Plan governance processes include board orientation and education, particularly with respect to specialized investment topics. Strategic decisions of the oversight committee and staff are reported to the board of directors and included in the financial reporting to the plan beneficiaries to ensure transparency. External experts are asked to participate in the process as necessary. Additional steps delineated in the plan document include separation of functions, definition of roles and responsibilities, periodic internal and external audits, and regular ethics and professional development training for staff.

Qualification, selection, and operation of governing bodies

Within a pension fund, the governing body—usually a board of directors or a board of trustees—generally has ultimate responsibility and accountability for carrying out the fund's mandate. The qualifications of governing body members and the processes used to select them work together with operating standards and processes to create incentives for the integrity, efficiency, and effectiveness of the governing body—an essential part of a pension fund's governance structure.

The supervision of pension funds by the Australian Prudential Regulation Authority (APRA), suggests APRA's Ross Jones, provides a useful reference point for regulatory standards governing the qualification, selection, and operation of governing bodies. Under the Australian regulatory model, trustees hold pension fund assets on behalf of fund members according to a specified trust structure and have a legal fiduciary duty to members. Core skills are required of all trustees, and these skills requirements are constantly evolving, especially with changes in the law and changes in investment markets. Operating standards are also important, with trustees required to comply with operating standards in several areas: fitness, propriety, adequacy of resources, outsourcing arrangements, risk management, and capital requirements. While fitness can, to a large extent, be considered on a collective basis, propriety must be met on an individual basis, and a disqualified person may not act as a trustee, investment manager, or custodian of a superannuation entity. Pension fund boards in Australia must have robust conflict of interest policies that, at a minimum, specify the manner in which potential conflicts are identified, assessed, and managed. Each fund must submit to the APRA a risk management plan that deals, at a minimum, with the risks to the investment strategy and financial position of the fund, and any risks associated with outsourcing arrangements.

Jai Parihar of the Alberta Investment Management Corporation (AIMCo), an institutional investment company that manages a significant amount of public pension assets, conveys the details of AIMCo's key principles for the qualification, selection, and operation of its governing body and identifies how these principles are supported through multiple processes and standards. AIMCo's key principles emphasize the importance of a qualified board through the application of suitability standards and establishment of a robust selection and appointment process, effective oversight, qualified professional investment and operations staff, separation of responsibility, and accountability. The key principles by which the suitability of board members are assessed include competence, skills, experience, understanding of the organization, independent thinking, understanding fiduciary responsibility, compatibility, and diversity of background. The selection and appointment process of AIMCo's board requires development of a competency profile matrix which includes, among other things, financial literacy, legal expertise, investment management experience, and public company governance experience. Ongoing education of board members is also an essential part of AIMCo's governance processes. Finally, AIMCo administers a code of conduct that includes parameters concerning conflict of interest.

Operational policies and procedures

Policies and procedures are mechanisms that ensure the proper functioning of a pension fund's governing body, managing institution(s), and any other institutions party to the governance process. Policies and procedures form the means by which incentives for prudent behavior are operationalized and form one of the elements for sound judgment and decision making. This is a complex area analyzed from the perspectives of pension board members, consultants, and regulators.

Anne Maher, formerly of Ireland's Pensions Board, provides the perspective of years of experience as a pension fund executive. She suggests that good governance starts with good legislation and is essential to managing risk, controlling costs, and achieving long-term returns. Key policies and procedures include those that support good governance structures and processes, accountability, transparency, independent oversight, a clear investment policy and strategy, risk identification, controls and monitoring, and a cost control process. A good governance structure has several major characteristics including the appointment of a responsible party, at the individual and collective levels, which in turn must be accountable to another body—ideally, the country's parliament. The responsible party should be comprised of high-caliber individuals who possess an appropriate level of expertise, skills, and professionalism and who have the integrity to remain independent from political pressures. Maher also recommends that sound appointment and removal procedures of the governing body be instituted, and that procedures for conflict identification and management be established. It is also critical that the governance structure and the governing body be subject to regular governance reviews by an external party.

Samuel W. Halpern of Independent Fiduciary Services, drawing upon his experience in advising governing boards and managers of public pension funds, suggests that the key elements that the governing fiduciaries and upper management of a pension fund must address in order to effectively structure and oversee their investment program include essential practices and procedures for good governance, developing a sound asset allocation, monitoring and reporting investment performance, and controlling investment costs. He reviews the importance of (1) identifying and addressing aspects of a pension fund's investment operations, organization and portfolio necessary to control undue risk, undue expense, or inefficiency, and achieve the desired net long-term return; (2) evaluating a pension fund's organization and procedures relative to peers and industry best practices; and (3) finding ways to enhance public trust and confidence in the pension funds system. Finally, he points out that measurement and evaluation of governance rests on the integrity, timeliness, accessibility, and detail of the underlying data. He also suggests that the inventory of critical subjects regarding a pension fund's investment program is extensive and that the governing body is ultimately responsible for assessing and overseeing them all. An expert, objective evaluation of such matters may assist the governing body in fulfilling its fiduciary duty.

Ross Jones of APRA provides a regulatory perspective on operational policies and procedures, risk management, and cost controls. He explains the approach used by APRA to undertake its governance assessment, including the employment of risk-based and outcomes-focused approaches. He suggests that assessing governance risks should focus on (1) the role, responsibilities, composition, and functioning of trustees and subcommittees, including the audit committee, and implementation of appropriate reporting lines; (2) review of risk management standards and risk management plans, including verification of how such standards are embedded in the business, applied, and reviewed; and (3) review of the compliance framework, and other internal or independent functions in place to assess the adequacy of and adherence to operational controls and risk management policies and procedures. Two supervisory tools, the Probability and Impact Rating System (PAIRS) and the Supervisory Oversight and Response System (SOARS), are the centerpieces of APRA's risk-based approach to supervision. They are used together to assess the supervisory capacity of individual entities regulated by APRA.

Managing fiscal pressures in defined-benefit schemes

This section examines different perspectives on how defined-benefit pension schemes can manage potential funding risks with the objective of achieving long-term sustainability. The multicountry perspective of the Organisation for Economic Co-operation and Development (OECD) is examined alongside the individual fund experience of the Ontario Municipal Retirement System (OMERS), and those of Japanese defined-benefit pension funds.

Looking at countries in the OECD, Juan Yermo of the OECD identifies several reforms intended to bring about more sustainable defined-benefit promises in the private sector. He suggests that policy action is needed to make funding regulations more countercyclical and to avoid introducing excessive volatility in pension accounting standards, and that regulators should strengthen governance and risk management requirements, especially in countries where there are clear deficiencies in these areas. Pension plan sponsors and employees should also think about more sustainable and meaningful pension promises via hybrid pension arrangements that provide benefit predictability to plan members and employers while reducing the volatility of contributions and funding requirements. The portability of pensions is also a basic requirement for making hybrid plans attractive to plan members.

Examining the experience of an individual fund, Andrew Fung of OMERS suggests that a complete and sustainable funding framework is needed to withstand the risks of a potential financial crisis while maximizing returns according to an established risk profile. Achievement of such objectives requires full collaboration between the plan sponsors and the administrator and the utilization of three funding levers—contribution rates, benefit levels, and investment strategy. A sound funding framework requires a certain element of defined metrics to trigger actions and avoid behavioral bias, and a consensus on principles that may include benefit security, contribution stability, and intergenerational equity. Such a framework does not replace professional judgment and also needs to reflect the practicalities of administration and communication.

An examination of the experience of Japanese defined-benefit pension funds by Masaharu Usuki of Japan's Government Pension Investment Fund, on the other hand, suggests that the recent global financial crisis offers four lessons related to fiscal pressures: (1) strategic asset allocation—suitably revised whenever asset class parameters change for the pension fund's target investment horizon—and a disciplined rebalancing process are important tools in prudently managing assets within a risk budget framework; (2) liquidity and the benefits of risk diversification both decline in times of market turmoil, reinforcing the importance of conservative, conscious liquidity management at all times; (3) quantitative methodologies, especially ones that depend on the normality of return distribution, need to be tempered with a greater awareness of the potential severity of rare events (or tail risk) as well as measures available to mitigate their impact; and (4) sharing a proper understanding of investment beliefs with stakeholders makes it much easier to formulate and select countermeasures to cope with market turmoil. Even during periods of severe fiscal pressure, Usuki maintains, it is critical for public pension funds to use a consistent strategic asset allocation and to uphold the investment belief that risk taking yields rewards in the long term. It is also important for funds to simultaneously manage short-term and medium-term risks, to apply various quantitative and qualitative analytical methods, and to not limit their analysis of fiscal pressures to a methodology that depends on the variance-covariance matrix derived from the normal distribution assumption of return.

Policy responses to turbulent financial markets

The financial crisis of 2008–09 had significant negative impacts on the financial wealth of pension funds around the world, and its effects will be felt for years to come. On the other hand, the crisis has also provided an important stress test of pension funds' governance structures and processes and has heightened attention to funds' governance frameworks, driving both interim and permanent policy changes.

Robert Holzmann and Richard Hinz of the World Bank apply modeling techniques to explore the magnitude of the effects of the financial crisis on national pension systems and consider some of the policy responses the crisis has elicited. They find that for funded defined-contribution schemes, the primary impact has been on individuals close to retirement age, while for public defined-benefit schemes—most of which are financed on a pay-as-you-go (PAYG) basis—the greatest impact will be on future retirees through changes in the level of benefits they receive. Further projections by Holzmann and Hinz, however, suggest that the long-term impact of the crisis on public PAYG defined-benefit schemes is likely relatively small compared to the challenges presented by population aging. This, it is suggested, can be perceived as strengthening the argument for multipillar pension systems, as the utilization of multiple sources of old-age income support can be more effective in managing exposure to risks.

Juan Yermo of the OECD suggests that the impact of the global financial crisis of 2008–09 on the financial wealth accumulated by pension systems in OECD countries depended largely on the level of equity exposure. Pension funds with a high ratio of equity to total holdings were hit much harder than funds with a low ratio of equity to total holdings. Pension funds' investment responses and policy makers' reactions to the crisis have also depended on the nature of the pension scheme. For defined-benefit plans and other plans that offer return or benefit guarantees, the crisis has had a doubly negative impact in that not only have returns been negative, but in many instances the discount rates used for calculating liabilities for regulatory purposes have fallen. Policy initiatives in response to the financial crisis among PAYG schemes and public pension reserves have included proposals to increase pension age, old-age payments as part of economic stimulus packages, and strengthening of safety nets. In contrast, pension funds are witnessing major policy shifts aimed at strengthening risk management systems and enhancing solvency (in defined-benefit funds) and facilitating adequate investment choices by individuals (in defined-contribution funds). These policy reforms are generally causing a move toward more conservative investment portfolios and leading to increased demand for risk-hedging instruments.

Anne Maher, formerly of Ireland's Pensions Board, traces measures taken by the Irish government to support macroeconomic stability in response to the crisis, finding that they may have come at the expense of the independence of the Irish National Pensions Reserve Fund. Specifically, the government of Ireland amended the governing legislation for the Irish National Pensions Reserve Fund in order to permit "directed investment" aimed at recapitalizing two of Ireland's largest banks. The diversion of investment capital into bank preference shares created a precedent and concern over possible future interventions in the face of other pressing economic circumstances. It is of particular importance to the public pension fund governance agenda because it illustrates that, in the face of a crisis, a previously established independent pension authority and a disciplined investment policy may have to be compromised to satisfy other urgent and pressing economic policy priorities. The issue, which remains open for Irish policy makers, is how to retain the independence and disciplined investment policy of the National Pensions Reserve Fund while at the same time raising the urgent funds needed for macro-economic stability.

In contrast to the case of Ireland, Mercedes Bourquin of the Argentine Ministry of Labor, Employment, and Social Security suggests that the so-called nationalization of the Argentine pension scheme in November 2008 was more a culmination of a gradual series of steps moving away from the privatized scheme than a specific policy reaction to the global financial crisis. Nevertheless, the decline in asset values that came with the crisis resulted in a decrease in pension fund asset values that was immediately transferred to pension benefits and accounts. The government decided to absorb the pension funds (individual savings accounts) to the state PAYG scheme and recognize the acquired rights of affiliates to the individual account pension funds as if they had always been making contributions into the state PAYG scheme. Bourquin points to political motivations behind closing the individual savings accounts scheme that dated back to 2003. By 2008, there was widespread support for the changes that took place.

Arporn Chewakrengkrai of the Government Pension Fund (GPF) of Thailand suggests that the lessons of the 1997 Asian crisis helped prepare the country for the shocks of the 2008 crisis, so that financial institutions did not require recapitalization or nationalization. The strategic response of the GPF to the recent crisis has been to reduce investment in equities both in domestic and global markets, reduce the ratio of corporate bonds and credit in the fixed-income portfolio, postpone investments in certain alternative assets (global private equity and global real estate), allocate new contributions to "highly secure" assets, and establish a new strategic asset allocation with less risky assets. No changes were made to the

GPF's investment risk and return objectives in the face of the crisis. While these responses did not entirely protect the GPF from negative outcomes, they significantly decreased the impact of the crisis.

Investment Management: Key Messages

Sudhir Rajkumar, Head of Pension Advisory, World Bank Treasury

The stock of pension assets, including voluntary pensions, has been estimated to be as much as 50 percent of world gross domestic product (GDP) (Palacios and Pallares-Miralles 2000). A recent report by Towers Watson (2010) estimates that just the world's 300 largest pension funds held assets of $11.3 trillion as of 2009. These numbers are likely to increase in coming years, as demographic trends of an aging population become more pronounced and as more countries choose to partially or fully prefund their liabilities. As a case in point, more than 50 countries have changed from a pay-as-you-go pension system to a partially or fully funded system over the last decade. Pension assets are an important share of the financial system's assets in many countries. The quality of pension asset management therefore has increasing indirect effects on the overall economy, especially when the size of pension assets is large relative to domestic capital markets.

At the same time, research shows that public pension funds are often used to achieve objectives other than providing pensions, are difficult to insulate from political interference, and tend to earn poor rates of return relative to relevant benchmarks. One World Bank study, for example, using surveys of annual pension fund returns across 22 countries over 1960–2000, found that average (unweighted by asset size) real annual returns were *−6.7 percent* (Iglesias and Palacios 2000). Deficiencies in governance structures for asset management and in strategic asset allocation choices were found to be particularly important in explaining the low level of returns. Turbulent financial markets—and recurring market crises—add to this challenge. Towers Watson estimates (2010) find that the assets of the world's 300 largest (and presumably, relatively sophisticated) pension funds declined by 12.6 percent in 2008 and have yet to return to precrisis levels.

The rationale for any pension system's existence is its ability to pool, and thereby diversify, individual investment and longevity risks and to take advantage of the huge economies of scale available in investment management. In this context, how can public pension funds overcome the governance and investment management challenges identified in the above-referenced World Bank study and successfully deliver affordable pensions to their beneficiaries? Publicly managed pension schemes cover approximately 800 million people, or roughly one-third of the world's total labor force, so this is not an inconsequential question.

While part three of the book focuses on the governance of pension assets, part four seeks to provide some insight into these issues by delving into different facets of the investment management process. However, as will quickly become clear to even the casual reader, it is difficult to neatly separate governance and investment management into distinct compartments. Several key messages gleaned from the perspective of practitioners focusing on investment management are discussed below.

The quality of investment outcomes is inextricably linked to and affected by the quality of governance structures

Keith Ambachtsheer of Canada's Rotman International Centre for Pension Management states that clear linkages between mission, governance, management, and results are the hallmarks of excellence in pension fund management. When integrated appropriately, these elements facilitate the conversion of retirement savings into pension payments in an efficient, cost-effective manner. Ambachtsheer also discusses "Integrative Investment Theory," which explicitly broadens traditional investment theory to include agency issues, governance quality, investment beliefs, operational and strategic risk management, and implementation capability as the key drivers of investment outcomes for institutions such as public pension funds.

Masaharu Usuki provides a perspective from the world's largest pension fund—Japan's Government Pension Investment Fund (GPIF)—on how to achieve an appropriate balance between separating the fund's investment policy from political influence while ensuring that it remains consistent with overall pension plan design. Despite significant governance reform in recent years, which made GPIF less vulnerable to criticism during the 2008–09 global financial crisis than it was during the market crisis of 2000–02, Usuki believes there is room for further improvement. The centrality of appropriate and adequate governance structures that accomplish their functions effectively is a continuing theme throughout part four—be it from the perspective of developing the investment policy framework, strategic asset allocation, effective management of internal portfolio managers and external service providers, currency policy, or investment in nontraditional assets.

Investment management costs are as important as investment returns in their effect on the value of pensions

Liew Heng San of Singapore's Central Provident Fund (CPF) states that a 1 percent administrative charge on assets over the course of 40 years could erode returns at a member's retirement age by 25 percent. CPF's annual administrative cost per member in 2008 was $21 (less than 0.05 percent of the average balance in each participant's CPF accounts); the fund's management is still exploring steps to further reduce administrative costs. Lars Rohde of Denmark's ATP (Arbejdmarkedets Tillaegs Pension) makes much the same point: higher annual asset management costs of 0.8 percent over a 40-year period may reduce benefits available to members by almost one-fourth.

There appears to be a growing recognition of this aspect. Jolanta Wysocka of the Mountain Pacific Group highlights a growing trend among large U.S. pension funds toward internal management of assets, driven by a need to reduce costs, among other factors. Ambachtsheer goes even further, stating that funds with low cost structures generally outperform funds with higher cost structures (adjusted for differences in investment policies) and that higher-than-necessary costs are a primary indicator of a shortfall in fund management excellence.

Defining the investment policy framework, and by implication the risk-return profile of the pension fund, is one of the most important functions of the governing board—one that cannot be delegated to staff or external consultants

Roger Urwin of Towers Watson points out that the weakness in the pension system is mostly the result of a misdirected focus in the value chain: too much of a typical governing board's time is spent on individual asset managers, while not enough time is spent on higher-level investment policy issues. Urwin observes that an Internet search for "great investment managers" yields hundreds of results, while "great investment committees" yields only a few. Krishnan Chandrasekhar of the World Bank Treasury refers to a study showing that 90 percent of a pension fund's total risk has historically been attributable to its strategic asset allocation, which is embodied in the investment policy.

Key elements of defining this framework include appropriately articulating the fund objectives, investment horizon, and risk tolerance of the pension fund, writes Chandrasekhar. Samuel W. Halpern of Independent Fiduciary Services in the United States suggests that all pension funds should issue an investment policy statement articulating the views of the governing body on the fund's mission and purpose, investment objectives and investment horizon, risk tolerance, asset allocation policy, and related policies and procedures.

Multiple, conflicting objectives are common to pension funds worldwide but do not preclude the use of a systematic process to develop an optimal investment policy

Sergio B. Arvizu of the United Nations Joint Staff Pension Fund (UNJSPF) outlines how his organization has developed a risk-tolerance framework incorporating quantitative measures and translated them into three risk-tolerance philosophies. This is despite the complex mandate of the UNJSPF, which includes providing pension and other benefits covering investment and longevity risks, cost-of-living adjustments, disability, death, and survivorship in 190 countries, 15 currencies, and with an elective two-track adjustment feature to protect purchasing power in local currencies. An actuarial valuation discipline, a long-term view, a prudent philosophy, and a funded approach since the UNJSPF's inception have resulted in surpluses over the last six consecutive valuations, maintaining the financial viability of the pension system.

Adriaan Ryder of Australia's Queensland Investment Corporation (QIC) states that QIC defines risk not as a statistical measure, but as a failure to meet five (often conflicting) portfolio objectives set by its governing body when formulating its investment policy. Peter Vlaar of the Netherlands' All Pensions Group—the largest pension fund in Europe—details how its governing body makes trade-offs between fulfilling its indexation targets while avoiding binding solvency requirements imposed by regulators, all the time striving to keep the contribution rate low and stable. Finally, Urwin states that best-practice funds reconcile multiple, conflicting objectives by having a clear primary objective and a number of defined secondary objectives that enable all parties to match operational goals with the mission.

Determining the strategic asset allocation embodied in a pension fund's investment policy should explicitly factor in the nature of the fund's liabilities; this can be done in several ways

Arjan Berkelaar of KAUST Investment Management Company (and until recently with the World Bank Treasury) states that experience from the two financial storms of the past decade—the collapse of the technology bubble in 2000–02 and the global financial crisis of 2008–09—supports the use of liability-driven investing (LDI) in an environment where pension liabilities are marked to market. LDI effectively hedges unrewarded risks and provides a framework for taking rewarded risks, in the process targeting the volatility of surplus (or assets minus liabilities) instead of the traditional asset-only volatility. Berkelaar also writes that the use of derivatives (such as interest rate and inflation swaps) for hedging liabilities can increase a pension fund's surplus return, though derivatives also increase exposure to counterparty credit risk and require strong operational capabilities to manage cash collateral.

John Oliphant of South Africa's Government Employees Pension Fund (GEPF), the largest pension fund in Africa, details how GEPF goes about developing an in-depth understanding of its current and long-term pension payment obligations, and sets the cash flows of its liability portfolio as the benchmark for evaluating optimal investment policy. Oliphant states that this LDI approach has worked well for GEPF—even during the 2008–09 crisis—and has ensured that its assets and liabilities move in a synchronized manner in the same direction, contribution rates remain relatively stable, and commitments to its members have been honored by granting inflation-related increases. Rohde shows how Denmark's ATP has been able to target high investment returns within a low risk-tolerance framework by minimizing uncompensated risks through its liability hedging portfolio. Chandrasekhar, Arvizu, Usuki, Vlaar, and Ryder all touch on the theme of explicitly incorporating liabilities into the investment policy process.

An asset-liability approach to strategic asset allocation may, however, increase asset-only volatility even as it reduces the more relevant surplus volatility, as Berkelaar shows. This requires ongoing education of policy makers and targeted communication efforts with key stakeholders so that the focus remains on the correct metrics by which to evaluate a pension fund's performance.

Mean variance optimization used for strategic asset allocation has significant limitations, is extremely sensitive to inputs, and should be tempered by qualitative judgments; use of forward-looking capital market assumptions over the appropriate investment horizon is important

Both Chandrasekhar and Halpern stress the inadequacy of mean variance optimization models. Halpern states that the output of such models should be used by governing bodies as a starting point for evaluating asset allocation policy, not as an endpoint prescription. Chandrasekhar emphasizes that while it is important to analyze historical return data for different asset classes, it is also important not to use such data in a mechanical fashion—rather, they should be used as an input in making informed, forward-looking projections, for which several methodologies are available. Chandrasekhar also shows how the historical returns and volatility of various asset classes look very different over different holding periods, thereby reinforcing the importance of evaluating asset classes over the investment horizon appropriate to a particular pension fund, which in most cases is significantly longer than the typical reporting horizon of one year.

Usuki cautions against the assumption of normal return distributions which underlies traditional quantitative portfolio construction methods and advises the use of several countermeasures available to mitigate the impact of rare but severe events (or tail risk). Rohde advocates buying insurance against extreme market events; however, this insurance needs to be purchased when it is inexpensive—that is, when markets are calm.

Defined-contribution pension schemes present specific challenges in managing members' investment and longevity risks; several options are available to address these risks effectively

Rohde points out that the move from defined-benefit schemes to pure defined-contribution pension schemes (individual accounts) entails a massive transfer of investment and longevity risks to individuals. If this risk transfer was indeed the objective, Rohde questions whether it could not be achieved quite efficiently by individuals' savings for old age being placed in banks within well-regulated environments, thereby obviating the need for defined-contribution pension schemes altogether. Yvonne Sin of Towers Watson adds that little consideration has been given in this process to individuals' ability to ride out such risks, while Liew highlights a study showing individuals would need to set aside 40–80 percent more assets to address longevity risks in the absence of risk pooling.

Sin suggests that sound investment options for members must take into account more than the relatively widespread linear shift to safer assets (such as bonds) as members age—including factors such as wealth, health, number of dependents, and future earning potential. Augusto Iglesias, Chile's vice minister for social security, adds that members in defined-contribution schemes face risks both at retirement (in schemes featuring mandatory annuitization at retirement) and after retirement, in addition to those incurred during the accumulation phase.

As a result, both Sin and Iglesias advocate the offering of several investment strategies with different asset mixes to individuals with the same investment horizon (the "multifunds" approach prevalent in Latin America and some parts of Europe), in addition to an age-based, automatic allocation strategy. However, as Sin states, in-depth knowledge of member profiles is needed in order to design improved investment choices; this requires strong engagement and ongoing communication with members. Iglesias also suggests that mandatory annuitization at retirement be replaced by a more flexible menu of options (including "programmed withdrawals" and variable timing of annuitization), and that members be allowed to choose among these options and combine them. Iglesias stresses the need for quality regulation and supervision in this context—in particular, the need to mitigate retirees' exposure to intermediary solvency risks.

Liew illustrates a different approach taken by Singapore's CPF to mitigate investment and longevity risks, including guaranteed minimum interest rates on members' balances and the ability to participate in a Lifelong Income Scheme for the Elderly (LIFE) to varying extents. Providing an interesting perspective on the debate about allowing investment choices to members versus mandatory default investment options, Liew says that, historically, CPF members exercising their self-investment options would have been better off leaving their assets with CPF. Finally, Rohde points out that ATP's implementation of a hybrid pension model in 2008 ensures security and lifelong stability for individual members without resorting to a low-return, conservative investment strategy. Rohde also suggests that several other hybrid pension models successfully address individuals' exposure to investment and longevity risks.

International investments by pension funds provide significant diversification benefits and help overcome the constraints of small domestic capital markets; overcoming political impediments to diversifying internationally requires a gradual approach developed in tandem with supportive regulators

Tørres Trovik of Norway's Storebrand (until recently with the World Bank Treasury) shows that investing in international equity markets can reduce the risk of a pension fund's overall portfolio; this remains true even as equity returns in different countries have become more correlated in recent years. The benefits from international diversification, however, appear to be more pronounced for pension funds outside the United States, which may be due to the generally higher risk in equity markets that are smaller and less diversified than the U.S. market. Further, the benefits of diversification appear to be exhausted once a portfolio is invested in six or seven equity markets. Wysocka, Iglesias, and Vlaar all agree that investing in foreign markets can mitigate country-specific economic and political risks and improve the risk-return profile of a pension fund's overall portfolio.

Vlaar considers the ability to invest internationally especially important if the domestic economy or capital markets are small relative to a pension fund's size. Oliphant mentions how GEPF owns, on average, 10 percent of issued shares of every publicly traded South African company, constraining it to a passive management strategy. GEPF is not authorized at present to invest internationally, and recognizes that it has a suboptimal portfolio in view of regulatory constraints. One option to address this issue would be to quantify the opportunity costs of these constraints and highlight them to key policy makers, in addition to the gradual approach to liberalization suggested by Iglesias in the following paragraph.

Vlaar suggests that domestic regulators seek to limit international investments in order to sustain development of domestic capital markets; Iglesias points to broader motivations, including the need to finance public deficits, concerns about impact on the domestic currency's value, the existence of currency controls for other investors, political opposition, lack of supervision capacity, and lack of experience with international investing. Iglesias suggests the optimal regulatory approach in such situations may be to develop a gradual strategy to liberalize international investments, authorize transactions in preselected markets, establish rigorous reporting requirements, and coordinate with domestic monetary authorities.

Development of a sound and comprehensive currency hedging policy, explicitly approved by the governing board, is recommended as soon as international investments become a significant proportion of a pension fund's portfolio

Trovik suggests that pension funds should focus on a global hedge ratio for their overall portfolio (domestic and international); separate hedge ratios for individual asset classes should be avoided. Due to some diversification benefits from currencies, a 100 percent hedge ratio is rarely optimal. Using the example of a pension fund whose home currency is the Korean won, Trovik concludes that the optimal hedge ratio is quite low (or even zero) when the allocation to foreign markets is less than 20 percent of the overall portfolio, although he cautions against generalizations, as each case is different. Wysocka, on the other hand, states definitively that in the experience of the Mountain Pacific Group, a formal currency hedging policy becomes necessary only when international equity assets exceed 20 percent of the overall portfolio.

Vlaar, Trovik, and Wysocka agree that developing optimal hedge ratios should take into account the costs and liquidity implications of currency hedging. The cost of currency hedging is generally higher for pension funds whose home currency is pegged or where domestic foreign exchange markets are not well developed. In such cases, broadly diversified exposure to a basket of currencies may be the next-best option. Iglesias points out, however, that in Chile, the market for currency hedging instruments has developed rapidly in response to increasing demand, which may be due, in particular, to the existence of a strong banking sector, a flexible exchange rate system, and open capital markets.

Wysocka states that the considerations that determine a currency hedging policy can differ greatly based on a pension fund's individual circumstances; there is no "right" policy or universally correct answer. Similar to investment policy, development of a currency policy falls squarely within the functions of the governing board or its investment committee. Articulating the goals of currency policy, listing all potential factors that can affect currency policy, and assigning an appropriate weight to each factor may be one way to proceed. There is a need to educate key stakeholders that currency hedging is not speculation; the goal is to reduce preexisting currency risk. An interesting development in recent years has been the exploration of options to hedge both home and foreign currency exposures by pension funds whose home currency is the U.S. dollar, euro, or Japanese yen, with the goal of maintaining the overall purchasing power of their assets.

In-house management of pension assets is usually more cost-effective than external management, but public pension funds must consider the constraints inherent in their public sector status and the governance challenges and other risks that accompany this activity

Wysocka highlights the benefits of in-house management of pension assets, including lower costs, strengthening the capability to effectively monitor external investment managers, and maintaining the confidentiality of major investment decisions. Risks include the difficulty of attracting and retaining appropriate staff in a public sector environment and the vulnerability of investment decisions to political pressures. The ability to apply the same governance rigor to internal portfolio managers as external investment managers in the event of bad performance is also a challenge. Headline risks emanating from one bad but visible investment by a pension fund's internal staff may take up a disproportionate amount of governance focus and time. As a result of these factors, internal investment management typically focuses on relatively low-risk, index, or quasi-index domestic fixed-income and equity strategies.

Ryder approaches this issue from a very different perspective: given the wealth of specialized, accessible investment expertise globally, public pension funds need to justify the development of an internal investment management team. This is particularly true in relation to the dynamic asset allocation strategy followed by QIC, where certain asset classes may be embraced and discarded fairly quickly, creating high transaction costs and necessitating rigorous governance in building, motivating, and dismantling in-house investment teams as needed. Ryder focuses on some alternative asset classes, which remain attractive during all parts of a market cycle, and where there may be a premium attached to maintaining confidentiality, as appropriate for building in-house expertise. The prime motivation in such cases is lower costs.

Investment in alternative asset classes can reduce portfolio risk due to low correlation with traditional investments; given their different characteristics and risks, such investment should be made gradually and within a disciplined evaluation framework as capabilities are built

Jai Parihar of Canada's Alberta Investment Management Corporation states that alternative or nontraditional investments (private equity, real estate, infrastructure, absolute return strategies or hedge funds, commodities, and timber) share some common characteristics: low correlation with traditional asset classes, relative illiquidity, difficulty in determining current market values, limited historical risk and return data, a requirement for more extensive analysis than for traditional asset classes prior to investment decisions, and relatively high transaction costs. Parihar goes on to enumerate the specific characteristics and risks of each of these asset classes, and emphasizes that distinctive management and risk mitigation approaches are thus required in each case.

Ryder states that QIC employs a disciplined framework to evaluate each of these asset classes, analyzing the nature of the risk premiums, including the illiquidity premium. As part of this evaluation, QIC examines the relationship of each asset class to key economic variables, looking for evidence of long-term structural breaks or strategic trends. Challenges involved in this approach include deconstructing these asset classes and their drivers, determining the current level of risk premium, and developing the capacity to select the best managers or funds to obtain the desired exposure.

The importance of proactive communication with key stakeholders (for defined-benefit funds) and strong engagement and ongoing communication with members (for defined-contribution schemes) cannot be overemphasized

The importance of communication with key stakeholders and plan members is a theme that runs through many of the contributions in this book. Multiple investment options targeted to the different circumstances of members of defined-contribution schemes require an in-depth knowledge of member profiles, which does not appear to be currently available. Continuing education of policy makers and a proactive communication strategy with key stakeholders of defined-benefit pension funds has been flagged as an important issue in the context of formulating the investment policy framework (objectives, investment horizon, risk tolerance, and other areas), strategic asset allocation in an asset-liability context, currency hedging decisions and the development of currency policy, and managing headline risks related to many facets of the investment process.

References

Iglesias, A., and R. Palacios. 2000. "Managing Public Pension Reserves Part I: Evidence from the International Experience." Social Protection Discussion Paper Series, Human Development Network. Washington, DC: World Bank.

Palacios, R., and M. Pallares-Miralles. 2000. "International Patterns of Pension Provision." Social Protection Working Paper Series, Human Development Network. Washington, DC: World Bank.

Towers Watson. 2010. "P & I/TW 300 Analysis: Year End 2009." www.towerswatson.com/assets/pdf/2728/PI-TW-300-survey.pdf.

PART TWO

Key Principles of Governance and Investment Management

Managing Public Pension Funds: From Principles to Practices

Lessons for Pension Funds on the Governance of Investments

Managing Public Pension Funds: From Principles to Practices

Keith Ambachtsheer, Director, Rotman International Centre for Pension Management, Canada

Strong, clear linkages between mission, governance, management, and results are the hallmarks of excellence in pension fund management

All pension funds have a mission and a governance structure by which to achieve that mission. In some cases, these missions and governance structures are clear and transparent. In other cases, they are not. An important benefit of clarity and transparency is that the logic and soundness of the governance structure can be readily assessed. Also, the connections between fund governance and how the fund is actually managed become readily apparent. In short, strong, clear linkages between mission, governance, management, and results are the hallmarks of excellence in pension fund management. When integrated appropriately, these elements facilitate the conversion of retirement savings into pension payments in an efficient, cost-effective manner. Effective pension fund management can also contribute to financial assets being priced efficiently in terms of risk and expected return.

How close is the real world of pension fund management to this ideal world of excellence? If there is an "excellence shortfall," why does it exist? And how can it be eliminated?

Higher-than-necessary costs are a primary indicator of a shortfall in fund management excellence

Once the parameters of excellence are established in pension fund management, funds that fall short of excellence may be identified more easily. A primary indicator that an excellence shortfall in fund management exists is that the fund's cost structure is higher than necessary. In his 2008 presidential address to the American Finance Association, Kenneth French pursued this cost question. He estimated the annual investment costs (management fees and trading costs) paid by all investors in U.S. equity markets over 1991–2006 amounted to 77 basis points of their investments, or $115 billion in 2006. Of that $115 billion, French estimated that total costs would have been about $15 billion (10 basis points) if the entire pool had been passively managed, leaving the remaining $100 billion (67 basis points) as the incremental cost of active management to investors in that year.

In 2006, total management and trading costs paid by all investors in U.S. equity markets amounted to 77 basis points, or $115 billion. Of this amount, $100 billion (67 basis points) constituted the incremental cost of active management to investors.

It is likely that price discovery costs are too high in equity and other asset classes

The question French's work allows one to pose is: what value did that incremental $100 billion in active fees and trading costs create for participants in pension, mutual, and hedge funds in 2006? The correct economic answer is "price discovery." In other words, in the absence of active management, stock prices would have no economic basis. Thus, the economics-based question becomes: how much money should be spent on active fees and trading costs in order to maintain "fair value" pricing in U.S. equity markets? And the economics-based answer is: up to the point where an incremental dollar spent does not have a sufficient incremental expected economic payoff.

In this context, how likely is it that $100 billion was the "right" amount to spend in 2006 if the goal is price discovery in the U.S. equity market? In the view of the author, not very likely, as calculations suggest that this goal of price discovery could have been achieved at one-tenth of that cost. In short, the likelihood that price discovery costs are too high in markets for other asset classes in the United States and many other countries indicates that hundreds of billions of dollars are likely drained out of the pockets of investors each year for which there is no economic quid pro quo. In other words, excellence shortfall is likely a serious economic reality.

High turnover of portfolios by investment managers, and plan sponsors who are not acting in the stakeholders' best interest, both contribute to increased management costs in pension funds

At present, the majority of the hundreds of billions of dollars in annual excellence shortfall is likely borne by retail mutual fund investors, as that is where there is the greatest informational asymmetry between buyers and sellers of investment services. Two recent studies, however, indicate that pension fund beneficiaries are not immune from incurring these unnecessary costs, and that there is some amount of dysfunction in the decision-making process within pension funds.

First, IRRC and Mercer (2010) find that most active managers investing pension assets have higher turnover rates in their portfolios than anticipated. When asked why they seemed to be engaged in self-defeating "short-termism," the managers cited volatile markets, adversarial hedge fund trading, mixed signals from clients, and short-term incentive systems. Interestingly, many seemed to recognize the negative consequences of what they were doing but felt they were locked into these value-destroying behavior patterns.

Second, Stewart and others (2009) find that "plan sponsors are not acting in their stakeholders' best interests when they make rebalancing or reallocation decisions concerning plan assets." Investment strategies in which plan sponsors allocate new money tend to underperform after the money is allocated, while strategies in which plan sponsors withdraw money tend to outperform after the money is withdrawn. Stewart and his colleagues estimated that the cost of these faulty rebalancing decisions ran into the hundreds of billions of dollars over five-year periods for the universe of funds they examined.

How should institutions invest?

The important question of how institutions such as public pension funds *should* invest is sidestepped in traditional investment theory, as noted in Ambachtsheer (2005). To derive elegant solutions using traditional theory, "animal spirits," informational asymmetry, agents willing to take advantage of that asymmetry, and complex organizational structure challenges present in the real world were simply assumed away. Thus, pension funds' "rational" investment decisions in traditional investment theory were derived solely from a universe of investment opportunities, their return distributions and covariances, and the degree of investor risk aversion. To transform traditional theory into a broader "Integrative Investment Theory," Ambachtsheer (2005) uses the function

Client/beneficiary value = F{A, G, IB, R, IMPL}, where:

A = *agency considerations*, such as potential misalignment of interests between clients/beneficiaries and the organizations providing investment services. Any such misalignment creates the risk that fund assets will be managed to cater to political interests or the financial bottom lines of service providers. This could hurt the financial interests of clients/beneficiaries.

G = *governance quality considerations* that recognize that bad fund governance is likely to lead to bad management and to bad investment outcomes. As an example, pension funds often have trustee board members who mean well but who are not equipped to deal with the complexities surrounding public pension funds.

IB = investment beliefs, which go beyond just specifying return expectations. The governing boards of pension funds should consider what predictive power specific investment beliefs are likely to have, and how behavioral issues such as short-termism should be addressed. Productive investment beliefs likely focus on acquiring long-horizon cash flows at reasonable prices in both public and private markets, and on nurturing those cash flows to produce sustainable long-term growth.

R = risk management, which should go well beyond specifying return covariances and understanding investor risk aversion. Risk management should also delve deeply into what risk really means, how risk is borne, and how it is best measured. Such thinking leads to understanding risk management as a 360-degree endeavor, encompassing both operational and strategic elements.

IMPL = implementation, which is a real-world issue that cannot be ignored. In practice, decisions involving implementation frequently include whether to outsource investment management services, whether to use derivatives, and whether to base compensation on performance.

Client/Beneficiary Value = F{A, G, IB, R, IMPL}

Empirical research confirms that all five of these considerations can materially affect client/beneficiary value creation—for better or for worse.

Research reveals that good governance and investment beliefs based on observed market behavior are key sources of value added, and economies of scale matter significantly in investment management

Using mutual fund databases and its own pension fund databases, the research firm CEM Benchmarking Inc. confirms that mutual fund investors endure significantly higher agency costs than pension fund beneficiaries. Good governance in pension funds has been shown to be a source of return value added, as have investment beliefs that incorporate realities such as the 10–20-year mood swings in investor mindsets (that is, from pessimism to optimism and back again). On the implementation side, funds with low cost structures generally outperform funds with high cost structures (adjusted for differences in investment policies), and internal management generally outperforms external management (for similar mandates, on a net excess return basis).

Sources of Return Value Added—Key Research Findings

- ◆ Mutual fund investors bear higher agency costs than pension fund beneficiaries.

- ◆ Good governance in pension funds is a source of return value added.

- ◆ Investment beliefs that incorporate the realities of investor behavior add value to pension fund returns.

- ◆ Funds with low cost structures generally outperform funds with higher cost structures (adjusted for differences in investment policies).

- ◆ Internal managers generally outperform external managers for similar mandates.

Implicit in the latter two implementation findings is the fact that economies of scale matter. Fund management and pension administration are both activities that can greatly benefit from scale. Take, for example, the finding from the CEM database that internal management generally outperforms external management. Cost differentials are a major driver here, especially in private market areas such as real estate, infrastructure, and private equity. However, avoiding the heavy external "2 and 20" haircut by going in house is only an option for pension funds that can staff up to place tens of billions of dollars in these market segments. Scale really does matter.

The Ontario Teachers' Pension Plan provides a good example of turning Integrative Investment Theory into practice

It is one thing to design the ideal public pension fund on paper, and quite another to actually create and manage one. Assessing whether actual value creation results match expectations would be best done by comparing a large sample of "ideal" funds to a large sample of "non-ideal" funds over a multidecade evaluation period. The necessary data to perform such a test are decades away, as there are probably only 10–15 funds using the "ideal" design (the Integrative Investment Theory described above), and the number of funds with multidecade performance records using such a design are even fewer.

One fund that has used Integrative Investment Theory over a multidecade period is the Ontario Teachers' Pension Plan (OTPP), which has achieved significant scale since its inception in 1990. OTPP's investment design was set out in a study by the Ontario Government Task Force on the Investment of Public Sector Pension Funds (1987), and the fund's evolution over 20 years recounted by its chief executive officer upon his retirement (Lamoureux 2008). A follow-up article by colleagues Bertram and Zvan (2009) explains how OTPP's incentive compensation scheme evolved over time, and a subsequent presentation by Zvan (2009) sets out the evolution of OTPP's risk management system.

Golden Rules of the Ontario Teachers' Pension Plan

◆ Choose the best board members possible.

◆ Do not engage in politics; the organization's only goal is to deliver good pensions at an affordable price.

◆ Hire the best people possible and agree on clear goals.

◆ Reward those people so that incentives and goals are aligned.

◆ Ensure the organization has the right resources to get the job done.

◆ Run the investment program as a team effort.

◆ Treat plan members and employees the way you would want to be treated.

◆ Give people real responsibilities and don't be afraid to take risks.

◆ Listen to plan members, employees, and the board.

◆ Communicate constantly and clearly.

◆ Never give in to the temptation, as Keynes put it, "to fail conventionally rather than succeed unconventionally."

In terms of investment performance, OTPP has outperformed its policy benchmark portfolio by a highly material 2.2 percent annually over its 20-year history. On the pension administration side, the OTTP's initial Quality Service Index score in 1993 was 8.1 on a 1–10 scale. The score rose steadily through the 1990s, broke through 9.0 in 2002, and has remained well above 9.0 since.

All pension funds have the ability to choose excellence

Opportunities to design a public pension fund from scratch do not arise very frequently. Far more often, pension fund managers inherit existing organizations, each with unique strengths and weaknesses that have accumulated over many years. Yet even in inherited organizations, pension fund leaders have the choice between simply maintaining the status quo or steering the organization toward excellence.

References

Ambachtsheer, K. 2005. "Beyond Portfolio Theory: the Next Frontier." *Financial Analysts Journal* 61 (1): 29–33.

Bertram, R., and B. Zvan. 2009. "Pension Funds and Incentive Compensation: A Story Based on the Ontario Teachers' Experience." *Rotman International Journal of Pension Management* 2 (1): 30–33.

IRRC (Investor Responsibility Research Center Institute) and Mercer. 2010. "Investment Horizons: Do Managers Do What They Say?" New York: IRRC and Mercer.

Lamoureux, C. 2008. "Effective Pension Governance: The Ontario Teachers' Story." *Rotman International Journal of Pension Management* 1 (1): 6–10.

Ontario Government Task Force on the Investment of Public Sector Pension Funds. 1987. "In Whose Interest?" Toronto: Queen's Printer.

Stewart, S. E., J. Neumann, C. Knittel, and J. Heisler. 2009. "Absence of Value: An Analysis of Investment Allocation Decisions by Institutional Plan Sponsors." *Financial Analysts Journal* 65 (6): 34–51.

Zvan, B. 2009. "The Financial Crisis and Pension Fund Management: Lessons Learned and Actions Implied in Risk Management." www.rotman.utoronto. ca/userfiles/departments/icpm/File/October%202009/Webposting%20 PDF/12b_Barbara%20Zvan.pdf.

Lessons for Pension Funds on the Governance of Investments

Roger Urwin, Global Head of Investment Content, Towers Watson

For institutional investors, governance is relatively easy to define but difficult to implement effectively

In institutional investment, "governance" describes the system of decision making and oversight used to invest a fund's assets. Responsibility for governance typically lies with trustees and other fiduciaries, who use such a system in making both high-level decisions (for which they typically take responsibility) and more detailed implementation actions (where delegating to others is more likely to be used and the trustees' role comes down to monitoring those actions). Successful investment governance involves the raw materials available to boards—their time, expertise, and organizational effectiveness—being appropriately applied to produce the desired governance performance.

One recent study suggests that pension funds worldwide have some tough lessons to learn about governance of their assets (Clark and Urwin 2010). The weakness in the pension system, the study finds, is mostly the result of a misdirected focus in the value chain. Specifically, governance of asset owners gets little attention compared to governance of asset managers. An Internet search for "great investment managers," for example, yields hundreds of results, while "great investment committees" yields only a few.

Though governance is typically perceived as a constraint, the Clark and Urwin study finds that it can be developed to meet high performance ambitions. The best-practice research carried out by Clark and Urwin cherry-picked funds from around the world that have built excellent reputations for governance and also delivered strong performance results. The research drew from highly detailed qualitative discussions on how these funds operated, what they considered success, and what made them successful.

In his 2001 book *Good to Great*, Jim Collins compared firms that made a leap from being a good company to a great company, to those that remained just good companies. Collins found that greatness was a matter of "conscious choice and discipline," and his lessons on how companies use governance to move from good to great

Governance—unsurprisingly difficult to change, yet surprisingly influential to results

are relevant for pension funds. According to Collins, one of the characteristics of a great firm is "getting the right people on the bus"—that is, employing the right people in leadership roles. Often, this is exactly the opposite of what happens in board member selection within a pension fund—pension fund board members are rarely chosen with investment skills and experience in mind. Although there were no simple formulas involved in their success, Collins repeatedly found focused, disciplined attendance to progress relative to a clear mission, especially in circumstances in which the measurement of that progress was inexplicit. This is very similar to the Clark and Urwin findings on investment governance.

Five factors are critical to the success of institutional funds

The Clark and Urwin study identifies five best-practice areas of critical importance for institutional funds, namely risk management, time horizon (focus on the long-term time horizon), innovative capabilities, clarity of mission, and effective management of external fund managers and other agents (figure 2.1). It also indicates that funds' success is dependent on their ability to manage these five areas successfully.

◆ *Risk management.* Decisions about how much risk to take on and how to manage that risk are critical to long-term value creation in a pension fund. Effective risk management, though, requires good governance to set strategy and monitor and control progress. And given that the investment world is dynamic and competitive, pension funds' governance resources need to be able to adapt to change to secure a competitive advantage. Best-practice funds have formed a very sophisticated view of the various risks they faced.

◆ *Time horizon.* The differences between short-term and long-term investing are significant. As most institutional funds have a long-term investment mission, their governance challenge is generally to manage according to the long-term plan but be resilient to short-term pressures that build up from time to time. Best-practice funds maintain a balance between the two.

◆ *Innovation capability.* The concept of early mover advantage is well known in the corporate world. In the context of investment markets, the concept involves successfully identifying and accessing markets and asset classes early in an investment cycle, ahead of the crowd. Funds investing in new, not-yet-popular asset classes or those with new strategies or managers, though, face more challenges than more traditional funds, placing significant demands on their governance, not least in terms of peer pressure.

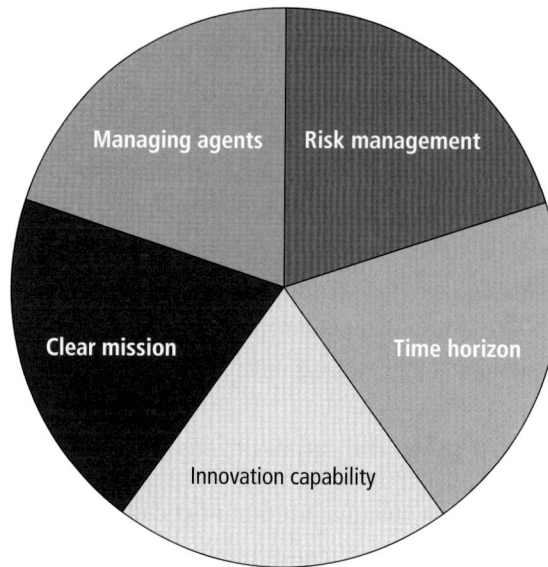

Figure 2.1 **Five Critical Factors of Successful Institutional Funds**

Source: Clark and Urwin 2010.

♦ *Clear mission.* Typically, institutional funds have difficulty with clearly establishing their missions. Because pension funds have a shared purpose of producing value for both members and sponsors, their particular complication in establishing a clear mission arises from their attempt to simultaneously satisfy the needs of those two parties. A clear statement of goals, though, is an important step in building alignment between parties and in identifying an appropriate investment risk profile and investment strategy. Best-practice funds tend to have a clear primary objective and a number of defined secondary objectives that enable all parties to match operational goals with the mission.

♦ *Managing agents.* Generally, pension funds do not have the resources to manage all of their activities in house, and consequently employ external agents in advisory and delegated roles. In turn, this outsourcing exposes funds to the risk that the goals of the agents do not align with those of the fund. Governance is critical in monitoring and controlling such misalignments, especially when pension funds maintain a large number of external agents. Best-practice funds are expert in managing these agents and building good alignment.

Even funds with exceptionally strong governance capabilities find it difficult to overcome certain constraints, particularly inherited regulations or systems of control and competing claims of multiple stakeholders. In addition, research shows that the industry is unprepared to consider in-house resources as anything other than highly visible costs, whereas external spending on managers and transaction costs tends to be seen as performance benefits (Clark and Urwin 2010). This has always seemed an extreme case of tortured logic.

The central goal of a 2008 Clark and Urwin study was to isolate 12 best-practice factors that are indicative of future success in meeting institutional goals (table 2.1). Six of these factors (called "core attributes") are considered within the reach of most institutional funds: mission clarity, effective use of time, investment committee leadership, strong beliefs, risk budgeting framework, and a manager lineup fit for the fund's purpose. The six other factors (called "exceptional attributes") are not easy for most funds to achieve: a highly competent investment executive, high-level board competencies, supportive compensation, real-time decision making, ability to exploit competitive advantage, and learning organization.

In terms of structure, leading funds tend to split key functions between a board, which governs, and an executive, who implements and manages. The board also appoints and supervises the chief investment officer (CIO). In most funds, the CIO tends to have a very high degree of investment expertise and be supported by strong researchers. In terms of processes, leading funds are extremely skilled at maximizing any sustainable comparative advantage they have over their competitors, and they tend to have impressively efficient decision-making structures.

Effective funds define governance as much more than simply "doing things right"

An important point addressed in Clark and Urwin (2010) is that effective funds define governance as much more than simply "doing things right." Rather, such funds view governance as doing the right things to optimize the trade-off between risk and reward, to maximize performance within a risk budget, and to create significant value for all stakeholders. These funds operate in a culture of controlled risk taking, where all team members—board and executives—share responsibility for dealing with risk intelligently.

Effective funds perceive **governance** as doing the right things to
◆ optimize the risk-reward trade-off,
◆ maximize performance within a risk budget,
◆ create significant value for all stakeholders.

Table 2.1 **Governance Success Factors**

	Factor	Description
Core input factor	Mission clarity	Clarity of the mission and commitment of the stakeholders to the mission statement
	Effective focusing of time	Resourcing each element in the investment process based on impact and required capabilities
	Leadership	Leadership, evident at the board/investment committee level, with the key role that of the investment committee chairman
	Strong beliefs	Strong investment beliefs commanding fund-wide support that align with goals and inform all investment decision making
	Risk budget framework	Frame the investment process by reference to a risk budget aligned to goals and incorporating an accurate view of alpha and beta
	Fit-for-purpose managers	Effective use of external managers, governed by clear mandates, aligned to goals, and selected on fit-for-purpose criteria
Exceptional input factor	Investment executive	Use of a highly investment-competent investment function with clear responsibilities and accountabilities to the investment committee
	Board competencies	Selection to the board and senior staff guided by numeric skills, capacity for logical thinking, ability to think about risk
	Supportive compensation	Effective compensation practices used to build team strength and align actions to the mission; different strategies according to fund context
	Competitive positioning	Frame the investment philosophy and process by reference to the institution's comparative advantages and disadvantages
	Real-time decisions	Utilize decision-making systems that function in real time, not calendar time
	Learning organization	Work toward a learning culture that encourages change and challenges commonplace assumptions of the industry
Output factor	Investment disclosures	Transparency and effective disclosure of investment philosophy, processes, strategy characteristics, and manager line-up
	Government disclosures	Transparency and effective disclosure of governance arrangements including structure and resources and policies
	Stakeholder accountability	Record of effective liaison with stakeholders that demonstrates accountability and clarity of priorities

Source: Clark and Urwin 2007.

The Clark and Urwin research also reveals the contrast between the seeming simplicity of the asset owner's business—long-term investment—and the complexity of the problems facing funds. Great funds are able to recognize difficult issues such as the following:

◆ Who, exactly, are stakeholders and what are their expectations?

◆ How should risk be viewed?

◆ How should the fund deal with uncertainty?

◆ How should the fund respond to agency issues?

Beyond being able to recognize these issues, the best funds are able to respond to them, in part by ensuring that the institution has appropriate talent in the team and on the board, and in part by constantly debating how to respond to these questions.

Responses to all of these issues call for adaptive skills and leadership. For best-practice funds, especially, there is evidence of strong leadership. A solid grasp of the wider context of fund circumstances, mission, and risk are critical for leaders, and board chairs are key to creating a strong risk management framework by shaping individual predispositions into collective belief systems. Additionally, strong leaders can marshal the different personal styles in board and organization, mediating among various approaches. Finally, clear and effective interaction among a fund's chief investment officer, chief executive officer, and the board, where the three act as counter-balances to one another, is particularly important.

Challenges for Pension Fund Leadership

◆ Increasing complexity in the markets and in the structure of investment vehicles

◆ A short supply of strong leaders in the funds industry

◆ A need for long tenure on boards in order to secure better organizational "memory" and commit to long-term horizons

---

The global financial crisis severely challenged pension funds' governance abilities in three areas

As demonstrated during the global financial crisis of 2008–09, institutional investors do not yet have the adaptability required to deal effectively with complex, fast-changing markets. Funds' most evident governance limitations during the crisis were in three areas:

◆ The ability of their boards to rapidly devote attention to crisis-related problems and to mobilize additional resources to solve them was insufficient. A simple test of pension fund reaction is to examine how many times a board met during a period of financial market distress.

◆ Funds' risk management abilities, from both quantitative and qualitative perspectives, were not up to the challenge of reacting to rapidly changing conditions during the crisis. Funds need to think of risk as dynamically variable rather than an orderly distribution characterized by a constant statistical measure.

◆ The investment belief structures of funds did not keep pace with the complexity of the financial crisis. Developing the appropriate foundations for these investment beliefs begins with assertions about critical aspects of the investment world such as the main drivers of risks, returns, and their relationship. Successful funds take the time to identify or clarify their stance in light of new evidence.

In stressed conditions, boards must remain above the noise and minutiae of issues. Though the temptation is to confuse urgent issues with important issues, time-challenged boards can alleviate this problem by developing dashboards to flag and prioritize issues requiring decisions and action. Despite the fact that these improvements are tremendously influential to results, it is quite difficult to change governance processes.

Sustainability of pension funds depends on more than just governance

Beyond good governance, pension funds can do much more toward ensuring sustainability, beginning with examining how successive generations of older beneficiaries who are no longer working will be affected by the pension environment. This "retirement sustainability" revolves around achieving retirement goals today without compromising the ability to do so tomorrow.

In the current environment of an aging population, retirement sustainability requires financing a pensioner population growing at 4–5 percent annually from the three pension pillars in which funded pensions are critical, given the slowing growth of young workers relative to the older dependents.

The contribution of workplace pensions to retirement sustainability is a function of pension design, contributions, retirement age, longevity, investment design, and execution in delivering consumption smoothing, insurance, income redistribution, and poverty relief—the traditional pension goals.

The most critical aspect of making this transformation efficient is exposing pension funds to an optimal amount of risk related to their ability to manage risk outcomes. This means finding a balance between safe, risk-free instruments and risk-taking investments, in particular locating the "sweet spot" at which risk produces a higher return stream without producing an inappropriate dispersion of outcomes.

A **sustainable retirement system** needs

◆ sufficient savings to achieve adequate retirement income given longevity trends,

◆ fair pensions deals and delivery that preserve intergenerational equity and incorporate the best features of both defined-benefit and defined-contribution plans,

◆ sustainable growth of assets given the current and future state of financial markets.

There are several possible sources of higher returns from risk taking. For one, there are macro-investment themes connected with emerging wealth and shifting long-term global macroeconomic trends; it is clear that direct investment in developing countries is potentially attractive. It is also possible that developing countries such as China and India will be buying the assets of retirees in developed countries, thus supporting the exit strategies of funds that would otherwise face an imbalanced world in which dis-savers would be stuck with their assets.

Pension funds can also seek sustainability via their investee companies. First, they can avoid companies that lack a sustainable business strategy or companies that seek short-term gains over long-term viability. Second, funds can avoid companies that seek profits without regard to externalities. And third, funds can engage with investee companies more productively.

The sustainable investing agenda includes the growing opportunities that exist in infrastructure and sustainable technology. Sustainable investing and its cousin, responsible investing, are often overlapped with the environmental, social, and governance influences on companies. In this context, it is the environmental considerations—such as companies' improvements in their carbon credits or taking advantage of specialized opportunities in alternative energy, energy efficiency, water, waste, and environmental support services—that matter the most.

Institutional investors need to play a bigger part in meeting sustainability challenges, and will need to strengthen their governance to do so. In this regard, it is important to recognize that pension funds are part of an interconnected system that includes governments, companies, and workers; all of these groups are critical to the success of the system. While there have been limited moves to date from any of these groups toward a more sustainable investing model, the pace of such change is expected to pick up considerably in the coming months and years.

It is clear that for many funds, the "governance gap"—insufficient governance for the complexity of the investment strategy pursued—is widening because a lack of focus on the core governance success factors (table 2.1) coincides with greater complexity of investment opportunities. The big performance advantage from strong governance, however, should be the motivator for investors to emphasize governance more than they currently do.

References

Clark, G. L., and R. Urwin. 2007. "Best-Practice Investment Management: Lessons for Asset Owners from the Oxford–Watson Wyatt Project on Governance." Cambridge, MA: Watson Wyatt. http://ssrn.com/abstract=1019212.

———. 2008a. "Best-Practice Investment Management." *Journal of Asset Management* 9 (1): 2–21.

———. 2008b. "Making Pension Boards Work: The Critical Role of Leadership." *Rotman Journal of International Pension Management* 1: 38–45.

———. 2010. "Innovative Models of Pension Fund Governance in the Context of the Global Financial Crisis." *Pensions: An International Journal* 15 (1): 62–77.

Collins, James C. 2001. *Good to Great: Why Some Companies Make the Leap…and Others Don't.* New York: Harper-Collins.

1. Governance Structures and Accountabilities

◆ Governance Process of the New Zealand Superannuation Fund

◆ Reforming Governance Structure and Accountabilities: The Experience of QSuper

◆ Governance Reform Proposals for the Republic of Korea's National Pension Service

◆ Governance of the World Bank Staff Retirement Plan and Trust

Governance Process of the New Zealand Superannuation Fund

Tim Mitchell, General Manager, Corporate Strategy, New Zealand Superannuation Fund

The Guardians of New Zealand Superannuation have established a detailed governance process supportive of its core competencies, values, endowments, and investment philosophy in managing the New Zealand Superannuation Fund. The role of the board of the Guardians has evolved as the organization has grown and board committees have been established and disestablished in response to ongoing assessments of their utility. At the same time, a series of established beliefs related to governance and investment objectives, asset allocation, asset class strategy and portfolio structure, manager and investment selection, and execution help cement ownership of decisions. Finally, the Guardians' high degree of transparency provides public accountability for its board's decisions.

The statute that established the New Zealand Superannuation Fund also established governance parameters

The New Zealand Superannuation Fund (the Fund) was established under a 2001 law passed in response to the challenges posed by New Zealand's aging population. The aim of the Fund is to smooth the tax burden of pension financing between generations by increasing the size of the Fund through returns generated by investing contributions received during its accumulation period.

The governance arrangements for the Fund provide guidelines for a clearly defined portfolio of assets owned by the Crown but managed by an independent governing body, the Guardians of New Zealand Superannuation (the Guardians). The Guardians have responsibility for investing the assets of the Fund in a prudent, commercial manner consistent with best-practice portfolio management; maximizing return without undue risk to the Fund as a whole; and maintaining New Zealand's reputation as a responsible member of the world investment community.

The statute that created the Fund and the Guardians also established that the board members of the Guardians be appointed by the governor general of New

Zealand upon recommendation of the minister of finance, who must, in turn, draw from recommendations made by an independent nominating committee. Board members are chosen based on experience, training, and expertise in the management of financial investments. The board must comprise at least five, but no more than seven, members. Each board member is appointed for an initial term of up to five years and is eligible to be reappointed. Other key provisions include the following:

♦ Prohibitions on the Fund controlling another entity

♦ Restrictions on borrowing or using derivative instruments without consent of the minister of finance

♦ Provisions for public accountability and independent review

♦ Specification of the board's powers to delegate certain responsibilities

Other than the broad provisions outlined above, the statute that established the Fund does not specify how the Fund's resources should be invested—that is, it does not set minimum or maximum criteria for particular types of assets. The statute does, however, provide New Zealand's minister of finance the power to direct the Guardians, but only in relation to the government's risk and return preferences, and not in such a way that would be inconsistent with the obligation to invest prudently and commercially.

The governance and committee structure of the Guardians is clearly delineated

The Guardians maintain a clearly delineated separation between the governance responsibilities of the board and the management responsibilities of the executive. The board has responsibility for the Guardians' corporate strategy, which includes reviewing and approving a strategic plan and the annual statement of intent; setting the risk tolerance for the Fund by endorsing the reference portfolio; agreeing on various value-adding management strategies; and setting policy statements outlining guidelines, particular responsibilities, and lines of reporting. Management, on the other hand, has responsibility for execution of value-adding strategies (including asset and investment manager selection), risk management, and reporting.

The board committee structure of the Guardians has been essential to the governance of the Fund. The board has established, and when appropriate disestablished, committees in response to ongoing assessments of the utility of each. When the board of the Guardians was first established in 2002, the organization had no staff. As the structure of the organization has developed, so has its committee structure (table 3.1).

Table 3.1 **Committee Structure of the New Zealand Superannuation Fund**

Committee	Established	Disestablished
Audit and governance	2002	
Manager selection	2003	2004
Responsible investing	2003	2009
Communications	2002	2004
Employee and remuneration	2002	
Private markets	2007	2008
Special purpose (various)	2007	

Source: New Zealand Superannuation Fund.

A range of governance and management processes is in place

The Guardians have an organizational vision of "a great team building the best portfolio." To support this vision, the Guardians integrate key inputs with a series of activities to deliver on their intended outcome: reducing the tax burden on future taxpayers. Key inputs in the Guardians' governance and management process are staffing, systems, competencies, values, and investment beliefs (figure 3.1). Investment management activities include portfolio research, investment manager and investment selection, treasury management, risk management, responsible investment, reporting, and monitoring. The sole output is management of the Fund, which includes determining the mix of asset exposures that best meets the Guardians' statutory duty to maximize returns without undue risk and then overlaying a series of value-adding activities. Those activities include private market diversification, active manager selection, strategic tilting (or dynamic asset allocation), and identifying implementation efficiencies.

Both internal and public accountability are strong

The Guardians' management reports to its board through a comprehensive dashboard of more than 20 reports completed at different frequencies. Such reporting reinforces management's accountability for execution of organizational and investment strategies. Ownership of the results of that execution is reinforced through a comprehensive performance-related remuneration system that links individual remuneration to achievement of key organizational performance

---

Figure 3.1 **Management Framework of the Guardians of New Zealand Superannuation**

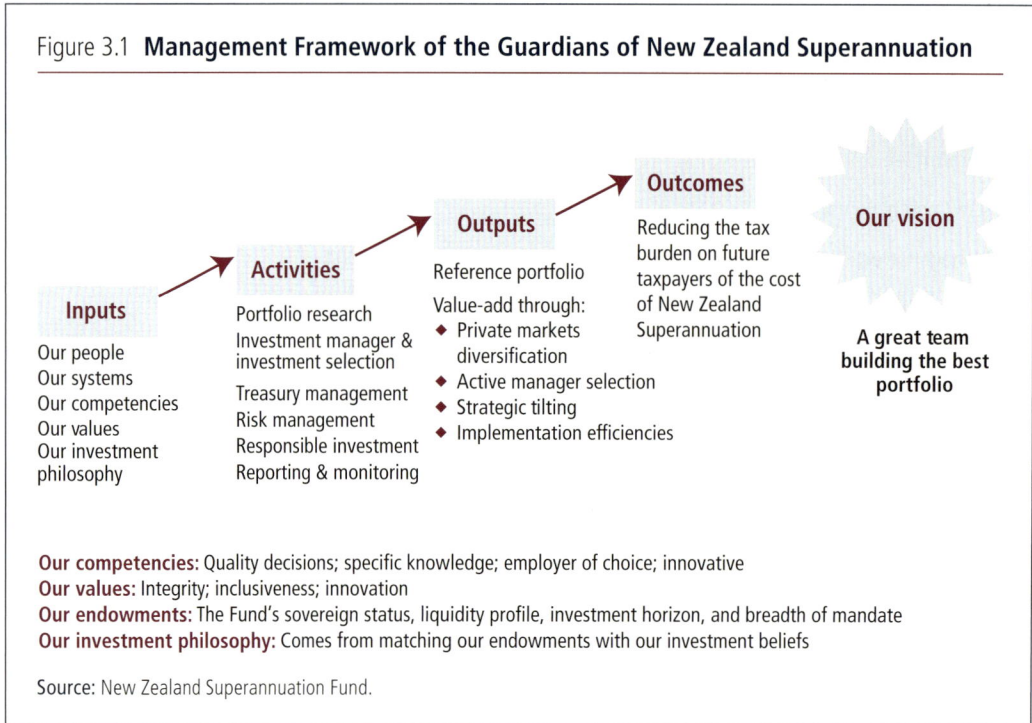

Inputs

Our people
Our systems
Our competencies
Our values
Our investment
philosophy

Activities

Portfolio research
Investment manager &
investment selection
Treasury management
Risk management
Responsible investment
Reporting & monitoring

Outputs

Reference portfolio
Value-add through:
◆ Private markets
    diversification
◆ Active manager selection
◆ Strategic tilting
◆ Implementation efficiencies

Outcomes

Reducing the tax
burden on future
taxpayers of the cost
of New Zealand
Superannuation

Our vision

A great team
building the best
portfolio

Our competencies: Quality decisions; specific knowledge; employer of choice; innovative
Our values: Integrity; inclusiveness; innovation
Our endowments: The Fund's sovereign status, liquidity profile, investment horizon, and breadth of mandate
Our investment philosophy: Comes from matching our endowments with our investment beliefs

Source: New Zealand Superannuation Fund.

---

indicators. To assist the board with approaching specific and complex issues, the Guardians have also launched a wide-ranging board education framework.

The Guardians' board is ultimately accountable to the minister of finance for the performance of the Guardians and the Fund. That accountability is delivered on through public disclosure of an annual statement of intent, an annual report, and a statement of investment policies. At the beginning of each fiscal year, the statement of intent sets out the objectives and financial forecasts for the Guardians and the Fund for the coming five years. The performance of the Guardians against the statement of intent is reviewed in the annual report. Both documents are presented to the parliament of New Zealand and made available on the Guardians' Web site. The information required to be in the statement of investment policies is contained in the governing statute. The statement is updated at least annually and is also posted on the organization's Web site. Additional information about the Guardians and the Fund—including a monthly performance and portfolio update—is also provided.

As an additional measure of internal accountability, the Guardians are subject to an annual financial review by a standing committee of the New Zealand Parliament. The meeting at which the review is conducted is open to the public, and the committee's conclusions are also made public on parliament's Web site (New

---

**Public Accountability Measures of the
New Zealand Superannuation Fund**

◆ Annual report   ◆ Statement of investment policies

◆ Statement of intent   ◆ Voluntary Web site

Zealand Parliament 2010). Finally, each year the Guardians' enabling statute provides for at least five independent reviews on how effectively and efficiently the Guardians are performing their functions. Two such reviews have been completed as of mid-2010 (New Zealand Superannuation Fund 2010).

Conclusion

The Guardians of New Zealand Superannuation are the governing body vested with the power to manage and administer the New Zealand Superannuation Fund. The board of the Guardians is responsible for setting the organizational strategy for the Guardians and for setting the risk tolerance for the Fund with the intended outcome of reducing the tax burden on future taxpayers in New Zealand. The Guardians' management is also responsible for executing the organizational and investment strategies, and the Guardians retain ultimate responsibility for monitoring and overseeing the performance of the Fund.

References

New Zealand Parliament. 2010. "Reports of Committees." www.parliament.nz/en-NZ/PB/SC/Documents/Reports.

New Zealand Superannuation Fund. 2010. "Independent Reviews." www.nzsuperfund.co.nz/index.asp?pageID=2145879295.

Reforming Governance Structure and Accountabilities: The Experience of QSuper

John Carpendale, Board Member, Queensland Superannuation Fund, Australia

Australia's Queensland Superannuation Fund has responded to changes in the governance requirements and investment management regulatory environment in Australian pension funds by undertaking a major reform of its governance structure. Prior to the reform, delegation of authority was disparate, with the governing body sometimes retaining decision-making responsibility and sometimes delegating it to a third party. Following the reform, roles and accountabilities of the governing body and investment staff are now clearly identified and separated. A range of mechanisms, processes, and practices has been put in place to supplement the structural changes.

QSuper recently came under the regulation of Australian Prudential Regulation Authority

The Queensland State Public Sector Superannuation Fund (QSuper), Australia's mandatory retirement fund for Queensland government employees, has more than $25.3 billion in assets and over 530,000 members (about 20 percent of Queensland's workers). More than 450,000 of the fund's members have a defined-contribution plan, while around 80,000 have a defined-benefit plan.

Under the Australian constitution, state retirement funds such as QSuper are excluded from the direct scrutiny of the Australian government regulator of pension scheme arrangements, the Australian Prudential Regulation Authority (APRA), unless they volunteer to be included. Following a period of consideration, the board of QSuper decided in 2009 that it would be in fund members' best interest if the fund forfeited its constitutional protection and QSuper became an APRA-regulated fund. Following the decision, QSuper has made major reforms to its governance structure. The arrangements, which have evolved over time, are modeled on the industry's best practice and provide a high level of protection for member interests.

QSuper has responded to changing needs in the pension system by adopting governance best practices

In 2009, QSuper entered into a fully regulated environment, which included much more rigorous requirements for investment governance. In addition, QSuper's board has sought to improve and strengthen its governance over the fund's investment, despite the fact that QSuper had developed a strong reputation for achieving high-quality pension fund outcomes in the preceding years: it was, for example, the recipient of a platinum (highest-level) award by SuperRatings, an Australian pension industry ratings agency, in 2007, 2008, and 2009.

At the QSuper strategic planning workshop in 2008, the board determined that it was time for it to assume full control and accountability for the fund's investment governance. In considering the governance model to be adopted, the board examined global best practices and, where practical, adopted such practices. In particular, the board took account of recent research work undertaken in Europe and North America.

In a landmark study, a Watson Wyatt Worldwide (2007) study identified characteristics of the world's best-governed institutional investors. The study examined the defining features of 10 investors that had consistently outperformed their peers. Results of this work are identified in six core best-practice factors and six exceptional best-practice factors (table 3.2). In developing its reformed governance model, QSuper adopted these best-practice factors as benchmarks.

In another paper, Ambachtsheer, Capelle, and Lum (2007) analyzed the findings of a survey on pension fund governance from an international group of 88 pension fund executives. The study concluded that there are five opportunities to improve pension fund governance:

◆ Redesign pension deals to eliminate the "competing financial interests" problem.

◆ Develop templates for ideal boards of governors composition, and integrate these templates into actual selection processes.

◆ Initiate board effectiveness self-evaluation processes.

◆ Achieve clarity between the respective roles of boards and management.

◆ Adopt high-performance cultures with competitive compensation policies.

QSuper's board adopted these recommendations alongside the Watson Wyatt Worldwide recommendations to guide the redesign of its investment governance model.

Table 3.2 **Global Best Practice in Investment Governance**

		Factor	Description
Core input factor	**Coherence**	Mission clarity	Clarity of the mission and commitment of the stakeholders to the mission statement
		Effective focusing of time	Resourcing each element in the investment process with an appropriate budget considering impact and required capabilities
	People	Leadership	Leadership, evident at the board/investment committee level, with the key role that of the investment committee chairman
	Process	Strong beliefs	Strong investment beliefs commanding fund-wide support that align with goals and inform all investment decision making
		Risk budget framework	Frame the investment process by reference to a risk budget aligned to goals and incorporating an accurate view of alpha and beta
		Fit-for-purpose manager line-up	Effective use of external managers, governed by clear mandates, aligned to goals, and selected on fit-for-purpose criteria
Exceptional input factor	**Coherence**	Highly competent investment executive	Use of a highly investment-competent investment function with clear responsibilities and accountabilities to the investment committee
	People	High-level board competencies	Selection to the board and senior staff guided by numeric skills, capacity for logical thinking, ability to think about risk and probability
		Supportive compensation	Effective compensation practices used to build bench strength and align actions to the mission; different strategies according to fund context
	Process	Competitive positioning	Frame the investment philosophy and process by reference to the institution's comparative advantages and disadvantages
		Real-time decisions	Utilize decision-making systems that function in real time, not calendar time
		Learning organization	Work toward a learning culture that deliberately encourages change and challenges commonplace assumptions of the industry

Source: Watson Wyatt Worldwide 2007.

QSuper's current investment governance framework covers strategic and operational functions

Table 3.3 identifies the eight broad functional roles in QSuper's current investment governance framework and briefly describes the type of activity undertaken at each level. The framework covers both strategic and operational functions and is generally hierarchical.

Table 3.3 **Current QSuper Investment Governance Framework**

	Function	Activity
Strategic	Investment philosophy and beliefs	Establish high-level investment vision and mission
	Investment governance	Develop governing structures/framework/budget and delegation statements
	Investment objectives	Establish risk and return objectives, budgets, controls, measures,and benchmarks
	Investment policy	Establish policy (for example, asset allocation, active/passive approach) to achieve objectives
Operational	Policy implementation	Establish implementation framework (for example, alpha/beta/omega; tactical asset allocation/dynamic asset allocation/rebalancing)
	Asset management	Decide investment management structure; appoint and terminate managers
	Investment administration	Establish administration framework (for example, custody, compliance, unit pricing, cash flow management)
	Performance monitoring	Establish reporting framework and review investment performance against benchmarks

Source: QSuper (adapted from Watson Wyatt Worldwide).

Prior to the 2009 reform, there was limited delegation of accountabilities within QSuper. As shown in table 3.4, the board of directors was the prime decision maker for six of the eight core investment functions, while the investment committee had no decision-making authority at all. Under these arrangements, the role of the internal investment staff was limited to analyzing and reviewing the inputs of external partners and advising the trustees of QSuper on same. The sole accountability of the investment staff was to monitor investment performance. At the same time, the investment knowledge and experience of the trustee board and the investment committee were limited. The investment committee, for example, held monthly meetings lasting one to two hours, during which there was little time, opportunity, or capacity for detailed analysis and discussion.

Several additional principles guided QSuper's governance reform

In 2008, the QSuper board developed and adopted five additional principles to guide the reform of its investment governance arrangements:

Table 3.4 **QSuper Governance Responsibilities prior to Reform**

Function	Trustee board	Board investment committee	Investment staff	External partners
Investment philosophy and beliefs	Decide	Recommend	Review	Propose
Investment governance	Decide	Recommend	Review	Propose
Investment objectives	Decide	Recommend	Review	Propose
Investment policy	Decide	Recommend	Review	Propose
Policy implementation	Decide	Recommend	Review	Propose
Asset management			Monitor	Decide
Investment administration			Monitor	Decide
Performance monitoring	Decide	Recommend	Implement	

Source: QSuper (adapted from Watson Wyatt Worldwide).

- Investments are arranged solely to satisfy members' interests.
- The board sets the investment agenda and gives clear direction to service providers.
- The board acts decisively to deliver on its duties to the fund's members.
- The board and the investment committee have clearly specified responsibilities and accountabilities and members who are highly competent in investment matters.
- QSuper either has or engages the skills and capacity to effect ongoing support for its investment activities for members.

During the months following the adoption of these principles, a subcommittee of the board, working with executive management and internal investment staff, developed proposals to reform the fund's investment governance structure. In late 2008, consistent with the guiding principles outlined above, the board approved the new investment governance accountabilities and delegations outlined in table 3.5. The new framework went into effect in January 2009.

Changes were also made to the investment committee and investment staff

Under the new governance arrangements, QSuper's investment committee is composed of seven members: four trustees and three external investment profes-

Table 3.5 **QSuper Governance Responsibilities after Reform**

Function	Trustee board	Board investment committee	Investment staff	External partners
Investment philosophy and beliefs	Decide	Recommend	Propose	
Investment governance	Decide	Recommend	Propose	
Investment objectives	Decide	Recommend	Propose	
Investment policy	Endorse	Decide	Recommend	
Policy implementation	Endorse	Decide	Recommend	
Asset management		Endorse	Decide	Implement
Investment administration		Endorse	Decide	Implement
Performance monitoring	Endorse	Decide	Implement	

Source: QSuper.

sionals. The chair of the investment committee is an external professional. A program for professional development has been established and is in the process of being implemented. Monthly investment committee meetings now last at least five hours, and an investment committee charter and agenda ensure detailed analysis and discussion of all relevant issues.

Previously, QSuper had four mid-level investment staff with no accountability for decisions. The internal investment team was primarily responsible for review and performance monitoring. Consistent with the guiding principles, a high-profile chief investment officer was appointed in late 2008. In 2009, a support staff of 20 was recruited. As indicated in the new governance arrangements (table 3.6), the internal investment team is accountable for providing inputs on all investment governance functions, both strategic and operational. In general, revisions in the governance structure have considerably increased the importance and accountability of the internal investment staff.

Changes in QSuper's investment governance framework also mean that the trustee board's decision-making authority is now restricted to high-level strategic issues. Accountability for investment policy setting, policy implementation, and performance monitoring has been delegated to the investment committee. The investment committee is also responsible for undertaking detailed analysis of and making recommendations on all strategic matters as well as the oversight of all functions performed by the investment staff.

The internal investment staff, meanwhile, is now responsible for decision-making related to asset management and investment operations. Investment staff also provide input on all investment governance functions. Under the revised governance structure, external partners have no direct governance accountability and are responsible for the implementation of only certain asset management functions and administration of investments (table 3.6).

Table 3.6 **Accountability and Ownership Changes within QSuper**

Entity	Activity
Governing body: **board**	◆ Decision making restricted to high-level strategic activities
Governing body: **investment committee**	◆ Decision-making accountability for policy, implementation, and performance ◆ Responsible for detailed examination of all strategic matters ◆ Oversight of all functions performed by investment staff
Investment staff	◆ Decision-making accountability for asset management and investment operations ◆ Ownership of input on all investment governance functions
External partners	◆ No direct accountability in new governance structure ◆ Responsible for implementation of some parts of asset management and investment administration

Source: QSuper.

Nonstructural mechanisms have also been undertaken to reinforce accountability and decision-making processes

To supplement the revised investment governance structure shown in table 3.5, QSuper is employing several nonstructural mechanisms to reinforce accountability and decision-making processes. The new governance responsibilities structure, for example, also serves as the board's simplified investment delegation statement, which is employed by the board to clarify and separate ownership of decision-making accountabilities (the complete, formal delegation statement is shown as table 3.7).

The board of QSuper also has approved an investment committee charter that clearly sets out committee responsibilities, accountabilities, and ownership obligations—specifically, membership composition, minimum skill levels and expertise, training and development, and committee performance review. The annual invest-

Table 3.7 **QSuper Delegation of Investment Functions**

Function	Board	IC	QSL	IMs	Description
Investment framework and philosophy					
Beliefs	A	R	P	—	
Framework: alpha and beta	E	A	R	—	
Investment governance					
Investment objectives scorecards	A	R	P	—	Includes objectives, risk controls, and measures of success
Delegations	A	R	P	—	
Beta management					
Asset allocation: PDS range, operational range	A	R	P	—	Formulate asset allocation ranges, including currency exposure; define benchmark or reference rates for each asset class
Intra-asset class guidelines	E	A	R	—	Establish controls for intra-asset class characteristics (cap, style, risk factors, and so on)
Dynamic asset allocation					Set exposure within the relevant range; includes allocations within intra-asset class guidelines; includes establishing risk budgets for alpha programs within overall beta context
PDS range	E	A	R	—	
Operational range	—	—	A		
Strategic risk management overlay	E	A	R	—	Fund-level optionlike exposures
Alpha management					
Alpha program guidelines	E	A	R	—	Establish fund-level alpha target and controls for volatility, beta sensitivity, capital, management expense ratio, and manager concentration
Establish alpha programs within guidelines	—	E	A	—	May be one or more programs within overall fund-level guidelines; these could contain one or more managers
Implementation (omega management)					
Policy implementation guidelines	E	A	R	—	Establish controls for cash flow, capital, tax policy, liquidity, counter-party management
Securities trading	—	—	A	—	
Asset management					
Manager selection guidelines	E	A	R	—	Establish parameters for use in appointing managers, including general characteristics, contractual principles, fee principles, and compliance policies
Manager selection					Establish parameters for internal and external manager selection, including appointments, terminations, documentation, investment management agreement, fee negotiation, monitoring, and reporting
Internal	E	A	R	—	
External	—	—	A	—	
Security selection	—	—	—	A	Selection of individual securities within risk constraints and policy

Source: QSuper.

Notes: IC = investment committee; IMs = investment managers; PDS = product disclosure statement; QSL = QSuper Limited Committee. A = approve; E = endorse; P = propose; R = recommend.

ment committee agenda (given for the year 2010 in table 3.8) ensures that decision-making ownership obligations are regularly revisited.

In addition to modifications in structures and accountabilities, QSuper has set out to change practices and procedures to aid accountability. For one, time allowed for

Table 3.8 **QSuper Investment Committee Example Agenda Plan**

Month	Governance	Investment strategy	Performance	Product management	Other
Feb.	Benchmarking policy Corporate governance policy	Strategy review	Performance report		Fiduciary training plans
March	Investment policy statement	Strategy review	Performance report Performance reporting capability plan	Investment entity structures	Custody Compliance capability plan
April	External manager appointment process	Strategy review External manager structure	Performance report	Management expense ratio review	
May	Provider capability update and risk assessment	Strategy review	Performance report Defined-benefit update		Liquidity risk review
June	Investment beliefs discussion	Strategy review Alpha plan	Performance report	Specific member option review	
July	Risk register briefing from an investment context	Strategy review	Performance report	Specific member option review	Environmental, social, and governance policy
August	Capital markets process	Strategy review	Performance report Defined-benefit update	Update on member research relevant to investments	
Sept.	Derivative risk management	Strategy review	Performance report	Management expense ratio review	
Oct.	Provider capability update and risk assessment	Strategy review	Performance report		Liquidity risk review
Nov.		Strategy review	Performance report Defined-benefit update	Product development update	Asset consultant policy
Dec.	Forward agenda plans	Strategy review	Performance report		

Source: QSuper.

discussion of investment matters has been lengthened to ensure that committee members fully understand the matters for which they are accountable. Investment professionals are now formally included in this process to bring a practical and informed perspective on accountabilities. Finally, a continuing professional development program has been instituted for trustees and an annual performance assessment for the board and committee members has been introduced.

Conclusion

Over the past several years, QSuper has undertaken significant governance structure and operational arrangement reforms to make itself consistent with global best practices. Roles and accountabilities of the board, investment committee, and investment staff are now clearly identified and separated in the investment delegation statement. A range of mechanisms, processes, and practices has been put in place to supplement the structural changes. As of early 2010, these arrangements have been in place for just over 12 months; as such, there is insufficient empirical experience to conclusively evaluate their efficiency or effectiveness in achieving best-practice investment performance outcomes. In due course, a formal review by an independent specialist will be undertaken to determine whether further governance refinement is needed.

References

Ambachtsheer, K., R. Capelle, and H. Lum. 2007. "The State of Global Pension Fund Governance Today: Board Competency Still a Problem." Toronto: Rotman International Centre for Pension Management, University of Toronto.

Watson Wyatt Worldwide. 2007. "Best Practice Investment Governance: Going from Good to Great." Watson Wyatt Worldwide, Australia. www.watsonwyatt. com/asia-pacific/media/2007-EU-0533.pdf.

Governance Reform Proposals for the Republic of Korea's National Pension Service

Seuran Lee, Director, Ministry of Health, Welfare, and Family Affairs, Republic of Korea

The National Pension Service (NPS) is the statutory body charged with the administration of the Republic of Korea's national pension system, including the investment of its pension assets. The pension assets of NPS (here referred to as "the Fund") are managed by investment staff in the Fund Management Center, presently housed within NPS. The governance structure of NPS, implemented in 1999, has been pivotal in increasing the efficiency and performance of Korea's national pension system for more than a decade. Further governance reform was proposed in 2009 and, as of mid-2010, is still being considered by Korea's National Assembly. The proposed reform focuses mainly on increasing the expertise and qualifications of committee members overseeing the Fund, with the objective of achieving a higher investment return during the Fund's growth period and securing the long-term financial stability of the Fund.

Governance of the National Pension Service is divided among several entities

In terms of assets under management, the National Pension Service (NPS) is the third largest sovereign pension fund in the world, with $312 billion as of September 2010.[1] NPS has an estimated 18.4 million participants and 2.4 million beneficiaries, and maintains a contribution rate of 9 percent of participants' salaries. Benefits are paid to NPS participants beginning at age 60 assuming a 20-year vesting period. The minimum income replacement rate is about 40 percent.

---

[1] Sovereign pension funds are established by national authorities for meeting pension liabilities. The ranking was calculated by Towers Watson as of end-2009 and is restricted to funds specifically sponsored by national authorities; it does not include other state-sponsored funds.

60

The Ministry of Health, Welfare, and Family Affairs oversees two nonpermanent governing bodies, the National Pension Deliberative Council and the National Pension Fund Management Committee (figure 3.2). The National Pension Deliberative Council determines pension benefits and contributions, and also governs NPS, which, in turn, is responsible for general management, including collections and disbursements. The National Pension Fund Management Committee is the Fund's investment management committee in charge of formulating its strategic asset allocation, strategic plan, and investment policy. The Fund Management Center is the specialist investment management organization charged with investment of the Fund. It is a part of NPS, but its investment activities are directly supervised by the Fund Management Committee. The Fund Management Center is responsible for the overall asset management and implementation of investment policies including strategic asset allocation, formulating outsourcing policies, and evaluating performance of internal and external asset managers.

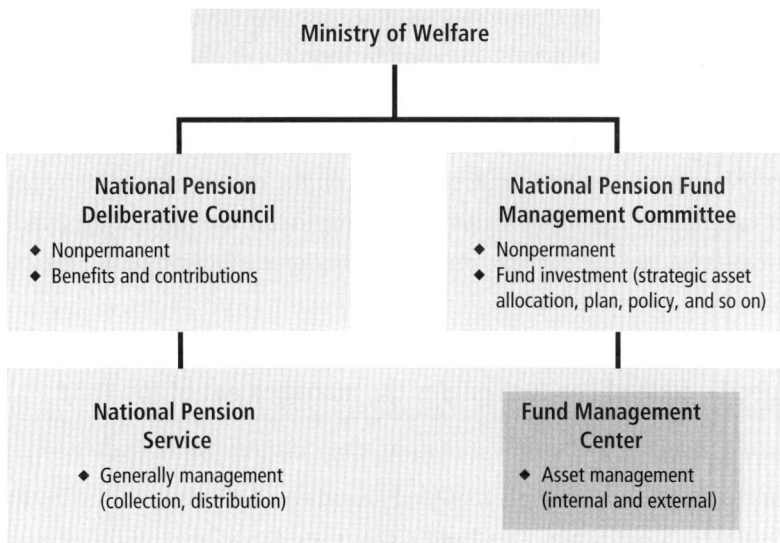

Figure 3.2 **Governance Structure of Korea's National Pension System**

Source: Ministry of Health, Welfare, and Family Affairs, Republic of Korea.

The Fund Management Committee represents government officials, employers, and employees

The Fund Management Committee consists of 20 members, 6 ex officio and 14 appointed, each nominated for a two-year term with a possibility of extension for one additional two-year term. Korea's minister of health, welfare, and family affairs serves as chairperson of the Fund Management Committee. The remaining five ex officio members include four government officials (from the Ministry of Finance, Ministry of Agriculture, Ministry of Labor, and Ministry of Knowledge Economy) and the president of NPS. Twelve of the 14 appointed members are recommended by groups representing NPS participants: 3 are employers representing the employers' association; 3 are employees representing a federation of workers' organizations (labor unions); 6 represent farmers' and fishermen's associations or associations of self-employed persons, consumer organizations, and civic groups. The remaining two appointed members are recommended by the Ministry of Health, Welfare, and Family Affairs.

Under the present arrangement, representative groups of NPS participants recommend suitable candidates for the Fund Management Committee to the minister of health, welfare and family affairs, who then appoints committee members from among those candidates. Nominees are generally presidents and vice presidents of their respective groups. Two members of the Fund Management Committee must be experts on public pension schemes.

The Fund Management Committee meetings are held at least four times a year. Six meetings were held in 2007, and eight in 2008. On an ongoing basis, the Fund Management Committee provides a number of reports to the minister of health, welfare, and family affairs: an investment policy statement, asset allocation targets, a performance evaluation, a settlement of accounts, and investment strategies by asset class. Other important matters pertaining to the operation of the Fund are carried out by the Fund Management Committee upon request by either the chairperson of the committee or one-third of the committee's members.

A specific code of conduct guides the management of the Fund

Governing legislation in Korea requires the minister of health, welfare, and family affairs to manage and operate the Fund according to the decisions of the Fund Management Committee. The Fund's objectives are to maximize investment returns for the purpose of securing long-term financial stability, to invest for the welfare of persons who are and were insured persons and beneficiaries as long as it does not endanger the security of the Fund's finances, and to comply with fiduciary duty.

Additionally, several rules in the code of conduct govern the Fund's management and governing bodies, namely that all members act honestly and in good faith, to the best interest of the Fund; that members with the possibility of conflict of interest have no voting right; and that information pertaining to the management of the Fund not be disclosed. All members must pledge to observe the code of conduct. Though compliance with the code of conduct is reinforced by the Fund Management Committee, tracking violations of the code are not the legal responsibility of the committee.

Several subcommittees with specific tasks have been established under the Fund Management Committee

Under the guidance of the Fund Management Committee, the Evaluation Committee for Fund Management conducts reviews that contribute to the Fund Management Committee's decision-making process. The Evaluation Committee consists of 20 members, 6 ex officio and 14 appointed (12 representatives are recommended by groups of NPS participants and 2 by the Ministry of Health, Welfare, and Family Affairs), each with a two-year term. The selection process is analogous to that for the Fund Management Committee with the exception of a qualification requirement for members. Evaluation Committee members must be licensed attorneys, accountants, or experts in social welfare, economics, or business.

Two additional committees—the Expert Committee on Voting Rights and the Expert Committee on the Evaluation of Performance Compensation—were established by the Fund Management Committee in 2005 and 2007, respectively. The former consists of nine members, each with a two-year term. Members are recommended by the government, groups of NPS participants, and academia. The latter consists of 12 members, also with a two-year term. Members are recommended by groups of NPS participants and experts.

The proposed governance reform incorporates five principles

The plan to reform the governance structure of the Fund was undertaken with a view toward supporting mechanisms to achieve higher investment returns during the Fund's growth period in an effort to secure the long-term financial stability of the Fund. A compounded increase of 1 percent in annual return on investment delays the Fund's projected depletion point from 2060 to 2069 or reduces the contribution rate by 2 percentage points from the current 9 percent. More generally, reform was needed to address the Fund's weaknesses, including lack of sufficient expertise and lack of independence from the government and other stakeholders.

The basic framework of governance reform focuses on increasing the expertise and qualification requirements among the various committees' members. Five principles were incorporated into the governance reform plan: a specific experience requirement for committee members (10 years of professional experience in finance or investment management), a secure government role, increased representation of NPS participants, transparency, and independence in decision-making processes (figure 3.3).

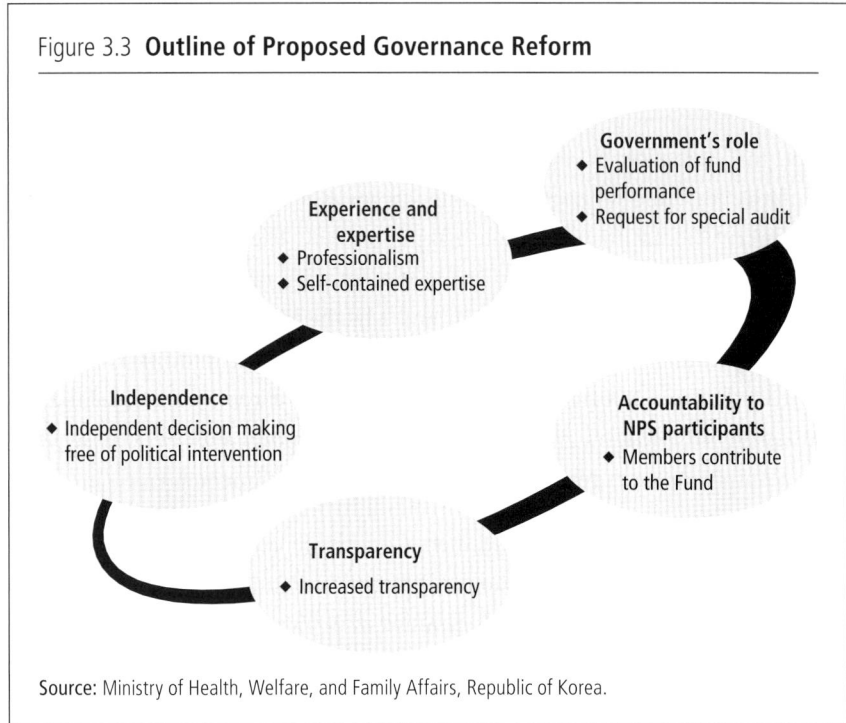

Figure 3.3 **Outline of Proposed Governance Reform**

Government's role
◆ Evaluation of fund performance
◆ Request for special audit

Experience and expertise
◆ Professionalism
◆ Self-contained expertise

Independence
◆ Independent decision making free of political intervention

Accountability to NPS participants
◆ Members contribute to the Fund

Transparency
◆ Increased transparency

Source: Ministry of Health, Welfare, and Family Affairs, Republic of Korea.

The 2009 reform proposal, which is awaiting the National Assembly's approval, also aims to separate the Fund Management Center from NPS, as the two bodies have different functions and therefore operate differently and require staff with a diverse set of skills. Under the proposed new structure, the Fund Management Committee would have dotted-line reporting to the Ministry of Health, Welfare, and Family Affairs and would consist of seven seasoned investment professionals (figure 3.4). Changes would also be made to the responsibilities of the Fund Management Center; though it would still oversee the Fund's asset management, it would be granted independence from the government, and become an independent entity distinct from NPS called the "Fund Management Corporation." Further, the chairman of the Fund Management Committee would not concurrently be chief executive officer of the Fund Management Corporation. This new Fund Management Committee (with membership reduced from the current 20 to 7) would serve as the governing board for the Fund Management Corporation.

The legislation would also shift the process of selecting governing bodies' members to a recommendation committee consisting of 11 members (the minister of health,

Figure 3.4 **Current versus Reformed Governance Structure of Korea's National Pension System**

a. Current structure

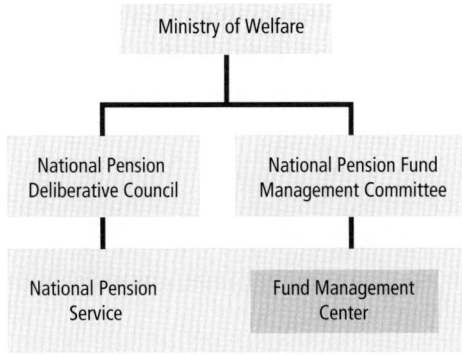

b. Reformed structure

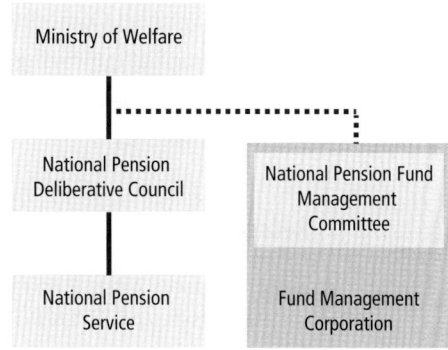

Source: Ministry of Health, Welfare, and Family Affairs, Republic of Korea.

welfare, and family affairs as the chairperson, 3 government officials, 6 representatives of NPS participants, and 1 finance expert). The president of Korea would appoint members to the Fund Management Committee for a three-year term.

Codes of conduct within the Fund Management Committee would be tightened after the reform

The reform would also lay out several specific requirements related to the code of conduct for members of the Fund Management Committee. First, the Fund Management Committee would be obligated to comply with the prudent investor principle and to act honestly and in good faith. Second, the committee's members would be held specifically accountable for revealing material insider information gained during the course of serving on the committee. Third, within one month of being appointed, new members of the Fund Management Committee would be required to disclose to the minister of health, welfare, and family affairs their personal securities holdings. Finally, each member of the Fund Management Committee would need to specifically agree not to vote on a resolution or participate in a discussion when he or she has a conflict of interest.

Conclusion

Korea's proposed reforms illustrate a deliberate program to establish a stronger governance structure and processes for its national pension system. This legislation, which is currently being considered by the National Assembly, follows reforms undertaken in past years, such as the establishment of the Expert Committee on Voting Rights Exercise and Expert Committee on the Evaluation of Performance Compensation. Separation of the newly transformed Fund Management Corporation from the NPS, under the oversight of the smaller and more independent Fund Management Committee, composed entirely of investment professionals, are all steps aimed at improving the governance and management of Korea's pension assets, which are already quite significant and expected to increase rapidly for the foreseeable future.

Reference

Towers Watson. 2010. "P & I/TW 300 Analysis: Year End 2009." www.towerswatson. com/assets/pdf/2728/PI-TW-300-survey.pdf.

Governance of the World Bank Staff Retirement Plan and Trust

John Gandolfo, Director and Chief Investment Officer, World Bank Pension Funds

The World Bank Staff Retirement Plan and Trust is a contributory, defined-benefit pension plan that covers most employees of the World Bank Group. Two main bodies, the Pension Finance Committee and the Pension Benefits Administration Committee, are respectively responsible for the management and investment of the plan's assets and for the administration of plan benefits. Significant decision-making authority, however, is delegated to Bank staff to develop, recommend, and implement asset allocation, investment management, and other policies for pension assets. This delegation of authority to staff encourages ownership, accountability, and role clarity. The Bank has designed and implemented an effective governance structure to mitigate potential risks associated with hiring external managers. Periodic, relevant, and reliable reporting is key to the Bank's pension governance processes.

The World Bank Treasury manages assets for a range of internal and external clients

The World Bank Treasury manages more than $100 billion for a diverse set of internal and external official sector clients, including $15 billion of pension and other retirement benefit assets. Treasury's mandates include *high-grade, global fixed-income* portfolios, usually managed in house; and *multi-asset class* portfolios managed by external managers or funds and covering developed and emerging market equities and fixed income, hedge funds, real estate, timber, commodities, infrastructure, and private equity (figure 3.5). As all participants in the investment management process have a fiduciary duty and designated responsibilities, the establishment of a proper governing body and of a satisfactory set of governance guidelines is essential.

The governance structure of the World Bank Staff Retirement Plan was established upon formalization of the plan

The World Bank Staff Retirement Plan was created by the International Bank for Reconstruction and Development (IBRD) board of directors in the form of a plan

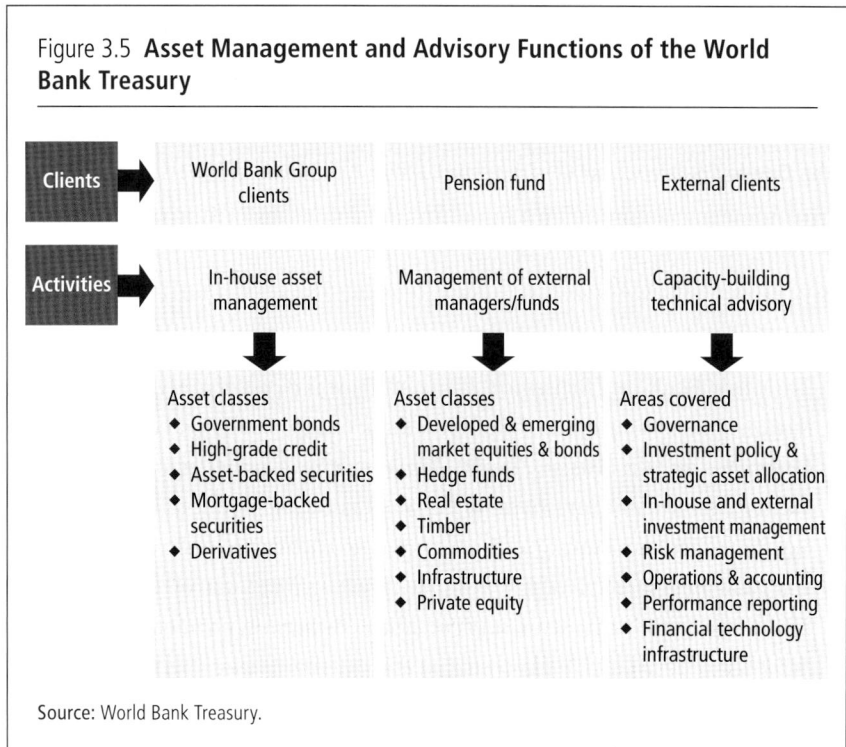

Figure 3.5 **Asset Management and Advisory Functions of the World Bank Treasury**

Source: World Bank Treasury.

document. In 2001, this plan was formalized as an explicit trust with IBRD as the trustee. Retirement plan assets are allowed to leave the trust only in the form of benefit payments or plan management expenses. Under the plan document, two committees are given responsibility for oversight of the retirement plan: the Pension Finance Committee and the Pension Benefits Administration Committee (figure 3.6). The Pension Finance Committee is in charge of investment oversight and review, approval of investment and funding policies, determination of contribution levels based on an actuarial valuation of the plan's liabilities, and budget approval. The Pension Benefits Administration Committee oversees administration of the plan.

Specifically, the Pension Finance Committee is responsible and accountable for the following investment decisions:

◆ Setting investment philosophy, objectives, and risk tolerance
◆ Establishing, reviewing, and revising the investment policy
◆ Establishing eligible asset classes and strategies
◆ Setting performance benchmarks
◆ Setting the risk budget for active management
◆ Reviewing portfolio strategies and performance

Figure 3.6 **World Bank Staff Retirement Plan: Governance Structure**

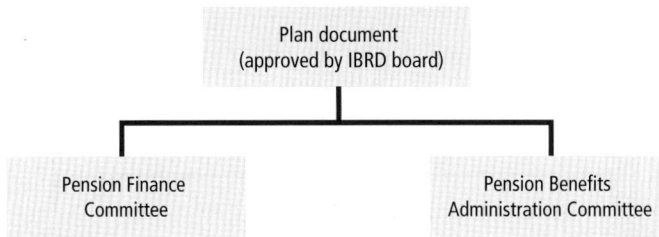

Source: World Bank.

Other investment-related decisions include the following:

- Internal versus external management of pension assets
- Portfolio construction
- Engagement of auditors and custodians
- Content and frequency of reporting to staff, investment committee, board, and stakeholders
- Budget for investment management

The Pension Finance Committee has 10 members representing different constituencies including 2 members of the World Bank's board of directors, 2 current World Bank staff, 1 retiree, and 5 members of executive management. All members of the Pension Finance Committee are appointed by the president of the World Bank.

The Pension Finance Committee delegates a significant amount of decision-making authority to Bank staff

As figure 3.7 illustrates, the Pension Finance Committee is supported by staff divided into three departments: the *investment department* is responsible for investment strategy, selection, and management of internal and external managers; the *risk and analytics department* is responsible for risk management; and the *operations and accounting department* is responsible for all accounting, middle-office, and back-office functions. In addition, a dedicated unit in the legal department of the World Bank provides specialized investment-related legal support to the plan.

The Pension Finance Committee meets on a quarterly basis to discuss asset allocation, investment performance, and all other issues brought to its attention by related departments. A significant amount of decision-making authority, however, is delegated to Bank staff. Staff develop, recommend, and implement the strategic

Figure 3.7 **Delegation of Duties to World Bank Staff by Pension Finance Committee**

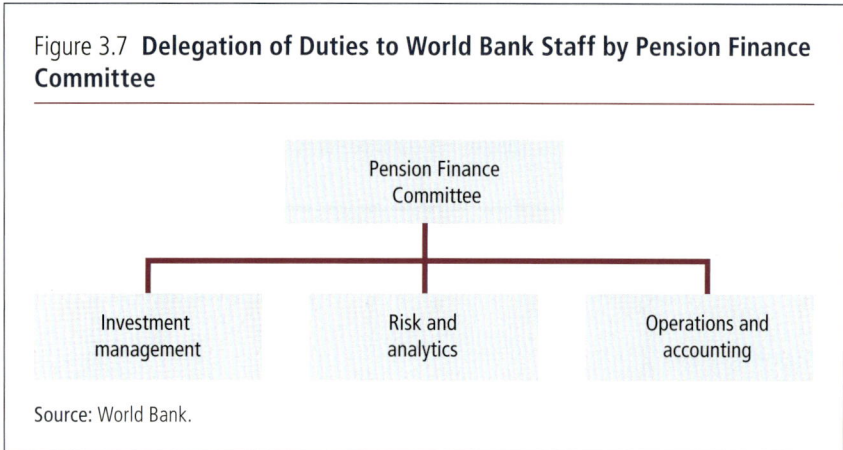

Source: World Bank.

asset allocation; select and monitor external investment managers; manage the active risk budget; track risk in various asset class portfolios; and provide reporting to various levels of management and the governing bodies.

The selection, monitoring, and oversight of external asset managers are critical to the implementation of the investment strategy of the plan, particularly for asset classes and strategies that require significant internal staff resources. This is particularly true in the area of alternative investments. In selecting external asset managers, staff consider whether managers fit the objectives of the portion of the portfolio they are to manage. The due diligence process involved in hiring external asset managers includes analysis of issues such as whether an environment supportive of the strategy can be created and whether the costs associated with the strategy can be sustained. Activities related to the hiring and management of external managers are undertaken in a well-segregated and specialized institutional environment by staff in the three departments under the Pension Finance Committee.

In addition to the investment functions overseen by the Pension Finance Committee, the World Bank employs a pension administration team, under the oversight of the Pension Benefit Administration Committee, that manages administration of plan benefits such as aiding staff in retirement planning.

Numerous steps have been taken to ensure good governance

Numerous policies, procedures, and processes support the governance structure of the Bank's pension plan. Chief among these is board orientation and education, particularly with respect to specialized investment topics, in order to ensure understanding of the board's fiduciary responsibilities and scope of authority, and to facilitate decision making and ownership of decisions. Separation of functions is another good governance mechanism. The Pension Finance Committee is governed by its own set of policies and practices, and strategic decisions of the oversight committee and staff are reported to the board of directors and included in financial reporting to the plan beneficiaries in order to ensure transparency. External experts are asked to participate in the process as necessary. Additional steps taken to ensure good governance within the plan are shown in figure 3.8.

Figure 3.8 **Good Governance Mechanisms**

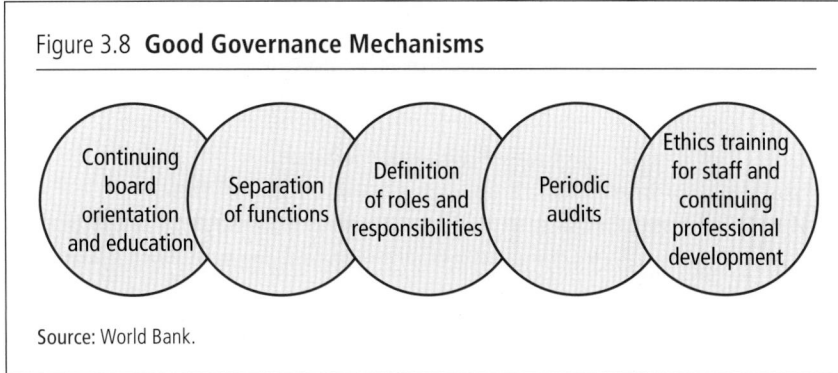

Source: World Bank.

Regular, accurate, and complete reporting is relevant to good governance and effective management of a pension plan

Reporting channels between all the entities involved in the governance of the World Bank Staff Retirement Plan are established with the object of ensuring the effective and timely transmission of relevant and accurate information. Appropriate processes are also in place to ensure that members of the governing body receive proper, timely, accurate, and complete information so they may discharge their responsibilities effectively and ensure that delegated responsibilities are fulfilled. Periodic, relevant, and reliable reporting is, therefore, key to good governance (figure 3.9).

Front-, middle-, and back-office staff are responsible for regular reporting, ongoing monitoring, and decision-making processes. They also prepare monthly reports for World Bank Treasury management on plan performance, risks, exposures, portfolio rebalancing, and cash requirements. The Pension Finance Committee meets and reviews reports quarterly, while reporting to the board of directors and beneficiaries is on an annual basis. Internal audits also play an important role in the periodic assessment of risks and controls, as well as in the assessment of the accuracy of the Pension Finance Committee's reporting to the board of directors.

Conclusion

The World Bank has invested substantial time and resources in designing and implementing a strong governance framework for its Staff Retirement Plan. The

Figure 3.9 **Reporting Structure within the World Bank Staff Retirement Plan**

Board of directors & beneficiaries: annually

Pension Finance Committee: quarterly

Treasury management: monthly

Front-, middle-, and back-office staff: daily/ongoing monitoring and decision making

Source: World Bank.

strong governance structure of the plan has ensured that all participants in the investment management process perform their fiduciary duty to act in the best interest of the plan beneficiaries. A notable aspect of the plan's governance structure is that the Pension Finance Committee delegates a significant amount of investment decision-making authority to Bank staff. The Bank has been able to attract staff and external investment managers with the talent and specialized skill sets required to manage traditional and alternative investments. Clear identification and separation of operational and policy/oversight roles, and the creation of appropriate reporting channels among all entities involved in the governance of the pension plan, have been major factors in ensuring good governance.

2. Qualification, Selection, and Operation of Governing Bodies

- ◆ Licensing Requirements and Operating Standards for Pension Fund Trustees in Australia

- ◆ Selection, Appointment, and Operating Processes for Board Members: The Case of Canada's AIMCo

Licensing Requirements and Operating Standards for Pension Fund Trustees in Australia

Ross Jones, Deputy Chairman, Australian Prudential Regulation Authority

A board of directors or board of trustees has ultimate oversight responsibility and accountability for the business affairs, operational policies, and financial health of a public or private pension plan. For pension funds based in Australia, the Australian Prudential Regulation Authority (APRA) maintains requirements related to the selection, qualification, training, and licensing of trustees, as well as conflict of interest and risk management policies within funds. Some of APRA's core requirements (character, honesty, integrity) apply to individual trustees, while others (understanding of investment and legal environment and maintenance of skills) apply to the trustees of a pension fund collectively.

APRA sets specific standards for the appointment and training of pension fund trustees

Under Australian law, the Australian Prudential Regulation Authority (APRA) supervises financial institutions including investment banks, commercial banks, insurance companies, and pension funds. In 2009, APRA-supervised financial institutions held approximately $3.6 trillion in assets for 22 million Australian depositors, policy holders, and superannuation fund members. APRA develops supervisory policies, including prudential standards under relevant legislation using a risk-based (as opposed to rules-based) approach. As Australian pension fund governance uses a trustee model, APRA dedicates substantial resources to how trustees are appointed, trained, incentivized, and held accountable for the results in the funds for which they are responsible.

Under Australian law, trustees of pension funds hold assets on behalf of fund members according to a specified trust structure and have a fiduciary duty to members. The trustees of a specific fund must be comprised of an equal number of members nominated by employers and employees (completely independent trustees, however, are not included in this requirement).

In general, Australian regulations are focused more on ensuring that pension fund trustees meet certain skills requirements in the course of carrying out their responsibilities than they are on ensuring that trustees meet a set of expectations prior to being appointed. If new trustees do not initially have the expertise, knowledge, or experience to oversee the operation of a pension fund, APRA expects them to undergo sufficient training to undertake their duties.

In 2004, Australia introduced new licensing requirements and operating standards for pension fund trustees. Trustees must now meet requirements including, but not limited to: compliance with the Registrable Superannuation Entities (RSEs) Licensee Law; proper and prudent performance of duties as trustees of RSEs; maintenance and compliance with the trustees' risk management strategy; and ongoing compliance with fit and proper standards, which at a most basic level require that trustees understand their responsibilities and act honestly.

APRA's governance requirements call for compliance with operating standards in five areas: fitness and propriety, adequacy of resources, outsourcing arrangements, risk management, and capital requirements

Operating standards are an important part of governance requirements for the financial institutions that APRA regulates. Successful licensees are required to comply with operating standards in several areas: fitness and propriety; adequacy of resources; outsourcing arrangements; risk management; and capital requirements.

APRA's licensing and supervision process includes a review of policies and processes that ensure the integrity of fund trustees. Licensing requirements are designed to ensure that the interests of fund members and beneficiaries are managed competently and honestly by trustees. Specifically, trustees must comply with the requirements of a "fit and proper" standard and possess attributes that enable them to carry out their duties in a prudent manner. These attributes include, but are not limited to: competence, diligence, experience, honesty, integrity, and good judgment. Collectively, trustees should also have educational and technical qualifications, knowledge, and skills relevant to the duties and responsibilities of an RSE licensee.

Trustees of Australian pension funds must have a set of core skills and must maintain those skills

Core skills required of all pension fund trustees include an understanding of investments, insurance, the Australian legal environment, and Australian taxation requirements. Rather than mandating that trustees have tertiary or other specific education qualifications, APRA puts the onus on trustees to identify their need for continuing education and to undertake appropriate related training. Trustees' skill requirements are not imposed individually but are to be met collectively.

Because the skills required to administer a pension fund are constantly evolving, especially with regard to regulatory and investment market changes, all funds must have a policy that addresses how ongoing training needs are identified and satisfied. Funds must also have a formally documented training register. In cases in which one member of a fund's board has skills and knowledge such that in the person's absence the board would not meet its fitness requirements, the board must have a mechanism in place for succession of that key person.

Propriety standards for pension fund trustees must be met on an individual basis

While the fitness of an Australian pension fund's trustees can, to a large extent, be considered on a collective basis, propriety standards must be met on an individual basis. Governing legislation in Australia provides a minimum statutory test. According to the legislation, a disqualified person may not act as a trustee, investment manager, or custodian of a superannuation entity. Grounds for disqualification include conviction of a dishonesty offense, insolvency, or the existence of a civil penalty order against the person. APRA may, in addition, apply through the court system to disqualify an individual on the basis of breaching its regulations or failure to meet its "fit and proper" standards.

APRA's approach to trustee propriety is that each fund's trustee policy must specify a standard of behavior and conduct. Trustees must then conduct tests against their standard and have a process to deal with failure to meet their standard. Trustees must also have a policy regarding conflict of interest.

Pension fund boards must have robust conflict of interest policies

Within pension fund boards, each person should represent the interests of fund members as a whole, not the groups from which they are appointed. Boards also must maintain robust conflict of interest policies that, at a minimum, specify the manner in which potential conflicts are identified, assessed, and managed. APRA staff typically review funds' conflict of interest policies and examine both individual conflict declarations and funds' conflict of interest registers.

Risk management strategies are required at the trustee level and the fund level

All APRA-supervised funds must establish a risk management strategy and provide that strategy to APRA. At the trustee level, the strategy must cover governance and decision-making risks, outsourcing risks, risks arising from regulatory changes, and risks of theft and fraud. At the fund level, the risk management plan must deal, at a minimum, with the risks to the fund's investment strategy, financial position, and outsourcing arrangements. Risks must be identified, evaluated in terms of likelihood and consequence, managed, and measured.

Conclusion

Strong corporate governance is critical to the prudent financial management and soundness of financial institutions and in maintaining public confidence in the financial system. Observing that a solid governance structure can enhance a pension fund's investment performance, APRA has consistently strived to improve its regulatory and supervisory functions. The governance framework that APRA applies to the pension funds under its supervision establishes prudential standards that set out sound foundations for good governance, guidance on meeting these standards, and guidance on prudent practices.

Selection, Appointment, and Operating Processes for Board Members: The Case of Canada's AIMCo

Jai Parihar, retired Chief Investment Officer, Alberta Investment Management Corporation, Canada*

Under the notion that a qualified, independent board is critical to maintaining a strong governance framework within a pension fund and, in the long term, achieving better investment results, the Alberta Investment Management Corporation (AIMCo) has established systematic board selection, appointment, and governance practices. AIMCo's governance practices include ongoing education of board members, establishment of a solid code of conduct, and institution of a system to manage conflicts of interest.

AIMCo has established five key principles for achieving strong corporate governance

The Alberta Investment Management Corporation (AIMCo) of Canada is a public sector institutional investment manager that manages more than $67 billion on behalf of multiple clients. Approximately $40 billion of this amount is held in balanced funds, including public sector pension plans and endowment funds for the government of the province of Alberta; the remaining amount is held in short-term government assets. AIMCo invests in a range of asset classes in order to deliver appropriate investment options to clients with diverse risk appetites.

AIMCo has established five key principles for achieving strong corporate governance and, ultimately, better overall investment results, These are selection of a qualified board through the application of suitability standards and establishment of a robust selection and appointment process, effective oversight, qualified profes-

---

* The author would like to thank Carole Hunt of the Alberta Investment Management Corporation for participating in discussions about modifications to the selection and operating processes for AIMCo's board members.

sional investment and operations staff, separation of responsibility, and account-ability (figure 3.10).

Figure 3.10 **AIMCo's Key Indicators of Good Governance**

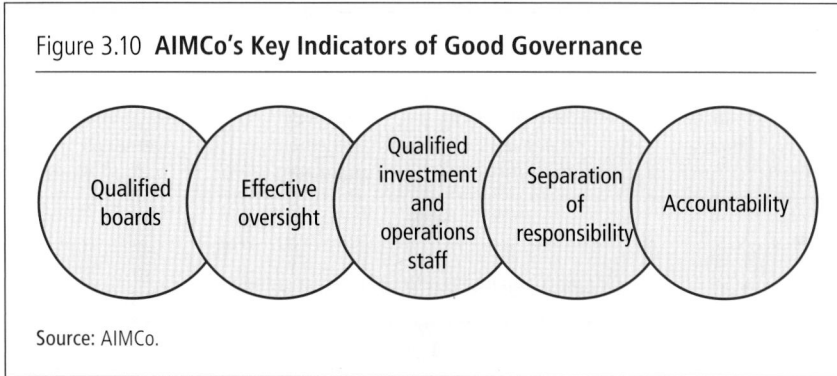

Source: AIMCo.

Specific standards have been set for selecting and appointing board members

Assessing the suitability of potential board members is important for AIMCo. Key suitability standards for board members include competence, relevant skills and experience, understanding of the organization, independent thinking, under-standing of fiduciary responsibility, compatibility, and diversity of background. Specific competencies assessed in the selection and appointment of AIMCo board members include financial literacy, legal expertise, investment management experience and public company governance experience. Candidates must also pass background checks and be assessed on several conflict of interest criteria. Human resource specialists may be used to assist in the selection and appointment process to access highly qualified candidates.

For each AIMCo board vacancy, a nominating committee must propose at least two potential candidates. The list is submitted to Alberta's minister of finance and enterprise, who then recommends one of the candidates to the Alberta Provin-cial Government Cabinet for their final approval. A summary of the nomination process is shown in figure 3.11.

The tenure of AIMCo board members is important to the incentive framework. Board members may serve up to three terms of three years each. Board member terms must be staggered to avoid more than one-third turnover in any year. The Alberta Provincial Government Cabinet appoints the chair of AIMCo's board. Board members and chairs of board committees follow a rigorous self-evaluation process to assess the effectiveness of the board as a whole.

Figure 3.11 **Selection and Appointment Process of AIMCo Board Members**

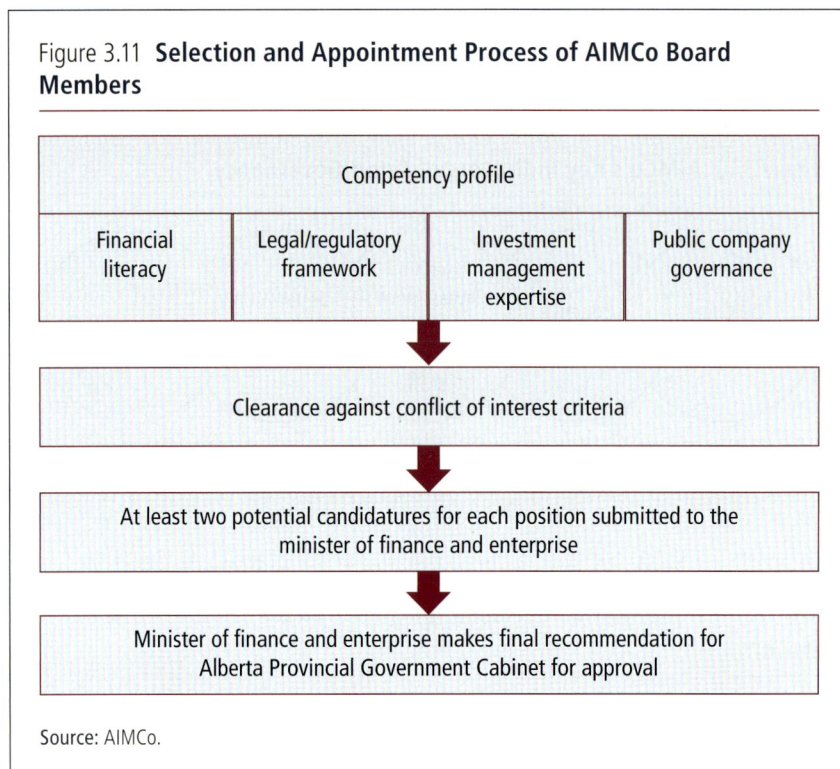

Competency profile

| Financial literacy | Legal/regulatory framework | Investment management expertise | Public company governance |

Clearance against conflict of interest criteria

At least two potential candidatures for each position submitted to the minister of finance and enterprise

Minister of finance and enterprise makes final recommendation for Alberta Provincial Government Cabinet for approval

Source: AIMCo.

Board members are expected to participate in ongoing education programs

Ongoing education of board members is an essential part of the processes used to ensure good governance practices among AIMCo board members. Education programs cover best practices in governance in particular. As needed, training is also provided in developing and strengthening skills in financial literacy, risk measurement and management, understanding the legal environment, and communication.

A clear code of conduct also has been established

AIMCo administers a code of conduct that applies to all AIMCo staff, including senior management. AIMCo's code of conduct also covers conflicts of interest that may arise as a result of material personal, financial, or commercial relationships involving a director, including directorships, employment, interest in business enterprises or professional practices, shared ownership (direct or indirect), existing professional or personal associations with the subject agency, professional associations or relationships, and family relationships. AIMCo maintains processes to carefully manage conflicts of interest in accordance with formal policies.

Key Elements of AIMCo's Code of Conduct

◆ Comply with all applicable laws and regulations.

◆ Always represent interest of clients.

◆ Act with honesty and integrity at all times.

◆ Do not use confidential information for personal benefit.

◆ Avoid taking inappropriate advantage of positions of trust and responsibility.

Conclusion

AIMCo has established key principles for the qualification, selection, and operation of its board. It supports these principles through multiple processes and standards applied to their operation. Recognizing the importance of good governance, AIMCo strives to select independent and qualified individuals who will add value and contribute to a dynamic, high-performing board.

3. Operational Policies and Procedures

◆ Policies and Procedures Needed to Implement Good Governance

◆ Key Ingredients in Developing Operational Policies and Procedures

◆ Effective Policies, Procedures, and Internal Controls: A Regulatory Perspective

Policies and Procedures Needed to Implement Good Governance

Anne Maher, former Chief Executive Officer, Pensions Board, Ireland

A number of policies and procedures are critical in maintaining good governance in public pension funds. Key elements of a good governance structure include solid legislation, appointment of a governance oversight committee, establishment of clear accountability guidelines and transparency measures, ongoing review of investment policy, appropriate identification and control of risks by supervisory authorities, and constant monitoring of cost controls.

Good governance in public pension funds begins with solid legislation and appointment of a governance oversight body

Good governance within public pension funds begins with solid legislation and is essential to managing risk, controlling costs, and achieving long-term returns. A good governance structure of public pension plans has several major characteristics (figure 3.12), starting with the appointment of a responsible party, at the individual and collective levels, which must be accountable to another body—ideally, the country's parliament. The responsible party must be independent from political pressure, and its governance structure should be openly disclosed. Governance of public pension schemes should follow current best-practice guidelines such as those proposed by the Organisation for Economic Co-operation and Development or the International Social Security Association.

The party responsible for good governance should have an unambiguous mandate and clearly defined responsibilities. It should be composed of high-caliber individuals who possess relevant expertise, professionalism, integrity, and the courage to remain independent from political pressures. The governing body should also have clear, sound appointment and removal procedures, and conflict identification and management processes. It is critical that both the governance structure and the roles and responsibilities of the governing body be subject to regular reviews by an external party.

Figure 3.12 **Good Governance: Key Policies and Procedures**

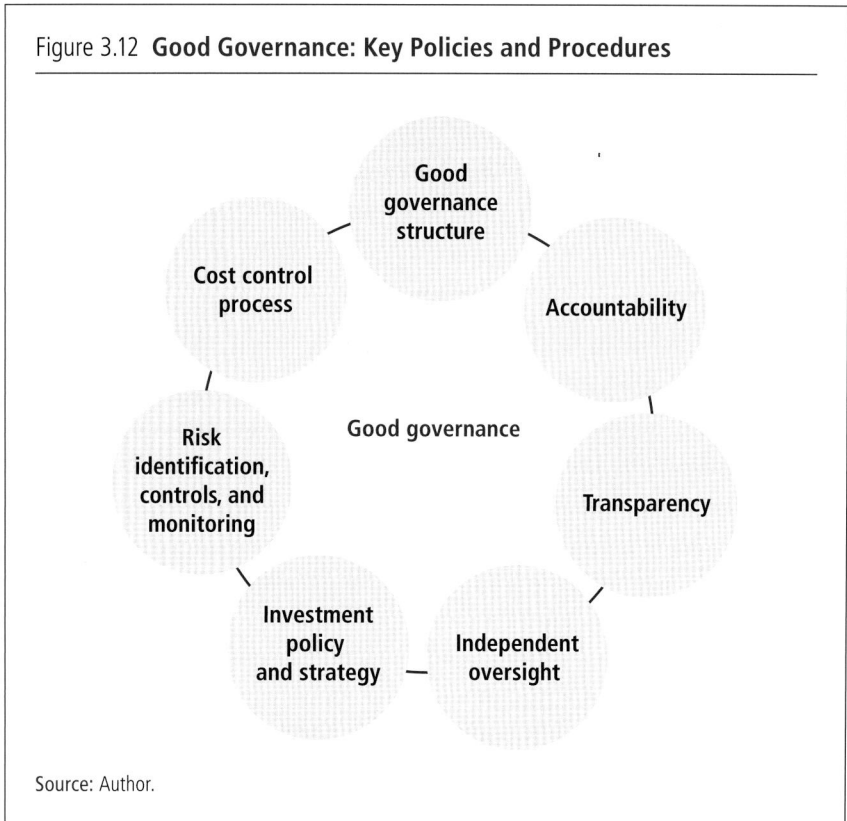

Though they are generally not required to comply with established accounting standards, public pension funds should implement several broad accountability guidelines

In general, public pension funds are not required to comply with national or international accounting standards. However, it is recommended that public pension funds implement the processes, as specified in figure 3.13, to ensure accountability.

Public pension systems also require measures to ensure transparency and independent oversight

Given that they are entrusted with public resources, public pension systems are expected to meet high fiduciary standards. In order to maintain public trust in them, pension systems should implement several processes to enhance transparency and accountability, as detailed in the box opposite.

Protection of the public interest should be further enhanced by exercising independent oversight over the governing body. The most common third-party oversight technique of public pension funds is the periodic auditing of procedures, processes,

---

Figure 3.13 **Processes Ensuring Accountability in Public Pension Schemes**

Accounts	Audits
◆ Accounts should be completed and issued at regular intervals ◆ Accounts should be done to the highest national and international standards ◆ Accounts should have prescribed contents	◆ Audits must be performed by independent, external auditors ◆ Audits must be regular ◆ Audits should adhere to the highest national auditing standards and should include actuarial evaluation

Source: Author.

---

and internal controls by independent, external auditors. In fact, it is often mandatory for public pension plans to have periodic actuarial reports, including valuation of assets and liabilities, prepared by independent, external actuaries. External validation of investment returns is another crucial element of good governance. Cooperation with independent examinations by the government or parliament and full compliance with regulatory requirements will further ensure a high standard of accountability of the governing body.

Ongoing monitoring of investment policy and strategy ensures the effectiveness of a pension fund's governance structure

Close monitoring of investment processes, policies, and strategies by a pension fund's governance oversight body ensures the effectiveness of the governance struc-

---

Processes to Enhance Public Transparency and Accountability

◆ Reports should be published at regular intervals.

◆ The contents of reports should be prescribed.

◆ A reporting mechanism needs to be in place to whomever a responsible party is accountable—preferably to the country's parliament.

◆ There should be public promulgation of reports.

◆ There needs to be a mechanism for the public to obtain relevant information.

◆ Specific information needs to be disclosed to individual beneficiaries, and this could include statements of benefits.

ture and of other parties involved in the operation and oversight of pension funds. The following processes and policies are critical to a strong investment policy and strategy:

- The party responsible for investment should be clearly identified—this may be the overall responsible party or a separate entity established for the purpose of investing.

- The investment mandate should be set out.

- The responsible party should clearly define the investment objectives.

- The responsible party should agree on a statement of investment principles which sets out its policy.

- Consistency between investment objectives and policy is essential.

- The responsible party should set an investment strategy based on its investment objectives and policy.

- The responsible party should determine appropriate benchmarks against which the investment return of the fund can be assessed.

- Investment performance reviews should be held regularly.

- A responsible investment policy might be considered based on the United Nations' Principles for Responsible Investment.

- Any restrictions on investment should be solely for prudential reasons.

- Restrictions should not be imposed for the purpose of achieving other unrelated objectives.

- Minimum restrictions should only be considered in exceptional circumstances.

- Maximum restrictions may be necessary for prudential reasons, for example, to avoid concentration of investments.

- Prudent person principle can work well and avoid the need for investment restrictions.[1]

- Procedures for implementation of investment policy and strategy are necessary.

- Resources and skills must be put in place to implement policy and strategy.

- External advice and support may be required.

---

[1] This principle is a legal requirement that a trustee, investment manager, or fiduciary (trusted agent) must invest funds with which he or she is entrusted as would a person of prudence—that is, with discretion, care, and intelligence.

Increasing their capacity to identify and control risks is important for many pension funds

Expanding public pension funds' ability to assess risk and enhance internal controls is another ongoing concern of many supervisory authorities and governing bodies. A crucial characteristic of a good governance structure is an adequate organizational framework that enables monitoring and control of risk-relevant business activities. A strong risk identification, control, and monitoring system also should be in place, one that includes relevant risk measures such as market risk, credit risk, liquidity risk, and operational risk (figure 3.14). An agreed-upon approach to measuring, monitoring, and managing all of these risks should be implemented.

Information technology systems and detailed control procedures, in line with industry best practice, are needed to further enhance the accountability of the governing body. An external body should be given custody of pension funds' assets, while the governing body must ensure that the external custodian is an independent, reputable provider of custody services. Pension funds' assets held by a custodian must be legally separate from the custodian's own assets. Though the external custodian may entrust assets in specific countries to subcustodians, the legal responsibility for safe custody of all assets should remain with the primary custodian.

Figure 3.14 **Components of Risk Identification, Control, and Monitoring System**

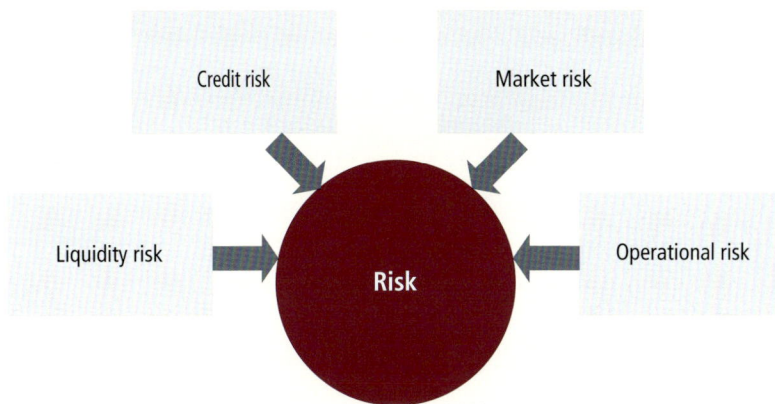

Credit risk

Market risk

Liquidity risk

Risk

Operational risk

Source: Author.

An ongoing cost control and review process should be in place

The expenses of managing and administering public pension funds, which are to some extent passed onto plan members, beneficiaries, and taxpayers, can significantly affect retirement benefits. Though monitoring of costs can be a major governance challenge for pension funds, cost reviews should be performed on a regular basis. Several standard best practices should also be used in regard to costs. Open procurement procedures should be used for all external services. Remuneration structures should be transparent and appropriate. All costs should be properly reported and clearly disclosed. Finally, public pension funds should engage the services of a reputable independent party to compare their own costs with those of other, similar funds.

Conclusion

Good governance, in its broadest sense, has become a key issue in the administration of public pension funds over the last decade. In light of the changing regulatory and market environment and the growing pension fund industry, ensuring that pension funds are run properly has become a major concern for supervisory authorities. It is critical, though, that good governance exist not just in legislation or in theory, but that it is also implemented in practice through operational policies and procedures.

Key Ingredients in Developing Operational Policies and Procedures

Samuel W. Halpern, President, Independent Fiduciary Services, United States

Governing fiduciaries and upper management of pension funds must address numerous areas in order to effectively structure and oversee their investment programs. These include setting out practices and procedures for good governance, developing sound asset allocation, monitoring and reporting investment performance, and controlling investment costs. In many cases, comparing investment management techniques and processes at the peer level can be helpful, as can considering best practices within the pension fund industry.

Pension funds' operational policies should cover three general areas

Well-functioning operational policies and procedures are an essential mechanism for ensuring linkages between pension funds' governance structure and management systems. With regard to operational policies, the management of all pension funds must (1) identify and address aspects of the fund's investment operations, organization, and portfolio necessary to control undue risk and expenses, minimize inefficiency, and achieve the desired long-term return; (2) evaluate the fund's organization and procedures relative to those of its peers and industry best practices; and (3) find ways to enhance public trust and confidence in the pension system.

Critical subjects to be addressed in pension investments are extensive and overlapping

In general, pension funds should address the following issues when establishing and carrying out their investment programs:

♦ *Governance policies and structure*, including the identity, appointment, and removal of governing fiduciaries; the roles of and relationships among members of the governing body, its committees, staff, and external service providers;

procedures for delegation of authority; charters and rules of order; policies regarding ethics, travel and entertainment, and personal securities trading; and internal controls and audit procedures.

◆ *Organizational structure*, including the legal framework defining the fund; the purposes, operations, and fiduciaries of the fund; the relationship of the fund to the sponsor (governmental, corporate, or otherwise), including the nature and degree of autonomy of the fund, its governing body, and upper management; and identification and liabilities of governing fiduciaries and related matters.

◆ *Nature, adequacy, and use of resources*, including internal staff, external professionals, and budgeting.

◆ *Personnel practices*, including the ability to attract and retain qualified staff with sufficient autonomy over hiring, compensation, benefits, and work conditions.

◆ *Investment policy*, including whether the governing body has developed a satisfactory written statement of investment policies that addresses and defines all essential elements of the investment program and its operations.

◆ *Processes for asset allocation*, including which methodologies are utilized, on what data and capital markets assumptions those methodologies are based, in light of what factors those methodologies are chosen (for example, the relationship between assets and liabilities, the need for cash flow and liquidity, and the investment horizon), and what procedures are in place for periodically rebalancing the portfolio.

◆ *Defining the responsibilities of investment consultants* (for example, those specializing in alternative assets), including the working relationship among the consultants, staff, and governing body; the specific tasks and topics assigned to the consultant; the consultants' legal status and liabilities; the structure and level of consultants' fees; and prevention of conflicts of interest.

◆ *Investment management structure*, including the number of investment managers and use of external versus internal asset management; active versus passive management; and separate accounts versus pooled vehicles such as limited partnerships, mutual funds, or bank collective trust funds.

◆ *Monitoring and evaluating investment performance*, including determining who monitors which aspects of performance (at the level of the total fund, by asset class, and by manager account), what data on which performance monitoring is based and relative to what benchmarks, how often performance is monitored, and to which internal controls performance is subject.

◆ *Investment performance reporting*, including what is reported, by and to whom, and how often.

- *Due diligence procedures*, including manager search and selection; subsequent monitoring of such managers; how monitoring should differ according to asset class, strategy, or investment account; and who performs what aspects of measurement and monitoring.

- *Investment program cost and fees*, including costs for asset management, custody, and operations.

- *Brokerage and trading practices*, including procedures for measuring and evaluating commission costs, quality of securities execution, manager transitions, and use of soft dollars and directed brokerage.

- *Nontraditional investment practices*, including those governing alternative assets such as private equity, currencies, and hedge funds; use and management of derivatives (both exchange traded and over the counter); and management of features ranging from valuation and legal risk to costs, illiquidity, and leverage.

- *Trust and custody arrangements*, including fees, securities lending, cash management, operational policies on securities clearance and failures, and reporting and analytical capabilities.

- *Investment accounting and operational controls*, including front-, middle- and back-office functions.

A pension fund's governing body is ultimately responsible for the fund's investment program

Within a pension fund, the governing body is ultimately responsible for the structure, operation, and oversight of the investment program of the fund. While the governing body—either a board of trustees or an investment committee—typically delegates a range of operational matters to internal staff or an external investment manager(s), the governing body still has ultimate responsibility for prudently structuring and monitoring (or arranging to monitor) all governance activities, from asset allocation to measuring and monitoring investment performance to containing investment costs.

One way for a governing body to prudently structure and oversee a fund's investment program is to conduct an independent, impartial evaluation of its essential policies and procedures relative to comparable funds. By assessing how its fund compares to common and best practices, a governing body can gain reassurance regarding which of its aspects compare favorably to other funds and establish a blueprint for implementing practical improvements where warranted. At the same time, this exercise should help establish—in the eyes of all stakeholders—that the governing body is prudently fulfilling its fiduciary responsibility to oversee and structure the investment program (see Halpern and Irving 2005).

All pension funds should issue an investment policy statement articulating the views of the governing body and formally documenting policies and procedures

An investment policy statement (IPS) is an industry standard foundational document for a pension fund's investment program. The essential purposes of the IPS are to articulate the consensus views of the governing body regarding the overall investment program and to document policies and procedures regarding major issues, including

- the fund's mission and purpose;
- investment objectives (including the investment horizon);
- risk tolerance (including liquidity needs);
- roles and responsibilities of key parties within the fund, including the board of trustees, staff, investment consultants, investment managers, and other service providers;
- the fund's asset allocation policy, including the rebalancing process;
- standards and measures of investment performance for each asset class and the portfolio as a whole;
- processes and policies for manager search and selection;
- broad portfolio and asset class investment guidelines, including allowable and prohibited investments;
- other pertinent polices, such as proxy voting and securities lending;
- the process for periodically reviewing the IPS.

Developing a complete IPS should help the governing body of a pension fund reach conclusions on the general investment rules and objectives and help shape the nature and operation of the investment program.

An optimal asset allocation strategy should not only conform to the fund's investment objectives and risk tolerance but take into account several other specific considerations

A pension fund's asset allocation should conform to its investment objectives, risk tolerance over a defined investment horizon, and permissible asset classes and strategies. In determining an optimal asset allocation, a pension fund's investment decision makers should strive to understand and evaluate (1) various methodologies of asset allocation (such as mean variance optimization—MVO) and their limitations; (2) the fund's cash flows, liquidity needs, and investment horizon;

(3) correlation between the fund's assets and liabilities; (4) the asset classes used in the process of asset allocation; (5) capital markets assumptions over the appropriate investment horizon for these asset classes (expected risk, return, and correlation inputs) used in such methodologies; and (6) how the portfolio will likely perform in varying economic scenarios.

The governing body is responsible for the pension fund's risk-return profile, which is primarily driven by its overall asset allocation. This function cannot be delegated to staff or external consultants, although consultants may assist in developing the asset allocation. Prudently determining an asset allocation strategy also requires that the governing body understand generally accepted methods for developing asset allocation, the limitations of such methods, and the judgments and policy decisions it should be prepared to make.

Mean variance optimization is commonly used in developing an asset allocation strategy by considering the trade-off between risk and return, though it has limitations

A commonly used methodology for developing an asset allocation strategy is MVO, a quantitative process based on assumptions for three inputs regarding capital markets: expected return for each asset class used in the process, expected risk for each asset class, and expected correlation of returns among asset classes (figure 3.15). The purpose of MVO is to assess various combinations of asset classes in order to identify combinations with sufficient probability of achieving a particular, expected, average long-term return at a given level of risk or, for any given level of expected risk, a sufficient probability of achieving the highest expected, average long-term return.

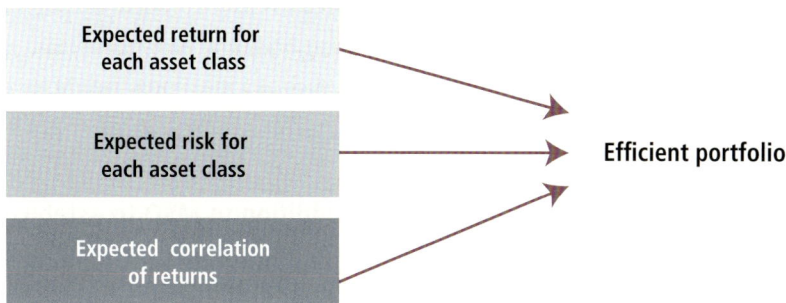

Figure 3.15 **Mean Variance Optimization Methodology Inputs**

Expected return for each asset class

Expected risk for each asset class

Expected correlation of returns

Efficient portfolio

Source: Independent Fiduciary Services.

Investment decision makers should use the output of **MVO** models as a starting point for evaluating asset allocation, not as an endpoint prescription

Despite its ubiquity, MVO suffers numerous limitations. First, the methodology is very sensitive to the inputs. Thus, defining an asset class and the capital markets assumptions for each asset class is critical. For example, whereas some practitioners distinguish between large- and small-capitalization publicly traded U.S. equities for purposes of MVO (and therefore use different assumptions for risk, return, and correlation for those categories), other practitioners define U.S. publicly traded equities as a single category with a single set of assumptions.

However asset classes are defined and whatever assumptions are used, the optimizer assumes the inputs are precisely accurate, when in fact they are only estimates, subject to a high degree of error over time. For illustrative purposes, table 3.9 sets forth the 2010 risk and return assumptions for a range of asset classes adopted by the investment advisory firm Independent Fiduciary Services for its MVO analysis.

Other limitations of MVO are that it assumes the expected returns are normally distributed (defined by their mean and standard deviation), which is very often not the case, and that all inputs and the interrelationships among them remain static over time, which is unrealistic (consider returns in 2008 and 2009, for example). Furthermore, "risk" in MVO analysis is typically defined in terms of variability of returns, as measured by standard deviation, but more severe tail risks may lie beyond that. MVO also does not specifically take into account considerations such as liquidity needs, operational and legal risks, asset management fees, and policy concerns, all of which may be significant in the real world. Considering all of these factors, the optimizer may produce portfolios that are unrealistic: for example, heavily weighted toward alternative assets without regard to other attributes of a particular asset class such as high fees, significant illiquidity, or extensive monitoring infrastructure which may be required to ensure prudent oversight. In light of this concern, the pension fund's governing body and investment team may impose subjective constraints on MVO output, such as a maximum weight for one or more asset classes.

Many pension funds use approaches in addition to MVO to establish an asset allocation strategy

Because of the limitations of pure MVO, many pension funds overlay an additional line of analysis, such as the expected performance of different types of assets in

Table 3.9 **2010 Risk and Return Assumptions for a Range of Asset Classes (%)**

Asset class	Return	Risk
Cash equivalents (short-term investment funds)	3.00	1.00
U.S. Treasury bonds (10-year)	3.50	7.00
Investment-grade bonds (core)	4.00	5.75
Below-investment-grade bonds	5.75	10.25
Inflation-linked bonds (Treasury Inflation-Protected Securities)	4.25	7.25
Global equities (developed and emerging markets)	8.00	19.00
U.S. equities	8.00	17.75
Non-U.S. equities	8.00	19.25
Hedge funds/active alternatives	7.00	8.25
Real estate (private, core)	7.00	10.75
Commodities (diversified, long only)	6.75	19.00
Private markets (leveraged buyouts, venture capital, mezzanine debt)	10.25	31.00

Source: Independent Fiduciary Services.

Note: For U.S. consumer price inflation, the central expectation is 3.00 percent with a standard deviation of 1.25 percent.

various economic climates and the economic factors underlying such performance. This approach develops the asset allocation methodology less in terms of capital allocation across asset classes and more in terms of risk allocation and economic factors.

As illustrated in figure 3.16, in a market environment of rising inflation and economic growth, commodities and inflation-protected securities are expected to generate the most satisfactory returns among various asset classes. By contrast, in an environment of rising inflation and a simultaneously contracting economy, inflation-protected securities are likely to perform best. Under a scenario of rising growth but falling inflation, equities are expected to perform best, whereas government bonds typically perform best when an economy is contracting and inflation is declining. This and similar lines of analysis enable pension funds to assess the extent to which their portfolios are premised on economic conditions that may (or may not) ensue and the risks of insufficient diversification.

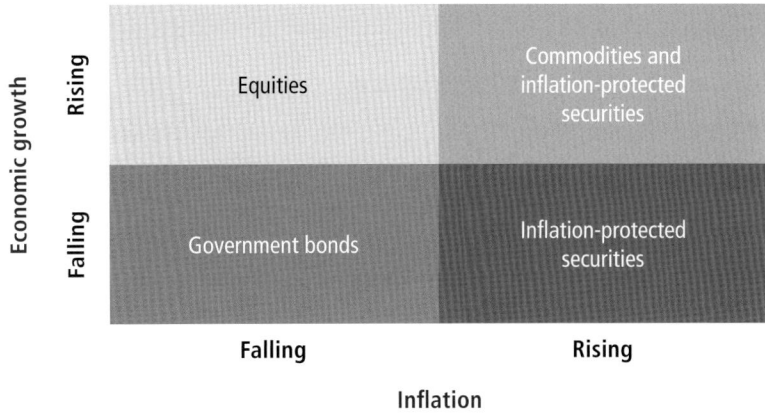

Figure 3.16 **Best Asset Class Performance, by Economic Environment**

Source: Independent Fiduciary Services.

Note: Falling/rising economic growth indicates economic contraction/expansion, not that the pace of growth is slowing/speeding up.

Monitoring a pension fund's investment performance can be done through several channels—performance reports, a policy index, evaluation of individual accounts, or ensuring adherence to guidelines

Providing an accurate assessment of a pension fund's investment performance is crucial for internal and external stakeholders, including fund participants, interested labor organizations, taxpayers, the media, and—in the case of public funds—the legislative and executive branches of the country in which the fund is domiciled. The governing body requires clear, concise, and practical reports concerning investment performance and risks in order to fulfill its fiduciary responsibility to oversee the investment program. Designing and implementing strong monitoring and reporting standards requires the governing body to develop sound policies and procedures related to what to measure and how, who measures and evaluates, against what benchmarks monitoring and reporting standards are measured, how often monitoring and reporting evaluations are conducted, on what data evaluations are based and who provides those data, how monitoring and reporting relate to governance, and reporting to different audiences.

Though investment performance is a far-reaching and complex subject, one way to begin addressing it is by distinguishing between measuring and evaluating the whole pension portfolio versus distinct asset classes and distinct accounts and, thereafter, by developing and applying different measures and benchmarks for each such component. To measure and evaluate the whole portfolio, including the effectiveness of asset allocation, two fundamental benchmarks are helpful: a *policy index* and an *asset allocation index*. The policy index is a static weighting of market indexes using the same percentages as for strategic target allocation—for example, 60 percent global equities and 40 percent global bonds. By contrast, the asset allocation index is a dynamic weighting—for example, 62 percent equities and 38 percent bonds at the end of the first quarter, but 59 percent equities and 41 percent bonds at the end of the second quarter.

The combination of these two benchmarks should assist in performance attribution—that is, it should enable the governing body to analyze which asset management decisions add to or impair investment results. The performance of the actual portfolio, however, may differ from that of the policy index as a result of fundamental policy decisions by the governing body or its delegates, such as how far to allow the portfolio's asset class weightings to vary from the static or strategic targets, or whether performance management is active or passive.

Identifying which of these factors has influenced portfolio performance requires applying both the policy index and the asset allocation index, as the asset allocation index effectively neutralizes most of the impact on portfolio performance of asset class "drift." The asset allocation index weightings move (with some unavoidable imprecision due to factors such as time lags) essentially in tandem with the portfolio's asset class weightings. If the global equities market index outperforms the global bond market index over a given time period and the governing body had previously decided to overweight its global equities, that decision, per se, should be additive to performance. If, on the other hand, the fund's actual global equity managers underperformed the global equity index, that would detract from performance. Applying the two indexes to assessments of portfolio performance enables more precise and informative performance attribution, and thus should lead the governing body to better-informed judgments regarding concrete action on decisions such as revising the asset allocation or terminating a particular investment account.

At the level of individual accounts, what investment performance dimensions are measured and how to evaluate those dimensions differ according to type of portfolio. For instance, assessing risks involved with an equity portfolio differs substantially from assessing risks involved with a fixed-income portfolio. Peer comparisons—such as how one active manager's performance compares to the performance of other managers overseeing similar accounts—are another useful tool at the level of individual accounts. Returns for a given account may be assessed over varying time periods, including single years or cumulative, trailing periods, and may be considered in terms of absolute returns or risk-adjusted returns (such as Sharpe ratios, Sortino ratios, alpha, and beta). For some purposes, returns should be measured gross of fees (that is, before deducting asset management fees), while for others they should be measured net of (after) such fees.

Another aspect of performance monitoring is properly enforcing adherence to investment guidelines. Typically, in connection with hiring a manager of a separately managed account, a pension fund should agree with the manager on a detailed set of written investment guidelines governing the nature, objectives, risks, and financial characteristics of the account. The precise content and degree of latitude suitable for the account will vary enormously with the particular mandate and overall circumstances. In all cases, the governing body should ensure that someone within the fund with sufficient resources, skills, and objectivity monitors whether the manager is indeed managing the account in conformance with such guidelines.

Three practical considerations are relevant for pension fund governing bodies in considering a fund's investment performance:

◆ All these measurements and evaluations of investment performance ultimately rest on the integrity, timeliness, accessibility, and level of detail of the underlying data. The format, clarity, and timeliness of information from the custodian is thus an essential foundation in building any system of performance attribution and risk management.

◆ The type, format, and frequency of reporting and analysis should reflect the particular user or audience involved. Information necessary and suitable for a fund's investment consultant or chief investment officer typically differs from (and is far more extensive and frequent than) information appropriate for the governing body.

◆ To ensure the integrity of the measurement and evaluation process, the governing body should ensure sufficient separation of functions among the parties responsible for *measuring* performance, the parties responsible for *generating* the performance (asset managers and asset allocators), and the parties responsible for *evaluating* performance. In pension funds with staff responsible for both some degree of internal asset management and oversight of external managers, this may present challenges.

Investment management fees should be subject to ongoing monitoring by a pension fund's governance body

Pension fund's investment management fees differ depending on the number and type of investment managers and how those managers interrelate. That said,

---

Investment Performance Monitoring

◆ The format, clarity, and timeliness of information from the custodian are an essential foundation on which to build any system of performance attribution and risk management.

◆ The type, format, and frequency of reporting and analysis should reflect the particular user or audience involved.

◆ The governing body should ensure a sufficient separation of functions among

   – the parties responsible for **measuring** performance,

   – the parties responsible for **generating** the performance,

   – the parties responsible for **evaluating** performance.

Source: Independent Fiduciary Services.

---

a fund's governing body should periodically monitor the appropriateness and consistency of fees and how they compare to fees incurred by other institutional investors, taking into account the fund's characteristics and operational environment. Funds may obtain comparative information from direct experience with and knowledge of other funds, as well as from third-party industry survey data.

When monitoring custodial costs, fiduciaries should consider the structure and level of contractually stated fees and the custodial agreement to determine whether the services are provided at a reasonable cost. Often, upon examination, the custody agreement allows for hidden costs such as unfavorable policies on fail float or crediting of income items, or excessive costs for cash management.

Conclusion

The inventory of critical subjects regarding a pension fund's investments program is extensive, and the fund's governing body is ultimately responsible for assessing and overseeing all of them. An expert, objective evaluation of such matters may assist the governing body in fulfilling its fiduciary duty. Some of the key elements requiring the governing body's focus include clearly articulated governance policies; a comprehensive, written investment policy statement; a well-thought-out asset allocation process; clearly defined and appropriate measures, monitoring processes, and reporting content/frequency for the fund's investment performance; and monitoring of investment costs in absolute terms and relative to the fund's peers.

Reference

Halpern, S., and A. Irving. 2005. "Identifying and Adopting Best Practices for Institutional Investors." In J. Clay Singleton, ed., *Core-Satellite Portfolio Management: A Modern Approach to Professionally Managed Funds.* New York: McGraw Hill.

Effective Policies, Procedures, and Internal Controls: A Regulatory Perspective

Ross Jones, Deputy Chairman, Australian Prudential Regulation Authority

Measures that assist in good governance within pension funds have more impact when they are backed by an effective regulatory body. One regulator, the Australian Prudential Regulation Authority (APRA), uses risk-based and outcomes-focused elements in evaluating the efficiency of pension fund governance. Specifically, APRA utilizes two key supervisory tools to measure the effectiveness of policies, procedures, and internal controls, and to ensure that operational risks are consistently and rigorously assessed and that supervisory interventions are targeted and timely.

APRA uses two risk assessment and governance oversight tools to evaluate governance effectiveness

Following the lead of banking and insurance sector supervisors, an increasing number of pension supervisory authorities have adopted a risk-based approach to governance. The Australian Prudential Regulation Authority (APRA), for example, utilizes two supervisory tools to ensure that governance risks within Australian pension funds are assessed rigorously and consistently and that supervisory interventions are targeted and timely: the Probability and Impact Rating System (PAIRS) and the Supervisory Oversight and Response System (SOARS). APRA's approach identifies key risks; determines appropriate supervisory activities; and ensures that risks are adequately measured, managed, and monitored.

APRA's primary method of risk identification and governance assessment includes on-site visits to trustees of pension funds. As illustrated in figure 3.17, assessing governance risks covers three primary areas: (1) the role, responsibilities, composition, and functioning of trustees and subcommittees, including the audit committee and implementation of appropriate reporting lines; (2) review of risk management standards and risk management plans, including verification of how

---

Figure 3.17 **Governance Risk Assessment in Pension Funds**

Trustees	**Risk management**	**Compliance**
◆ Roles, responsibilities, composition ◆ Reporting lines	◆ Risk management standards, policies, and procedures ◆ Risk mitigation plans	◆ Compliance framework ◆ Internal controls ◆ Independent management

Source: APRA.

such standards are embedded in the business, applied in practice, and reviewed to keep pace with changing business conditions; and (3) review of the compliance framework and other internal or independent functions in place to assess the adequacy of and adherence to operational controls and risk management policies and procedures. Governance assessment also includes a review of the skills, experience, resourcing, and effectiveness of independent review functions, including audit, actuarial and risk management, and compliance.

Based on analysis of governance risk in the three areas identified above, on-site work, and any prior knowledge, APRA supervisors compile an assessment of a pension fund's risk governance. Each fund is scored on a scale of 0–4, with 0 indicating very strong governance and 4 indicating extremely weak governance.

When APRA finds that a pension fund has "poor" risk governance, a series of actions may be taken:

◆ Requirements may be imposed by APRA in order to make improvements in areas where weaknesses have been identified.

◆ Recommendations for improvement may be made.

◆ If requirements/recommendations are not addressed effectively and on time, further action, such as imposition of conditions on a fund's license, may be implemented.

Risk governance is only one of several areas assessed by APRA. A 0–4 scale is applied to assess four other areas: operational risk, market and investment risk, strategy and planning risk, and liquidity risk. All of APRA's risk assessments are part of the PAIRS tool, which is designed to incorporate an importance factor

Characteristics of Strong Governance Used by APRA in Scoring Pension Funds' Governance

◆ Role and responsibilities of the board are clear

◆ Strong evidence that the board provides clear direction and leadership

◆ Risk management framework and statement are regularly reviewed and exceed minimum requirements

◆ Committee structure is well established and strong evidence that committees function effectively

◆ Audit committee is well established, exceeds prudential requirements, and functions effectively

◆ Performance of the board and committees is regularly reviewed

◆ Strong internal and external audit and actuarial functions

◆ Independent, high-quality staff that is adequately resourced and effective

◆ Strong compliance function that is independent, adequately resourced, and with clear and effective resolution processes

or significance weight to each key risk area according to the business profile of a regulated institution.

In addition to allocating a score to risk measures, APRA uses a weighting system that assigns a level of significance to each of the five risk areas. Risk governance has the highest weighting (on average, around 25 percent) and operational risk the second highest weighting, followed by market and investment risk. The high weight on governance reflects the importance APRA places on good governance in the trustee model.

The SOARS is intended to ensure that supervisory interventions are targeted and timely

APRA uses SOARS to determine how to act on supervisory concerns based on risk assessments made under PAIRS. SOARS is intended to ensure that supervisory interventions are targeted and timely. All APRA-regulated entities that are subject to PAIRS assessment are also assigned one of four stances under SOARS: *normal, oversight, mandated improvement,* and *restructure.* The supervision stance of a regulated entity is determined based on the PAIRS probability rating and impact rating matrix (table 3.10).

Table 3.10 **APRA's Assessment of Supervisory Concerns**

Probability rating

		Low	Lower medium	Upper medium	High	Extreme
Impact rating	Extreme					
	High					
	Medium					
	Low					

Normal *Oversight* *Oversight* *Mandated improvement* *Restructure*

Source: APRA.

Determining a supervision strategy is an integral component of APRA's supervision process

Once it establishes a risk profile and supervision stance for each pension plan, APRA determines its supervision strategy for each plan subject to PAIRS. The objective of a supervision strategy is to select the supervision activities to be performed over the supervision period. These activities are usually coordinated by the responsible supervision team. The supervision process incorporates a feedback loop, or a control cycle, as depicted in figure 3.18. In general, APRA's supervision strategy varies according to the fund's assigned supervision stance. If an entity's response to identified risks or prudential concerns is inadequate, its PAIRS risk rating will increase; this inadequacy is also reflected through more intense SOARS supervision. The SOARS categories of "mandated improvement" and "restructure"

Figure 3.18 **APRA's Supervision Process: Application of a Feedback Loop**

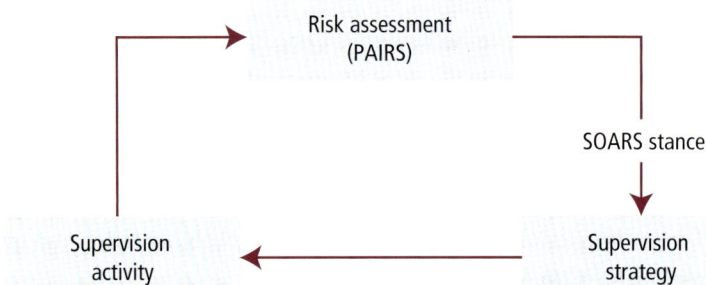

Risk assessment (PAIRS)

SOARS stance

Supervision strategy

Supervision activity

Source: APRA.

involve rigorous supervision activities such as changing of license conditions and enforcement actions. Supervision strategies are reevaluated after the PAIRS risk assessment has been updated.

Conclusion

A strong governance and prudential framework is an essential component of successful pension schemes, particularly employer-based schemes with a trustee-based design. Effective legislation, regulations, and supervision assist financial institutions in designing and implementing good governance models, including the processes, policies, and internal controls surrounding such models. APRA's duty as the prudential regulator of Australian pension funds is to protect the interests of beneficiaries and superannuation fund members and ensure that their interests are not compromised by the actions of the board and management of APRA-regulated institutions. Two supervisory tools, PAIRS and SOARS, are the centerpieces of APRA's risk-based approach to supervision. They assist pension fund governance bodies in making sound risk judgments, quickly and consistently taking supervisory actions where necessary, and improving oversight and reporting on problem entities.

4. Managing Fiscal Pressures in Defined-Benefit Schemes

◆ Building Sustainable Defined-Benefit Pension Schemes: The Landscape for Reform

◆ Creating a Sound Funding Framework: The Experience of OMERS in Canada

◆ Lessons from Defined-Benefit Pension Funds in Japan

Building Sustainable Defined-Benefit Pension Schemes: The Landscape for Reform

Juan Yermo, Head, Private Pensions Unit, Organisation for Economic Co-operation and Development

Several reforms are needed to make defined-benefit pension systems more financially sustainable. Policy action is needed to make funding regulations more countercyclical and to avoid introducing excessive volatility in pension accounting standards. Regulators should strengthen governance and risk management requirements, especially in countries where there are clear deficiencies in these areas. Pension plan sponsors and employees should think about more sustainable and meaningful defined-benefit promises via hybrid pension arrangements that provide benefit predictability to plan members and employers while reducing the volatility of contributions and funding requirements. The portability of pensions is also a basic requirement for making hybrid plans attractive to plan members.

Despite losing significant value during the financial crisis, defined-benefit pension plans can protect plan members from the volatility of financial markets

Defined-benefit pension funds were on the wane throughout much of the corporate world prior to the 2008–09 financial crisis. Their appeal to employer plan sponsors had diminished in line with a variety of structural trends—globalization and the entry of low-cost producers into world markets, the sectoral shift from manufacturing to services in many countries, and increasing life expectancy. In addition, regulatory and accounting reforms have created major pressures on employers sponsoring defined-benefit plans. In countries such as Ireland, Sweden, and the United Kingdom, the closure of occupational defined-benefit plans is well under way.

Despite dealing a heavy financial blow to defined-benefit plans, the financial crisis has also demonstrated that some types of defined-benefit plans can be of great value to plan members, protecting them from the volatility of financial markets. Three main messages for defined-benefit pension schemes seeking to address sustainability needs in the face of the financial crisis are as follows: (1) hybrid plans are one way to avoid growing costs of defined-benefit schemes and the uncertainty of defined-contribution schemes; (2) regulations and accounting standards are necessary to encourage long-term, countercyclical funding and investment policies; and (3) good governance and risk management are critical to sustainable pension promises.

Hybrid pension arrangements may alleviate the burden of growing costs to defined-benefit plan sponsors and decrease the uncertainty of benefits to defined-contribution plan members

Traditionally, defined-benefit plans afforded life benefits based on a member's final preretirement salary and provided some degree of indexation to prices or wages after retirement. Over time, however, these features have proven to be increasingly expensive to maintain. Simultaneously, regulations have become more protective of these benefit promises, increasingly treating them as contractual obligations rather than targets. Moving to a sustainable pension environment requires recognizing the value of benefit predictability to plan members and employers while selecting benefit designs that reduce the volatility of contributions and funding requirements. "Hybrid" pension plans may support financial sustainability and allocate risks of defined-benefit plans in a variety of ways. Hybrid fund features that support sustainability include

◆ benefits calculated based on career-average wages;

◆ conditional indexation of benefits, requiring that accrued benefits be indexed relative to the plan's funding status;

◆ linking of the minimum retirement age and minimum years of contributions required for a full pension or linking the pension benefit itself to life expectancy;

◆ as a last recourse, reductions in accrued benefits.

Such features are present in a variety of plans around the world, including conditional indexation and collective defined-contribution plans in the Netherlands and other European countries and cash balance plans in Japan and the United States.

Figure 3.19 illustrates how one Dutch pension fund, Pensioenfonds Zorg & Welzijn (PFZW), applies conditional indexation to its funds, where the indexation factor is based on average wage growth. PFZW's indexation ladder also depends on the fund's nominal and real funded ratios and is linked to wage inflation. PFZW does not provide indexation when the nominal funded ratio falls below 105 percent (the minimum required by law), and full indexation is provided when the funded ratio is above 130 percent. When the nominal funded ratio falls between 105 percent and 130 percent, partial indexation applies. Extra indexation is given when the real funded ratio is above 100 percent but indexation was not provided in the past because the 105 percent mark was missed.

Figure 3.19 **Conditional Indexation by PFZW**

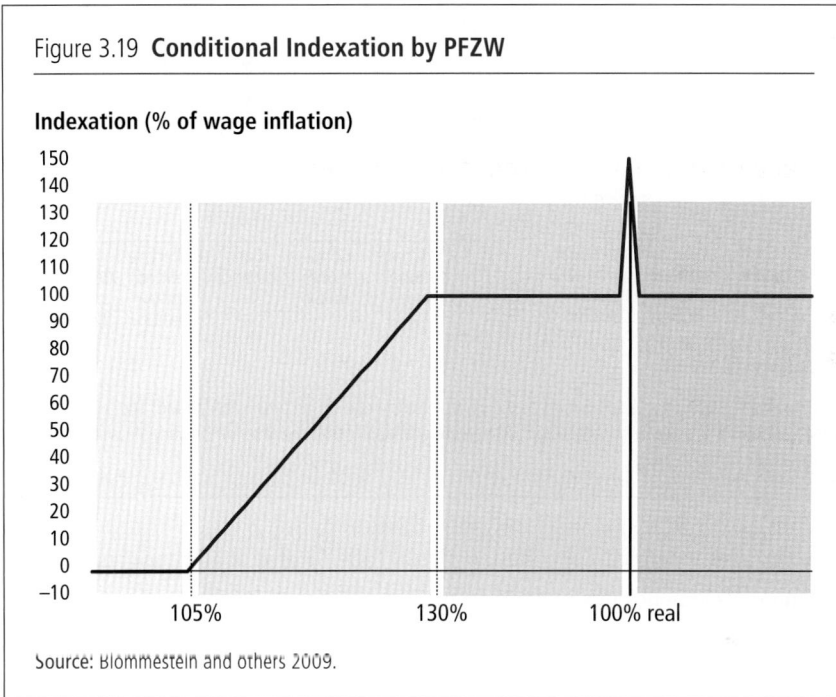

Source: Blommestein and others 2009.

Figure 3.20 illustrates the nominal funded ratios and income replacement rate projections at the end of a 40-year period for five types of pension plans: (1) a defined-benefit plan providing guaranteed or unconditional indexation, (2) a defined-benefit plan providing conditional indexation, (3) a cash balance plan, (4) a collective defined-contribution plan, and (5) an individual defined-contribution plan in which all risks are borne by the plan member.

Since the projections in figure 3.20 are based on a fixed contribution rate, the greater the security sought in the target replacement rate (that is, the range of possible outcomes is minimized), the greater the variability in the funded ratio. As depicted in the figure, the range of possible funded ratio outcomes and replacement rates is very large. Though a plan with unconditional indexation offers a replacement rate of around 70 percent under all scenarios, the corresponding nominal funded ratio ranges between 20 percent and nearly 490 percent (funded ratios below and above these levels each have a 5 percent probability). At the other

Figure 3.20 **Nominal Funded Ratio and Replacement Rate Projections for Various Pension Plans after 40 Years**

a. Nominal funded ratio

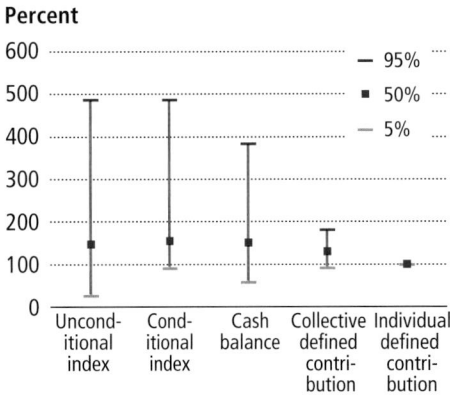

b. Replacement rate at 65

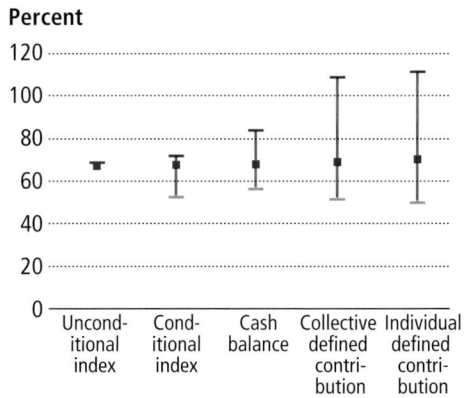

Source: Blommestein and others 2009.

Note: The cross marks in the figures depict the median level of the variable at the end of the projection period. The confidence interval for the variables is ±5 percent, indicating a 90 percent probability that the level of the variable will be within the bar shown in the figure after 40 years.

extreme, a pure defined-contribution plan is fully funded at all times but leads to income replacement rates ranging from 50 percent to 112 percent. By choosing a suitable hybrid arrangement, pension plan sponsors can maintain a certain level of predictability in benefits (which is valuable to plan members) while ensuring a low level of volatility in funding, and hence in contributions (which is valuable to sponsoring employers).

Funding regulations have the potential to encourage long-term, countercyclical funding and increase the security of members' benefits

Three essential goals of pension plan funding are the long-term viability, stability, and security of member benefits. Reform of funding regulations for defined-benefit pension schemes to make them more countercyclical can help achieve these goals while making defined-benefit schemes more attractive to plan sponsors, who are increasingly moving away from defined-benefit and toward defined-contribution plans.

If designed properly, funding regulations can help maintain defined-benefit systems for the long term and provide greater member security. Broadly speaking, funding regulations should (1) encourage deficit reduction contributions and appropriate buildup of surplus when plan sponsor finances are strong, (2) help maintain predictable costs and dampen volatility, and (3) give plan sponsors more control over risk management and costs. In general, pension policy reform should aim to make funding regulations more countercyclical in nature. Such measures have the potential to both strengthen the security of members' benefits in defined-benefit plans and help to maintain defined-benefit plans for future workers. Severinson and Yermo (2010) suggest several policy measures for maintaining this balance.

First, excessive reliance on current market values of pension assets and liabilities for purposes of determining contribution requirements should be avoided. Though disclosure to plan stakeholders based on current market prices may be appropriate to increase transparency, regulators should decrease the weight of volatility of market prices in determining contribution requirements.

Second, appropriate levels of overfunding in good economic times via flexible tax ceilings should be allowed. One possibility that could be explored in the wider context of country-specific regulation is for maximum contributions, or funding ceilings, to span a multiyear period rather than be set on an annual basis, allowing greater management of cash flows by the plan sponsor. Governments should also consider raising the maximum level of surplus before contributions must be suspended.

Third, contribution holidays and plan sponsor access to surplus should be limited. Regulators should consider restricting the extent to which plan sponsors can take contribution holidays, offer additional benefits, or withdraw a portion of pension fund surplus—for example, by allowing such actions only when funding reaches a certain amount above the minimum level.

Fourth, funding rules should incorporate flexibility that reflects the overall volatility of funding valuations. While plan member security must be maintained, funding regulations should be structured so as not to put undue pressure on plan sponsors at times when their own profitability, or even continuity, is under pressure. For instance, the recovery periods required for plan sponsors to elimi-nate funding deficits should reflect the overall volatility of funding levels. The level of flexibility in funding rules also depends on factors such as the extent to which the fund can rely on additional plan sponsor contributions and what other type of security mechanisms, such as pension guarantee or insurance schemes, are in place to protect scheme assets and members from the pension fund or plan sponsor's insolvency.

And fifth, overregulation and regulatory instability should be avoided. Plan sponsors crave predictability, stability, and simplicity in funding and accounting rules. Policy makers should therefore avoid continuously changing and excessively complex regulation, as this will discourage plan sponsors from making long-term pension promises.

Policy Measures That Aim Toward Making Pension Funds' Funding Regulations More Countercyclical

◆ Avoidance of excessive reliance on current market values of pension assets and liabilities for purposes of determining contribution requirements

◆ Allowance of appropriate levels of overfunding in good economic times via more flexible tax ceilings

◆ Limitation of contribution holidays and plan sponsor access to surplus

◆ Flexibility of funding rules in order to reflect the overall volatility of funding valuations

◆ Avoidance of overregulation and maintenance of a stable regulatory environment

---

Proposed changes to accounting standards are expected to affect pension funds in coming years

Accounting standards related to pension funds, in particular International Accounting Standard (IAS) 19 and similar standards used at the national and international level, are a major driving factor behind the decision of many corporations to discontinue their defined-benefit pension plans. The growing popularity in recent years of accounting standards with significant mark-to-market components, combined with periods of poor asset performance and low interest rates, has brought pension plans into serious focus in corporate board rooms. Even companies with relatively modestly sized pension plans can have pension obligations that dwarf other obligations in their financial statements. Though mark-to-market accounting rules have arguably increased transparency and comparability of corporate financial statements, the effect of defined-benefit systems on volatile corporate profits as actualized by mark-to-market accounting rules may increasingly dominate arguably more fundamental issues—such as long-term corporate profitability, corporate culture, regulatory environment, and long-term financing strategies—as the biggest driver behind how and in what manner corporations remunerate their employees.

Certain aspects of widely used pension accounting standards are controversial. For instance, large swings in funding levels can be caused by relatively small shifts in bond rates, rather than by inherent changes to the solvency position of corporate-sponsored defined-benefit pension plans. The International Accounting Standards Board (IASB) has proposed several limited-scope amendments to IAS 19 and the pronouncement is pending for a fundamental review of all aspects of post-employment benefit accounting. In particular, IASB is expected to prohibit smoothing features allowed under the current standard and replace them with the requirement to immediately recognize actuarial gains and losses.

Critics of smoothing argue that it obscures the true financial position of the pension plan and that its elimination would ensure a transparent, unbiased disclosure of the impact of defined-benefit pensions on a company's financial statement. On the other hand, defined-benefit pension plans are long-term contracts between a company and its employees, and thus the valuation of these promises according to market prices as if they were being held for trading creates unwarranted volatility on a company's balance sheet. In reality, pension promises can have very different values, depending on whether one expects the plan to continue in the future. For plan members, the main concern is the extent to which the pension promises would be covered by existing plan assets if the sponsor went bankrupt. For shareholders, accounting disclosures should as far as possible act as a reliable predictor of future changes in pension contributions for an ongoing plan. As noted in Severinson (2008), it is far from clear that the proposed changes to IAS 19 would achieve these goals.

Strengthening governance and risk management is essential

Good pension fund governance is an essential precondition for sustainable pensions. At the helm of all pension funds is a governing body, a board of trustees or the equivalent, that has responsibility for managing funds in times of crisis. These boards set, or at least approve, the strategic investment policy of the fund, which determines its exposure to risky assets and hence critically affects its performance both during the crisis and in the long term. A high level of knowledge and expertise on investment matters is therefore essential to ensuring that boards properly assess the pros and cons of their chosen investment strategy.

Much work remains to be done in the area of pension fund governance, however. In many countries, pension fund trustees are often chosen for their role as representatives of employers or employees rather than their specific knowledge of pension and investment matters (Stewart and Yermo 2008). Policy initiatives have been aimed mainly at promoting trustee training. A good example of such training is the United Kingdom's Pensions Regulator's Trustee Toolkit, a free, online training facility. That said, there are limitations to what such training programs can achieve. Stricter regulations surrounding licensing or certification of trustees may be required—as are under way in Australia, among other countries. A radical governance reform could be to transform current employer and employee representatives into an oversight body and assign fiduciary responsibilities on a professional management board. Such a dual board structure is already common in Germany, for example.

Good governance also calls for adequate risk management systems. Above all, it is imperative that risks faced by defined-benefit pension funds are clearly identified. Once the risks are identified, the next step is to determine the institutions' stance with respect to the risk. Is the risk to be tolerated, mitigated, or (to the extent possible) eliminated? The final step is to establish processes and reporting mechanisms to ensure adequate monitoring, control, and disclosure of the risks. Funds must also have a written risk management strategy covering these three stages.

On the investment front, risk managers are reviewing their models to take tail risks, or extreme events, into greater account. Stochastic modeling, stress testing, and other tools to simulate extreme negative events are increasingly being used by pension funds, and in fact are a regulatory requirement in countries such as Denmark and Germany. While useful, such tools also have limitations, as correlations between various asset classes observed during past crisis may fail to materialize during future adverse events. As often observed, the future may look very different from the past. In the end, prudent management of pension funds is a tall order. In all cases, pension funds should avoid relying on a single indicator of their risk exposure or a specific tool to manage risk. Similarly, it is critical to develop a risk management culture throughout the organization and ensure appropriate reporting and disclosure of the main risks to which the institution is exposed.

The need for strengthening risk management is all the more necessary as defined-benefit pension funds increasingly use hedging techniques involving the use of derivatives and invest part of their assets in alternative investments (such as private equity, hedge funds, and commodities) that may suffer from low levels of liquidity, poor disclosure of underlying investment strategies, and short performance track records. Pension funds' risk management strategies should specifically address how risks related to derivatives and alternative investments will be monitored and managed.

Conclusion

The outlook for defined-benefit plans can be improved considerably if the stakeholders involved engage in a dialogue to identify the features of benefit design and regulation that have made these plans increasingly expensive for plan sponsors without necessarily improving their attractiveness to plan members. Benefit designs that incorporate hybrid features are increasingly seen as part of the solution, but policy makers must also contribute to a solution by introducing countercyclical funding regulations that provide stability and predictability to funding requirements. Stricter governance and risk management requirements should also be on the policy agenda.

Two other major policy issues that should be considered are the need for portability of benefits in defined-benefit plans, so that when workers switch employers they can transfer their accrued rights to the new plan; and the interaction between funding requirements, the plan sponsor's financial strength, and protection schemes designed to insure pension benefits against bankruptcy of the plan sponsor.

References

Blommestein, H., and others 2009. "Evaluating the Design of Private Pension Plans: Costs and Benefits of Risk-Sharing." OECD Working Papers on Insurance and Private Pensions No. 34. Paris: OECD. www.oecd.org/dataoecd/23/31/42469395.pdf.

OECD (Organisation for Economic Co-operation and Development). 2009. "OECD Guidelines on Pension Fund Governance." Paris: OECD. www.oecd.org/dataoecd/18/52/34799965.pdf.

Sender, S. 2009. "IAS19: Penalising Changes Ahead." EDHEC Risk and Asset Management Research Centre, Nice, France.

Severinson, C. 2008. "Recent Developments in Pension Accounting." Paris: OECD. www.oecd.org/dataoecd/60/54/40954137.pdf.

Severinson, C., and J. Yermo. 2010. "The Impact of the Financial Crisis on Defined Benefit Pension Plans and the Need for Counter-Cyclical Funding Regulations." OECD Working Paper on Finance, Insurance and Private Pensions No. 3. Paris: OECD. www.oecd.org/dataoecd/22/11/45694491.pdf.

Stewart, F., and J. Yermo. 2008. "Pension Fund Governance: Challenges and Potential Solutions." OECD Working Papers on Insurance and Private Pensions, No. 18. Paris: OECD. www.oecd.org/dataoecd/18/29/41013956.pdf.

Creating a Sound Funding Framework: The Experience of OMERS in Canada

Andrew Fung, Vice President, Ontario Municipal Employees Retirement System, Canada

For pension funds, a complete, sustainable funding framework capable of weathering the effects of financial crisis requires close collaboration between plan sponsors and the administrator. The full power of such a framework can be unleashed only if there is willingness to fully utilize the three funding levers—contribution rates, benefit levels, and investment strategy. A sound funding framework also requires a certain element of defined metrics to trigger actions and avoid behavioral bias, as well as consensus on principles which may include benefit security, contribution stability, and intergenerational equity. Such a funding framework should not, however, replace professional judgment, which needs to reflect practicalities of administration and communication.

OMERS has a relatively long history and a solid governance structure

Established in 1963 as a defined-benefit plan, the Ontario Municipal Employees Retirement System (OMERS) is currently the second largest pension plan by asset base in the province of Ontario, Canada. It is funded by contributions from employers and employees and by investment earnings. OMERS serves employees of cities, towns, villages, school boards (nonteaching members), libraries, police and fire departments, children's aid societies, and other municipal agencies across the province. The plan represents more than 400,000 members (291,000 active and 109,000 retirees) working for approximately 900 employers. As a multiemployer pension plan, OMERS provides lifetime retirement income along with survivor benefits and inflation protection. The plan is regulated, and full prefunding is required.

Between OMERS's inception in 1963 and 2006, the government of the Province of Ontario served as the plan's sponsor. This situation was revised under the OMERS Act, 2006, which established the OMERS Sponsors Corporation (a body that represents employer, employee, and retiree members of OMERS) as the plan's sponsor. The OMERS Act is precise in regard to the responsibilities of each body within its governance structure. Governance responsibility for OMERS is shared by the Sponsors Corporation and the Administration Corporation (figure 3.21). The

Figure 3.21 **The Governance Structure of OMERS**

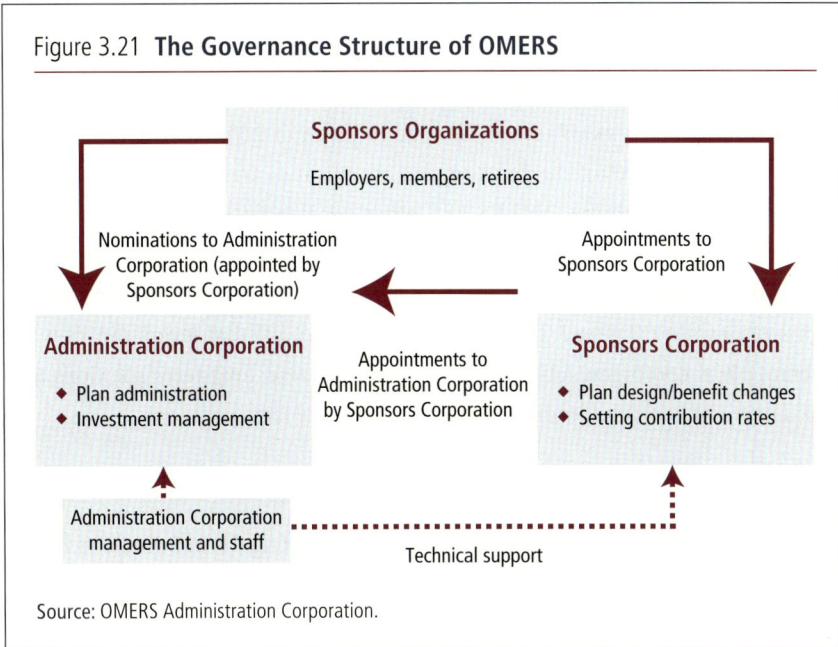

Sponsors Organizations

Employers, members, retirees

Nominations to Administration
Corporation (appointed by
Sponsors Corporation)

Appointments to
Sponsors Corporation

Administration Corporation

Appointments to
Administration Corporation
by Sponsors Corporation

Sponsors Corporation

- ◆ Plan administration
- ◆ Investment management

- ◆ Plan design/benefit changes
- ◆ Setting contribution rates

Administration Corporation
management and staff

Technical support

Source: OMERS Administration Corporation.

Sponsors Corporation is charged with plan design, including adjustments to benefit provisions, contribution rates, and changes to the reserves. It also has responsibility for setting compensation levels and amending the appointment protocol for both itself and the Administration Corporation. The Administration Corporation is responsible for pension administration, investment strategy, and preparation of the plan actuarial valuation.

Losses incurred during the crisis mean that OMERS will have a larger minimum funding requirement in the coming years

Like other public pension plans, OMERS did not escape the steep downturn in stock markets caused as the result of the financial crisis of 2008–09. OMERS utilized a standard Canadian actuarial technique to smooth the impact of market fluctuations on pension plan funding: spreading annual gains or losses over a five-year period. As a result, OMERS reported a deficit of only $0.3 billion as of the end of 2008, and is expected to recognize a 2008 net deferred loss of $6.0 billion in the funded position of the plan over the four years between 2008 and 2012. As a consequence of these forecasted losses, OMERS anticipates needing a sizable increase in its minimum funding requirement unless the fund earns a consistent double-digit return over the coming several years.

As a regulated pension plan, an actuarial valuation of OMERS must be filed with the regulators every two to three years. Filing with the currently projected deficit, however, will trigger a hefty increase in the minimum funding requirement. Though improving OMERS's funding situation is no doubt a short-term priority, it is more important to establish a long-term solution that will allow the plan to sustain future "black swan" events similar to those of 2008–09. Identifying the fundamental objectives of the pension plan is critical in arriving at the long-term funding solution, both for OMERS and other pension funds. Once the funding objectives and target are in place, benefit levels, contribution rates, and investment and funding policies can be appropriately leveraged to navigate the plan to long-term sustainability (figure 3.22). Ownership of these different levers can vary for different plans and organizations. Seeking collaborative, long-term solutions also would have the benefit of leading to appropriate short-term solutions.

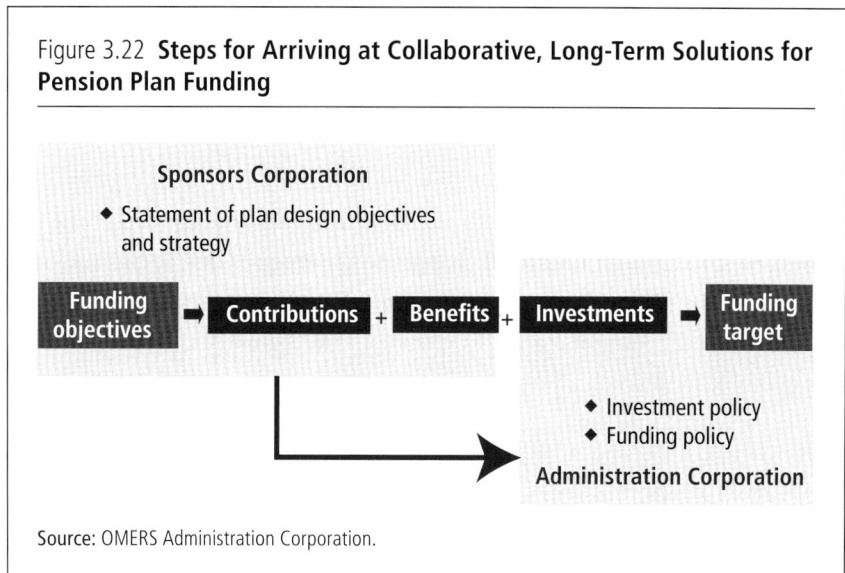

Figure 3.22 **Steps for Arriving at Collaborative, Long-Term Solutions for Pension Plan Funding**

Source: OMERS Administration Corporation.

Pension plans' funding gaps can be resolved by assessing three core funding objectives: benefit security, contribution stability, and intergenerational equity

Resolution of pension plans' funding gaps can be addressed through a review of each of the plan's core funding objectives: benefit security, contribution stability, and intergenerational equity. These objectives must then be operationalized and translated into tangible terms. In general, solicitation of input from various stakeholders should be considered.

Though a common core objective of many defined-benefit plans is *benefit security*, the more appropriate objective is *benefit security at a predetermined minimum level*.

Achieving this objective involves evaluation of appropriate trade-offs between the higher level of security associated with a lower level of benefits versus the lower level of security associated with a higher level of benefits. Setting a lower target does not necessarily mean lower benefits, however; higher benefits are simply subject to affordability of the plan. For OMERS, choosing the appropriate level of benefits is especially important because benefits, once accrued, cannot be reduced under the current pension regime in Ontario. The idea is to build leeway and to avoid being boxed in. Properly addressing this objective involves several considerations:

◆ Different target benefit levels for different groups (due to the diversity of the membership of the plan)

◆ Prioritization of the order of benefit enhancements above the target

◆ Evaluation of current benefit levels versus the maximum allowable benefits under the current pension regime

The *contribution stability* of pension funds is an easy objective to achieve if one ignores affordability. Again, the more appropriate core objective should be *contribution stability at a predetermined, affordable level*. Achieving this objective involves evaluation of appropriate trade-offs between high stable costs and reasonable (albeit more volatile) lower costs. Stability can be achieved by maintaining a target range of acceptable contributions between minimum and maximum levels, a target or a desired range of ratios of contributions to benefit levels, or both targets. Properly addressing the contribution stability objective involves the following considerations:

◆ Prioritization of contribution reduction and benefit enhancements, recognizing that the contribution level affects active members and employers only, not current retirees

◆ The impact of an aging population on costs

Intergenerational equity means the avoidance of significant transfer of costs or liabilities or surplus from one generation of members or taxpayers to another. Successful achievement of this objective hinges on two key criteria:

◆ Timely resolution of the projected deficit and allocation of surpluses or rising normal costs

◆ Evaluation of the sustainability of current benefits and contributions and any proposed changes to those areas

When a pension fund's surplus is spent by increasing benefits or reducing contributions, the contributions-to-benefits ratio will drop. Similarly, deficit funding by decreasing benefits or increasing contribution will cause the ratio to rise.

Performing a periodic rebalancing of contributions and benefits over a reasonable period of time is thus important. Waiting too long to rebalance or rebalancing over a prolonged period of time leaves the fund at risk of inequity, while rebalancing too frequently or over too short a period of time leaves the fund subject to drastic actions and adjustments.

A pension fund's regulatory framework should allow for ranges of surplus accumulation and deficit diminishment before requiring that contribution or benefit levels be adjusted

Once a pension fund reaches an excess surplus, it must scale back contributions or increase benefits to comply with Canadian regulations. On the other hand, if a fund is in deficit, it must by law increase contributions or reduce *future* pension benefits (accrued benefits cannot be reduced). In either situation, the funding objectives are compromised—any decisions made would be very short term and focused on compliance. Opportunity lies between these two extremes. A policy framework is needed to build leeway (that is, to avoid, to the extent possible, falling into either side of the spectrum when flexibility is taken away). Ideally, there should be a range in which the plan's sponsors feel comfortable letting the surplus accumulate without taking any actions to adjust benefits or contributions. That surplus creates a cushion to provide for long-term contributions and benefits. But as the surplus either grows larger or starts to diminish (see the red areas in figure 3.23), sustainability of long-term contributions and benefits becomes questionable and sponsors may feel that action is warranted in order to protect the long-term objectives.

When the surplus continues accumulating, plan sponsors must evaluate whether to increase target benefits or reduce contributions based on a set of agreed priorities. Sponsors also need to assess if such adjustments are sustainable temporarily or permanently (figure 3.24). Presumably, sponsors will act if there is a large enough reserve to provide them comfort. A permanent change signifies a change to the underlying long-term objective—a decision that should not be taken lightly. A temporary change would presumably be made on the basis of intergenerational equity. On the other hand, when the surplus diminishes, sponsors need to decide whether to reduce future target benefits or increase contributions.

It is possible that sponsors could be of the view that there is a high probability that the target benefits and contributions could be impaired and inaction would result in inappropriate intergenerational imbalance. The reality, however, is that it is difficult to entertain any benefit reduction or contribution rate increase before hitting a real deficit. Such changes require foresight, courage, collaboration, and discipline.

Figure 3.23 **Pension Plan Management Spectrum**

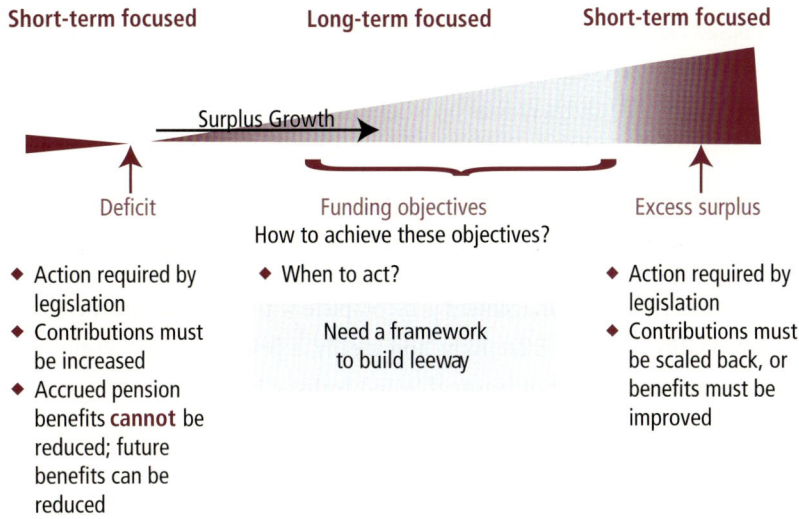

Short-term focused　　　　**Long-term focused**　　　　**Short-term focused**

Surplus Growth →

Deficit　　　　Funding objectives　　　　Excess surplus
How to achieve these objectives?

- Action required by legislation
- Contributions must be increased
- Accrued pension benefits **cannot** be reduced; future benefits can be reduced

- When to act?

  Need a framework to build leeway

- Action required by legislation
- Contributions must be scaled back, or benefits must be improved

Source: OMERS Administration Corporation.

Figure 3.24 **Achieving Funding Objectives**

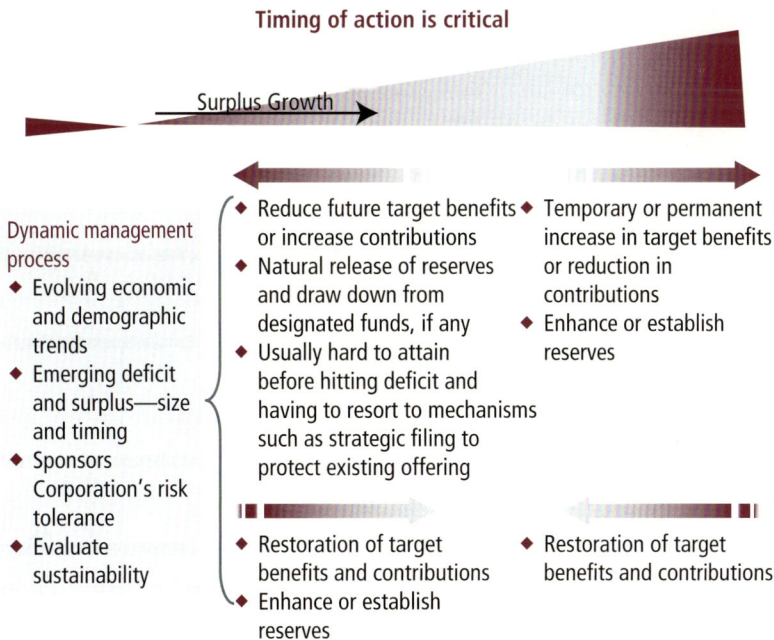

Timing of action is critical

Surplus Growth →

Dynamic management process
- Evolving economic and demographic trends
- Emerging deficit and surplus—size and timing
- Sponsors Corporation's risk tolerance
- Evaluate sustainability

- Reduce future target benefits or increase contributions
- Natural release of reserves and draw down from designated funds, if any
- Usually hard to attain before hitting deficit and having to resort to mechanisms such as strategic filing to protect existing offering

- Temporary or permanent increase in target benefits or reduction in contributions
- Enhance or establish reserves

- Restoration of target benefits and contributions
- Enhance or establish reserves

- Restoration of target benefits and contributions

Source: OMERS Administration Corporation.

When the deficit diminishes, the sponsors should focus on restoring the target benefits and contributions, again based on agreed priorities. The trigger for any adjustments centers on sponsors' level of risk tolerance and should be institutionalized based on defined metrics; otherwise, behavioral bias will make it difficult to make a change when one is needed. This dynamic management process focuses as much on where the fund is now as on where the fund is heading.

Determining the fiduciary role of a pension fund's administrator is a key part of establishing a long-term funding framework

The picture of funding management is incomplete without including the fiduciary role of the administrator. Effectively, and ideally, a pension plan's funding objectives should result in a set of reasonable and realistic boundaries of target contributions and benefits, among other things (figure 3.25). Though periodic review of these objectives by the plan sponsors to ensure that they remain valid and current could lead to a new set of boundaries, frequent changes should be avoided. The administrator exercises its fiduciary duty by managing the fund toward these boundaries through its funding and investment policies. These policies, in effect, provide another level of risk management, complementing that of the sponsors through their contribution and benefit management process. This is where collaboration comes into play, as each party's views with respect to risk influence the approach not only of their own policies but also of the other party.

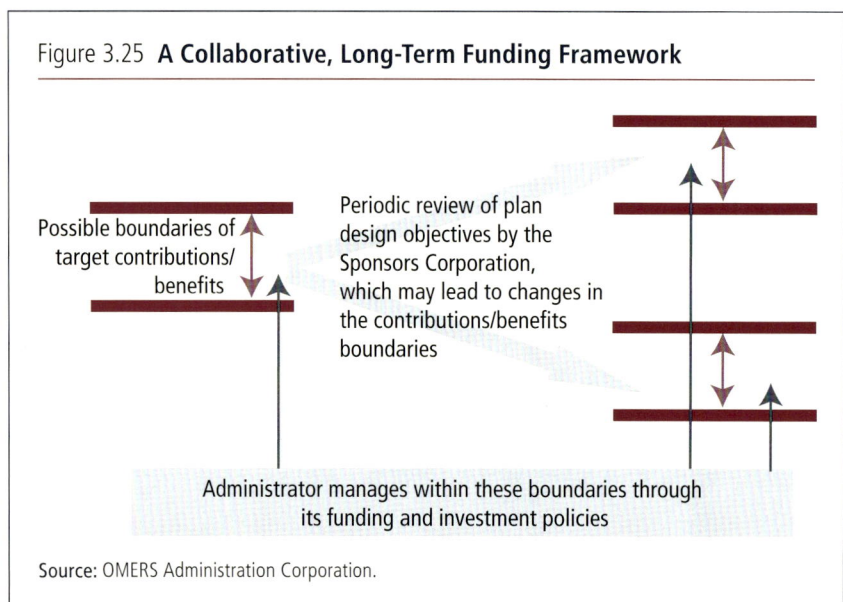

Figure 3.25 **A Collaborative, Long-Term Funding Framework**

Possible boundaries of target contributions/ benefits

Periodic review of plan design objectives by the Sponsors Corporation, which may lead to changes in the contributions/benefits boundaries

Administrator manages within these boundaries through its funding and investment policies

Source: OMERS Administration Corporation.

Conclusion

A complete funding framework for a pension fund—including detailed funding objectives such as benefit security, contribution stability, and intergenerational equity—needs time to develop. However, not all elements of a strong and effective funding framework need to be developed or resolved at once. Though a sound funding framework uses defined metrics to trigger actions and avoid behavioral bias, it does not replace professional judgment, which should reflect the practicalities of administration and communication. Periodic review of a funding framework is encouraged, while abrupt and frequent changes should be avoided given the long-term focus of the objectives.

Lessons from Defined-Benefit Pension Funds in Japan

Masaharu Usuki, Member of Investment Committee, Government Pension Investment Fund, Japan

Recent market turmoil has highlighted several problems in the conventional method of managing defined-benefit pension plans in Japan. In particular, four important lessons have emerged from the recent crisis: (1) strategic asset allocation and a disciplined rebalancing process are important tools to prudently manage assets; (2) both liquidity and the benefits of risk diversification decline in times of market turmoil, thereby reinforcing the importance of conservative, conscientious liquidity management at all times; (3) quantitative methodologies, especially those that depend on the normality of return distribution, need to be tempered with increased awareness of the potential severity of rare events and the measures available to mitigate the impacts of such events; and (4) sharing a proper understanding of investment beliefs with stakeholders makes it much easier to formulate and select countermeasures to cope with market turmoil.

Recent market turmoil offers several lessons for pension funds in Japan

Both public and private pension funds in Japan suffered significant depreciation in portfolio asset values and a decrease in funded ratios during the global financial crisis that began in 2008. The crisis, however, offers numerous lessons that may help mitigate such negative outcomes in the future. For public pension systems, the four most important lessons are the following:

- The need to rebalance portfolios and revise the strategic asset allocation whenever asset class parameters change for the target investment horizon

- The importance of explicitly incorporating liquidity management—stress tested for crisis scenarios—as part of overall risk management

- The need to supplement traditional quantitative portfolio construction methods relying on normality of distribution by countermeasures to address tail risk, or the potential for occurrence of unlikely events

- The importance of communication with stakeholders, including the sharing of investment beliefs and timely disclosure of events and performance

The timing of changes to strategic asset allocation is important

Revision of a pension fund's strategic asset allocation should be undertaken only if the asset class parameters (expected return and covariance matrix) change for the target investment horizon. Judging when those changes have occurred, however, is not an easy task. Table 3.11 illustrates the pros and cons of two methodologies for asset allocation revisions, namely periodic revision every three to five years and ongoing revision in accordance with changes in the portfolio, economy, or market conditions.

Table 3.11 **Pros and Cons of Two Methodologies for the Strategic Asset Allocation Revision**

	Revise every 3–5 years	Revise at any time
Pro	◆ Prudent and careful judgment ◆ Lower transaction costs ◆ Consistency with periodic actuarial valuation	◆ Easy to adjust to changes in economy and market
Con	◆ Slow adjustment to changes in economy and market	◆ Excessive influence of market ◆ Inconsistency with periodic actuarial valuation ◆ Increase in transaction costs

Source: NLI Research Institute

Rebalancing rules are an integral part of pension funds' strategic asset allocation

Questions have arisen around whether to rebalance a public pension plan's investment portfolio in the face of a crisis. The rebalancing rule is an integral part of the strategic asset allocation. Ideally, as long as the expected return and covariance matrix are constant, a portfolio should be rebalanced instantaneously to abide by its risk budget limit. In practice, however, constant rebalancing is usually too expensive due to high transaction costs. In Japan, it became evident in hindsight that many pension funds that suspended rebalancing and avoided reallocation to equity toward the end of 2008 were unable to enjoy gains from the stock market recovery in 2009. A certain amount of portfolio deviation from the strategic asset allocation thus is and should be permissible. In order to decide the permissible range of deviation, the pension fund needs to quantitatively assess the costs and benefits of constant and instantaneous rebalancing against rebalancing within a permissible range.[1]

Risk diversification becomes less effective as a risk management tool during financial crisis

The effectiveness of risk diversification as a downside risk management tool during times of financial crisis is questionable. Importantly, correlation coefficient values are unstable in times of market turmoil. This tendency can be observed by examining the "exceedance correlation" (figure 3.26).[2] In general, correlation between risky asset classes (domestic equity versus foreign equity, domestic equity versus hedge funds, and domestic equity versus long-short equity hedge funds) has a tendency to increase and become larger than the theoretical values during periods of market turmoil. Correlation between risky asset and safe asset classes (domestic equity versus domestic investment-grade fixed income), on the other hand, has a tendency to decrease and become smaller than the theoretical correlation during periods of market turmoil.

Liquidity management during market turmoil depends on asset classes

When liquidity dries up during times of market turmoil, illiquid asset classes (real assets and other alternative asset classes) are especially vulnerable to downside price uncertainty. If a pension fund needs to dispose of assets to raise cash, it must accept fire-sale prices. But in cases in which external investment managers use a significant amount of leverage (borrowing), they have a tendency to refuse the pension funds' requests to redeem shares. To satisfy the pension fund's redemption request, investment managers would have to deleverage. Usually, however, the value of collateralized assets is less than the borrowed amount. As a result, a portion of other asset classes or securities must be disposed of at fire-sale prices in

---

[1] One method for quantitatively examining the appropriate deviation range is a simulation in which selected deviation ranges are applied to the return distribution experienced in the past. The tracking error and/or information ratio (additional return divided by tracking error) could be used as a criterion for the selection of the most suitable deviation range.

[2] Exceedance correlation is defined as the correlation between pairs of returns that are above (or below) a given positive (or negative) threshold value, as in Longin and Solnik (2001). The x-axis for each of the four correlation figures shows that threshold value. For example, the correlation coefficient value at negative 0.5σ is calculated from the subsample of monthly return data in which both asset class returns are below the full sample mean by 0.5 times the standard deviation of all samples.

Figure 3.26 **Correlation of Returns of Various Asset Classes**

a. Domestic equity versus domestic fixed income (1980–2007)

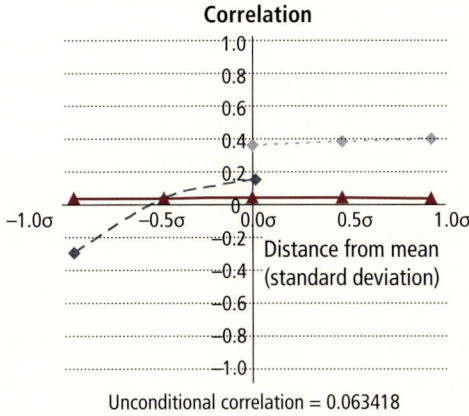

Correlation

Distance from mean (standard deviation)

Unconditional correlation = 0.063418

b. Domestic equity versus foreign equity (1985–2007)

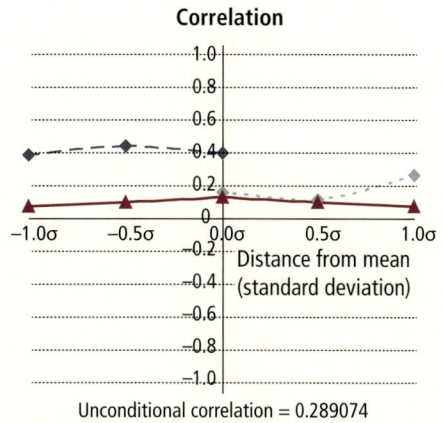

Correlation

Distance from mean (standard deviation)

Unconditional correlation = 0.289074

c. Domestic equity versus hedge funds (1993–2007)

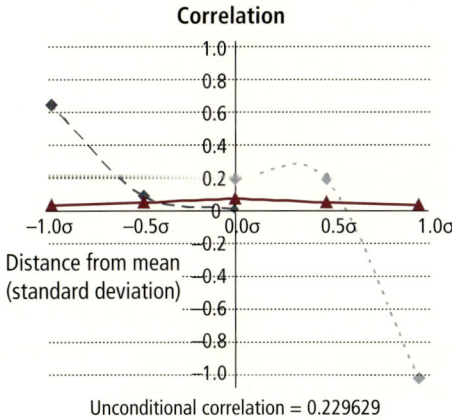

Correlation

Distance from mean (standard deviation)

Unconditional correlation = 0.229629

d. Domestic equity versus long-short equity hedge funds (1993–2007)

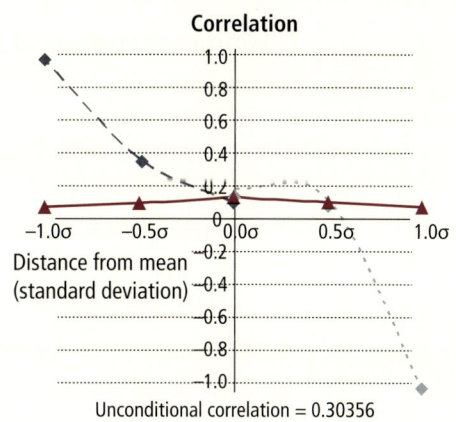

Correlation

Distance from mean (standard deviation)

Unconditional correlation = 0.30356

—◆— Historical value (−)   —◆— Historical value (+)   —▲— Theoretical value

Source: Ibbotson Associates.

Note: The theoretical value lines represent the exceedance correlation coefficient derived from the (unconditional) correlation coefficient shown at the bottom of each figure. Theoretical exceedance correlation values are calculated using pairwise subsample return data generated by Monte Carlo simulation under the assumption of binomial normal distribution, with the unconditional correlation coefficient shown below each figure.

the market turmoil, unless investment managers can persuade the pension fund to suspend the redemption request.

The illiquidity of alternative asset classes became an impediment to portfolio rebalancing during the market turmoil in the last quarter of 2008. Specifically, the value of public equity fell faster than that of alternative assets. To rebalance their portfolios, pension funds would have had to sell off alternative asset classes and purchase equity. Market conditions, however, were such that alternative assets could be sold only at fire-sale prices. Moreover, pension funds had to sell their most liquid asset—public equity—in order to satisfy the liquidity needs to pay benefits. This caused further deviation from strategic asset allocation because pension funds could not increase the equity allocation. In the end, many pension funds suspended their portfolio rebalancing efforts.

For defined-benefit pension systems, it is also noteworthy that once the funded ratio falls below 100 percent, benefit payments, which decrease assets (numerator) and liabilities (denominator) by the same amount, lead to further decline of the funded ratio. In order to maintain the same funded ratio, a pension fund's asset return must then surpass its liability return.

Quantitative analysis of portfolio returns is necessary but has limitations

The conventional method of portfolio optimization assumes a normal distribution of return and derives risk and return parameters from historical market data. These parameters, however, may be unreliable with respect to market turmoil events because such events are much more frequent than is implied by the normal distribution. For example, using the average asset allocation of Japanese private sector pension funds and index return data of each asset class, the recent financial crisis would have made the funds report a 36.4 percent drop in portfolio value between the peak in July 2007 to November 2008 (30 percent on an annual basis). Assuming an expected annual return of 4.5 percent and a standard deviation of 8 percent, the probability of incurring such a loss falls between 3σ (0.135 percent probability) and 4σ (0.00317 percent probability).[3] This very low probability can be construed as evidence of the reality of "fat tail" events and the unreliability of the normal distribution assumption.

---

[3] In the 100 quarters between the first quarters of 1985 and 2010, the same portfolio suffered five quarters of returns that deviated more than two standard deviations from the mean, something that should happen only once in 100 quarters assuming a normal distribution.

Measures are available to mitigate the risk of fat tail events

Countermeasures to address this fat tail risk include

◆ nonparametric optimization utilizing, for example, bootstrap econometric techniques;

◆ optimization by applying a lower partial moment;[4]

◆ utilization of dynamic hedging techniques;

◆ stress testing simulations;

◆ deliberate neglect, an important technique for pension funds because they are long-term investors and therefore can benefit from the long-term nature of their liability structure.

While various quantitative analyses should be applied to mitigate as many risks as possible, such analyses also have limitations.

Communication with stakeholders is critical

An important aspect of a pension fund's accountability, particularly during exceptional market turmoil, is timely disclosure of relevant information to stakeholders such as board members and representatives of plan participants. Most important, however, is for stakeholders to have similar investment beliefs and similar ideas about how to apply those beliefs to market conditions. It is also critical that misunderstanding surrounding investment beliefs be avoided (see table 3.12). For example, risk premiums are not always positive, and the effect of diversification depends on market conditions. In order to manage pension plans consistently, especially during market turmoil, pension fund managers should continuously share these investment beliefs as well as their proper understandings with stakeholders.

Conclusion

Even during periods of severe fiscal pressure, it is critical for public pension systems to abide by a consistent strategic asset allocation and to uphold the investment belief that risk taking yields rewards in the long term. It is also important for pension systems to simultaneously manage short-term and medium-term risk, to apply various quantitative and qualitative analytical methods, and to not limit

---

[4] *Lower partial moment* refers to the arithmetic mean or variance (square of standard deviation) of the subsample of return data with a value below a certain target. This is a useful measure of downside risk, especially when the return data are asymmetric above or below the mean.

Table 3.12 **Examples of Investment Beliefs to Be Communicated to Stakeholders**

Investment belief	Common misperceptions
Risk premium (compensation for risk) does exist.	◆ Risk premium is positive in every investment period. ◆ Historical level of risk premium is a reliable indicator of future level. ◆ Standard deviation or value at risk assuming the normal distribution of risk premium is the sole risk measure.
Diversified investment is free lunch to improve efficiency.	◆ Diversification means investment in different asset class (no labels). ◆ Correlation among asset classes is stable.
Short-term market timing requires special skills, while a long-term investment horizon has more chances of success.	◆ Strategic asset allocation can be revised only at set intervals, even if market conditions change significantly.
Illiquidity bears a risk premium.	◆ Premium for (il)liquidity is positive and stable in any period.

Source: NLI Research Institute.

risk analysis to examination of the variance-covariance matrix derived from the normal distribution assumption of return.

Looking ahead, due to the decline in risk-taking capacity of investors such as investment banks and hedge funds, risk premiums will rise in the long run. Until higher risk premiums are factored in by markets, instability of securities prices will continue. During that period, premiums earned from investment in risky assets, which should lead to lower funding costs in defined-benefit plans, will be very unstable. It is thus desirable for pension managers to pay more attention to the risk management side of investment operations than to the return generation side.

After the market has adapted to the lower level of risk tolerance, investors with a long-term investment horizon, such as pension funds, may expect to enjoy higher returns for the same amount of risk. That said, it may take several years for the market to yield higher risk premiums.

Reference

Longin, F., and B. Solnik. 2001. "Extreme Correlation of International Equity Markets." *Journal of Finance* 55 (2): 649–76.

5. Policy Responses to Turbulent Financial Markets

◆ Adjustments and Risk Mitigation in National Pension Systems

◆ Key Lessons for Pension Policy Makers: An OECD Perspective

◆ The Case of the Irish National Pensions Reserve Fund

◆ Renationalization of Argentina's Pension System

◆ Thailand's GPF: From the 1997 Asian Crisis to the 2008 Global Financial Crisis

Adjustments and Risk Mitigation in National Pension Systems

Robert Holzmann and **Richard Hinz,** Pension Policy Advisers, World Bank

While the financial crisis of 2008–09 was detrimental to funded and unfunded pension systems, its effect is relatively small compared to underlying demographic pressures such as increasing longevity and old-age dependency rates, unaffordable accrual rates, and insufficient indexation policies. Ironically, in the long term, the crisis may serve as a catalyst to improve the financial status of many pension systems—though this will come at a cost to real benefit levels and may create pressures elsewhere in pension systems. Young pension systems with reserves will experience a decline in assets (which is likely to be offset on the liability side), highlighting the need for a long-term investment strategy that considers solvency targets and cash flow needs. Mature pension systems, on the other hand, will need to solve short-term cash flow deficiencies, and will need to do this without losing the benefits of multipillar diversification or taking on excessive future liabilities.

Funded and unfunded pension systems were both hit hard by the global financial crisis, though in different ways

Both funded and unfunded pension systems were hit hard by the global financial crisis of 2008–09, albeit in different ways. For funded *defined-contribution schemes*, the primary impact was on individuals close to retirement age. In public *defined-benefit schemes*, most of which are financed predominantly on a pay-as-you-go (PAYG) basis, the impact will be largely through changes in the level of benefits received by future retirees.

Although this effect will be relatively small compared to the challenges existing pension systems face in terms of population aging, the financial crisis can be perceived as strengthening the argument for multipillar pension systems, as diversification of old-age income support is more effective in addressing exposure to risk than is utilization of a single source.

In general, economic crises deeply affect pension systems and government budgets—mostly through lower contribution and tax revenues. Table 3.13 summa-

Table 3.13 **Peak-to-Trough Changes during Severe Financial Crisis**

Indicator	Cumulative change (%)	Duration (years)
Housing prices	−36.0	5.0
Equity prices	−56.0	3.4
Unemployment	−7.0	4.8
GDP per capita	−9.3	1.9
Change in public debt +86 percent after three years		

Source: Reinhart and Rogoff 2009.

Note: The data are for 19 financial crises that occurred between 1899 and 2007.

rizes peak-to-trough changes for several indicators during past crises. The deterioration in government finances is particularly alarming: on average, public debt rises 86 percent in the three years following a crisis.

Simulations of the impact of the financial crisis on public pension systems can be useful in predicting actual outcomes

To evaluate the impact of the crisis on public defined-benefit systems, World Bank staff simulated a number of short-term and long-term implications of the financial crisis on the financial status and benefit levels of several stylized public defined-benefit systems using the Pension Reform Options Simulation Toolkit (PROST) model. Four crisis scenarios—a precrisis base case and three crisis scenarios—illustrate the range of outcomes of financial crises of varying depth (figure 3.27). The precrisis baseline scenario assumes a gradual slowing of the very high 5 percent gross domestic product (GDP) growth rates seen in recent years to a long-term rate of 2 percent. The crisis scenarios assume an initial shock that produced a 2 percent contraction in GDP for a mild crisis, followed by a rapid return to a long-term growth rate of 2 percent. The two severe crisis scenarios assume a 6 percent initial contraction with either a fast or a prolonged recovery. The three scenarios assume similar paths of economic recovery, albeit from different levels. In all three scenarios, GDP growth is assumed to have recovered by 2027. Employment is assumed to follow the GDP recovery path, while asset prices were assumed to recover more quickly.

As shown in figure 3.27b, the cumulative effect of projected shocks—even those associated with a mild crisis—results in a GDP level substantially below the

Figure 3.27 **Effects of Stress Test Scenarios on GDP Growth and GDP Level**

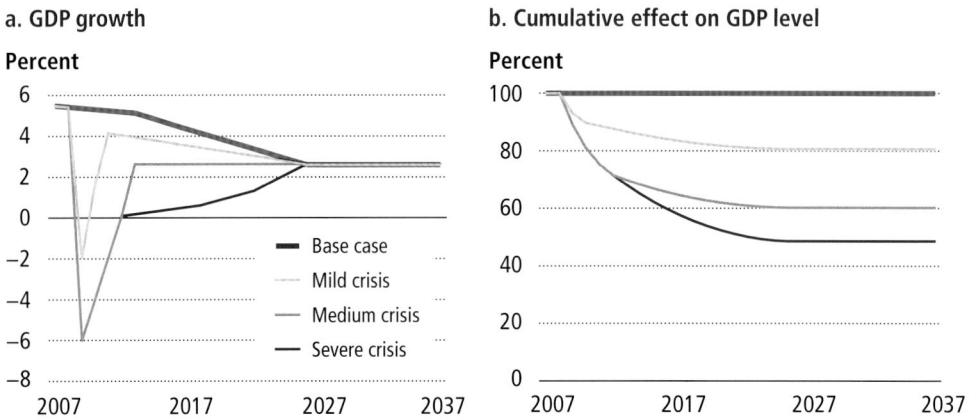

a. GDP growth

Percent

b. Cumulative effect on GDP level

Percent

Base case
Mild crisis
Medium crisis
Severe crisis

Source: World Bank.

precrisis expected path. Because the covered wage bill is assumed to be a constant relative share of output, the change in GDP path implies a similar adjustment to future path of wages. And because the benefit (and therefore expenditure) levels and revenue flows are a function of the path of covered earnings, a financial crisis can result in potentially significant changes in the financing flows and fiscal balances of the pension system and the level of benefits and income replacement that it provides to future retirees.

The macroeconomic impacts of financial crises play out in a complex manner

Results of the stress tests show that short-term projected revenues decline rapidly as wages decline in response to the overall deterioration in the economy. In most cases, the decline in aggregate earnings and the covered wage base is proportionally greater than the decline in output as wage levels and employment decline and workers transition to informal employment. Projected decreases in annual revenues are proportional or even greater than the declines in the earnings base due to anticipated informalization of labor and evasion of pension contributions.

While pension contribution revenues are projected to decline, current expenditures are projected to remain stable or increase in nominal terms. There is a lagged adjustment to wage and employment changes, however, which extends for a long period. Early retirement and disability benefits are anticipated to increase in response to declines in employment. Although such benefits remain at a nominally similar level, expenditures on them represent a significantly greater share of GDP than before the crisis because GDP is smaller.

The decline in revenues proportional to GDP, combined with the increase in expenditures as a share of GDP, opens up a transitory financing gap that represents the most dramatic and immediate impact of the crisis. Over the longer term, however, expenditures decrease as new retirees reach retirement age with lower wage levels and shorter work histories. Moreover, the level of nominal liability may decline, even though its proportion of GDP may be stable or increasing.

In addition to changes in annual flows, there is an impact on any funded reserves or individual accounts if they are included in the system. Though these are expected to decrease in value during a crisis far more than earnings, they also should return to precrisis levels more quickly.

Impacts of Financial Crises on Pension Systems

- ♦ Revenues decline rapidly.
- ♦ Current expenditures remain stable or increase in nominal terms.
- ♦ Long-term stock of liabilities decreases.
- ♦ Current value and rate of return on reserves decline.

The impact of the financial crisis and resulting fiscal pressures depends on the design and maturity of the pension system

Projections find that the impact of the financial crisis and resulting fiscal pressures depend on the design and maturity of the pension system. Three stylized examples characterize different systems:

- ♦ *Mature pension systems in transition economies*, such as those in Central and Eastern Europe, generally operate on PAYG basis with no reserves, have a small funded pillar to diminish future unfunded obligations, have high rates of accrued benefit obligations, are characterized by an aging population, offer an increase in benefits in response to high growth and wage increases, and are indexed based on wages or mixed wage/price benefits.

- ♦ *Young systems in developing countries*, such as those in the Middle East and North Africa, typically cover a first generation of members who are still working, face growing populations with relatively high fertility and low life expectancy, have low system dependency rates, and accumulate reserves in anticipation of future costs.

◆ *Maturing systems in developed countries*, such as in the United States, typically offer less generous benefits, have additional established private pension systems, have less pronounced demographic change, and are partially funded with reserves in public debt.

For mature pension systems in transition economies, simulations suggest an immediate, steep drop in revenues

The simulations suggest a number of impacts of the financial crisis on mature systems in transition economies. First, revenues are projected to decline as the crisis unfolds, reflecting changes in the covered wage bill. Typically, revenues are a 25 percent tax on a covered wage bill of 40 percent of GDP. An optimistic 10 percent decline in covered wages would result in a revenue decline of 1 percent of GDP below expectations. A more severe crisis could double this level.

Mature pension systems in developing countries can be expected to operate with increased deficits for 5–15 years following a financial crisis, depending on the path of crisis and the recovery. A very severe crisis with a slow recovery in a very mature system could face an additional financing gap of 3–4 percent of GDP compared to the precrisis expected path.

Expenditures, on the other hand, are projected to remain constant or increase in nominal terms but to increase as a share of GDP (because of the reduction in GDP). Benefit adjustments are projected to lag revenue losses—especially given resistance to negative benefit indexation. With no liquidity in reserves, mature pension systems in developing countries are projected to face severe cash flow crises for a number of years before reaching a new equilibrium. The net effect can be a substantial additional financing gap within the system (compared to a noncrisis path) of 0.5–2.5 percent of GDP per year for several years following a crisis (figure 3.28). A prolonged recovery period in which revenues remain low can result in a very significant cumulative financing gap.

The underlying demographically induced deficit within mature pension systems will be exacerbated by a financial crisis, as these systems tend to have existing underlying structural financing gaps due to the relatively generous benefits and unfavorable demographics in which the ratio of contributors to retirees is steadily declining.

Over the long run, lower benefit levels for future retirees and a rebound in wages after the crisis will restore the system to a similar annual financing status. This can be expected to take 5–10 years depending on the speed of the recovery. Over the very long run, a reversal of the initial process occurs when lower wage levels during the crisis years translate into lower benefits for future retirees and revenue rebound with earnings. Interestingly, this slightly improves the annual financing balances, but with a much smaller margin than the gap that emerges in the short term.

The impact of a financial crisis does not materially change the long-term status of mature pension systems' finances, however. The underlying demographic deficit is only marginally affected. As indicated in figure 3.28, the deterioration in financial status resulting from a crisis, while substantial in the immediate aftermath of a crisis, does not greatly alter the long-term path of the system. This is due to the offsetting effects of lower benefit levels in the future.

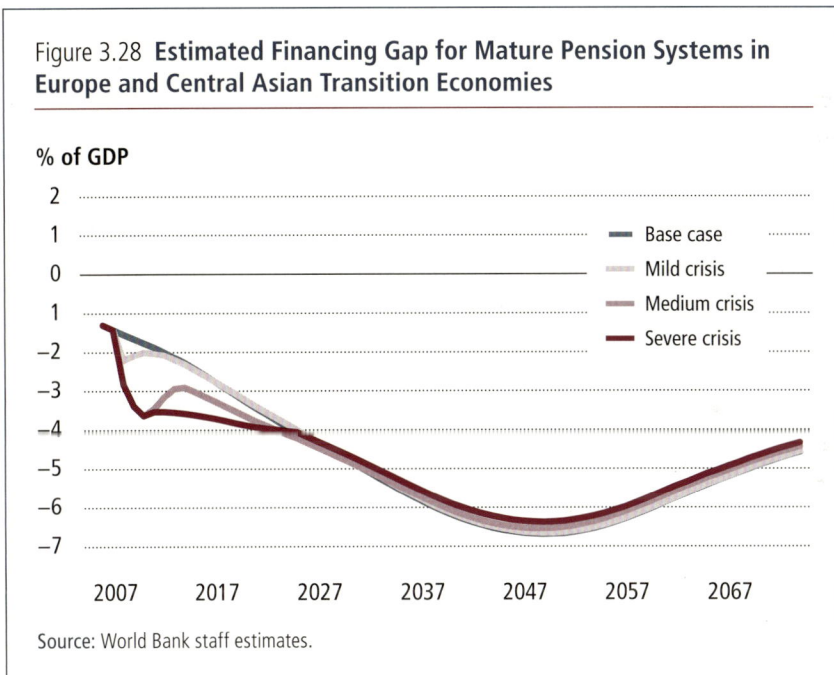

Figure 3.28 **Estimated Financing Gap for Mature Pension Systems in Europe and Central Asian Transition Economies**

Source: World Bank staff estimates.

For young pension systems in developing economies, long-term solvency impacts are expected to be more important than short-term impacts

For young pension systems in developing countries, such as those in the Middle East and North Africa, projected cash flows remain positive during the short and medium term in spite of the crisis, meaning that the more important concern is long-term solvency (figure 3.29).

Figure 3.29 **Estimated Financing Gap for Young Pension Systems in the Middle East and North Africa**

% of GDP

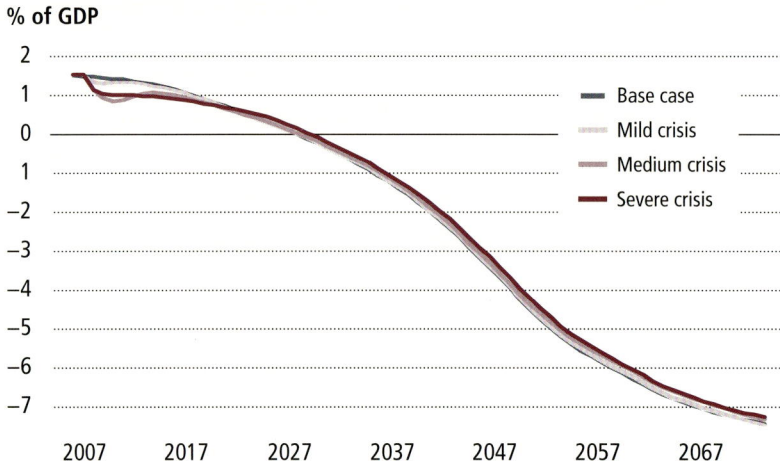

Source: World Bank staff estimates.

Public pension schemes in the Middle East and North Africa had a present value of liabilities of 80 percent of GDP and reserves of 19 percent of GDP before the crisis, implying a funded ratio of 23 percent. During a crisis, asset values are projected to decline by about 20 percent in the current year and move to a lower path in the next decade, as returns may be lower and additions to reserves diminish as operating surpluses decline. Thus, while projected changes in the present value of liabilities are immediate and large, future expenditures are projected to remain constant in relation to GDP but at a lower nominal level. This results in a large reduction in the present value of liabilities that could increase funded ratio above current levels.

Young pension systems in developing countries are less likely than mature systems to face short-term cash flow problems due to their young populations and relatively small number of beneficiaries. In fact, these systems are projected to remain in surplus during their current accumulation phase, and the projected impact on net cash flows is a lower share of GDP for young, small systems than for mature systems. The primary effect on young systems is a marginally lower path of reserve accumulation.

In the short term, funded ratios are projected to increase due to large changes in the present value of benefit obligations (figure 3.30). A return to the prior path is expected within 10 years as flows and returns diminish and obligations increase. Projected long-term fund exhaustion dates for young pension systems remain largely unaffected by the crisis.

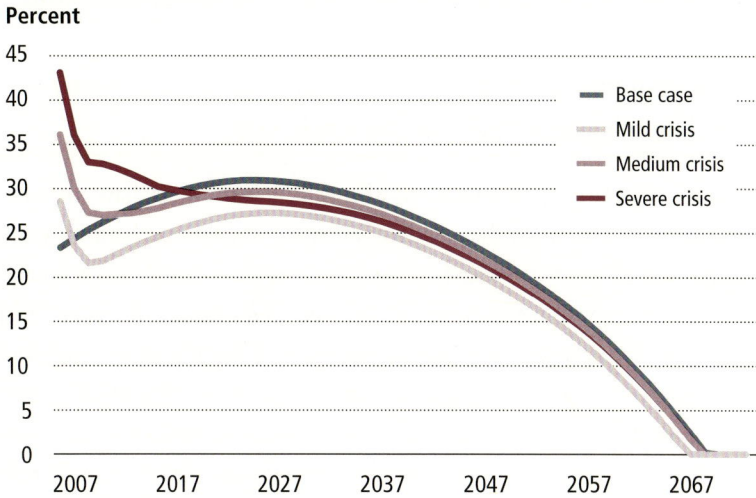

Figure 3.30 **Estimated Funded Ratios for Young Pension Systems in the Middle East and North Africa**

Source: World Bank staff estimates.

For mature pension systems in developed countries such as the United States, demographic changes will be more consequential over the long term than the financial crisis

For mature pension systems in developed countries, the employment effects of a financial crisis are likely to be greater than wage effects due to rigidities in labor markets. Current operating surpluses of the U.S. Social Security system, for example, are expected to deteriorate due to a decline in the taxable wage base, resulting in permanent loss to reserves. As of 2009, the Social Security trust fund is expected to be exhausted in 2037.

For the U.S. Social Security system, the net effect of all factors changing in 2008 would be to move forward cash flow reversal by 1 year from 2017 to 2016, move forward exhaustion of reserves by 4 years from 2041 to 2037, increase unfunded obligation over 75 years by 0.1 percent of GDP to 0.7 percent, and increase estimated actuarial deficit from 1.7 percent of covered wages to 2.0 percent (U.S. Social Security Administration 2009).

Only half of the projected 0.3 percentage point increase in the actuarial deficit is attributed to the economic crisis. The remainder is a result of projected life expectancy increases of about half a year. Stated differently, in-depth analysis of the U.S.

system concludes that the impact of the financial crisis is roughly equivalent to an overall increase in life expectancy of one-half of a year. This is similar to the observation that the underlying demographic conditions in mature pension systems are likely to be far more consequential over the long term than the financial crisis.

Pension-related policy responses to the financial crisis differ by region and by the type of pension system in use

In response to short-term financing challenges, governments have sought to deploy public funds, including the resources of public pension funds and sovereign pension and wealth funds, to alleviate the effects of the current financial crisis. Nonetheless, even private pension funds have not been immune to governments' pressure in this financial turmoil, and several have either closed or temporarily diverted all or part of their second-pillar contributions to the first pillar. Governments, however, are also using the crisis to push for long-envisaged but delayed difficult policy decisions such as increase in retirement age, equalization of retirement ages between men and women, and elimination or curtailment of early retirement programs. Table 3.14 presents the various policy actions taken or considered in a number of countries in Europe and Central Asia.

In mature pension systems in transition economies, major short-term challenges encountered during the financial crisis include

◆ filling a cash flow gap (over the long term, benefits adjust downward, but this takes at least a decade),

◆ mobilizing fiscal transfers due to declining overall revenues at a time of loss of access to borrowing and other competing demands for scarce resources (see table 3.14).

Several policy responses have been undertaken in mature systems in response to the crisis. First, governments have increased contribution rates, frozen benefits at current levels, or limited access to funds. Diversion of revenues or assets from funded systems has emerged as another common response, including closing of a funded system (Argentina), permitting voluntary switchbacks (Slovak Republic), or temporarily or permanently diverting funded contributions (Estonia and Lithuania). In other cases, the contribution rate to the second pillar has been decreased (Latvia) or made voluntary for new entrants (Slovak Republic).

In the long term, the crisis may create an opportunity to tackle demographic challenges through parametric reforms such as a switch to price indexation, which will have short-term costs but also result in a net long-term improvement or changes to minimum retirement age (for example, in Hungary, Latvia, and Poland), actuarial adjustment to benefits, or establishment of an automatic stabilizing device.

Pension funds have much to learn from financial crises but should not ignore future challenges

While there are many lessons that public pension funds can learn from the recent financial crisis, continued challenges still lie ahead. No pension scheme is immune to risks, and ex ante risk analysis does not always hold up to current political pressure and economic realities. That said, the projected effect of the financial crisis is relatively small in relation to the impacts of demographic pressures. Increasing longevity and old-age dependency rates, unaffordable accrual rates, and indexation policies will overshadow the effects of the current economic shock for many years to come.

Ironically, the long-run effect of the current crisis could improve pension systems' financial status in many countries. This will come at a cost, however, to real benefit levels that may create pressures elsewhere, such as for minimum or social pensions. Mature pension systems will need to solve short-term cash flow needs, yet the challenge will be to do this without losing the benefits of multipillar diversification or taking on excessive future liabilities. Younger systems with reserves will probably suffer a blow to the value of their assets, but this is likely to be offset on the liability side, highlighting the need for a long-term investment strategy that considers solvency targets and cash flow needs.

Two Pension-Related Questions Policy Makers Should Ask When Facing a Financial Crisis

- ◆ Will the crisis accelerate the move toward defined-contribution plans?
- ◆ Will attempts to unload risks on individuals lead to pressure for governments to take on a larger role in pension systems?

Public pension funds should raise questions as to whether there might be a better way to distribute risks (both ex ante and ex post), what options could be applied to improve risk management ex ante (risk prevention and mitigation), and what measures might be employed for improving risk sharing and management. The first and most important option in terms of risk sharing and management is to establish policy designs in which retirement income is derived from multiple sources, such as through multipillar hybrid defined-benefit and defined-contribution systems.

Table 3.14 **Policy Actions in Response to the Financial Crisis (as of January 1, 2010)**

Policy action	Legislated	Considered
Change in over-all contribution rate	◆ **Romania:** 27.5% in 2008 to 31.3% ◆ **Russian Federation:** 20% to 26% starting in 2011 ◆ **Macedonia:** 21.5% in 2008 to 19% (2009), 16.5% (2010), and 15% (2011) ◆ **Bulgaria:** 28% to 26% as of January 1, 2010	◆ **Bulgaria:** further gradual reduction from 26% to 23% by 2013
Adjustment to second pillar contribution rate	◆ **Romania:** contribution rate to the second pillar frozen at 2% (instead of legislated increase to 2.5%) ◆ **Lithuania:** contribution rate to the second pillar reduced from 5.5% to 2% in 2009 and 2010, to increase to 6% for 2012–14 and revert to 5.5% in 2011 ◆ **Estonia:** all second-pillar contributions diverted to first pillar in 2009 and 2010; second-pillar contribution reverting to 2% in 2011 and 4% in 2012, with the possibility of higher second-pillar contributions of 6% in 2014–17 to compensate for the current reductions ◆ **Latvia:** contribution rates to the second pillar reduced from 8% to 2% in May 2009; increasing to 4% in 2010 and to 6% in 2011 and remaining at this level (instead of 10% in 2010 originally planned)	◆ **Romania:** restoration of second-pillar contribution rate at 2.5% in 2010; increase in contribution rate by 0.5% every year until it reaches 6%
Allowing opting in/out of second pillar	◆ **Slovak Republic:** first option (January–June 2008) and second option (January–June 2009) to switch in/out of the second pillar ◆ **Hungary:** Beneficiaries older than 52 on December 31, 2008 will be allowed to switch back to the first pillar only until December 31, 2009	
Making second pillar voluntary to new Entrants	◆ **Slovak Republic:** second-pillar participation for new participants voluntary as of January 2008	

Policy action	Legislated	Considered
Changing indexation/minimum and basic pension/benefit cuts	◆ **Serbia:** suspension of indexation for 2009 and 2010 ◆ **Hungary:** abolishment of 13th pension; indexation to be set between Swiss or pure inflation indexation depending on GDP growth ◆ **Croatia:** suspension of indexation in 2010 ◆ **Latvia:** reduction in benefits (nonworking beneficiaries 10%, working beneficiaries 70%) found unconstitutional; underpayments in 2009 pad back ◆ **Macedonia, FYR:** pension indexation at 20%–50% gross wage–CPI indexation from July–December 2009; back to 50%–50% indexation in 2010 ◆ **Lithuania:** old age pension reduction between 3.3% and 12.4% as of January 1, 2010 ◆ **Turkey:** in addition to regular price indexation, low pensions increased by 60 lira (additional 16% increase for minimum pension recipients) ◆ **Russian Federation:** increase in basic pension from 1,560 to 2,562 rubles (64%) starting January 2010	◆ **Latvia:** elimination of wage indexing of contributory pensions ◆ **Estonia:** change of indexation if negative growth or first pillar deficit more than 1% of GDP ◆ **Romania:** gradual shift from wage indexation to inflation indexation ◆ **Ukraine:** suspension of indexation in 2010 ◆ **Moldova:** suspension of indexation in 2010
Increase in retirement age	◆ **Hungary:** increase in retirement age from 62 to 65 by 2012 ◆ **Azerbaijan:** gradual increase in retirement age for men and women starting in 2010, to reach 63 for men by end-2011 and 61 for women by end-2015	◆ **Ukraine:** increase in retirement age to 62 for both men and women ◆ **Romania:** equalization of retirement age of women with that of men at 65 ◆ **Croatia:** increase in retirement age for women to 65
Measures to address early retirement	◆ **Poland:** elimination of numerous early retirement schemes (previously available to some 1 million people) ◆ **Hungary:** increase in penalties for early retirement and introduction of bonuses for delayed retirement ◆ **Latvia:** reduction of early retirement pensions from 80% of normal retirement pension to 50% of normal retirement pension; early retirement will no longer be an option as of January 1, 2012	◆ **Ukraine:** gradual elimination of special and early pension regimes ◆ **Romania:** reforms related to special regimes and early retirement
Guarantees of second pillar contributions	◆ **Kosovo:** guaranteed nominal value of contributions for those retiring in late 2008 and 2009	

Source: World Bank.

Second, asset allocation limits should be linked to an asset-liability management framework in the case of defined-benefit schemes. Third, the so-called life-cycle funds and asset allocation limits should be established according to age and income for defined-contribution funds.

Public pension funds should also consider other ways to mitigate risk, such as (1) improved governance, accountability, and transparency; (2) minimum benefit provisions or guarantees; or (3) risk-sharing arrangements for extreme upside or downside events (performance and mortality) such as insurance against extreme events (sponsor default or performance guarantees) in defined-benefit schemes and minimum performance guarantees (by sponsors, third parties, or the government) in defined-contribution schemes.

References

Hinz, R., A. Zviniene, S. Biletsky, and T. Bogomolova. Forthcoming. "The Long-Term Impact of the Financial Crisis on Public Pension System Financing: Stress Testing Models of Mandatory Pension Systems in Middle Income and Developing Countries Social Protection." Discussion Paper Series. Washington, DC: World Bank.

Reinhart, C., and K. Rogoff. 2009. "The Aftermath of Financial Crises." *American Economic Review* 99 (2): 466–72.

U.S. Social Security Administration. 2009. "The 2009 Annual Report of the Board of Trustees of the Federal Old-Age and Survivors Insurance and Federal Disability Insurance Trust Funds." U.S. Social Security Administration, Washington, DC. www.ssa.gov/OACT/TR/2009/trTOC.html.

Key Lessons for Pension Policy Makers: An OECD Perspective

Juan Yermo, Head, Private Pensions Unit, Organisation for Economic Co-operation and Development

The impact of the global financial crisis in 2008–09 on the asset values in pension systems of Organisation for Economic Co-operation and Development (OECD) member countries depended largely on the level of equity exposure. Though pension funds in some countries reduced their equity exposures before the crisis, others had increased their equity risk before the crisis. Funds' investment responses and policy makers' reactions to the crisis have also depended on the type of pension system in operation in particular countries. In general, social security funds had greater freedom than did pension funds to stick to their long-term asset allocations, as their assets played a relatively small role in the financing of public pension systems. In contrast, pension funds witnessed major policy shifts aimed at strengthening risk management systems and enhancing solvency (in defined-benefit funds) and facilitating adequate investment choices by individuals (in defined-contribution funds). These policy reforms have led to a move toward more conservative investment portfolios and increasing demand for risk-hedging instruments.

The financial crisis hit pension systems in OECD countries hard

The financial crisis of 2008–09 dealt a heavy blow to the financial wealth of pension systems. Collectively, pension funds in Organisation for Economic Co-operation and Development (OECD) countries posted a return of −21.4 percent in nominal terms in 2008 (−24.1 percent in real terms), though performance varied substantially by country (figure 3.31). Private pension arrangements were more affected than public pension systems, as private systems rely heavily on asset accumulation to finance pension benefits.

Though public funds traditionally have relied largely on pay-as-you-go (PAYG) financing, over the past decade many countries have introduced reserve or buffer funds to meet part of the additional benefit expenditure required as a result of their aging populations. According to OECD (2009) figures, public pension reserve funds in most countries also posted double-digit negative returns during the crisis,

Figure 3.31 **Pension Fund Returns 2008–09**

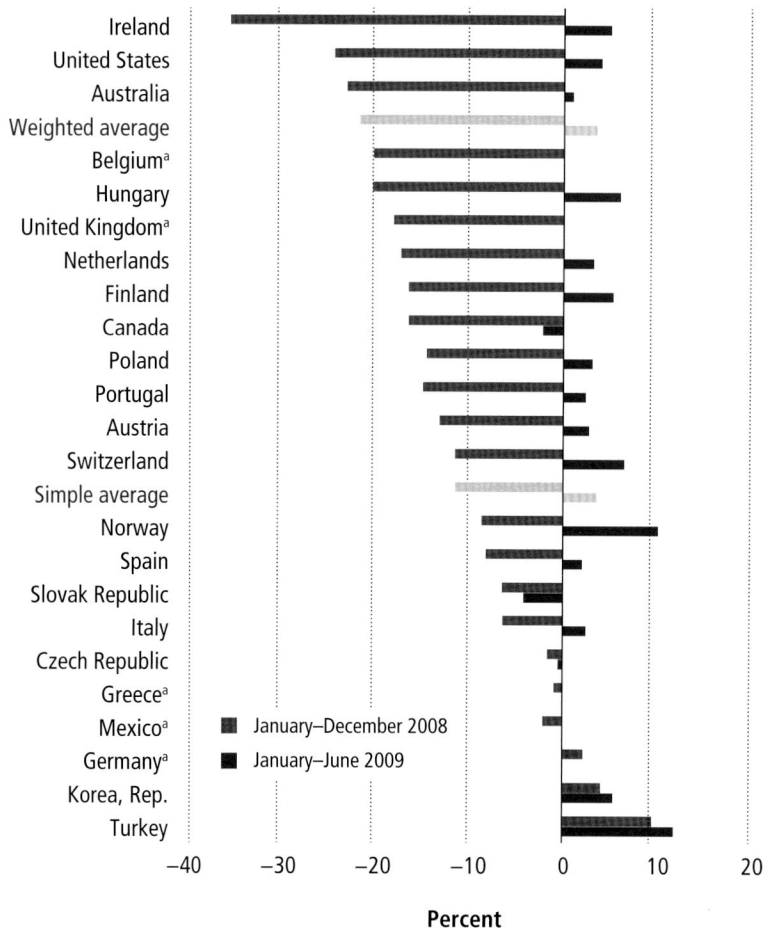

Source: OECD 2009.

Note: For Ireland, January–June 2009 investment rate of return is an OECD estimate. For United States, estimate includes IRAs. For Australia, data refer to Australian Prudential Regulation Authority (APR)–regulated entities with more than four members and at least AU$50 million in total assets; return on assets is net earnings after tax divided by the average assets for the period. For Hungary, data refer to mandatory pension funds; return data for voluntary pension funds are 4.63 percent (−10.67 percent for 2008). For United Kingdom, January–December 2008 investment rate of return is an OECD estimate. For Canada, data refer to the period January–March 2009. For Switzerland, data refer to January–August 2009. For Norway, data relate to a selection consisting of the largest private and municipal pension funds, accounting for about 80 percent of aggregate total assets. For Slovak Republic, data refer to the second pillar pension funds; return data for third pillar pension funds are −0.16 percent (−1.93 percent for 2008). For Italy, data refer to contractual pension funds; return data for open pension funds are 3.0 percent (−14.0 percent for 2008). For Czech Republic, data are estimated; the net return for investors = 0.34 percent for 2008, after extra funding by the fund managers.

a. No data for 2009.

ranging from −14.4 percent in Canada to −30.4 percent in Ireland.[1] Contrast this with the experience of Spain and the United States, where reserve funds posted positive return over the same period; in those two countries, assets are fully invested in government bonds. Though 2009 saw a major recovery in investment returns (15 percent, on average, as estimated by the OECD), the first decade of the 21st century remains one of the worst in history in terms of pension fund performance.

The impact of the financial crisis on pension funds' asset values varied a great deal according to funds' level of equity exposure. In several OECD countries, pension funds reduced their equity exposure before the 2008 crisis (figure 3.32). A similar trend occurred among several public pension reserve funds, particularly those most heavily exposed to equities, such as Ireland and New Zealand (figure 3.33). In countries where equity allocation increased substantially, such as Norway and the Republic of Korea, this increase took place from relatively low levels, as reserve funds traditionally have had rather conservative asset allocations, with heavy exposure to bonds.

Figure 3.32 **Variation in Equity Allocation of Pension Funds in Select OECD Countries, 2001–08**

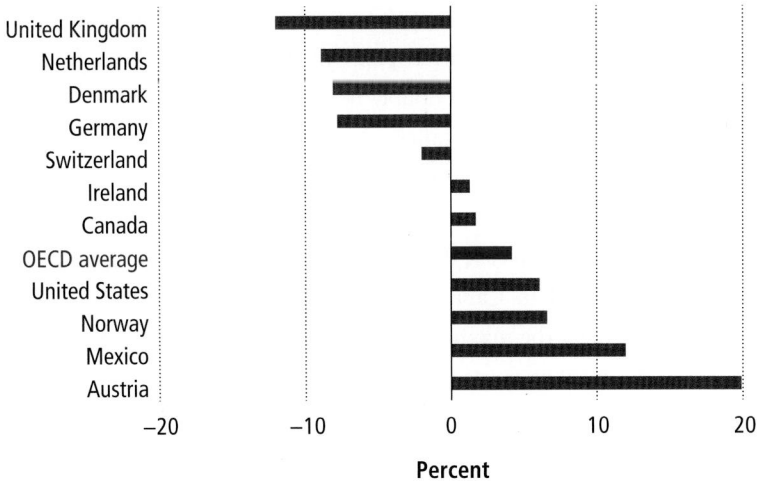

Source: OECD.

_____

[1] For a detailed analysis of the financial impact of the crisis on both public pension reserve funds and pension funds, see Pino and Yermo (2010).

Figure 3.33 **Equity Allocation of Public Pension Reserve Funds in Select OECD Countries, 2004–08**

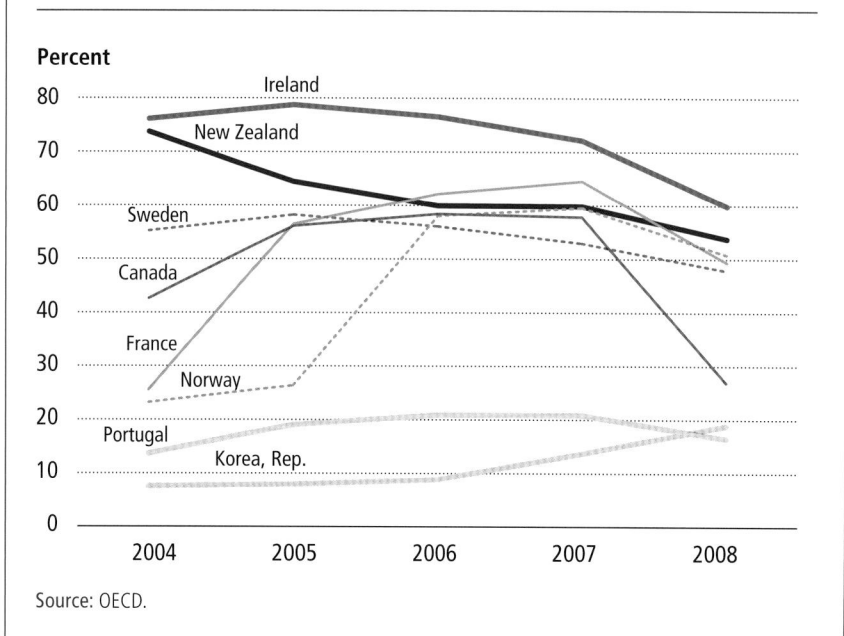

Source: OECD.

The crisis had an especially negative impact on defined-benefit pension funds

For defined-benefit and other pension plans in the OECD offering guaranteed returns or benefits, the crisis had a doubly negative impact in that not only were returns negative, but in many instances the discount rate used for calculating liabilities for regulatory purposes fell. The resulting funding deficits triggered regulatory requirements for higher contributions, leading many countries to put in place temporary measures to ease the burden on plan sponsors. A popular policy response—one employed in Canada, Ireland, and the Netherlands—has been to extend by a few years the maximum recovery period allowed to eliminate the funding gap. Japan went so far as to set a moratorium on pension contributions. Meanwhile, Finland relaxed solvency rules, and Denmark departed temporarily from mark-to-market valuation methods in order to avoid fire sales of equities and mortgage securities. Despite the swift reaction by policy makers, the crisis has heightened employers' concern over their pension risk exposure and is likely to accelerate the shift toward defined-contribution funds.

One means of assessing the financial situation of defined-benefit pension funds is to look at their funded ratio. Due to changes in accounting laws, assets and liabilities increasingly must be valued at their fair-market values. Figure 3.34 shows

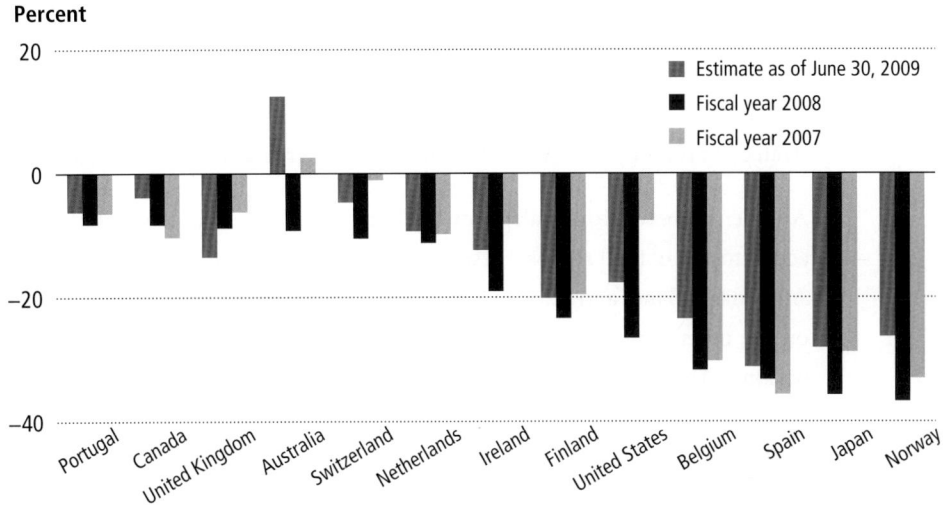

Figure 3.34 **Estimated Median Surplus/Deficit of Companies' Aggregate Defined-Benefit Obligations, by Country of Domicile**

Source: OECD 2009.

estimated median funding levels of the aggregate defined-benefit obligations of publicly traded companies as reported in their annual financial statements for fiscal years 2007 and 2008, and an estimate of the level for the first half of 2009.[2] As detailed in the figure, the median funding level for these companies deterio rated from a 13 percent deficit as of the fiscal year 2007 to a 24 percent deficit as of fiscal year 2008 before improving to an estimated 18 percent deficit as of the end of June 2009. Funding levels improved in most countries in 2009, as stronger market performance increased asset levels and higher bond yields decreased liabilities. The United Kingdom was an anomaly, however, where the funded ratio worsened from a 9 percent deficit in December 2008 to a 13 percent deficit in June 2009.

Losses from defined-contribution pension funds affected those close to retirement age the most

Though defined-contribution pension funds in OECD countries suffered directly from the crisis in terms of accumulated wealth, the losses materialized mainly

---

[2] It is important to note that the funding levels found in corporate financial statements are most often reported on a global aggregate basis and thus can serve as only a broad indication of what has happened on a plan-specific or country-specific basis.

for those who were close to retirement and were preparing to buy an annuity. In countries such as Ireland and the Netherlands, the relaxation of annuitization requirements helped reduce the extent to which these paper losses translated into permanent cuts in benefits. The crisis has also demonstrated the benefits of a life-cycle investment approach, under which exposure to risky assets is reduced as the member approaches retirement. Various countries, including Chile, Hungary, and Mexico, have recently adopted such an approach as their default investment strategy in recent years, and Colombia and Israel are in the process of doing so.

Another, more controversial, policy reaction has been the decision to allow workers access to part of their retirement savings in order to alleviate immediate needs (as in Australia, Ireland, and Spain). Countries such as Estonia, Lithuania, and Romania, on the other hand, have reduced the amount of the mandatory pension contribution to the defined-contribution system in order to bolster the finances of the social security system. While possibly necessary, such actions should be carefully restricted and monitored, as they may ultimately jeopardize the security of payouts to beneficiaries.

Several policy initiatives involving public pension reserve funds were undertaken

Policy initiatives for PAYG schemes and public pension reserves during the financial crisis have included (1) proposals to increase the age at which pension benefits can be accessed (for example, in Finland and the Netherlands), (2) incorporation of old-age payments into economic stimulus packages (for example, in Australia, Greece, and the United Kingdom), and (3) strengthening of safety nets (for example, in Finland, France, and Spain). A direct link between public pension reserves and pension benefits was observed only in Sweden's nonfinancial defined-contribution system. In particular, largely as a result of the losses suffered by the country's AP Funds, Swedish pensioners will suffer a cut in their pension benefits in 2010. Public pension reserves have also been used for crisis mitigation measures in countries such as Ireland and Norway.

Governance can be strengthened by establishing a dual board structure

For all public pension reserve funds, one potential long-term hurdle is the possibility of undue government influence in the management of the fund. Though institutional safeguards have been introduced to address political interference in many OECD countries, many funds around the world face governance problems that are often compounded by the presence of board members with a political or personal agenda. Going forward, two main options for removing such governance problems are establishing stricter requirements under a single governing body structure or establishing a dual board structure with tripartite stakeholder representation (government, employers, and employees) only in an oversight body.

Conclusion

Prudent management of social security and pension funds is a tall order. Using modeling, stress testing, and other tools (now a regulatory requirement in countries such as Denmark and Germany), risk managers can simulate extreme negative events. While useful, such tools have limitations, as the correlations between different asset classes observed during past crises may fail to materialize during future adverse events. In general, institutions should avoid relying on a single indicator of their risk exposure or a specific tool to manage risk. It is also critical to develop a risk management culture throughout the organization and ensure appropriate reporting and disclosure of the main risks to which the institution is exposed.

For regulators and other policy makers, the financial crisis has shown the value of clear rules and flexibility. Swift reactions in several countries helped prevent a worsening of the crisis and limited fire sales of equities and annuity conversions at the worst possible moment. There is, however, much work still to be done, particularly in strengthening the governance and risk management requirements of these institutions.

References

OECD (Organisation for Economic Co-operation and Development). 2009. "Pension Markets in Focus, No. 6." Paris: OECD.

Pino, A., and J. Yermo. 2010. "The Impact of the 2007–2009 Crisis on Social Security and Private Pension Funds: A Threat to Their Financial Soundness?" *International Social Security Review* 63 (2): 5–30.

The Case of the Irish National Pensions Reserve Fund

Anne Maher, former Chief Executive Officer, Pensions Board, Ireland

In the face of the global financial crisis of 2008–09 and the Irish banking crisis, the government of Ireland amended the governing legislation for the Irish National Pensions Reserve Fund in order to permit "directed investment" aimed at recapitalizing two of Ireland's largest banks. Such measures addressed the urgent need for macroeconomic stability at the expense of the independence and disciplined investment policy of the National Pensions Reserve Fund. The diversion of investment capital into banks created a precedent and concern over possible future interventions in the face of other pressing economic circumstances. This is of particular importance to the public pension fund governance agenda because it illustrates that in the face of a crisis, a previously established independent pension authority and a disciplined investment policy may have to be compromised to satisfy other urgent and pressing economic policy priorities.

The global financial crisis in 2008–09 resulted in the need to recapitalize the Irish banking system

In 2008, in response to the global financial crisis and a serious domestic banking crisis, the government of Ireland set about increasing taxes and reducing expenditure. The resolution of the banking crisis, in particular, was viewed by the government as vital to the national recovery plan. As a first step, a bank guarantee scheme was introduced in September. Irish banks continued to be heavily affected, however, by turbulence in the global economy and financial markets and by public uncertainty about their capital adequacy. In December 2008, the government agreed to recapitalize the Irish banking system. The aim of recapitalization was threefold: (1) to reinforce the stability of the financial system, (2) to increase confidence in the Irish banking system, and (3) to facilitate the banks' involvement in lending to the Irish economy. As the government did not want to increase its sovereign debt, it identified the Irish National Pensions Reserve Fund (the Reserve Fund) as the source of funding for the recapitalization.

The Reserve Fund was at the heart of the solution to the banking crisis

Established as an independent entity in 2001, the Reserve Fund has the objective of meeting as much of the costs of social welfare and public service pensions as possible from 2025 onwards, when pension costs are forecast to increase considerably due to aging of Ireland's population. By law, the Irish government is required to contribute 1 percent of its gross national product (GNP) annually to the fund.

The investment mandate of the Reserve Fund was clear from the outset—namely, to maximize returns within acceptable risk levels in anticipation of increased payouts between 2025 and 2055. The size of the fund is projected to peak at about 50 percent of GNP in 2040. The fund's only investment restrictions are that it may not invest in Irish government securities nor acquire a controlling interest in any company. The investment strategy focused on building a diversified portfolio of equities and other real assets with an original split of 80 percent equity and 20 percent fixed-interest investment. The Reserve Fund's assets totaled $27.0 billion (€21.2 billion), or 13.4 percent of GNP, before the recent government intervention.

"Directed investment" by the Reserve Fund required a change in legislation

Despite the Irish government's desire to use the Reserve Fund as a source of funding to recapitalize domestic banks, the National Pensions Reserve Fund Act 2000 did not allow this (no withdrawals were to be made from the fund until 2025). The government then proposed amendments to the legislation that would permit "directed investment." The proposition was approved by the Irish Parliament, allowing the minister for finance to take certain actions in the public interest for either or both of two purposes: to remedy a serious disturbance in the economy, or to prevent potential serious damage to the financial system and ensure the continued stability of that system.

Armed with legal backing, the minister for finance directed the National Pensions Reserve Fund to contribute the necessary funds for bank recapitalization. Ireland's two largest banks, Allied Irish Banks and Bank of Ireland, each received $4.5 billion (€3.5 billion) in core Tier 1 capital. The recapitalization program was funded as follows: $5.1 billion (€4 billion) from the fund's current resources and the balance of $3.8 billion (€3 billion) was provided by front loading Department for Finance contributions to the fund for the years 2009 and 2010. In return, the fund received preferred shares in the banks with a fixed dividend of 8 percent payable in cash or ordinary shares and gained certain powers over the bank boards. In hindsight, this intervention happened in the context of a low level of political and public interest in or appreciation of the fund and its objective.

The Irish Government's Regulatory Response to the Global Financial Crisis

◆ Amendment of the National Pensions Reserve Fund Act to allow for directed investment

◆ Minister for finance given authority to direct National Pensions Reserve Funds assets to bank recapitalization

---

In the time since the intervention, the Reserve Fund's asset allocation has been split into a discretionary investment portfolio and a directed investment portfolio, the latter of which includes the preferred shares in the banks. In 2009, the discretionary portfolio, which amounts to two-thirds of the total assets of the fund, earned a return of 20.9 percent. When the preferred shares and related warrants are taken into account, however, the fund's return was 11.6 percent. Several new developments have arisen in 2010. First, cash dividends to the fund from the two recapitalized banks have been suspended following a European Union directive that said that no cash payments were to be made while the European Union is considering larger plans for bank restructuring. As a consequence, the fund has received a stock dividend which increased the fund's holding to 15.7 percent of the ordinary stock of Bank of Ireland. Second, new capital requirements have been introduced for Irish banks and must be in place by the end of 2010. The new requirements obligate Allied Irish Banks and Bank of Ireland to raise additional capital, a situation that, paradoxically, could result in additional bank funding being required from the fund.

Conclusion

Though international observers and regulatory bodies have commented extensively on whether the response of the Irish government in directing the National Pensions Reserve Fund to invest in the banks was an appropriate policy move, the issue that remains open for Irish policy makers is how to retain the independence and disciplined investment policy of the fund while simultaneously raising the urgent funds needed for macroeconomic stability in the face of the crisis. Questions for the fund remain whether investments in preferred bank shares are optimal from the viewpoint of its long-term investment objectives and achievement of its overall purpose. Finally, the diversion of capital into bank recapitalization creates a precedent and raises concerns over possible future interventions in the face of pressing economic circumstances.

Renationalization of Argentina's Pension System

Mercedes Bourquin, Director, Ministry of Labor, Employment, and Social Security, Argentina

An initiative to nationalize the Argentine pension system in November 2008 can be seen more as the culmination of a gradual series of steps to move away from the privatized scheme rather than a specific policy reaction to the global financial crisis. Political motivations behind the closing of individual savings accounts date back to 2003. By late 2008, there was widespread support for this change, sparked by the global financial crisis, the prevalence of reform proposals since 2003, and the importance of these reforms in the government's political platform. Societal mistrust of the private pension fund administrators resulted in little objection to nationalization proposals.

Renationalization of Argentina's pension system in 2008 was intended to protect individuals from losing their savings and provide the government with access to short-term financing

By November 2008, it was clear that the global financial crisis was having detrimental impacts on the value of assets held within Argentina's pension system. That month, the Argentine government began nationalizing the country's 10 mandatory private pension funds, which at the time had collective assets under management of around $30 billion. Prior to that, affiliates had to choose between contributing to one of the existing private pension funds or to a pay-as-you-go (PAYG) scheme for their salary-related pension.

To many observers, the government's action seemed to serve a dual purpose: to protect individuals from losing their savings and to provide the government access to short-term financing. There is a case, however, for considering the so-called nationalization of the Argentine pension system as the culmination of a gradual series of steps to move away from the private scheme rather than as a specific policy reaction to the global financial crisis.

Argentina's pension system has existed for more than 100 years, and the 2008 renationalization followed a long series of reforms to the system

Argentina's public social security system dates back to 1904. Until the 1950s, the system was fragmented—a partially funded and defined-benefit set of schemes covering a range of occupational pension systems. In the 1950s, efforts were made to unify provincial schemes into a PAYG defined-benefit scheme. Though the system continued to mature during the 1970s and 1980s, it also became increasingly financially unbalanced. In 1993, a major structural reform was put in place (figure 3.35), introducing individual savings accounts as part of a dual second pillar with several objectives, some of them beyond standard pension scheme goals.[1] An important objective of the 1993 reform was to develop Argentina's capital markets through the introduction of mandatory pension funds. For the pension system itself, a first-pillar flat benefit was established for all old-age pensioners; all workers (both employees and self-employed) were required to choose between contributing to the state PAYG earnings-related scheme or an individual retirement account managed by a pension fund company, the Retirement and Pension Fund Administrators (AFJP). Under the dual system, employers were still required to make contributions to the first pillar administered by the government.

In 2001, Argentina went through a major social, economic, and financial crisis caused in part by incomplete consideration of transition costs of the 1993 pension reform. The crisis resulted in external and internal debt renegotiation; the end of the decade-long peso-U.S. dollar peg; and, for the pension system, a continuous decline in coverage rates and benefits from the first and second pillars. The national pension scheme saw an increase in uncertainties for affiliates and beneficiaries resulting from the decline in real pension benefits due to the lack of a benefit indexation mechanism taking into account the change in the purchasing power of Argentina's currency after the devaluation in 2002 and inflation in subsequent years.

Further pension reforms involving several simultaneous objectives were begun in 2003. On the one hand, there was a clear intention to recover the state's role

---

[1] The 1993 reform introduced a three-pillar scheme. The first pillar was a flat-amount basic pension benefit. The second pillar (the income- or contribution-related part of the benefit) offered affiliates two options: the existing privately owned pension funds (the Retirement and Pension Fund Administrators, or AFJPs) or the state PAYG scheme. When new entrants to the labor market did not express a preference, their workers were by default assigned affiliation with one of the AFJPs. The third pillar offered the possibility of making additional voluntary contributions to one of the privately owned funds.

Figure 3.35 **Mechanism of Financial Transfers in Argentina's Social Security System**

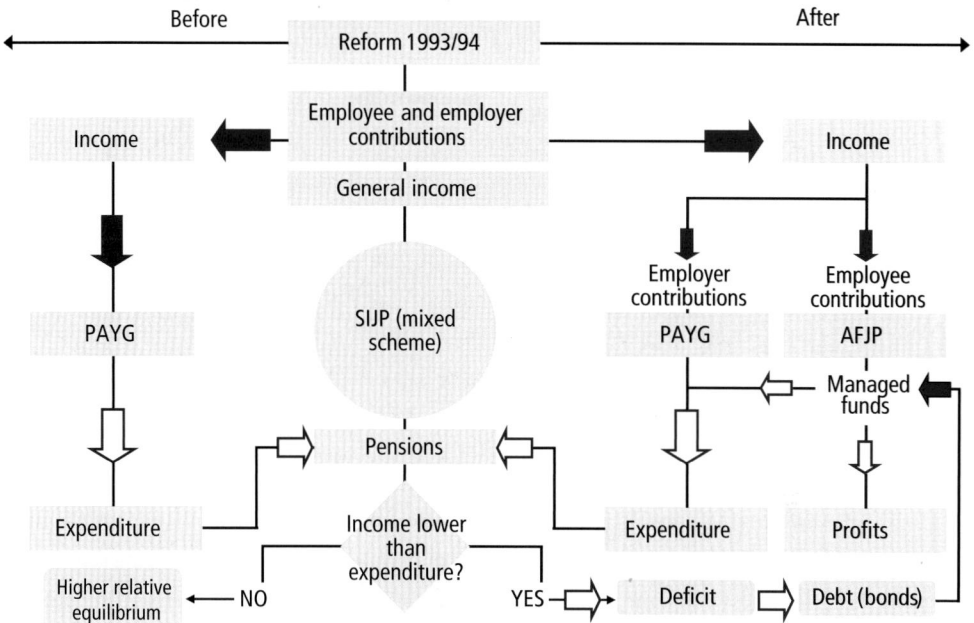

Source: Ministry of Labor, Employment, and Social Security.

in the social security system. At the same time, there was an implicit objective to improve coverage by making the requirement for accessing pension benefits from the PAYG scheme more flexible and to improve the adequacy of the benefit that made an increase in pensioners' spending power possible. (Pensioners' spending had declined considerably during the previous several years.) A further modification in the pension law in 2007 allowed affiliates of any of the pension funds to change their affiliation to the national PAYG scheme.

In November 2008, Argentina enacted a law that eliminated private pension funds altogether, transferring all their assets to the Sustainability and Guarantee Fund (FGS) of the Argentine Integrated Pension System (SIPA). As a result, the second pillar was completely nationalized, with contribution and benefit accumulation reverting to the national PAYG defined-benefit scheme (figure 3.36). The contributions, which had gone to the former first pillar, were then received by different pension funds during the period 1993–2008. These fund accumulations resulted in 50–70 percent of the second pillar's portfolio being invested in government bonds.

Over time, several issues affected the second pillar and the politics surrounding it. These included increasing the minimum benefit provided under the PAYG scheme,

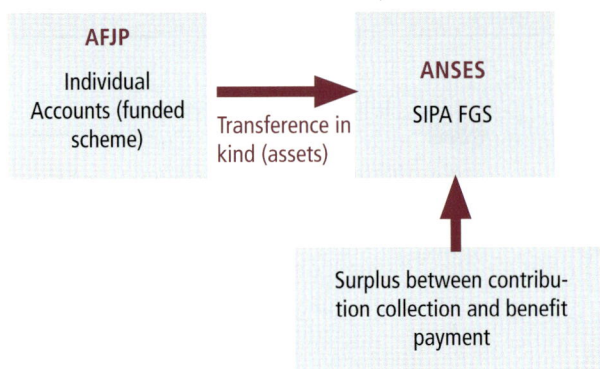

Figure 3.36 **Renationalization of the Integrated Argentine Social Security System**

Source: Ministry of Labor, Employment, and Social Security.

improving benefits and other parameters of the PAYG scheme, including guaranteed minimum benefits for affiliates of private pension funds, making requirements to access pensions more flexible, reinstating some "special" pension schemes, and revising labor incentive policies to reduce informality in the labor market.

Argentina's Pension System Policy Responses to the Global Financial Crisis

◆ Elimination of the second pillar system of individual retirement accounts managed by private pension funds (AFJP)

◆ Transfer of AFJP assets to a new government fund (SIPA)

◆ Creation of a bicameral legislative commission and oversight panel to supervise the administration of SIPA

Political motivations for the 2008 reform originated in 2003

The political motivations behind the nationalization of the second pillar of Argentina's pension system date to a political platform announced in 2003, in which pension reform was a key part. By 2008, there was widespread support for changes including elimination of the individual savings account scheme, despite vehement objections by the financial industry and lobbying against reform by AFJPs. In the end, the global financial crisis was the catalyst for introduction and passage of the November 2008 reform. The societal mistrust in the private pension scheme and in pension fund administrators that had built up in preceding years resulted in few objections being made to the nationalization proposals upon their submission to the Argentine National Congress. Even the opposing political parties were not against the basics of the reform. Quick adoption of the reform limited pension funds' risks at a time of rapid declines in the value of the assets they held.

Current pension system governance is similar to that of the pre-2008 system but with several key changes

Under the reformed pension system structure, the National Social Security Administration (ANSES), which manages FGS and invests its portfolio, is financially and economically self-governed with assistance of an executive committee. Supervision of the ANSES is provided by a bicameral commission (six senators and six deputies) within the Argentine National Congress. A committee to monitor the resources of the FGS has also been created. The committee's members include representatives of government, pension beneficiaries, workers, employers, banks, and parliamentary representatives.

The size of the FGS has increased considerably with the addition of resources previously invested in Argentina's 10 terminated private pension funds. Restrictions on FGS's investments, though, are the same as those that were in place for the pension funds except for the addition of a prohibition on investing abroad that was included in the last reform. That last reform also prohibited charging commissions for managing FGS investments. FGS is responsible for guaranteeing the payment of pensions; since 2009, the fund's returns may also be used to pay benefits from a new family allowance program.

FGS invests according to three basic criteria: security, transparency, and return. On the security criteria, most FGS assets qualify as investment grade by local and international rating agencies. On transparency, ANSES and the FGS are subject to several control, audit, and supervision policies. On return, FGS's track record thus far has been good: after one year of functioning, the annual rate of return was 41.5 percent.

As of February 2010, 62.6 percent of FGS's portfolio was invested in bonds issued by the government and other domestic public entities, 11.2 percent in private assets and other private investment, 7.1 percent in fixed-term deposits, 6.9 percent in productive and infrastructure projects investments, and 12.2 percent in investment funds and bank deposits. The share of productive and infrastructure projects investments increased 6 percentage points between to November 2008 (before the nationalization) and February 2010, demonstrates that FGS makes financing the real economy a priority.

Conclusion

The renationalization of the second pillar of Argentina's pension system was not a policy that arose from the global financial crisis. Rather, it was a milestone in a longer-term change to the concept of social insurance and the division of roles between the government, workers, employers, and society as a whole. It is important to emphasize that although Argentina's pension reform has been one of the most vital in recent years, even at a worldwide level, it has not solved all the difficulties and problems of the country's pension scheme in terms of inter- and intra-generational equity, solidarity, and financial sustainability. The reform should therefore be considered one of a series of steps taken by the government to improve the pension scheme. Though they are not always recognized as such, pensions are a political issue very much influenced by ideological perspectives.

Thailand's GPF: From the 1997 Asian Crisis to the 2008 Global Financial Crisis

Arporn Chewakrengkrai, Chief Economist, Government Pension Fund, Thailand

The lessons of the 1997 Asian financial crisis had a major impact on the responses of Thailand's Government Pension Fund (GPF) to the global financial crisis in 2008. Having experienced crisis a decade prior, the Thai financial system was relatively well prepared for the shocks of the turmoil and did not require recapitalization or nationalization. The strategic response of the GPF to the crisis included shifting its asset allocation, delaying investment in certain types of assets, and allocating new pension contributions to highly secure assets. No changes were made to the GPF's investment risk and return objectives in the face of the crisis.

Thailand's Government Pension Fund has relied on solid investment techniques and rules since its inception

Established in 1997 as a compulsory, defined-contribution pension scheme for government officials, Thailand's Government Pension Fund (GPF) has grown to become one of the country's key institutional investors. The GPF held assets of $11.2 billion as of the end of 2008, a fivefold increase from $2 billion in 1997 (figure 3.37).

The investment philosophy of the GPF has six main goals: (1) safeguarding the fund's principal, (2) producing returns that outperform the long-term inflation rate, (3) selecting appropriate asset allocation, (4) diversifying investments so that they are capable of weathering perpetually changing globalization trends, (5) providing efficient investment control, and (6) supervision of the investment process. All these factors help counterbalance cyclical economic effects and generate satisfactory returns for GPF members.

GPF's Investment Committee is required to comply with a set of stipulated rules and investment limits. The investment guidelines direct that no less than 60 percent

Figure 3.37 **Total Asset Growth of the GPF**

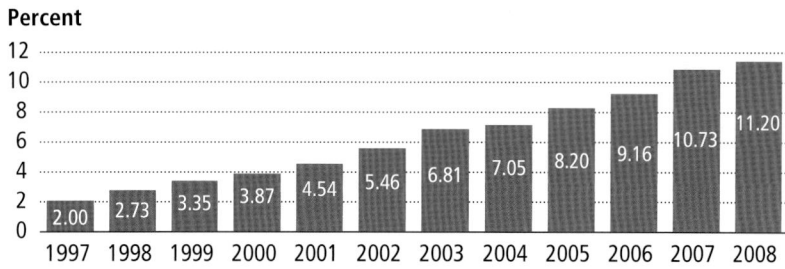

Percent

Year	Value
1997	2.00
1998	2.73
1999	3.35
2000	3.87
2001	4.54
2002	5.46
2003	6.81
2004	7.05
2005	8.20
2006	9.16
2007	10.73
2008	11.20

Source: GPF.

of the total portfolio be allocated to "secure assets." These include bank deposits, government bonds, state enterprise bonds with a government guarantee for both principal and interest, and high-grade private sector bonds. Allocations to other asset classes may not exceed the following limits: 35 percent for equity, 25 percent for global assets, and 8 percent for real estate.

The GPF regularly reviews its asset allocation to ensure that it is in line with its investment policy and to effectively respond to changing economic conditions. Investment evaluation benchmarks are regularly adjusted to reflect the fund's performance level. Compliance with investment recommendations prescribed by the framework of the Government Pension Fund Act and applicable ministerial regulations are also regularly monitored, and investments are made prudently and efficiently in order to maximize returns.

The GPF has successfully weathered several domestic and external shocks

The GPF's investment strategy is based on a 10-year investment time horizon. The long-term (10-year) return objective is inflation plus 2.75 percent, while the short-term return objective is based on a market benchmark (table 3.15). The fund's risk tolerance is based on a projected 65 percent probability of achieving the long-term return objective and a 17 percent probability of a negative annual return (that is, once every six to seven years).

Between 1996 and 2008, the GPF weathered a number of internal and external shocks, including the political turmoil and coup in 2006 and the global financial crisis in 2008. The Thai stock index dropped by 34 percent between September and October 2008 and fell 47 percent for 2008 as a whole. Foreign investors withdrew

Table 3.15 **GPF Investment Profile**

Factor	Target
Retirement age	60 years
Investment time horizon	10 years
Long-term return objective	Inflation +2.75%
Short-term return objective	Market benchmark

Source: GPF.

approximately $7.2 billion from the Thai market between July 2007 and the end of 2008.

Having experienced the severity of the 1997 Asian financial crisis, however, the Thai financial system was better prepared for the shocks of the 2008–09 crisis than the financial systems of many Western countries. Thai banks did not require recapitalization or nationalization. For its part, the GPF posted a cumulative nominal return of 236 percent between 1996 and the end of 2008, against 146 percent inflation over the same period (figures 3.38 and 3.39).

The GPF response to the 2008 global financial crisis has been strategic

The strategic response of the GPF to the 2008 crisis was fivefold. (1) reducing equity holdings in both domestic and global markets, (2) reducing the ratio of corporate bonds and credit in the fixed-income portfolio, (3) delaying investment in global alternative assets; (4) allocating new contributions to lower-risk assets, and (5) establishing a new strategic asset allocation with less risky assets. GPF's reduction in exposure to Thai and global equities between end-2007 and March 2009 is shown in figure 3.40.

During the first quarter of 2008, the GPF Investment Committee revisited its strategic asset allocation and investment benchmark during a scheduled biannual review. Taking into account the changing investment environment in global financial markets, the committee made several adjustments in the GPF's asset allocation.

As a result of this review, almost 78 percent of the GPF's portfolio assets were allocated to lower-risk assets, an increase of 15 percentage points compared to the 63 percent allocation to such assets as of the beginning of 2008. Compared to the January 2008 allocation of assets, the December 2008 asset allocation represented a substantive increase in Thai bond holdings; a decrease in Thai equity holdings;

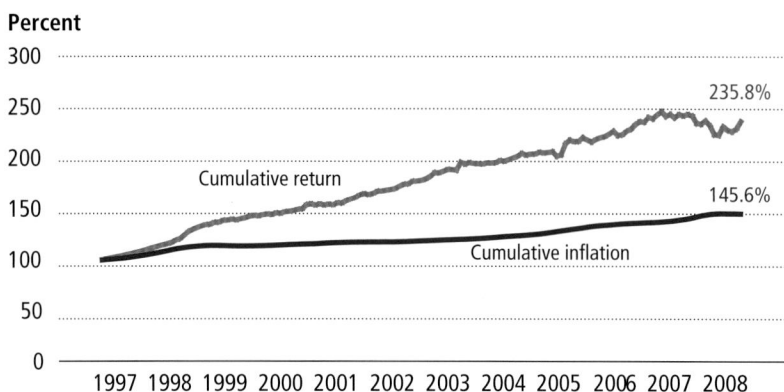

Figure 3.38 **GPF Returns versus Inflation**

Percent

- 235.8%
- 145.6%

Cumulative return

Cumulative inflation

Source: GPF.

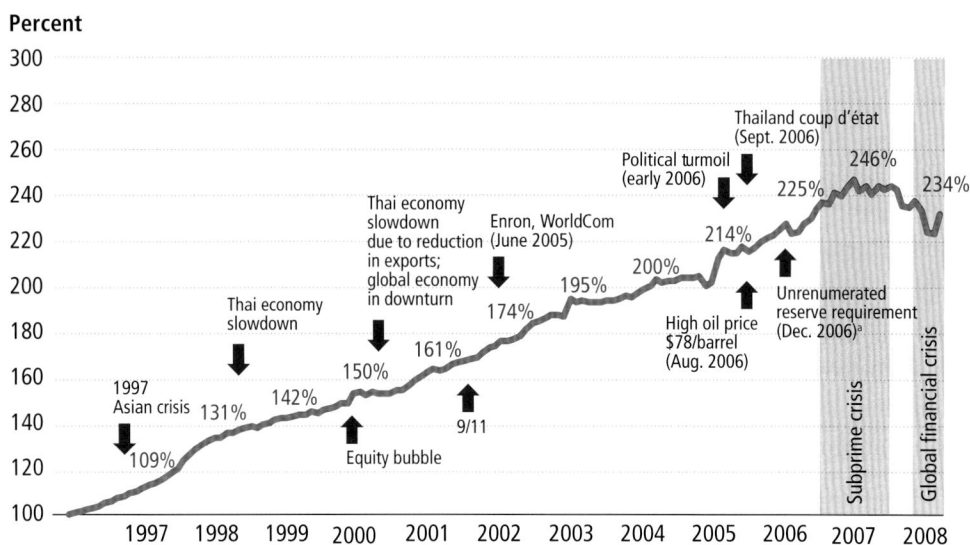

Figure 3.39 **Accumulated GPF Returns**

Percent

Thailand coup d'état (Sept. 2006)

Political turmoil (early 2006)

246%

234%

Thai economy slowdown due to reduction in exports; global economy in downturn

Enron, WorldCom (June 2005)

225%

214%

200%

195%

Thai economy slowdown

174%

Unrenumerated reserve requirement (Dec. 2006)[a]

161%

High oil price $78/barrel (Aug. 2006)

150%

1997 Asian crisis

131%

142%

9/11

109%

Equity bubble

Subprime crisis

Global financial crisis

Source: GPF.

Note: Data are as of December of each year.

a. On December 18, 2006, the Bank of Thailand implemented an unremunerated reserve requirement on short-term capital inflow. In general, 30 percent of foreign currencies bought or exchanged against the Thai baht were withheld by financial institutions.

and a decrease in global equity, private equity, and real estate holdings (figure 3.41). For 2008 as a whole, the GPF posted a 5.2 percent loss, a relatively small amount compared to other public pension funds.

Figure 3.40 **Reduction in Equity Investments by the GPF**

a. **Thai equity**

Percent

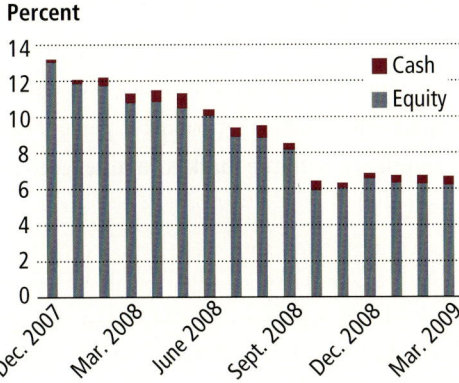

b. **Global equity**

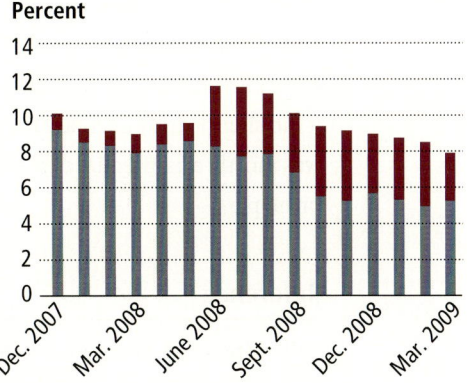

Percent

Source: GPF.

Figure 3.41 **GPF's Asset Allocation**

a. **January 2008**

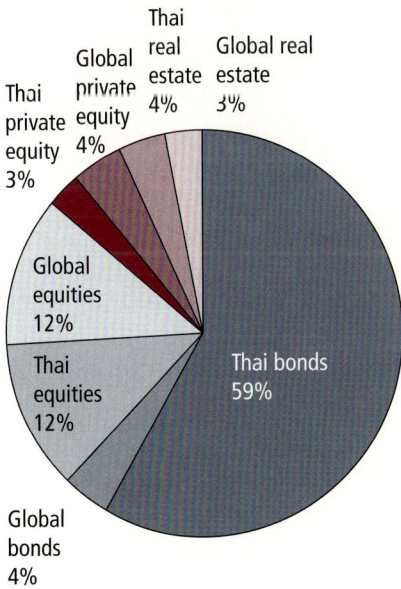

b. **December 2008**

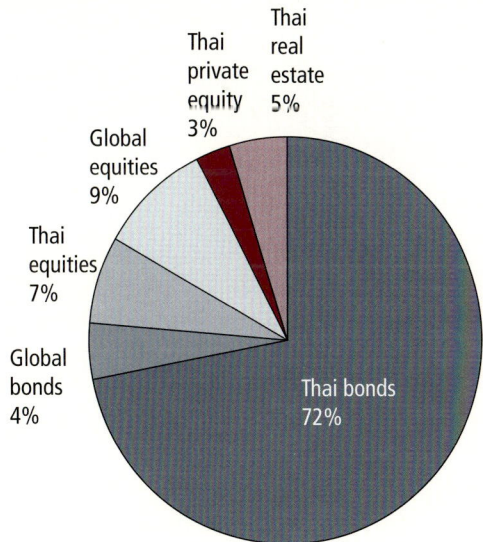

Source: GPF.

Conclusion

Thailand's GPF has successfully weathered the effects of the 1997 Asian financial crisis, the political turmoil and coup of 2006, and the global financial crisis of 2008. In both 2006 and 2008, the GPF rapidly reduced its exposure to domestic and global equities in favor of retaining more cash. Though this response to the global financial crisis has not entirely protected the fund from negative outcomes, it did significantly decrease their impact. The negative return of 5.2 percent in 2008 was mostly an unrealized loss, in compliance with the mark-to-market accounting principle.

Reference

GPF (Thailand Government Pension Fund). 2008. "Annual Report." www.gpf. or.th/download/annual/annual2008_eng.pdf.

PART FOUR

Investment of Public Pension Assets

1. Defining the Investment Policy Framework for Public Pension Funds

2. Managing Risk for Different Cohorts in Defined-Contribution Schemes

3. An Asset-Liability Approach to Strategic Asset Allocation for Pension Funds

4. In-House Investment versus Outsourcing to External Investment Managers

5. International Investments and Managing the Resulting Currency Risk

6. Alternative Asset Classes and New Investment Themes

1. Defining the Investment Policy Framework for Public Pension Funds

- ◆ The Investment Policy Process: A Perspective from the World Bank

- ◆ Designing Investment Policy to Ensure Long-Term Solvency: The U.N. Joint Staff Pension Fund

- ◆ Making Investment Policy Consistent with Overall Pension Plan Design: Japan's GPIF

- ◆ Linking Risk Tolerance and Pension Liabilities with Investment Strategy: Denmark's ATP

The Investment Policy Process: A Perspective from the World Bank

Krishnan Chandrasekhar, Senior Manager, World Bank Treasury

Strategic asset allocation is important to the construction and performance of a pension fund's overall investment portfolio. Within the World Bank Staff Retirement Plan and Trust, specification of several parameters have gone into the establishment of an investment policy, including the investment objectives and investment horizon, risk tolerance and risk constraints, and eligible asset classes given the fund's predefined investment objectives. A key component of the strategic asset allocation exercise is to determine long-term capital market expectations relating to risk and return for major asset classes, while the end goal is to agree upon a policy mix of assets that is both optimal in terms of returns and realistic given the long-run investment objectives of the fund.

Strategic asset allocation is a key element in designing and implementing an efficient investment policy framework for pension funds

Four elements are crucial to designing and implementing an efficient investment policy framework for pension funds: (1) understanding the role of strategic asset allocation (SAA) in the long-term investment performance of pension assets; (2) following a systematic investment policy process; (3) appropriately articulating the objectives, investment horizon, and risk tolerance of the pension fund; and (4) implementing the SAA and constructing the policy portfolio taking organizational capabilities into account.

SAA is a process by which a pension fund determines its appropriate neutral asset allocation at any point in time to achieve its long-term investment objectives. Appropriate SAA should

◆ be neutral, rather than driven by short-term market views;

◆ be reviewed periodically as conditions—both external market conditions and internal fund specifics—change;

◆ involve well-considered trade-offs between return and risk;

◆ be embodied within a clearly articulated investment policy statement.

Historically, SAA has outweighed all other determinants of pension funds' portfolio performance, with more than 90 percent of the portfolio's total risk being attributable to it (Brinson, Hood, and Beebower 1991). As such, it ranks high in the hierarchy of investment decisions and defines the overall return-risk profile of a pension fund's portfolio. In fact, the SAA process should be the focal point of portfolio strategy making, be managed at the highest managerial level within the fund, and be supplied with adequate resources.

Figure 4.1 summarizes the five steps in the investment policy process followed by the World Bank Staff Retirement Plan, from articulating objectives and the investment horizon to deciding on a neutral asset allocation and implementing the SAA.

Figure 4.1 **Steps in the Investment Policy Process**

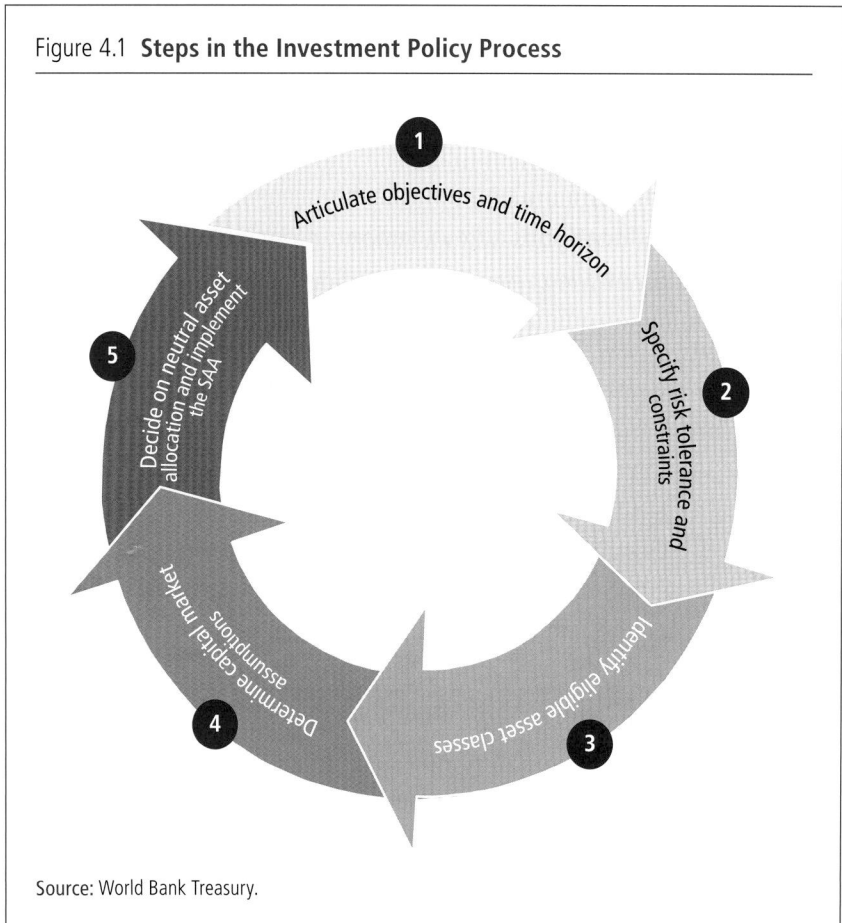

Source: World Bank Treasury.

The investment objectives of a pension fund should depend largely on the liabilities of the fund

The overall objectives of a pension fund depend on the nature of the fund's liabilities. Defined-benefit plans prefund future employee benefits, allow sponsors to spread financial obligations over time, provide security to plan beneficiaries, and allow pooling of investment and other risks. Defined-contribution plans, on the other hand, help accumulate wealth to meet retirement income needs. In both cases, it is important to take advantage of the long-term investment horizon and (hopefully) low short-term liquidity needs to extract long-term risk premiums on a diversified pool of assets.

In general, the main investment objective of a defined-benefit pension fund is expressed in one of two forms: maintenance and growth of the plan surplus (the difference between the value of assets and liabilities) and maintenance and growth of the funded ratio (the ratio of assets to liabilities). Liabilities are key in defining a pension fund's investment objectives, and the asset allocation strategy chosen by the fund's investment managers thus depends on the characteristics of the liabilities (for example, whether they are indexed to inflation), liquidity needs arising from such liabilities, and the plan's funded status.

Defined-benefit plans typically have a fairly long investment horizon, which may, however, be affected by regulatory and accounting considerations. The investment horizon depends on the plan's maturity (the ratio of retiree members receiving benefits to active employee members contributing to the plan), and the time pattern of the projected benefit cash flows. Defined-contribution plans also have a fairly long investment horizon, though the investment horizon of an individual's account depends on the individual's age. Defined-contribution plans maintain different horizons for different cohorts of participants, and declining horizons over time for the same cohort of participants.

Though defined-benefit pension funds generally use the same two key measures of risk, the objectives and risk tolerance of different stakeholders in the fund may not be the same

Defined-benefit pension plans are funded through sponsor and employee contributions and investment returns. The objective of the contribution and investment policies is to ensure that the plan sponsor is able to honor its obligations to current and future beneficiaries. In general, there is a trade-off between the size of contributions and the amount of the investment risk that is taken: a low-risk portfolio would secure plan assets but lock in a high level of contributions, while a higher

171

risk portfolio could potentially require lower contributions if expected returns are realized, but could also jeopardize the security of the plan's assets in the event of unfavorable investment returns.

Defined-benefit pension funds use two key measures of risk, which are interrelated: minimum acceptable funded ratio levels and maximum acceptable contribution rates. As figure 4.2 indicates, a common objective of a public pension fund's governing body is to maximize investment returns and, in turn, maximize the wealth of the fund; however, the objectives of a plan's stakeholders may be contradictory. The objective of the plan sponsors is generally to maintain contributions at a constant and relatively low level, while the objective of plan members and retirees is generally to achieve security by avoiding low funded ratios.

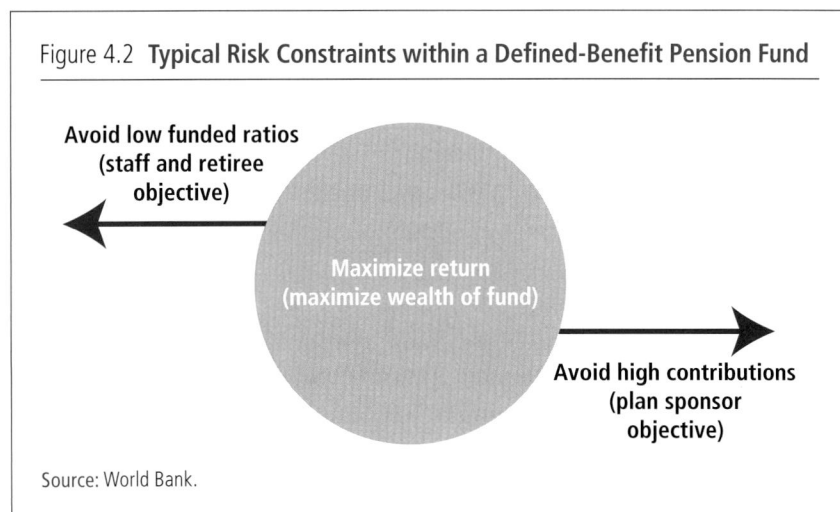

Figure 4.2 **Typical Risk Constraints within a Defined-Benefit Pension Fund**

Avoid low funded ratios
(staff and retiree
objective)

Maximize return
(maximize wealth of fund)

Avoid high contributions
(plan sponsor
objective)

Source: World Bank.

There is also a difference between an institution's ability to take risk and its decision makers' willingness to take risk. The *ability to take risk* refers to the amount of risk appropriate for achieving long-term goals and is driven by plan objectives, funded status, institutional constraints, and human resources (for example, capacity and skills of staff members). *Willingness to take risk*, on the other hand, can be driven by emotions, peer pressure, herd behavior, and financial literacy of key stakeholders. Low willingness to take risk may create opportunity costs, while high willingness may result in excessive risk taking and negative results (figure 4.3).

Pension funds have a typical set of eligible asset classes and considerations influencing the choice of those asset classes

The typical universe of eligible asset classes for pension fund investments includes *fixed-income instruments* (sovereign bonds, government agency bonds, mortgage-

Figure 4.3 **Willingness versus Ability to Take Risk**

Willingness to take risk	Ability to take risks
◆ Can be driven by – Emotions and noise – Peer pressure and herd behavior – Financial literacy of key stakeholders ◆ Low willingness may create opportunity costs ◆ High willingness may result in excessive risk taking and negative surprises	◆ Refers to the appropriate amount of risk to achieve long-term objectives ◆ Can be driven by – Plan objectives – Funded status – Institutional constraints and human resources (for example, staff capacity and skills)

Source: World Bank.

backed and other asset-backed securities, and corporate bonds); *equity* (public equity and private equity); *real return instruments* (inflation-linked bonds, real estate, commodities, infrastructure, and timber); and *absolute return instruments* (hedge funds).

Considerations influencing choice of eligible asset classes usually include investment objectives and risk-return considerations, headline/reputational risk issues (related to hedge funds, for example), legal and political constraints (for example, relating to international investments and "directed investments"), staff capabilities and skill mix (including public sector constraints), and overall capacity and sophistication (for example, investment in alternative asset classes or private markets).

Forward-looking capital market assumptions for different asset classes over the appropriate investment horizon are key to developing a strategic asset allocation

Capital market assumptions are a key ingredient in the SAA process. Assumptions include expected returns for each asset class, volatility of returns (which measures potential dispersion in returns), and correlations across asset classes. Though it is important to analyze historical return data, it is also important not to use such data in a mechanical fashion—rather, they should be an input in making informed, forward-looking projections. Quantitative models frequently used in this capacity include *factor models* (regressions or building-block models); *autoregressive models,* which account for mean reversion; and *Bayesian models*, which combine expected returns implied by an asset pricing model with investor views.

Besides developing forward-looking capital market assumptions, pension funds must assess the performance of various asset classes over different holding periods. Figure 4.4 shows the historical performance and volatility of various U.S. asset classes over holding periods ranging from 1 year to 20 years. Though equities are much more volatile than bonds or cash investments, especially over short holding periods, they also have the capacity to produce much higher returns than other asset classes over the long run. This emphasizes the importance of evaluating asset classes over the investment horizon appropriate to a particular pension fund—which in most cases is significantly longer than the typical reporting horizon of one year.

Figure 4.4 **Historical Performance of U.S. Asset Classes: Maximum and Minimum Returns over Various Holding Periods, 1926–2007**

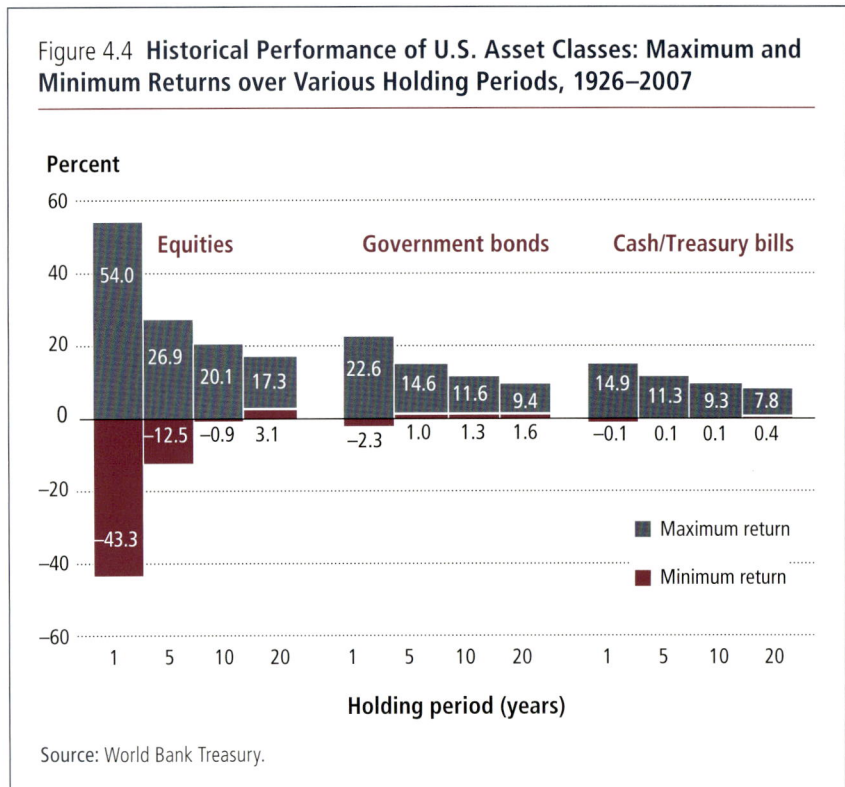

Source: World Bank Treasury.

Mean variance optimization is extremely sensitive to inputs and should be tempered with qualitative judgments

The most common approach employed by institutional investors and asset managers to determine optimal portfolios is to apply mean variance optimization (MVO), a quantitative analytical process that helps an investor determine a portfolio that maximizes expected return for a given level of risk. The basic philosophy behind the process is not to put all of one's eggs in one basket. A key assumption of MVO is that returns are normally distributed. Inputs for MVO analysis include the expected return of each asset class, standard deviation of each asset class, and correlation of returns among asset classes. The output of the analysis is an efficient frontier—that is, the set of portfolios with the highest expected return for a given level of risk. It should be noted that the results of MVO models are extremely sensitive to input assumptions and should be tempered based on qualitative judgments.

Conclusion

The process for optimal investment management of pension funds includes setting investment objectives, determining the investment horizon, determining risk tolerance and defining appropriate risk parameters in order to quantify this tolerance, identifying the universe of asset classes for investment, determining forward-looking capital market assumptions for these asset classes, and finalizing the fund's SAA using optimization techniques overlaid as needed by qualitative judgments. Long-term capital market expectations of risk and return for each asset class are generally framed in terms of expected returns, volatility of these returns, and correlations across asset classes. The reliability of MVO is dependent upon the accuracy with which the analytical inputs can be predicted. Merging the requirements of the investment policy process with well-thought-out, forward-looking capital markets expectations is essential to formulating SAA appropriate to the circumstances of a particular fund.

Reference

Brinson, G., L. Hood, and G. Beebower. 1991. "Determinants of Portfolio Performance" *Financial Analysts Journal* 47 (3): 40–48.

Designing Investment Policy to Ensure Long-Term Solvency: The U.N. Joint Staff Pension Fund

Sergio B. Arvizu, Deputy Chief Executive Officer, United Nations Joint Staff Pension Fund

In 2007, the United Nations Joint Staff Pension Fund (UNJSPF) conducted an asset-liability management (ALM) study with the objective of establishing a strategic, long-term asset allocation policy for the UNJSPF investment portfolio and assessing its long-term solvency vis-à-vis a range of stochastic, simulation-derived investment results. The results of the ALM study also helped the UNJSPF in evaluating its investment structure and enhancing the flow and interaction among its elements. Decision makers within pension funds should consider an ALM study as part of an evolving, continuous process of assessing the impact of key investment decisions upon the financial condition and performance of a pension plan.

The UNJSPF is a multifaceted agency with a record of prudent financial management

The United Nations Joint Staff Pension Fund (UNJSPF) is an interagency entity that was established by the General Assembly of the United Nations in 1949 with the objective of providing retirement, death, disability and related benefits for the staff of the United Nations and related international intergovernmental organizations. As of 2010, it serves 23 member organizations. It is a defined-benefit, fully funded public pension scheme with more than $32 billion in assets. The UNJSPF pools and invests participants' and employers' contributions (23.7 percent of pensionable remuneration) to help provide current and future pensions (as well as other related benefits) to participants and other beneficiaries. Benefits, which are paid in 190 countries and in 15 currencies, are determined based on the rights accrued according to an employee's grade and length of service and are not subject to individual investment risk.

In many respects, the UNJSPF is more like a life insurance company than solely a benefits payment administrator or investment manager. Working on the basic principle of solidarity, it pools contributions to provide pension and other benefits covering risks including investment, longevity, cost-of-living adjustment, disability, death (during United Nations service), and survivors (widow/widower). That said, the UNJSPF has features similar to those of defined-contribution plans, such as the right of members to up to one-third benefit commutation and portability. Finally, the UNJSPF offers an elective two-track adjustment feature to protect purchasing power in the local currencies in which it offers benefits. The two-track system is a feature of the UNJSPF's pension adjustment system whereby a member's pension is calculated and maintained in both U.S. dollars and in the currency of the country in which the member resides.

All pensions are calculated initially in U.S. dollars (the "dollar track"), which is then adjusted by the movement of the U.S. consumer price index. If a member then declares a country other than the United States as his or her residence, the UNJSPF establishes a local currency track pension for the member, which is then adjusted by the movement of the consumer price index of the member's respective country. Every quarter, the local currency equivalent of the dollar track (derived using the quarterly exchange rate) is compared to the local track amount; generally, the member is entitled to the higher of the two amounts.

Partially as a result of its unique features, the UNJSPF has become increasingly complex to manage in recent years. As of end-2008, the UNJSPF had approximately 110,000 active participants and 59,000 beneficiaries. In 2008, it received $1.6 billion in contributions and made nearly 700,000 pension benefit payments equivalent to $1.8 billion. The gap between contributions and benefits remains low (figure 4.5).

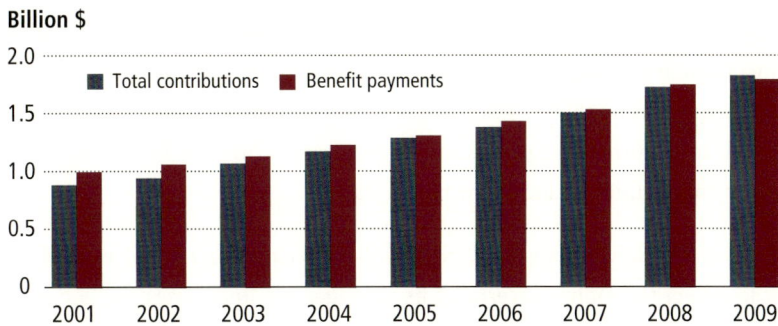

Figure 4.5 **UNJSPF Contributions and Benefit Payments**

Source: UNJSPF.

An actuarial valuation discipline, a long-term view, a prudent philosophy, and a funded approach since the UNJSPF's inception have resulted in surpluses over the last six consecutive valuations (figure 4.6). The most recent actuarial valuation, conducted in 2007, showed a 0.49 percent surplus, down from a 1.29 percent surplus in 2005. The decline reflects higher costs related to growth in longevity, which increased by an average of three years from the original estimate.

Figure 4.6 **Evolution of UNJSPF's Actuarial Situation Since 1990**

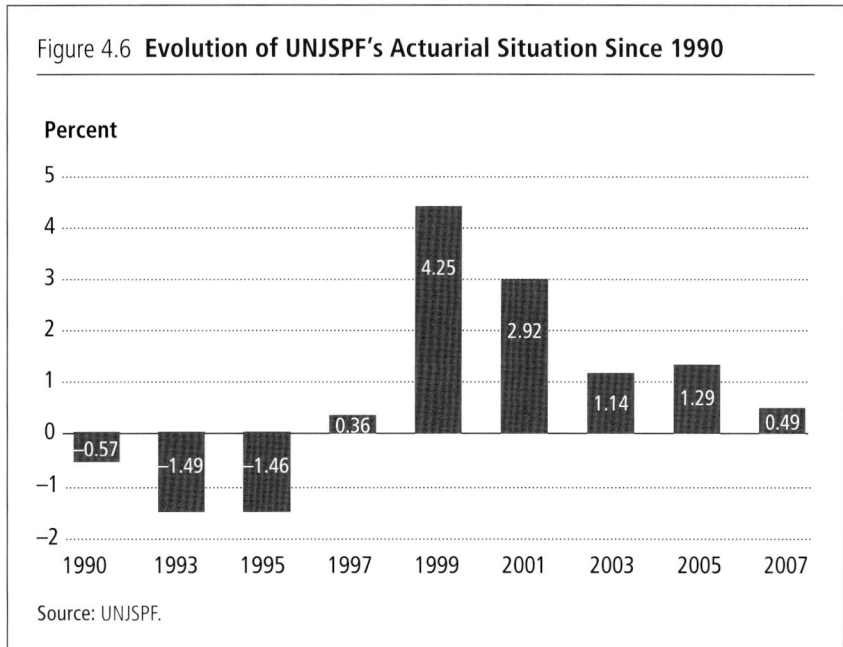

Source: UNJSPF.

The UNJSPF has developed a risk-tolerance framework incorporating quantitative measures and translated them into three risk-tolerance philosophies

In 2007, the UNJSPF undertook an asset-liability management (ALM) study that used stochastic forecasting to simulate projected benefits and actuarial costs as a percentage of active payroll costs based on different asset allocations. The outcomes of those simulations suggested very wide ranges for both benefit payments and costs of operating the fund (figure 4.7). The reason for such high volatility lies mainly in the two-track feature of the pension adjustment system and the impact of currency volatility on liabilities for locally recruited staff.

As part of the ALM study, the UNJSPF also developed a risk-tolerance framework to reflect the main concerns of its management and governing bodies. The framework uses sets of specific quantitative measures associated with four factors: actuarial costs, funded ratio, real-term investment returns, and assets-to-benefits

Figure 4.7 **UNJSPF Stochastic Simulation Model Results**

a. Benefit payments

b. Costs

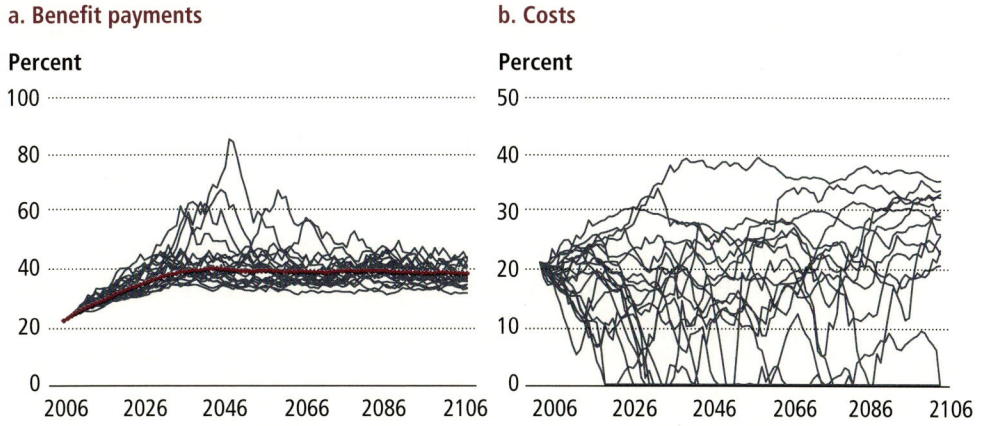

Source: UNJSPF.

Note: Red line in 4.7a shows projected benefits as a percentage of the active payroll.

ratio (figure 4.8). Those factors, in different combinations and assigned different weighting, translate into three risk-tolerance philosophies:

Figure 4.8 **Risk-Tolerance Framework within the UNJSPF**

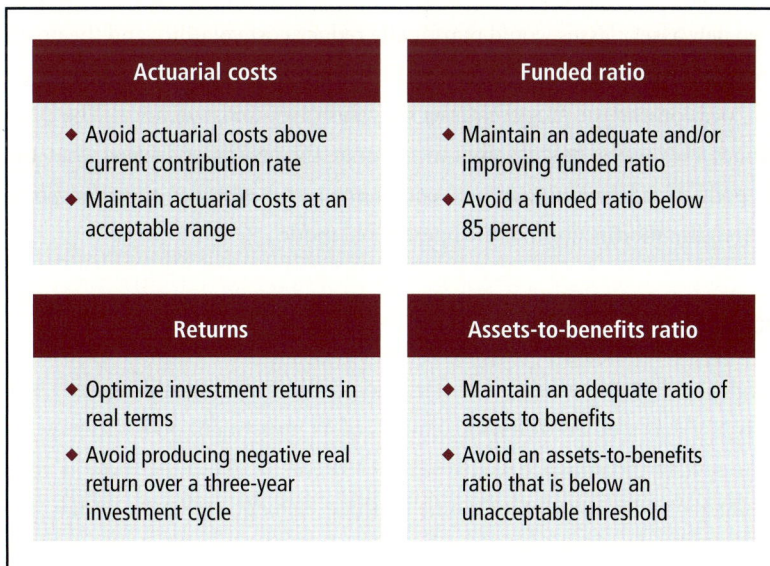

Actuarial costs	**Funded ratio**
◆ Avoid actuarial costs above current contribution rate ◆ Maintain actuarial costs at an acceptable range	◆ Maintain an adequate and/or improving funded ratio ◆ Avoid a funded ratio below 85 percent
Returns	**Assets-to-benefits ratio**
◆ Optimize investment returns in real terms ◆ Avoid producing negative real return over a three-year investment cycle	◆ Maintain an adequate ratio of assets to benefits ◆ Avoid an assets-to-benefits ratio that is below an unacceptable threshold

Source: UNJSPF.

◆ *Prudent funding* places a high priority on improving the funded status of the plan while also focusing on protecting long-term plan solvency.

◆ *Return-oriented* places a high priority on achieving a favorable long-term real return while stressing the importance of avoiding sustained negative real returns.

◆ *Defensive* places a high priority on maintaining low plan cost volatility and avoiding deterioration in long-term solvency of the UNJSPF.

The ALM study shows that adding two new strategic asset classes to the UNJSPF's portfolio would marginally reduce cost volatility and the potential for insolvency

Results of the ALM study showed that all optimized asset allocations (that is, allocations that maximize expected portfolio returns with a given amount of risk or that minimize risk given an expected level of return) have an expected long-term investment return higher than the 3.5 percent real return required by the (deterministic) actuarial valuation. Currently, the UNJSPF's asset allocation policy covers four broad strategic asset classes: global equities, global fixed income, real estate, and short-term assets (table 4.1). These broad asset classes contain other key investment segments including, but not limited to, emerging market equity and fixed income. Following input from the ALM steering committee, the study considered two new strategic asset classes: real return assets and private equity.

Further analysis shows that extending UNJSPF's asset allocation policy to include the two new asset classes would marginally reduce cost volatility and the potential for insolvency (figure 4.9). In terms of the funded ratio, the results of the current asset allocation and the proposed asset allocation are almost identical. The UNJSPF continues to examine how it might incorporate the new asset classes; what are the legal, political and organizational constraints; and whether the incorporation would require modification of the operational model.

Conclusion

Through an ALM process and the interaction of its governing and advisory bodies, the UNJSPF has studied different elements of its investment policy framework in order to review and enhance its investment structure and evaluate how its components interact with each other. Some of these elements are plan design, governance, risk tolerance, funded ratio, volatility of liabilities and assets, investment horizon, and the inherent constraints of its investment model. The UNJSPF has also (1) developed a risk-tolerance framework (using four sets of specific quantita-

Table 4.1 **UNJSPF Asset Classes and Risk-Return Statistics (%)**

		Prudent funding		Return oriented		Defensive	
		Current classes	All classes	Current classes	All classes	Current classes	All classes
Asset class as % of holding	Short-term investment	3	3	3	3	3	3
	Developed market fixed income	26	26	29	26	32	32
	Emerging market fixed income	0	0	0	0	1	2
	UN real estate	7	7	7	5	7	7
	Real return investment strategies	0	3	0	3	0	3
	Developed market equities	57	51	55	53	54	47
	Emerging market equities	7	7	6	7	3	3
	Private equity	0	3	0	3	0	3
	Total	100	100	100	100	100	100
Risk-return statistics	Expected annual return	7.9	8.0	7.8	8.0	7.6	7.7
	Expected 1-year standard deviation	10.5	10.4	10.1	10.6	9.5	9.2
	Expected 10-year standard deviation	3.3	3.3	3.2	3.3	3.0	2.9

Source: UNJSPF.

Figure 4.9 **UNJSPF Asset Allocation: Current Asset Classes versus Proposed Asset Allocation**

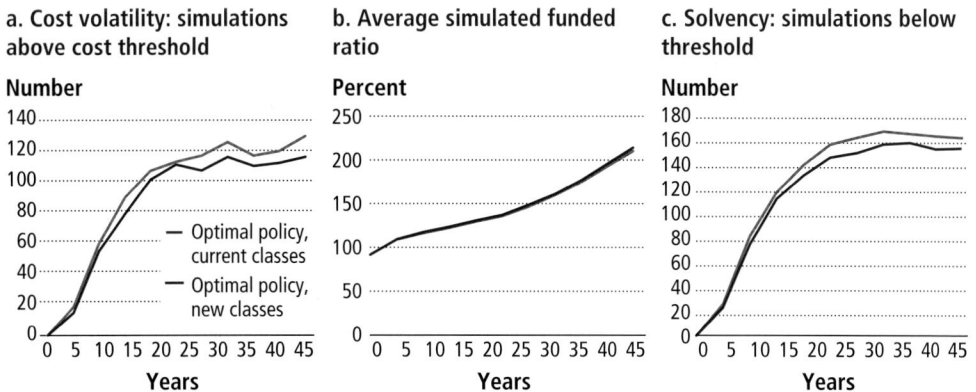

a. Cost volatility: simulations above cost threshold

b. Average simulated funded ratio

c. Solvency: simulations below threshold

— Optimal policy, current classes
⋯ Optimal policy, new classes

Source: UNJSPF.

Note: Proposed asset allocation includes current assets plus real return assets and private equity.

tive measures) and used this framework to construct and choose a risk-tolerance philosophy; (2) conducted an ALM exercise to test the actuarial valuation process, assess the asset allocation mix, and estimate the funded ratio; and (3) explored two new asset classes, private equity and real return.

As a result of these analyses, the UNJSPF has determined that the expanded universe of asset classes provides further diversification and marginally better results. However, the UNJSPF also recognizes that several organizational, political, and even legal constraints must be addressed before any change is adopted. With this in mind, the UNJSPF is currently revisiting its investment mode.

Though the UNJSPF's governance process is rather complex, it has functioned relatively well for many years and has provided adequate checks and balances. Moreover, it has allowed stakeholders, with advice from experts in different disciplines, to review and discuss different aspects of pension management, including investment policy.

Making Investment Policy Consistent with Overall Pension Plan Design: Japan's GPIF

Masaharu Usuki, Member of Investment Committee, Government Pension Investment Fund, Japan

In order to formulate and implement a public pension fund investment policy with prudence and expertise, those responsible for investment management should be separated from those responsible for political decisions about pension design. On the other hand, it is desirable that some components of investment policy, such as strategic asset allocation, are consistent with the overall pension plan design, especially with actuarial assumptions. Achieving an appropriate balance between separation from political influence and integration with overall pension plan management is of paramount importance in the governance design of the pension system and investment of pension assets. Japan's Government Pension Investment Fund offers an example of how to balances these two considerations in the formulation of pension funds' investment policy.

Japan's public pension system has two tiers: fixed-amount benefits available to all members and earnings-related benefits available to public and private sector employees

Japanese law requires that all individuals age 20 and older must participate in the public pension system in some form. Currently, there are 69 million pension plan participants, of which 20 million are self-employed persons and 10.4 million are nonworking spouses of private or public sector employees. Both of these groups are covered only by the basic pension, known as National Pension Insurance (NPI).[1] The two other parts of the public pension system are Employees' Pension Insurance (EPI), which covers 34.4 million private sector employees, and the Mutual Aid, which covers 4.5 million public sector employees (figure 4.10).

---

[1] Some irregular and part-time employees are included in the NPI (rather than the EPI) due to the negligence of employers.

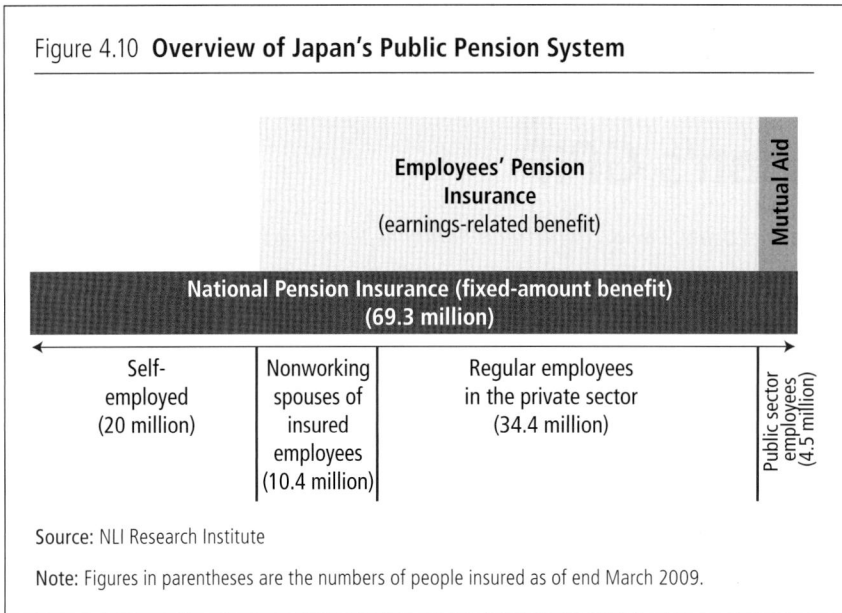

Figure 4.10 **Overview of Japan's Public Pension System**

Source: NLI Research Institute

Note: Figures in parentheses are the numbers of people insured as of end March 2009.

Japan's public pension benefit system has two tiers. The lower tier refers to the basic pension (NPI), which provides a fixed-amount benefit to all 69 million members. The upper tier is an earnings-related benefit provided to the participants of EPI and Mutual Aid. Contribution amounts (social security tax) are calculated as a fixed percentage of wages in EPI and Mutual Aid, and as a fixed amount for self-employed NPI participants.[2]

Public pension schemes in Japan are financed on a pay-as-you-go basis, with two stipulations. First, every pension plan maintains a certain amount of reserves. The reserves of EPI and NPI amounted to $1.7 trillion and $0.1 trillion, respectively, as of March 2009.[3] Second, one-third (one-half from 2010) of the basic pension is subsidized by general government revenue.

---

[2] Nonworking spouses of EPI or Mutual Aid participants are covered by NPI but do not pay contributions. Legally, their contribution is construed as being included in their spouse's contribution. For EPI and Mutual Aid participants, contributions to NPI are included in their EPI/Mutual Aid contributions, calculated as a fixed percentage of their wages.

[3] The value of EPI assets includes the value of the reserve for the substitution (contracted-out) portion of the Employee Pension Funds (EPFs). EPFs are occupational pension plans that manage a part of EPI. EPFs are supposed to pay out part of EPI benefits corresponding to the EPI contributions diverted to them. This system, similar to the contract-out scheme in the United Kingdom, is called the substitution portion.

Reforms to Japan's pension system in 2004 introduced defined-contribution elements to a system facing financial difficulties caused by an aging population

Prior to 2004, Japan's public pension system was a defined-benefit system. In 2004, facing growing financial difficulty caused by an aging population, Japan began a reform of its public pension system that encompassed two new rules. The first rule called for a gradual increase in the EPI contribution rate, from 13.58 percent in 2004 to 18.3 percent in 2018, and an increase in the NPI monthly contribution from $163 in 2004 to $200 in 2018. The second rule, a benefit adjustment rule, reflected the decreasing number of active workers and increasing longevity of beneficiaries. It is estimated that the rule will decrease the real benefit amount by approximately 0.9 percent per year (0.6 percent for the decrease in active participants plus 0.3 percent for the increase in longevity of beneficiaries). The adjustment will remain in effect until parity between plan assets and liabilities is reached (figure 4.11).

Figure 4.11 **The Benefit Adjustment Rule Used by Japan's Public Pension System**

a. Rule activates if balance is not achieved

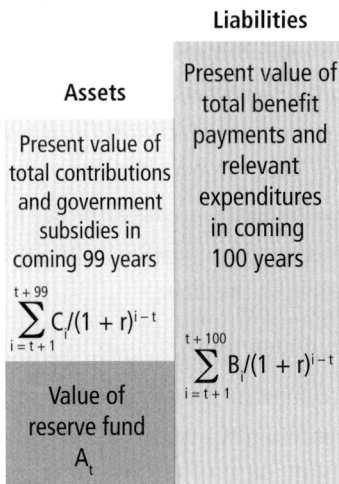

Assets — Liabilities

Present value of total contributions and government subsidies in coming 99 years

$$\sum_{i=t+1}^{t+99} C_i/(1+r)^{i-t}$$

Value of reserve fund A_t

Present value of total benefit payments and relevant expenditures in coming 100 years

$$\sum_{i=t+1}^{t+100} B_i/(1+r)^{i-t}$$

b. Rule deactivates if balance is achieved

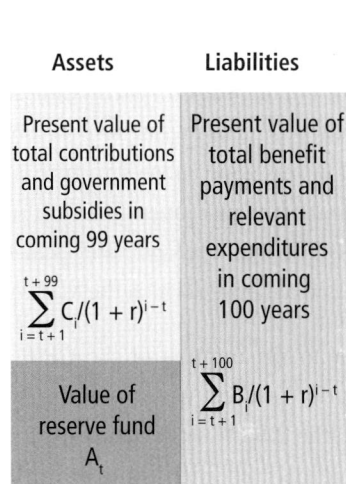

Assets — Liabilities

Present value of total contributions and government subsidies in coming 99 years

$$\sum_{i=t+1}^{t+99} C_i/(1+r)^{i-t}$$

Value of reserve fund A_t

Present value of total benefit payments and relevant expenditures in coming 100 years

$$\sum_{i=t+1}^{t+100} B_i/(1+r)^{i-t}$$

Source: NLI Research Institute.

Note: Assets are defined as the sum of the present value of projected contributions and government subsidies over the coming 99 years and the value of the reserve fund. Liabilities are defined as the present value of projected total benefit payments and relevant expenditures over the coming 100 years. A = value of reserve fund; B = expenditures (benefits and relevant expenditures); C = revenue (pension insurance tax and government subsidies); r = discount rate.

The Japanese Ministry of Health, Labor, and Welfare (MHLW) estimates that the benefit adjustment will terminate in 2025, when a single-income couple, in which the working partner ends a 40-year career with an annual income of $81,000 (the average for all employees) will receive a benefit of $33,000. The $33,000 represents an income replacement ratio of slightly less than 50 percent assuming that the couple's after-tax income is $67,000.[4] This estimate is subject to change, however, depending on how long the adjustment rule is in place. The timeline of the rule is dependent, to a substantial degree, on investment results and the plan's asset value. In other words, as a result of the 2004 reform, the Japanese public pension system has taken on one of the main characteristics of a defined-contribution plan, where investment results increase or decrease the benefit level.

Governance of the pension system is overseen by the Ministry of Health, Labor, and Welfare

The MHLW, as the insurer of NPI and EPI, holds ultimate responsibility for governance of Japan's public pension system (figure 4.12). Its responsibilities include pension plan design, setting of benefit and contribution levels, validation of the financial feasibility of pension plans based on actuarial forecasts, and supervision of the Government Pension Investment Fund (GPIF) and Japan Pension Service. The GPIF, in turn, is responsible for investment management, which includes formulation and implementation of investment policy, including strategic asset allocation (SAA); selection of an investment manager; and liquidity management. The GPIF itself is not a pension institution but is more like an investment division of the public pension system. Collection of contributions, benefit verification, and benefit payments are the responsibility of the Japan Pension Service. The primary goal in this governance structure is to maintain an appropriate balance between separation of investment policy from political considerations and influence from the MHLW on the one hand, and integration of investment policy with overall pension design for which the MHLW is responsible on the other.

Prior to the creation of the GPIF in 2006, the MHLW, along with the Social Security Council, were responsible for formulation of an SAA. Under this structure, the MHLW was accountable for investment results. Under the current governance scheme, which stands at arm's length from the MHLW, the GPIF formulates an SAA and is responsible for investment management. In the new structure, three bodies play important roles in the governance of the GPIF—the MHLW, the presi-

---

[4] Salary and benefit figures are represented at 2004 constant prices.

Figure 4.12 Governance Structure of Japan's Public Pension System

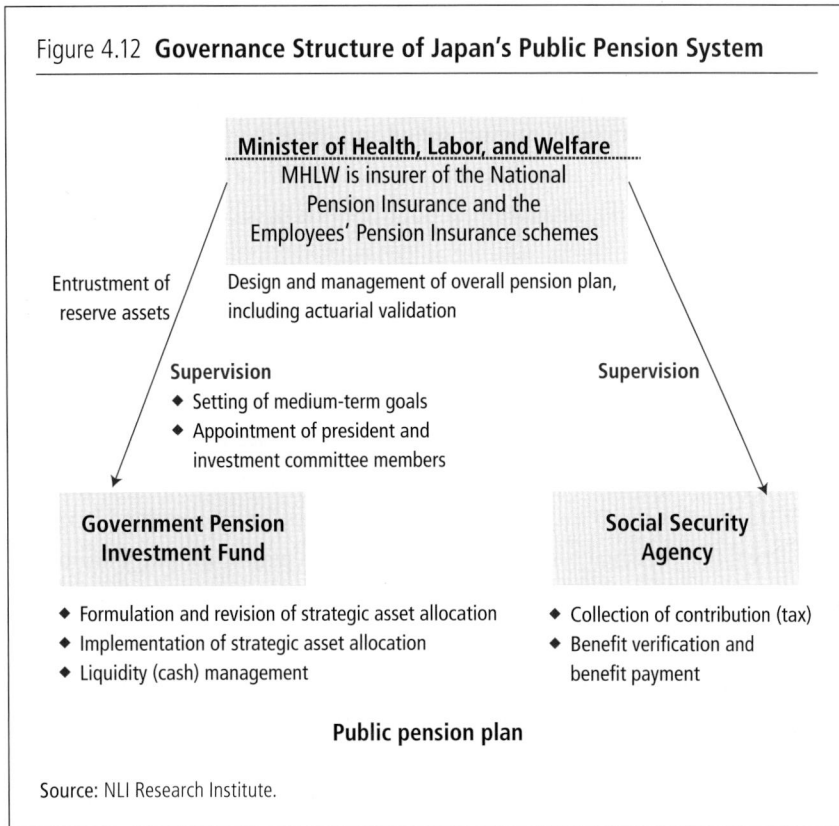

Minister of Health, Labor, and Welfare
MHLW is insurer of the National
Pension Insurance and the
Employees' Pension Insurance schemes

Entrustment of
reserve assets

Design and management of overall pension plan,
including actuarial validation

Supervision
◆ Setting of medium-term goals
◆ Appointment of president and
  investment committee members

Supervision

**Government Pension
Investment Fund**

◆ Formulation and revision of strategic asset allocation
◆ Implementation of strategic asset allocation
◆ Liquidity (cash) management

**Social Security
Agency**

◆ Collection of contribution (tax)
◆ Benefit verification and
  benefit payment

Public pension plan

Source: NLI Research Institute.

dent of the GPIF, and the investment committee of the GPIF. The breakdown of governance duties is as follows:

◆ The MHLW supervises GPIF management by setting midterm goals, evaluating GPIF results, and appointing the GPIF president and investment committee members. The MHLW evaluates GPIF performance from the standpoint of being the insurer of EPI and NPI and, if necessary, issues decrees to the president.

◆ The GPIF president is responsible for all GPIF investment decisions and operations. Specifically, the president is accountable for formulation and implementation of the midterm plan and the SAA, and appointment and management of staff, including other executives. The president has a duty to carry out these responsibilities prudently and with loyalty to the GPIF.

◆ The investment committee of the GPIF can have up to 11 members, of which 2 are representatives of management and labor and the remainder are experts in finance, economics, or investing. The committee's primary function is to extend opinions and advice to the president on the midterm plan, SAA, and other important matters pertaining to investment operations.

187

Medium-term goals for the plan are set by the MHLW. The set of goals that covered the period April 2006 through March 2010 are as follows: promote operational efficiency and cost reduction, enhance expertise and fiduciary responsibility, conduct thorough disclosure, conduct sound and efficient management of reserve funds, formulate the SAA and revise it as necessary, exercise appropriate control of investment risks, and rely primarily but not wholly on passive (index) funds.

With regard to the GPIF's investment management of reserve funds, the MHLW has issued more specific goals: (1) secure a real return on investment of 1.1 percent above wage growth through the long-term investment horizon, (2) exceed market index returns in each asset class, (3) control risks through diversification and other measures, (4) avoid exercising unnecessary influence in the market and in the management of private enterprises,[5] (5) secure liquidity sufficient for pension benefit payment, and (6) formulate specific guidelines for reserve fund management. The GPIF president formulates a medium-term plan to achieve these objectives and then establishes annual goals for each of the years covered by the medium-term plan. Progress toward fulfilling the goals set out in both the medium-term and annual plans is evaluated by the MHLW. One of the most noteworthy results achieved in the course of this process is the disclosure of information. The GPIF's role, structure, and investment results, for example, are disclosed regularly (table 4.2), mainly through its Web site. In general, disclosure is an essential element in creating accountability for the investment management process.

The GPIF uses a four-step process to formulate its strategic asset allocation and was given additional discretion in 2009 on selection of eligible asset classes and estimation of asset class parameters

The GPIF's current SAA, formulated in 2004 and covering the period April 2005 to March 2010, was set out as follows: domestic fixed income (67 percent), domestic equity (11 percent), foreign fixed income (8 percent), foreign equity (9 percent), and cash (5 percent). The annual expected return is 3.37 percent and standard deviation (risk measure) is 5.55 percent. The process involved in establishing this SAA involved four steps:

◆ *Estimating parameter values.* The expected return had to be consistent with the macroeconomic model used in the MHLW actuarial validation, while risk and correlations were estimated from historical data.

---

[5] Considering the size of the GPIF (more than $1 trillion), a decision to change its asset allocation by as little as 1 percent can have a significant impact on capital markets.

Table 4.2 **Items Periodically Disclosed by the GPIF**

Item	Interval of disclosure
Details of investment operation	Annually
Investment goal and strategic asset allocation	
Investment results: return and income/loss	
Comparison with long-term goal	
Asset amount and allocation to asset classes	
Cash flow	
Risk control operation	
Investment results by asset class and comparison with benchmarks	
Management structure	
Fees and commissions	
Evaluation of external investment managers	
Amount of asset and investment performance by managers	
Exercise of voting rights by external managers	
Evaluation of custodial operation	
Results of investment operation	Quarterly
Investment results: return and income/loss	
Investment results by asset class and comparison with benchmarks	
Asset amount and allocation to asset classes	
Periodic plan	Annually
Midterm plan	
Annual plan	
Evaluation of achievement of midterm plan	
Evaluation of achievement of annual plan	
Financial statements	Annually
Compensation for executives and officers	Annually

Source: GPIF.

- *Drawing an efficient frontier on the risk-return axes under two constraints.* The allocation to foreign fixed-income assets had to be less than the allocation to foreign equity, the allocation to foreign equity had to be smaller than the allocation to domestic equity, and the allocation to cash was 5 percent.

- *Selecting 2 out of 11 portfolios.* The two portfolios with the highest Sharpe ratios, with expected returns from 3.2 percent to 3.7 percent (target return), and with risk no higher than that of domestic bonds were selected.

- *Choosing one of the two portfolios.* Finally, the portfolio with the lowest short-fall probability in the simulation was chosen.

In this and previous SAA formulation processes, the portfolio target return and total risk (risk budget) were decided in the MHLW actuarial validation process, making it possible to have an SAA consistent with overall pension design and management. By setting the target return and risk budget a priori, however, the GPIF was not left much room for discretion. In 2009, a new SAA formulation process was begun. Although the target return[6] and risk budget are still decided by the MHLW through its actuarial validation process, the GPIF has discretion to set parameter values for each asset class's expected return and risk and to select asset classes for investment.

Despite changes in recent years, there is room for improvement in Japan's pension system

Even with the recent reforms, several additional changes would improve the functioning of Japan's pension system. For example, during the actuarial valida-tion process, the MHLW could consult with the GPIF president and investment committee about the expected return and risk of each asset class and of the total portfolio under current market conditions. This consultation process would enable the GPIF to reflect its view of the risk/return trade-off. Sharing of views about return and risk numbers would also encourage the MHLW to set more realistic midterm goals for the GPIF. In addition, both the MHLW and the GPIF could examine the risk/return trade-off in the context of the defined-contribution plan.[7]

---

[6] The target is a nominal return of 4.1 percent and real return (return above wage growth) of 1.6 percent.

[7] On average, as the risk/return ratio of the GPIF portfolio increases, the benefit adjust-ment period shortens and the final replacement ratio increases. However, in low-proba-bility downside cases, the length of the benefit adjustment period will increase and income replacement ratio will decrease by a larger margin.

Conclusion

Since its establishment as an independent administrative agency in 2006, the GPIF has borne responsibility for the pension system's investment management process, while the MHLW, as the insurer of the system, has been responsible for the overall public pension system. The purpose of this governance structure was to devolve responsibility for investment management from the MHLW, which was apt to be the target of political criticism. The GPIF has made efforts to be accountable for its investment process and results to the MHLW and general public through reporting and disclosures. As a result, Japan's pension system was less vulnerable to reputational risk and political criticism during the market turmoil of 2008–09 than it was during the turmoil of 2000–02. On the other hand, the MHLW now chooses the target return and risk budget in order to make the investment policy and SAA consistent with overall pension plan management, especially with actuarial validation. This leaves less room for discretion by the GPIF. Despite these substantial governance and structural changes in Japan's pension framework, there is room for improvement in the functioning of its public pension system.

Linking Risk Tolerance and Pension Liabilities with Investment Strategy: Denmark's ATP

Lars Rohde, Chief Executive Officer, ATP, Denmark

Pension funds need to design and implement an investment framework that not only explicitly ties together the fund's objectives, risk tolerance, and nature of its pension liabilities, but can also withstand tail risks arising during financial market crises in a robust manner. Since it is required to be fully funded at all times, Denmark's ATP (Arbejdmarkedets Tillaegs Pension) has a low tolerance for risk. ATP addresses this constraint by using its risk budget judiciously and minimizing uncompensated risks in its investments through its hedge portfolio. ATP also allocates risk equally among various risk classes, with the objective of creating an investment portfolio that provides stable returns under all economic conditions. The main features of ATP's investment strategy include a dynamic risk budget that protects the scheme's solvency, a hedge portfolio to minimize uncompensated risks, a focus on diversification and allocation of risk rather than asset allocation, and methods for minimizing tail risks.

ATP is a contributory, funded supplement to Denmark's state-funded old-age pension system that is independent of the government

Denmark's ATP (Arbejdmarkedets Tillaegs Pension, or Labor Market Supplementary Pension) was established in 1964 as a contributory, funded supplement to the state-funded old-age pension system. ATP manages a portfolio of $76 billion on behalf of 4.6 million members, providing a lifelong pension to its contributing members. The fund is managed and directed by a board composed of representatives of employer and employee organizations and hired professional management. It is also independent from the government, including in the areas of investments and budget. Supervision and accounting standards are similar to those prevailing for other Danish pension funds and insurance companies.

Over the past decade, ATP has strived to develop an investment framework that enables the fund to provide high real pensions in an environment of aging populations, stricter regulatory standards, and mark-to-market accounting. The challenge lies in the fact that the combined effect of these changes results in a need to generate higher returns with less risk.

ATP's objectives, risk tolerance, and business model are somewhat different from those of other pension funds

Before determining an investment framework, it is necessary for a pension fund to get its basic building blocks right. First, it is crucial to be very clear about what the fund wants to accomplish. ATP's objective is to secure the highest possible real value of future pensions. At a minimum, ATP aims to increase pension values by at least as much as the level of inflation and to compensate for increases in longevity. This is an ambitious target. Second, a pension fund should determine how much money it would be willing to lose—that is, its risk tolerance. ATP's risk tolerance is quite low. Without a sponsor, and with a regulatory requirement to remain fully funded, it is imperative for ATP to avoid solvency problems at all times. This translates into an operational rule that says that the risk of failing the supervisor's minimum surplus requirement test (the "red light test") on a three-month horizon may never exceed 1 percent. And third, it is imperative that a pension fund understand the precise nature of its liabilities, as they constitute the true benchmark of its investments. ATP focuses on how much money is being earned from members' point of view. This implies a focus on absolute investment returns, and as a consequence, ATP has abandoned traditional market benchmarks that focus on relative returns.

ATP's business model emphasizes the inextricable links between objectives, pension liabilities, and investment strategy (figure 4.13). The strong focus on interdepen-

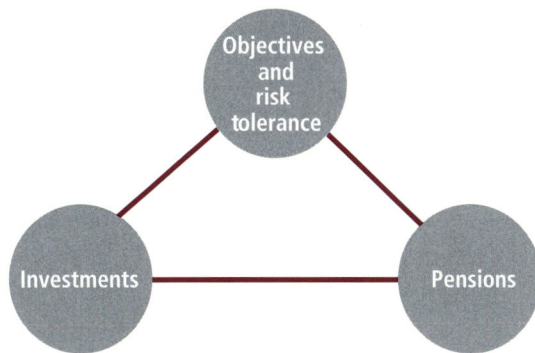

Figure 4.13 **ATP's Model for Pension Excellence**

Investment policy reflects objectives and liabilities (liability-driven investments)

But equally important to optimize liability structure (investment-driven liabilities)

Objectives and risk tolerance

Investments

Pensions

Source: ATP.

dencies distinguishes ATP from most other pension funds. Several interesting corollaries result from ATP's approach, in which interdependence is not only reflected in the fund's investment strategy, but also in the way it structures pension liabilities or designs pension products. Given its objectives and investment framework, ATP applies an *investment-driven liabilities* approach. ATP's ability to tie members' accrual of pension liabilities to prevailing market interest rates at the time of receiving each contribution provides it an additional degree of freedom (which is not normally available to pension funds) in determining its investment strategy. ATP's approach also has important organizational implications, as it results in investment managers and actuaries working alongside each other in a single department.

ATP's investment strategy is crafted with respect to its ambitious return target, its low tolerance for risk, and the nature of its pension liabilities without endangering its solvency. Four elements of ATP's investment approach ensure that it generates its targeted investment returns without endangering its solvency at any point in time: (1) the dynamic risk budget protects solvency, (2) the hedge portfolio minimizes uncompensated risks, (3) diversification works when needed, and (4) tail risks are accounted for realistically.

Dynamic risk budget protects ATP's solvency

Because owning risky assets may result in higher volatility, investors who own them require a buffer in the form of reserves. A decline in the size of the buffer means that less risk can be tolerated, while an increase in buffer size means that more risk can be tolerated. The riskiness of ATP's investments thus adjusts automatically if ATP's reserves change significantly due to circumstances such as a decline in the equity market. That said, ATP evaluates on a daily basis whether it has taken on too much risk given its funded ratio. If the amount of risk is indeed too high, ATP reduces the amount of equities and other risky assets it holds by 1 percentage point at a time until risk is within the allowed band. This "dynamic risk budget" (figure 4.14) provides very effective protection of ATP's funded status during times of financial market distress.

A hedge portfolio minimizes uncompensated risks

In theory, investors assume investment risk in order to earn a return. In practice, though, investors cannot expect to be compensated for all financial risks. ATP's main uncompensated risk is that related to the interest rate sensitivity of its liabilities, which are marked to market in Denmark. This means that the liabilities, similarly to bonds, go up in value when interest rates decline. ATP's pension liabilities are extremely sensitive to changes in interest rates. A decline in long-

Figure 4.14 **ATP's Dynamic Risk Budget**

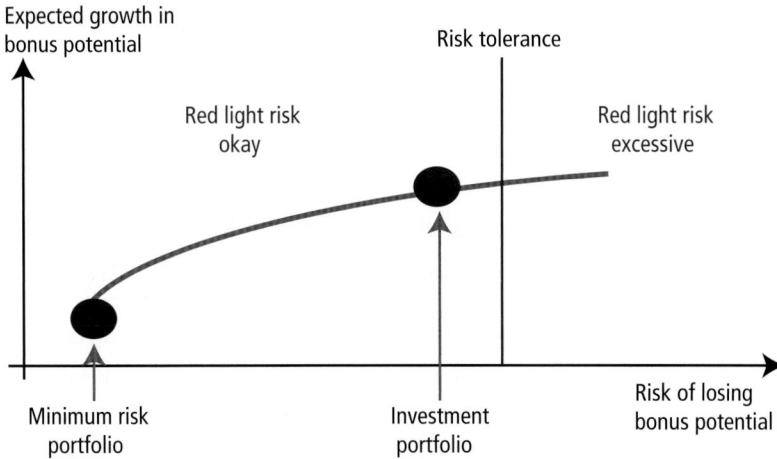

Source: ATP.

term interest rates of 1 percentage point, for example, increases ATP's liabilities by approximately $9 billion. If this risk were left unhedged, a fall in long-term interest rates of about 1.5 percentage points would wipe out all of ATP's reserves. ATP considers this an uncompensated risk, as it is unlikely that it would make money in the long term by being exposed to interest rate risk. For that reason, the interest rate risk of pension liabilities is fully hedged in a special hedge portfolio consisting of long-term government bonds and interest rate swaps.

Figure 4.15 shows how the hedge protects ATP against movements in short-dated as well as long-dated interest rates, meaning that the fund has enough assets to meet

Figure 4.15 **ATP's Assets and Liabilities with Hedge Protection**

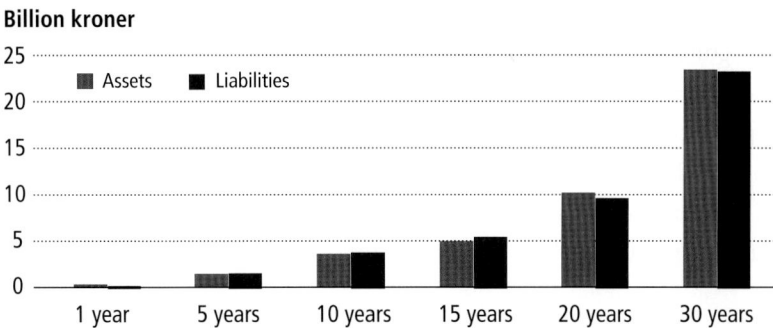

Source: ATP.

its short-term and long-term liabilities. This hedging strategy, together with ATP's finite risk budget strategy, creates the potential to make other expected positive return investments for ATP. These additional investments reside in a separate investment portfolio. All considered, the decision to begin hedging pension liabilities in late 2001 is probably ATP's most important investment decision to date. Without the hedge policy, ATP would likely have encountered solvency problems on several occasions in recent years.

Risk allocation, rather than asset allocation, and insurance against extreme market events are important elements of ATP's strategy

Because equities dominated many of their portfolios, pension funds and other institutional investors encountered serious difficulties following the large decline in the value of equities in 2008. In general, institutional investors tend to do well when equities do well, and vice versa. ATP, however, has chosen a different approach to its investment management. Seeking to produce its desired financial results regardless of the situation in the financial markets, ATP divides its investments into five broad *risk classes*: equities, interest rates, credit, inflation-linked investments, and commodities. The risk classes are characterized by the fact that their returns are driven by different underlying factors. For example, the return on government bonds will depend mainly on the level of interest rates, whereas equities will be more dependent on the ability of companies to generate income.

ATP's board determines a neutral allocation of risk among the five risk classes, focusing on allocating *risk* rather than money, as the board considers it a better assessment of the impact on the total portfolio. If, for example, an equal amount of resources is invested in bonds and equities, the return of the combined investment will be dominated by equities because their returns are so much more volatile than bond returns. A five-to-one ratio of bonds to equities, on the other hand, results in a much more balanced risk profile. ATP's neutral risk allocation is shown in figure 4.16. No single risk class dominates the picture and every risk class makes a meaningful contribution to total risk. This stands in stark contrast to the investment profile of many institutional portfolios, in which the risk contribution from equities is 80 percent or more. In addition, ATP does not have a specific "alternatives" risk class. Instead, the specific alternative investment is included in the most relevant risk class. For example, private equity resides in the equity risk class, as ATP considers private equity returns to be driven by the same underlying factors as public equity.

For ATP, diversification is also a question of balancing liquid and illiquid investments. During the financial crisis, many institutional investors ran into grave problems due to the illiquidity of their portfolios. In many instances, this led to

Figure 4.16 **ATP's Neutral Risk Allocation**

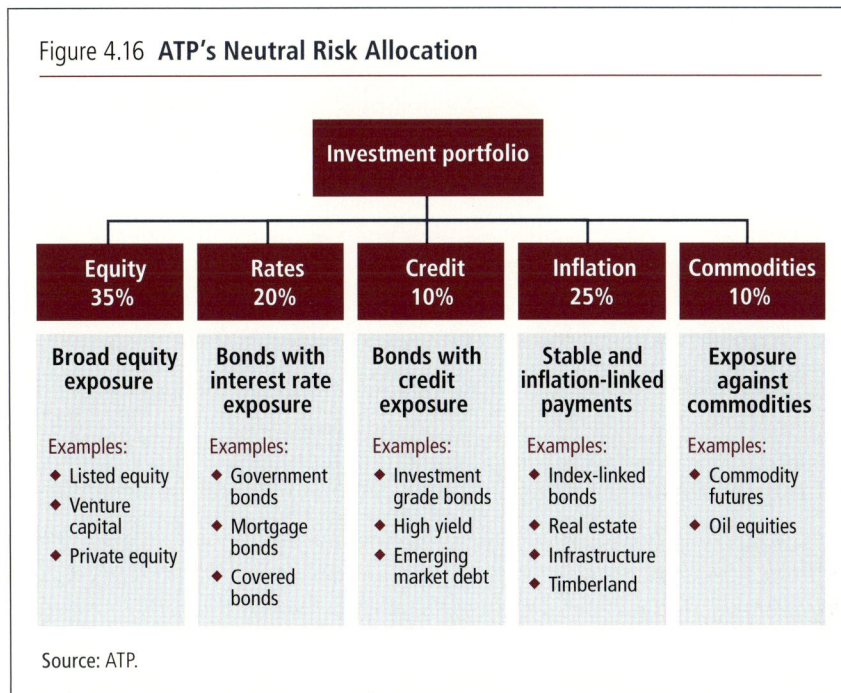

Investment portfolio				
Equity 35%	**Rates 20%**	**Credit 10%**	**Inflation 25%**	**Commodities 10%**
Broad equity exposure	**Bonds with interest rate exposure**	**Bonds with credit exposure**	**Stable and inflation-linked payments**	**Exposure against commodities**
Examples: ◆ Listed equity ◆ Venture capital ◆ Private equity	Examples: ◆ Government bonds ◆ Mortgage bonds ◆ Covered bonds	Examples: ◆ Investment grade bonds ◆ High yield ◆ Emerging market debt	Examples: ◆ Index-linked bonds ◆ Real estate ◆ Infrastructure ◆ Timberland	Examples: ◆ Commodity futures ◆ Oil equities

Source: ATP.

large losses and dramatic portfolio adjustments, including fire sales of assets in order to generate urgently needed cash. Beyond diversification, the fact that ATP had insurance against certain extreme events prior to the financial crisis saved it from experiencing a severe negative impact on its portfolio. In fact, ATP benefited handsomely in 2008 from having bought out-of-the-money put options on equities and oil investments. It is important, however, that this insurance be purchased when it is inexpensive—that is, when the markets are calm.

Conclusion

The onset of the 2008 financial crisis was the fiercest test of ATP's investment framework thus far. With a funded ratio of nearly 120 percent at the end of 2009, not only has ATP shrugged off the losses of 2008, but it is better off than before the crisis. The main lesson learned during this process is that public pension fund managers should always formulate explicit investment objective and risk-tolerance parameters. Other lessons include the need for pension funds to focus on the full pension model, rather than resorting to viewing investment issues in isolation. Separating decision making and staying disciplined in the face of adverse markets can assist in this process. In addition, it is important to recognize that absolute risk targets are more critical than benchmarks, and that risk allocation is preferable to asset allocation. Finally, unwarranted and uncompensated risk, including tail risk, should be eliminated.

2. Managing Risk for Different Cohorts in Defined-Contribution Schemes

- ◆ A Glide-Path Life-Cycle Fund Approach

- ◆ A Hybrid Approach to Managing Members' Investment and Longevity Risks: Singapore's CPF

- ◆ An Age-Based Multifunds Regulatory Approach for Latin American Funds

- ◆ Using a Hybrid Pension Product in a Collective Framework to Distribute Risk: Denmark's ATP

A Glide-Path Life-Cycle Fund Approach

Yvonne Sin, Head of Investment Consulting China, Towers Watson

Historically, members have borne all the risks in a defined-contribution pension plan, though little consideration has been given to their ability to ride out such risks. Assuming they are well informed about the risk profiles of their membership, however, plan sponsors may be in a better position to design retirement schemes for different types of members. The "glide-path life-cycle" strategy to risk management makes use of this knowledge to improve upon the basic life-cycle model. Through incremental transitions from growth assets to safe assets during the accumulation phase, the glide-path strategy steadily reduces exposure to investment risk as members approach retirement, while remaining focused on customizing asset allocation to member circumstances. Integral to this approach is "journey planning," a concept that aligns all key areas of retirement plan management—including plan objectives and thresholds, investment assumptions and methods, investment strategy, funding strategy, legacy benefits, exit strategy, and ongoing benefit strategy—with the possibility of rebalancing members' portfolios along the way to ensure successful delivery of expected retirement outcomes.

There must be a balance between financial inflows and outflows if a pension plan's long-term financial viability is to be maintained

The financial viability of a pension scheme, regardless of whether it uses a defined-contribution or a pay-as-you-go arrangement, depends on a balancing of financial flows into and out of the system. In general, drivers of success for defined-contribution plans include appropriate investment choices, informed investment decisions, and cost-effective management. To balance the defined-contribution pension equation, the sum of contribution revenues and investment earnings must be sufficient to pay for members' benefits and management costs.

Balancing the Defined-Contribution Pension Equation

Contribution revenues + investment earnings = Benefit payments + management costs

---

If the goal is to provide a pension that is a decent percentage of a plan member's final wage at retirement, the return on investments must be greater than wage growth while the pension assets are accumulating. Thus, defined-contribution plans not only need to be managed cost-effectively, but they need to be able to transfer sufficient knowledge to their members to help them make informed investment decisions.

The investment of pension assets, like all other investments, involves risk: the greater the potential return, the higher the risk. In conventional thinking, the number of years to retirement is the most reasonable yardstick by which to measure asset allocation decisions. The basic premise is that workers who have a long way to go before retirement can handle higher exposure to assets that have strong growth potential but bear substantial risk, such as equities, whereas workers closer to retirement should protect their capital by choosing safer investments, such as bonds and cash (figure 4.17).

Figure 4.17 **Allocation to Growth and Safe Assets by Years to Retirement**

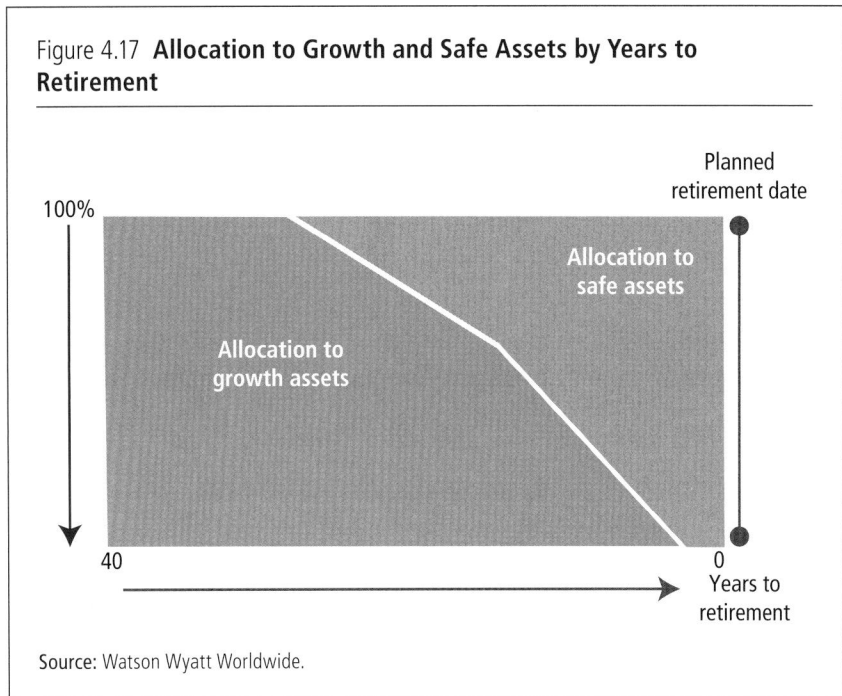

Source: Watson Wyatt Worldwide.

The traditional life-cycle method of asset allocation involves a shift from growth assets to safe assets as plan members approach retirement

The life-cycle method is a simple, sound asset allocation strategy that can assist members in their defined-contribution journey. Typically, it involves steadily adjusting the asset allocation of plan members' accounts to reduce investment risk exposure as a particular target date—usually retirement—approaches. The life-cycle model operates as a de-risking program that gradually and linearly switches member assets from growth to protection over a predetermined period, say 5, 10, or 15 years prior to retirement. The life-cycle approach also seeks to reduce the volatility of returns during that period of time and hence is able to protect investors who are close to retirement from extremely negative outcomes. From a risk-return perspective, the life-cycle approach is considered superior to many other strategies and can be modified to take into account individual preferences and circumstances (figure 4.18).

Figure 4.18 **Long-Term Income Replacement Rates of Various Asset Mixes**

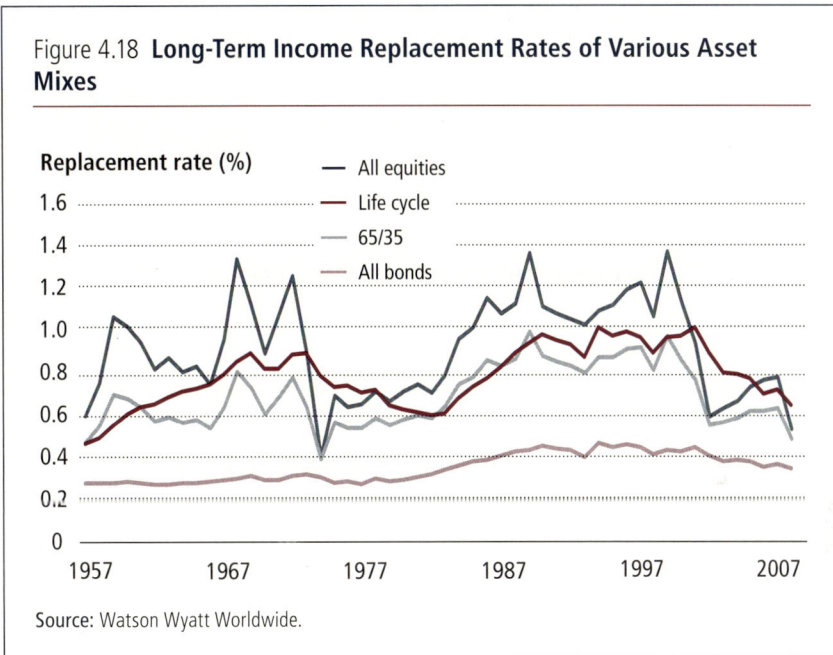

Source: Watson Wyatt Worldwide.

Sound investment strategies must take into account much more than a linear shift to safer assets as members age: wealth, health, number of dependents, and future earning potential are all important

There is more to defined-contribution investing than a linear shift from growth to safe assets as members move toward retirement, however. Historical experience suggests that most people are generally unwilling or unable to make investment decisions. Moreover, people who are most vulnerable in terms of exposure to investment risk tend to be those who are least equipped to manage their portfolios. Thus, pension plan designs need to address not just the size of the "pot" expected at retirement—although that is clearly important—but also the probability of reaching the desired outcome and the volatility around the expected return.

Many factors need to be analyzed to determine whether individual members of a retirement scheme should take investment risk and to what extent. Does the member have the flexibility to cope with an adverse investment outcome? Is there a long enough time horizon to respond to a series of negative outcomes? Is there sufficient time for diversification to spread out the potential risk? Besides time to retirement, individual characteristics such as wealth, health, dependents, future earning potential, and other lifestyle factors also influence risk-taking behavior. For the best results, a defined-contribution plan should take all of these factors into consideration (figure 4.19).

Figure 4.19 **Investment Risk Factors to Consider**

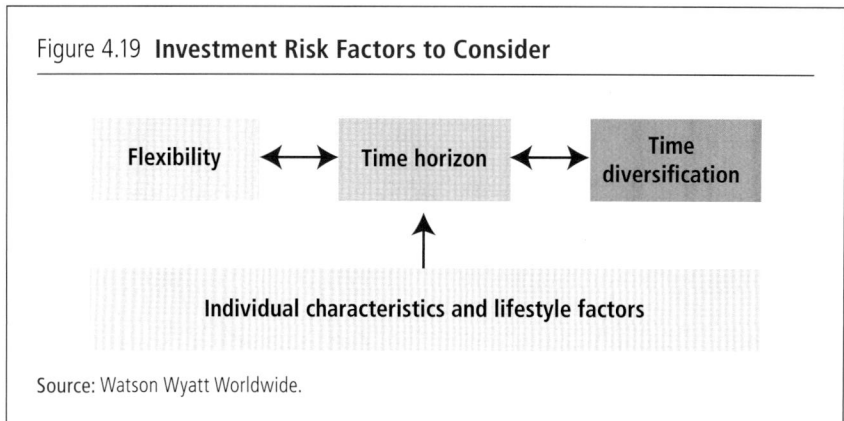

Source: Watson Wyatt Worldwide.

Defined-contribution plans generally have three types of members, the profiles of which allow plan sponsors to address member needs in targeted ways

A defined-contribution plan sponsor is in a better position to help plan members achieve their retirement objectives if it has access to more information about members' ability and willingness to tolerate investment risk. Defined-contribution schemes typically serve three types of members. The first group, *self-selectors*, is made up of members who make their own decisions and for whom the ideal investment approach would be tailor-made managed accounts that support personal preferences. The second group of members are *guided selectors*, those who are willing and able to make investment choices but choose not to. This group needs to be steered away from the default option of a life-cycle fund. Most fund members, though, belong to the third group, the so-called *true defaulters*, those who are both unwilling and unable to make investment decisions. This group would be best served by the life-cycle default method (figure 4.20).

Membership profiles allow defined-contribution plan sponsors to address member needs in targeted ways. For instance, given the close connection between the

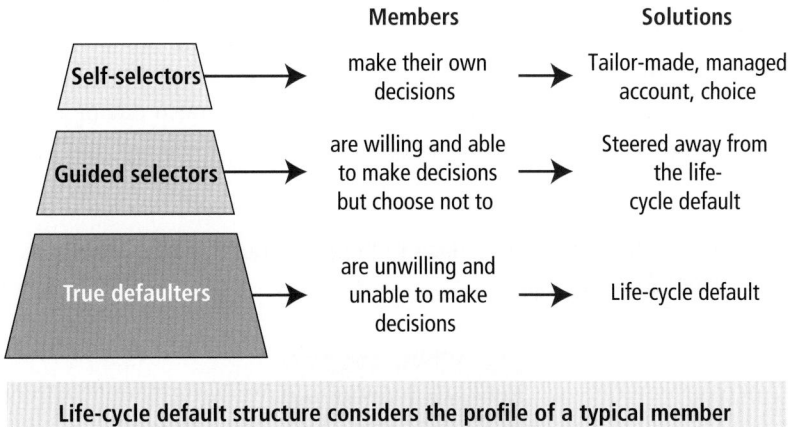

Figure 4.20 **A Stylized Typology: Members of a Defined-Contribution Plan**

	Members	Solutions
Self-selectors	make their own decisions	Tailor-made, managed account, choice
Guided selectors	are willing and able to make decisions but choose not to	Steered away from the life-cycle default
True defaulters	are unwilling and unable to make decisions	Life-cycle default

Life-cycle default structure considers the profile of a typical member

Source: Watson Wyatt Worldwide.

desired level of contribution and the ability and willingness of members to take on risk, is there any flexibility with respect to the contribution rate vis-à-vis the risk budget? Can the proportion of protection versus growth asset allocation be adjusted? How will investor preference or circumstances change the default life-cycle strategy? Would it be possible to revise the defined-contribution journey with a view to further reducing risk exposure as retirement approaches? Membership data clearly add value to plan design by making it possible to justify "nudges" away from the default structure and toward a more tailor-made structure in line with members' perspectives.

Using a personalized glide-path strategy alongside a standard glide-path strategy can be extremely effective

An innovative tool that can help defined-contribution plan members make more effective customized investment decisions is the charting of a long-term savings plan with a glide-path design. The standard glide-path strategy has a built-in de-risking process and recognizes the potential impact of investor preference as well as extraneous events on the default structure. But a personalized glide-path journey that transitions from growth assets to safe assets guided by the member's own game plan is a great improvement on the automated life-cycle method. Hence, the combined glide-path life-cycle approach may be deemed a "superior plus" strategy for defined-contribution schemes.

In the early part of a person's working life, when the ability to take on investment risk is generally high, a close to 100 percent allocation to growth assets is suggested under a glide-path life-cycle approach. As a person gets closer to retirement age, the emphasis is switched to income generation with lower volatility. Assuming that most members annuitize at retirement (with some flexibility), an individual member's portfolio should be close to 100 percent in low-risk protected assets by the time he or she retires, with the possibility of an accelerated rate of exposure reduction close to retirement (figure 4.21).

Figure 4.21 **A Glide-Path Approach to Steady Reduction of a Member's Investment Risk**

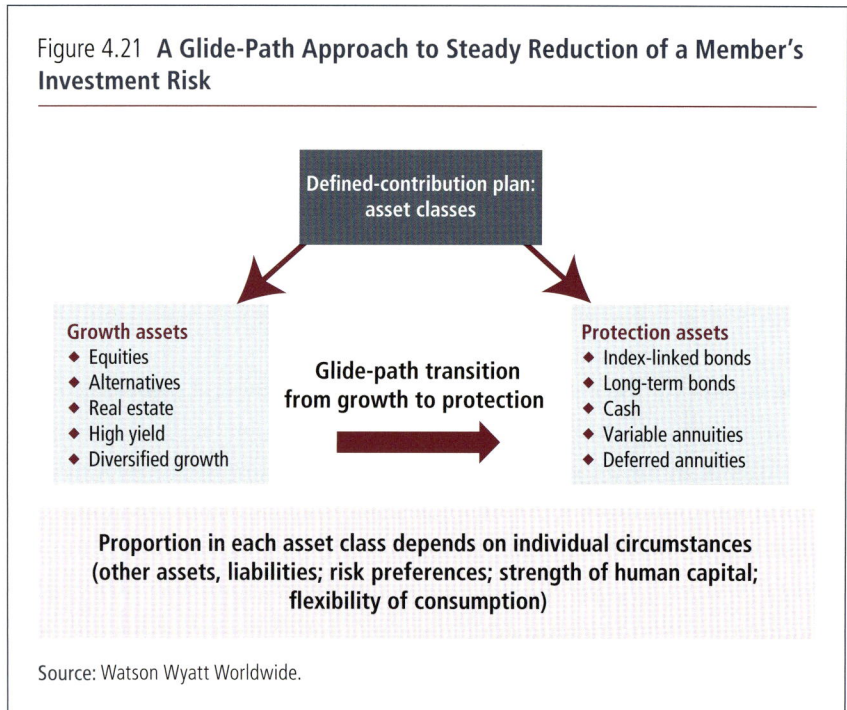

Defined-contribution plan: asset classes

Growth assets
◆ Equities
◆ Alternatives
◆ Real estate
◆ High yield
◆ Diversified growth

Glide-path transition from growth to protection

Protection assets
◆ Index-linked bonds
◆ Long-term bonds
◆ Cash
◆ Variable annuities
◆ Deferred annuities

Proportion in each asset class depends on individual circumstances (other assets, liabilities; risk preferences; strength of human capital; flexibility of consumption)

Source: Watson Wyatt Worldwide.

Development of a journey plan that allows for dynamic adjustments is important. Periodically, the plan member or an administrator (assuming that the decision-making power has been delegated to a third party) will rebalance the asset allocation of an individual plan by purchasing either more growth assets or more protection assets to ensure that the total package is consistent with the predefined life-cycle matrix. This two-way rebalancing policy enables the member to have increased or decreased exposure to growth assets, whereas one-way rebalancing tends not to increase growth asset allocations once the glide-path de-risking process has begun.

Several investment protection strategies can be applied to individual plans as an additional safeguard against adverse outcomes. These include gradually switching into safe assets and establishing annuity matching funds. Protection strategies are more likely to be implemented as an overlay by a member, rather than incorporated within a default life-cycle strategy. Downside protection could, in principle, be purchased explicitly by a member while a high exposure to growth assets is maintained (such as through option strategies). In practice, however, such protection strategies come at considerable cost, and it must also be noted that protection strategies tend to focus on capital protection rather than retirement income protection.

In-depth knowledge of member profiles can contribute significantly to design of improved investment choices; this requires strong engagement and communication with members on an ongoing basis

Defined-contribution pension plans should be able to deliver better investment results than defined-benefit plans if sponsors are able to use their knowledge of member profiles and construct the default or range of defaults with these specifications in mind. This is important not only because investment performance has been found to play a key role in pension wealth accumulation, but also because the greatest impact on retirement outcome attributed to asset allocation appears to be largely driven by the proportion invested in equities and other risky assets. Given that the global financial crisis has caused pension assets to lose significant value, it is imperative that pension funds pay more attention to risk management in fund design—particularly risk that is associated with members' personal circumstances. Success in this regard depends on strong engagement and communication with a fund's members at all times.

A Hybrid Approach to Managing Members' Investment and Longevity Risks: Singapore's CPF

Liew Heng San, Chief Executive Officer, Central Provident Fund, Singapore

As a fully funded defined-contribution pension fund, Singapore's Central Provident Fund seeks to protect its members from key risks, such as investment risk and longevity risk. Through minimum guaranteed returns and extra interest, members may earn up to 5 percent on their Central Provident Fund balances. To address longevity risk, the national longevity insurance scheme provides lifelong income for members during their retirement. Members may choose the extent to which they wish to risk-pool their assets, and are protected from low interest rates by a guaranteed minimum rate of return.

In defined-contribution pension funds, members bear the full brunt of investment losses

An important issue for all defined-contribution pension funds is the level of investment risk members can tolerate for their retirement income. Though building up adequate retirement savings sounds simple, it is in fact a daunting task that faces periodic setbacks. The recent financial crisis, for instance, erased $5.4 trillion (about 20 percent) of global private pension asset values in the year to December 2008, severely affecting both defined-benefit and defined-contribution pension funds (OECD 2008).

In pure defined-contribution funds, participants bear the full brunt of losses when investments perform badly. In such schemes, the onus is on the individual to optimize asset allocation, asset selection, and portfolio costs (expense ratios). Luck also plays an important role in determining whether an individual's retirement will be enjoyed or endured. As recent events have shown, even the savviest investor with the most sophisticated tools cannot predict when the next financial crisis will strike, or even when a bull market will start. Furthermore, it is difficult for individuals to address longevity risks on their own, as no withdrawal strategy can guarantee an income for life.

In numerical terms, savings run down at a withdrawal rate of 4 percent, for example, may last only 30 years; while at lower withdrawal rates, the right asset allocation could help reduce the probability of premature depletion. When the withdrawal rate reaches 6 percent, however, depletion is almost ensured (figure 4.22). So without risk sharing, individuals without significant retirement balances run the risk of withdrawing their savings at an unsustainable rate.

Figure 4.22 **Effect of Asset Allocation on Distribution Portfolios**

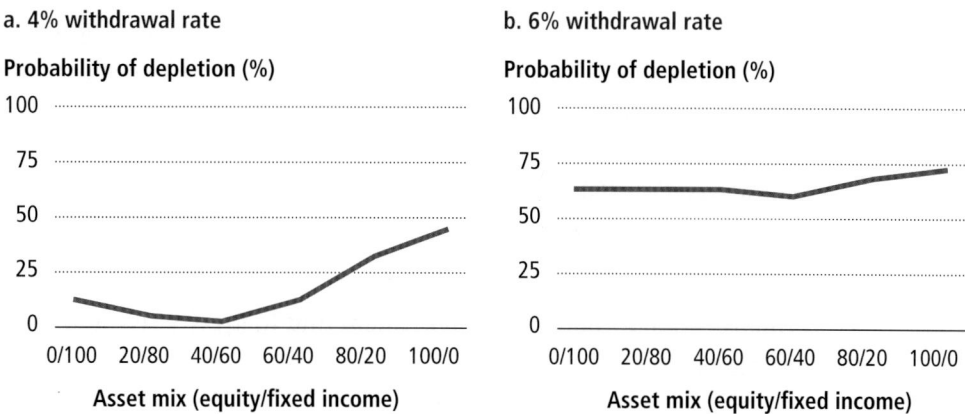

Source: Otar 2006.

There are ways to ameliorate the challenges posed by a pure defined-contribution model. During the accumulation phase, some financial planners advocate investing in life-cycle funds. The idea of life-cycle funds, also called target date funds, is to shift an individual's portfolio asset mix away from equities and toward more conservative asset classes as the person approaches retirement. This strategy, however, may still not be optimal. Some financial planners argue that as more assets are placed in fixed-income instruments over time, the portfolio's ability to participate in a secular strong upward trend in equity markets is diminished when it is needed most, in later years (Otar 2006).

Another way to address the challenges faced by defined-contribution plan participants is to integrate the accumulation and decumulation phases. Though a longer investment horizon provides greater flexibility in asset allocation and yields an untapped illiquidity premium, for an individual, these added benefits may still not be enough to guard against the risks of adverse exogenous events and outliving one's savings.

Risk pooling can help to protect defined-contribution plan participants from key risks

In 1960, life expectancy in Singapore was 60 years (UN 2002). Today, it is 80.6 years. Mortality tables from Singapore's Department of Statistics show that a 65-year-old Singaporean has a 66.4 percent chance of reaching the age of 80, a 47.4 percent chance of reaching 85, and a 27.5 percent chance of reaching 90. With postretirement averaging 20–25 years, the risk of a retiree outliving his or her source of income urgently needs to be addressed.

As no strategy to fully protect individual defined-contribution participants from investment and longevity risks exists, there is a need for risk pooling. Without risk pooling in the decumulation phase, individuals would need to set aside 40–80 percent more assets in order to finance their retirement income for the rest of their lives (Otar 2006).

Singapore's Central Provident Fund uses several techniques to help insulate Singaporeans from investment and longevity risk and reduce investment costs

As a case in point, Singapore has maintained, since 1955, a fully funded defined-contribution scheme—the Central Provident Fund (CPF)—with features that help insulate members from investment and longevity risks. Unlike a pure defined-contribution scheme, the CPF offers a minimum guaranteed return of 2.5 percent for assets kept with the fund (table 4.3). During the accumulation period, members can choose not to bear any investment risk at all if their assets are invested in risk-

Table 4.3 **Interest Earned by CPF Members**

Account type	CPF-guaranteed interest rates (%)[a]
Ordinary account	2.50
Special and Medisave accounts	4.00
Retirement account	4.00

Source: CPF.

a. Reviewed quarterly.

free government bonds called Special Singapore Government Securities. Members with higher balances and a higher risk appetite may opt to invest their CPF savings themselves in capital markets.[1] Historically, members who took on higher risks for potentially higher returns would have been better off had they left their assets with the CPF.

With regard to individual investments, the CPF considered the possibility that the fund's savings be managed in private pension plans to achieve possible higher returns—an option that would have required members to expose their CPF money to higher market risks and administration costs. Ultimately, however, the government of Singapore decided that it would be unwise to adopt this full investment option because the majority of CPF members do not have large balances. For members nearing retirement age, in particular, shifting their savings to private pension plans would have been too risky.

In hindsight, this decision has protected CPF members from the steep plunge in financial markets resulting from the financial crisis of 2008–09 and shielded them from excessive volatility in their asset values. Instead, to help members improve their retirement savings, an extra 1 percent interest is paid on the first $44,300 in combined CPF balances. This risk-free extra interest will benefit all members, especially those with small and average-size balances. Including this extra 1 percent, members have the potential to earn up to 5 percent interest on their CPF balances. And because a 1 percent administrative charge on assets over the course of 40 years could erode returns at a member's retirement age by 25 percent, the fund's management is exploring steps to reduce the current annual administrative cost (fiscal year 2008) of about $21 per participant.

Meanwhile, to address longevity risk, a national opt-in longevity insurance scheme called CPF Lifelong Income Scheme for the Elderly (LIFE) was established in September 2009. From 2013 onwards, LIFE will automatically enroll members meeting two parameters (those born after 1957 and with at least $29,500 in their retirement account) to yield a meaningful monthly income. Under LIFE, members will be able to choose the extent to which they wish to risk-pool their assets from four different plans.

LIFE was designed so that participants will not be permanently locked into a low interest rate due to market conditions when they purchase their LIFE plan. Rather, LIFE payouts adjust to reflect interest rate and mortality changes. At the same

---

[1] CPF members must first set aside $14,700 in their ordinary account and $22,145 in their special account before they can invest their CPF assets under the CPF Investment Scheme.

time, by investing in special government bonds, participants are protected from low interest rates by a guaranteed minimum rate of return, which limits the impact of falling interest rates on payouts.

Conclusion

The financial crisis of 2008–09 has highlighted that it is neither ideal nor sustainable for an individual to bear all the risks of saving for retirement. The CPF seeks to protect its members from investment and longevity risks by developing a retirement savings scheme that combines individualized savings with elements of risk pooling.

Specifically, the CPF is addressing longevity risk through a national opt-in longevity insurance scheme, while investment risk is being addressed through CPF-guaranteed interest rates on members' balances. As is increasingly clear, a challenge ahead for many countries is longevity risk. Such a massive challenge, though, cannot be met solely by solutions within the mandate of pension funds. Thoughtful, strategic, and forceful responses from society are needed. In this regard, it would be helpful to replace the artificial divide between work and retirement with flexible arrangements that allow individuals to remain active professionally, physically, intellectually, and socially. At the same time, there is a need to move beyond mere financial adequacy in pension systems to a mindset of "retirementality," as has recently been done in Singapore (Mitch 2006). Though all this is easier said than done, the sooner countries start thinking about retirement in a more holistic manner, the easier it will be to deal with the challenges ahead.

References

Bengen, W. 2006. "Sustainable Withdrawals." In H. Evensky and D. Katz, eds., *Retirement Income Redesigned*, pp. 217–36. New York: Bloomberg Press.

Department of Statistics. Singapore. "Complete Life Tables: Singapore Resident Population, 2003–2008." Singapore: Department of Statistics. www.singstat.gov.sg/stats/themes/people/demo.html.

Mitch, A. 2006. "Reinventing Retirement." In H. Evensky and D. Katz, eds., *Retirement Income Redesigned*, pp. 49–64. New York: Bloomberg Press.

OECD (Organisation for Economic Co-operation and Development). 2008. *OECD Private Pensions Outlook 2008.* Paris: OECD.

———. 2009. "Private Pensions Outlook 2008." Paris: OECD. www.oecd.org/document/60/0,3343,en_2649_34853_41770428_1_1_1_1,00.html.

Otar, J. 2006. "Lifelong Retirement Income: How to Quantify and Eliminate Luck." In H. Evensky and D. Katz, eds., *Retirement Income Redesigned*, pp. 77–96. New York: Bloomberg Press.

UN (United Nations, Department of Economic and Social Affairs, Population Division). 2002. *World Population Ageing 1950–2050.* New York: UN.

An Age-Based Multifunds Regulatory Approach for Latin American Funds

Augusto Iglesias, Vice Minister for Social Security, Chile

Determining the level of pension investment risk appropriate to an individual's age, time horizon, income, risk aversion, and other potential sources of retirement income, makes a significant difference to the value of retirement assets, as measured by their long-term, risk-adjusted rate of return. The greatest impact of investment performance on pension wealth is for workers close to retirement. Looking broadly at the second pillar of defined-contribution schemes in Latin America, it is evident that age-based allocation strategies, such as voluntary provisions and regulatory requirements for so-called default options, are important. Additionally, alternatives to traditional annuitization, such as those structured through programmed withdrawals, can help pension funds avoid the adverse effects of eroded asset values or low prevailing interest rates at the time a member's balances are annuitized. The risk of insufficient funds for longevity remains, however.

Investment and longevity risks mean that members of defined-contribution pension plans with similar employment histories can receive widely divergent pension benefits

Traditionally, funded defined-contribution pension programs have provided members with market rates of return on their balances but without protection from investment or solvency risks. Defined-contribution pension funds also rely on financial intermediaries to cover longevity risks, which can significantly affect the amount of pension benefits. During the accumulation phase, members face uncertainty about the rate of return on pension savings (figure 4.23). This insecurity escalates during the years immediately preceding retirement. At retirement, defined-contribution pension fund members face uncertainty about the value of their annuitized benefits. After retirement, members face uncertainty about rates of return on their pension savings (relevant for variable annuities and programmed withdrawals) and about longevity (relevant for programmed withdrawals). Investment risks also change over time for each cohort, and they can differ within cohorts.

Figure 4.23 **Member Risk at Different Stages in Funded Defined-Contribution Pension Plans**

Accumulation	At retirement	After retirement
◆ Rate of return on pension savings ◆ Investment or insolvency risks	◆ Value of annuitized pension benefits based on prevailing interest rates and mortality	◆ Rates of return on pension savings ◆ Longevity risks

Source: PrimAmérica Consultores.

In the context of a funded pension system, it is thus quite possible that individuals with similar employment histories will receive different levels of pension benefits.

Exposing members to investment risks through mandatory defined-contribution plans is more controversial in cases where such plans contribute a high proportion of total retirement income

Within a pension system, investment risks differ among cohorts and change over time for individual cohorts. The acceptability of these risks depends on factors such as the structure of the system, the relative contribution of funded pensions to overall retirement income, and the quality of regulation and supervision in the accumulation and decumulation phases. Figure 4.24 shows the contribution of government-sponsored defined-benefit and defined-contribution pension plans to total retirement income in selected Latin American countries. Total pension wealth at retirement is presented as a multiple of average earnings.

Efficiently protecting plan members from investment risks in funded defined-contribution pension plans involves several factors: (1) trade-offs between risk and return, (2) continued exposure to risks such as intermediary solvency risks, and (3) complex financial decision making (which most participants are not prepared to make). Most individuals are primarily concerned with their anticipated individual income replacement rates at retirement. Because they recognize that investment risks during the accumulation phase contribute to the value of total pension assets accumulated at retirement, they tend to limit investment risks.

In general, the higher the contribution of pension programs to total retirement income, the more controversial the issue of the mandatory pension's investment risks. Figure 4.25 shows the proportion of pension wealth from government-run

Figure 4.24 **Contribution of Different Pension Programs to Retirement Income**

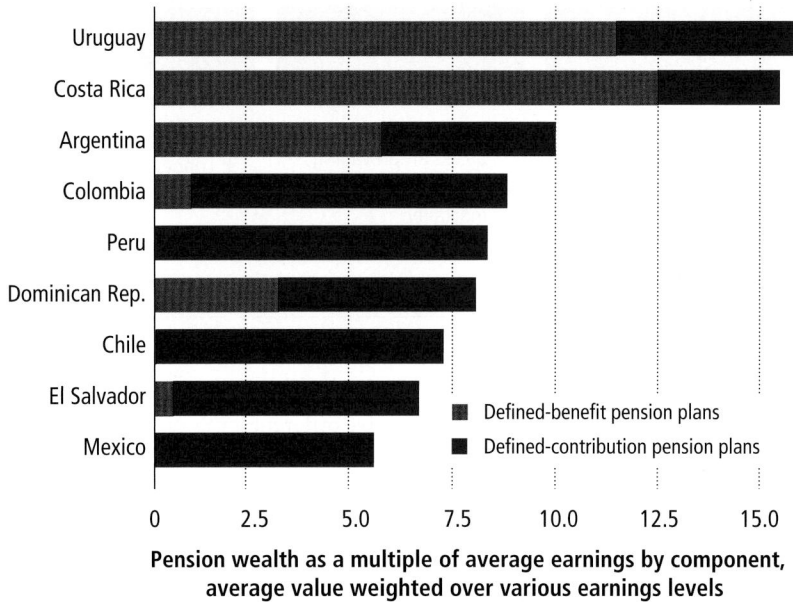

Pension wealth as a multiple of average earnings by component, average value weighted over various earnings levels

Source: PrimAmérica Consultores.

Figure 4.25 **Pensions from Pay-As-You-Go Defined-Benefit Programs**

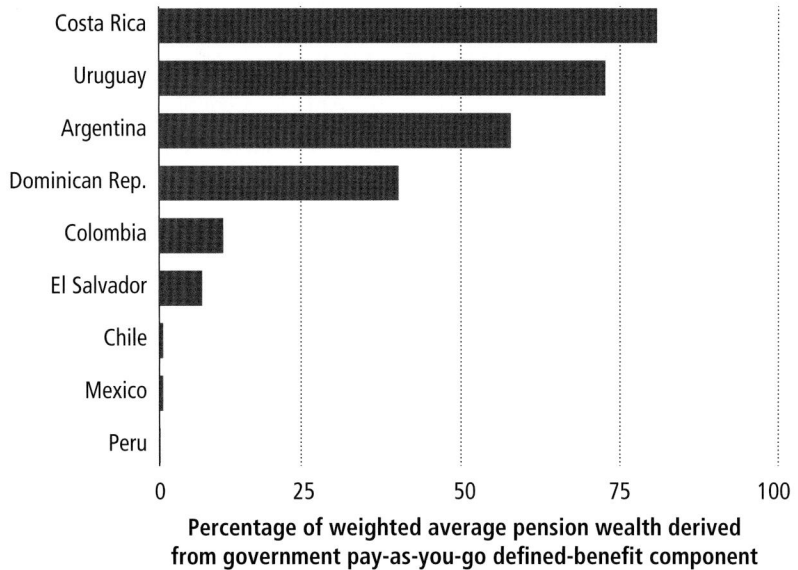

Percentage of weighted average pension wealth derived from government pay-as-you-go defined-benefit component

Source: PrimAmérica Consultores.

defined-benefit programs (which protect pensioners from investment risk) in a set of Latin American countries. In each case, the balance of pension wealth thus comes from defined-contribution programs (that is, programs in which members are exposed to investment risk). Of the set of countries examined here, Chile, Mexico, and Peru expose their members to the most investment risk, while Costa Rica exposes its members to the least. In all cases, protecting pensions from investment risk may come at a cost. At the same time, pension programs that do not expose their members to any investment risks may expose them to other types of risks, such as solvency risks; an example of this is where governments are forced to break their defined-benefit promises due to lack of financial resources. In sum, there is a trade-off between risk and return that means that in some cases, it may be efficient for a country to authorize mandatory pensions to accept investment risks. In such cases, efforts should be made to design and implement regulations that minimize such risk exposure and provide basic protection to workers (and cohorts) who cannot fully mitigate investment risks during their work lives.

During the accumulation phase, the volatility of cumulative investment returns up to retirement age is the critical risk to be managed

For most individuals, pension systems aim to maximize income replacement rates at retirement relative to a given contribution level. Thus, the investment risk to be managed during the accumulation phase is the volatility of the cumulative investment returns up to retirement age. Appropriate management of investment risk is important for several reasons:

◆ Variability in the prices of equities and bonds can translate into very different cumulative rates of return for different cohorts of pension plan members (figure 4.26).

◆ Returns in the years close to retirement will have a disproportionate impact on total accumulated pension wealth.

◆ Cumulative returns are influenced by reinvestment risks, particularly when there is not a well-developed market for long-term instruments.

◆ There can be a positive correlation between investment return risks and labor-related risks (specifically, the risk of loss or reduction in income).

Pension investment regulations should promote investment policies that efficiently manage volatility risk during the accumulation phase. Modern finance theory can help guide pension fund managers in this regard. In particular, regulations should recognize that (1) pension program participants have different investment

Figure 4.26 **Ratio of Assets to Earnings Using a Target Date Fund, 1911–2008**

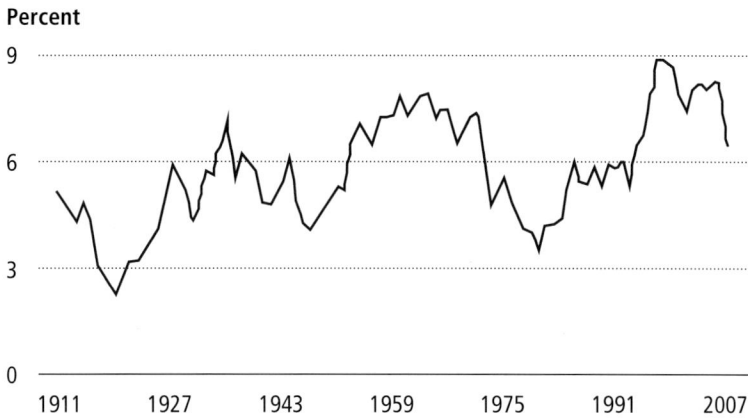

Percent

Source: Munnell, Webb, and Golub-Sass 2008.

Note: Figure shows the ratio of assets to average (age 54–58) earnings for individuals who enter the labor force at age 22 and retire at age 62.

horizons, and the longer the horizon, the greater the reinvestment and inflation risks; (2) different asset classes have different expected cumulative returns and cumulative volatility; (3) labor-related risks should be taken into account (the higher the labor-related risks, the more conservative a portfolio should be); and (4) the greater the relative importance of an individual's financial wealth in determining his or her retirement income, the more conservative the optimal portfolio mix should be. Moreover, wages and income are volatile over the course of pension fund members' careers, so the optimal asset mix for those with safe sources of labor income becomes more conservative as the individual ages.

Regulation of optimal investment policies for defined-contribution pension programs should recognize that

- ◆ the younger the participants, the longer the investment horizon;
- ◆ cumulative returns and volatility for each asset class over the relevant investment horizon are the most appropriate risk measure;
- ◆ the higher a participant's labor-related risks, the more conservative their investment portfolio should be;
- ◆ the higher the relative contribution to total retirement income from this program, the more conservative their investment portfolio should be.

Because individuals have different investment time horizons and risk preferences at different times of their lives, the optimal mix of assets for a single cohort also changes over time, and optimal portfolios are different for cohorts of different ages. A second challenge of risk management within pension funds is therefore to design portfolios that take into account the investment horizon and the risk preferences of members. Age-based portfolio allocation strategies may be appropriate in this regard.

Under an age-based allocation strategy, asset allocation is a function of the investor's time horizon, the portfolio is periodically rebalanced to adjust to a target asset mix, and the target mix depends on the target date of the portfolio (the closer the target date, the more conservative the target mix).

Age-Based Allocation Strategy

◆ Asset allocation as a function of the investor's time horizon

◆ Portfolio periodically rebalanced to target asset mix

◆ Asset mix becomes more conservative closer to target date

Defined-contribution pension plans should offer several portfolio strategies with different asset mixes to individuals with the same investment horizon, in addition to an age-based, automatic allocation strategy

Age-based allocation strategies (with default options for individuals who cannot— or do not want to—choose a strategy) can substantially decrease the variance in investment risks (that is, variance in accumulated rates of return) for funded defined-contribution pension plan participants. Nevertheless, individuals' risk preferences do not depend only on age. Since individuals with the same investment horizon (those in the same cohort) have different employment histories, different degrees of uncertainty regarding future wages, and different levels of wealth, the structure of their retirement incomes will also vary. Defined-contribution pension plans should therefore offer several portfolio strategies with different asset mixes to members with similar investment horizons. Regulations for mandatory pension fund investments that allow for different investment portfolios ("multifunds") should also be encouraged, and an age-based, automatic allocation portfolio should be made available. And because individuals are often not prepared to make difficult investment decisions, plan managers should offer default options. Mandatory funded pension plans with these kinds of regulations exist in Chile, Mexico, Peru (table 4.4), as well as in Estonia, Hungary, Latvia, and the Slovak Republic.

Table 4.4 Age-Based Allocation Strategies in Selected Latin American Pension Funds

	Fund	Limit on investment in equities (as % of total assets)		Default option by age[a]		
		Minimum	Maximum	Men & women < 35	Men 36–55; women 36–50	Men 56–65; women 51+ & pensioners
Chile	E	0	5			
	D	5	20			▓
	C	15	40		▓	
	B	25	60	▓		
	A	40	80			

	Fund	Minimum	Maximum	Members < 27	Members 27–36	Members 37–45	Members 46–55	Members > 55
Mexico	SB1	0	0					▓
	SB2	0	15				▓	
	SB3	0	20			▓		
	SB4	0	25		▓			
	SB5	0	30	▓				

	Fund	Minimum	Maximum	Members < 60	Members > 60
Peru	Type 1	0	0		▓
	Type 2	25	45	▓	
	Type 3	30	80		

Source: PrimAmérica Consultores based on data from International Federation of Pension Funds Administrators 2009.

a. Default option is shaded.

The following insights are useful with respect to investment rules in the context of life-cycle funds (Viceira 2008).

◆ For fixed-income instruments:
  – Short-term bonds and cash are not necessarily safe assets because they can involve material reinvestment risks.
  – Inflation risk needs to be managed, particularly over the medium and long term; some preference for indexed long-term bonds is therefore warranted.

- Government bonds present important risks even though in many countries they represent the deepest and most liquid fixed-income market.

◆ For equity instruments:

- International equity diversification helps to decrease portfolio risk at the country-specific level.

- Stock returns seem to be mean reverting.

At retirement age, forced annuitization can have an adverse impact on income replacement rates

It is possible that individuals will reach retirement age after a period of low returns or retire during a period when annuitized benefits are relatively low as a result of prevailing interest rates. In both cases, forced annuitization, particularly in the case of fixed annuities, will have an adverse impact on income replacement rates. Lump-sum distributions are not a solution to this problem: if returns have been low, then pension savings would have been eroded. Programmed withdrawals,[1] on the other hand, which allow individuals to keep pension savings in their respective accounts until a better moment to annuitize arrives, can be a good alternative to forced annuitization upon retirement.

Additional observations on investment risks and options during retirement follow:

◆ Differences in short-term rates of return for different portfolios can be vital during retirement, suggesting the importance of rigorous investment management during the payout phase.

◆ Since consumption during retirement is generally denominated in the local currency, benefits should be disbursed in local currency and, at this stage of the life cycle, pension assets should be mostly denominated in local currency.

◆ Inflation can quickly erode the purchasing power of pensions, so inflation-indexed annuities should be considered if the markets can provide such instruments.

◆ To decrease investment risks during retirement years, pension savings should be invested in portfolios with very low volatility, made up mostly of inflation-

---

[1] Programmed withdrawals are calculated according to local regulations, which typically divide the balance in an individual's account by the number of years of life expectancy. The annual payout not only includes assumptions of life expectancy but also incorporates a discount factor and anticipated future returns on pension fund balances. The annual payout can be recalculated annually in accordance with actual accumulation and decumulation of the account balance.

indexed bonds denominated in the local currency, with a maturity close to the time horizon of pension payments.

Investment risks continue during retirement

Almost all pension modalities expose pensioners to some kind of risk. Fixed nominal annuities, for example, provide protection against longevity risks and investment risks, but do not protect against inflation risk. Variable annuities may maximize returns yet expose retirees to some level of investment risk. Programmed withdrawals protect against neither investment risk nor longevity risk.

Fixed real annuities seem, then, to be the pension mode that offers the pensioner full protection against financial risks during retirement years. In this case, however, financial risks are transferred to the providers of these annuities, leaving pensioners exposed to the solvency risk of the financial intermediary. The financial intermediary solvency risk can be mitigated by the strength of regulation and supervision of such intermediaries, the depth of inflation-indexed securities available to invest in for such annuitants, and the existence of any guarantee or insurance provisions provided by third parties.

To protect participants from investment risk at and after retirement age, different pension modalities should be available, and pensioners should be able to choose among them and to combine them.

References

Munnell, A., A. Webb, and A. Golub-Sass. 2008. "How Much Risk Is Acceptable?" Brief 8-20. Boston: Center for Retirement Research at Boston College.

Viceira, L. 2008. "Life-Cycle Funds." In A. Lusardi, ed., *Overcoming the Saving Slump: How to Increase the Effectiveness of Financial Education and Saving Programs*. Chicago: University of Chicago Press.

Using a Hybrid Pension Product in a Collective Framework to Distribute Risk: Denmark's ATP

Lars Rohde, Chief Executive Officer, ATP, Denmark

While it can be argued that the reason for any pension system's existence is its ability to diversify individual risks into collective risks, a global trend of transferring risks—both longevity and financial—back to the individual is under way. ATP's (Arbejdmarkedets Tillaegs Pension's) use of a hybrid pension product design, however, manages the risk profile of different cohorts of members in a collective framework, guaranteeing a minimum nominal pension that includes lifelong pension guarantees (to fully mitigate longevity risk) with conditional indexation in addition to insurance elements. Collective schemes such as ATP take advantage of huge economies of scale to offer affordable pensions. As a result, individuals covered under such plans can look forward to receiving secure and stable pensions and, in the long run, potentially higher pensions than under other types of plans.

ATP is a critical part of the Danish pension system

Established by a 1964 law as a funded supplement to the tax-funded old-age pension, Denmark's ATP (Arbejdmarkedets Tillaegs Pension, or Labor Market Supplementary Pension) now manages a portfolio of close to $76 billion on behalf of 4.6 million members. All employees and recipients of government transfer income pay a flat rate ATP contribution corresponding to approximately 1 percent of the income of an average worker. ATP, in turn, provides a lifelong pension. Though its supervision and accounting standards are similar to those stipulated for other Danish pension funds and insurance companies, ATP must be fully funded at all times, as it has no sponsor.

ATP's role in the Danish pension system is described in figure 4.27, which illustrates the pyramid structure of the pension system in Denmark. The first layer of the pyramid consists of old-age pensions that are tax-financed on a "pay-as-you-go" basis, and the ATP pension. This first layer can be seen as a protection against

Figure 4.27 **Denmark's Pension Pyramid**

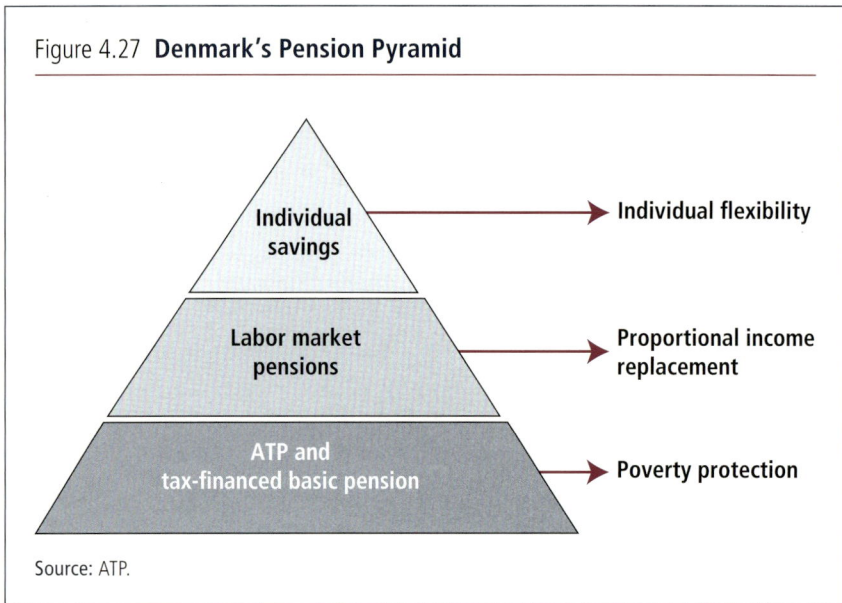

Source: ATP.

poverty. The second layer has been created through the labor markets (in the form of employment-related pensions) with the objective of providing proportional income replacement. The third layer consists of individual savings.

Though it resembles the three-pillar pension system used in many countries, Denmark's three-pillar system is unique in several ways

While the Danish pension pyramid resembles the classic three-pillar model found in many countries, it is different in a number of ways. For one, the public pension system is universal, and its objective is to provide effective poverty protection. Accordingly, the Danish public pension system is not intended to ensure a certain replacement rate. This task is assigned to the second and third layers of the pyramid—that is, employment-related pensions and individual savings.

Second, the accumulation of pension rights in funded schemes in Denmark is unique. At the start of the accumulation process, a pension contribution is immediately converted to a lifelong pension guarantee. The size of the guarantee depends on actuarial assumptions about mortality and other metrics and on interest rates. If investments subsequently generate a surplus in excess of the guaranteed pensions, the surplus is returned in the form of bonus and thus higher pensions. Furthermore, Danish employment-related pensions must be accumulated outside the company. Once the pension contribution has been made, the future credit quality of the employer has no impact on the security of the pension. This is quite different from the Anglo-Saxon model.

For Danish pension savers, the biggest risk is not that their employer defaults, but that their pension provider encounters solvency problems. The Danish authorities have addressed this issue in various ways. When mark-to-market accounting was introduced for pension funds, it had an effect akin to turning on the lights in a dark room, making balance sheet risks in pension funds much more visible. Furthermore, there has been a strong focus on solvency by the introduction of conditions such as minimum surplus requirements for pension funds. These changes have spurred a minor revolution in the risk management practices of Danish pension funds, including ATP.

With the pyramid structure, Denmark provides multiple pension instruments with varying levels of importance by income decile. Figure 4.28 presents government projections of the relative importance of the three layers of the pension pyramid in 2045. For the lower-income deciles, the basic old-age pension and ATP will remain the dominant sources of retirement income even in the long term.

Figure 4.28 **Contribution of Various Sources of Pension Income by 2045**

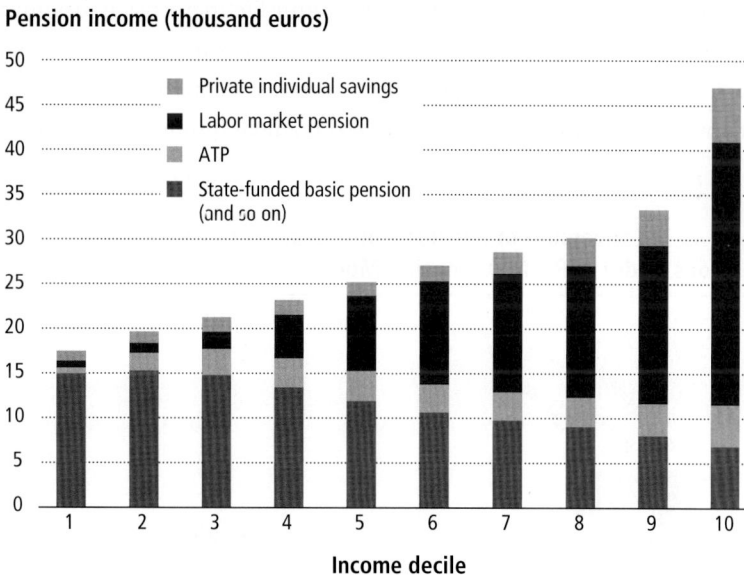

Pension income (thousand euros)

Legend:
- Private individual savings
- Labor market pension
- ATP
- State-funded basic pension (and so on)

Income decile

Source: Denmark Ministry of Economic Affairs.

Modifications to ATP's pension model focus on retaining security and stability without producing low pension returns

In recent years, there has been a move from defined-benefit schemes to pure defined-contribution schemes (individual accounts). The reasons for this shift are easy to understand in light of population aging and recurring financial crises, but policy makers should not overlook the fact that it entails a massive transfer of risk from pension providers (companies) to individuals. The modification also leaves open the question of the purpose and objectives of a pension system, since individuals' savings can be quite efficiently handled by banks in well regulated environments.

ATP's recently implemented pension product ensures security and stability for the individual member without resort to a low-return, conservative investment strategy.

In early 2008, ATP implemented a new pension model focusing on retaining security and stability for the individual without resorting to a conservative investment strategy with low expected returns. Specifically, this new pension feature retains guaranteed minimum nominal pensions based on market interest rates. It splits pension contributions into a guaranteed part, which ensures a minimum pension, and a bonus part, which provides an option to have pensions indexed in future. On an aggregate level, 80 percent of an individual's contributions for each year are converted into a guaranteed nominal future lifetime pension (beginning at age 67 in the example shown in figure 4.29). The amount of this guaranteed nominal future lifetime pension can vary from year to year, since it is based on prevailing long-term interest rates. The total guaranteed nominal future lifetime pension is,

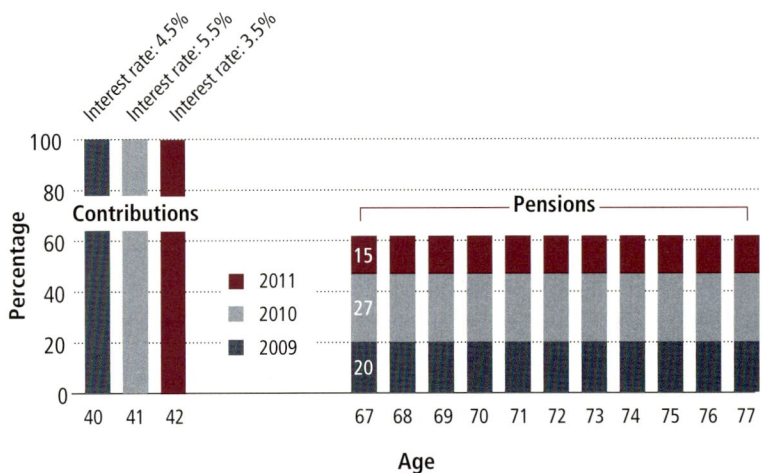

Figure 4.29 **Conversion of Pension Contributions to Guaranteed Pensions under ATP's New Pension Model**

Source: ATP.

therefore, an aggregate of these annual guarantees. The remaining 20 percent of an individual's contribution goes to the bonus reserves. Figure 4.29 illustrates how each year's pension contributions are converted to a guaranteed nominal future lifetime pension based on long-term interest rates prevailing at that time.

As demonstrated by ATP's model, security and predictability do not result in low pensions. First, the guaranteed portion of pensions is based on long-term market interest rates, and all pension guarantees are fully hedged by long-term government bonds and interest rate swaps. Long-term bonds offer higher expected returns than money market rates, and this return premium is captured by the liability hedging, thus improving the probability of meeting expected pension returns essentially risk-free. Second, the 20 percent bonus contribution provides risk capital for new pension rights. Free reserves serve the dual purpose of financing indexations and providing risk capital for investments. With new contributions adding to risk capital, there is room to pursue an investment strategy with a higher return target. Furthermore, due to large economies of scale, collective schemes like ATP offer affordable pensions. Figure 4.30 illustrates that even small differences in asset management cost make a significant impact on the terminal value of pension savings.

Collective schemes offer affordable pensions by taking advantage of economies of scale. Higher annual asset management costs of 0.8 percent over a 40-year period may reduce benefits available to members by almost one-fourth.

ATP's new pension feature explicitly balances longevity risk among fund members using a cohort mortality model. As such, tariffs are calculated, updated, and fixed for all contributions made that year, taking the trend in longevity into account. A unique feature is that the trend is estimated using international data, which is much more robust than using only observations from Denmark.

Hybrid pension models may better protect members' income replacement needs by taking into account members' time to retirement and risk aversion

ATP's pension model is not the only possible solution. One could, for example, envision a hybrid model for the future based on three elements. First, investments for younger cohorts would be nonguaranteed. These cohorts would invest with a relatively high degree of risk. Second, there would be a gradual transfer to a guaranteed lifelong annuity. For example, the middle-aged cohorts from age 55 could have

Figure 4.30 **Impact of a Small Difference in Asset Management Cost on Pension Savings Value**

Basis points

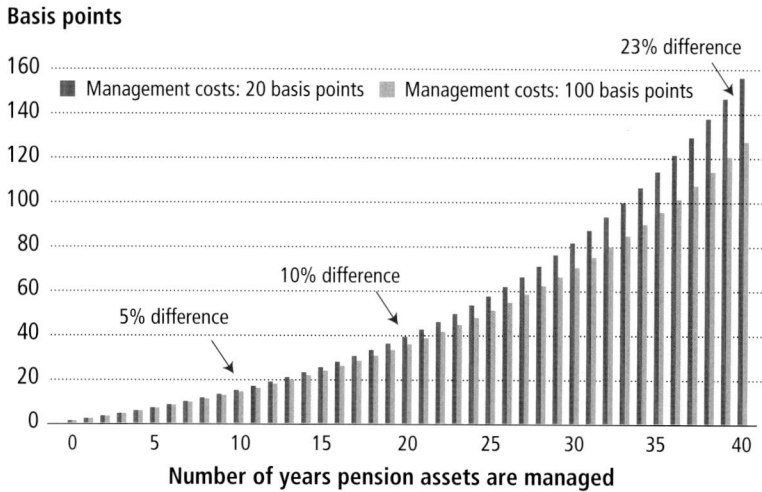

Number of years pension assets are managed

Source: ATP.

10 percent of their savings switched to annuities every year. Finally, a 100 percent guaranteed lifelong annuity would be provided for retirees beginning at pension age—that is, at 65 years.

Conclusion

The most fundamental role of a pension system is to manage longevity and other difficult-to-assess individual risks in a collective framework, diversifying risks within and between generations and making life more predictable in the older years along the way. ATP's pension model shows that it is possible to provide basic pension products that offer individual savers important benefits, demonstrated in particular by the fact that it has retained lifelong pensions with a minimum nominal guarantee based on market interest rates. This model allows individuals to manage longevity risk efficiently while also providing intergenerational solidarity. For the ATP member, such an arrangement ensures secure and stable benefits and potentially higher pensions in the long run.

3. An Asset-Liability Approach to Strategic Asset Allocation for Pension Funds

- ◆ Liability-Driven Investing: Hype or Hope?

- ◆ Strategic Asset Allocation as a Risk Management Exercise: A Perspective from the QIC

- ◆ Using Asset-Liability Analysis to Make Consistent Policy Choices: The Approach in the Netherlands

- ◆ Determining Investment Strategy from the Liability Structure: South Africa's GEPF

Liability-Driven Investing: Hype or Hope?

Arjan B. Berkelaar, Head of Investment Strategy and Risk Management, KAUST Investment Management Company, United States*

In an environment where pension liabilities are marked to market, pension funds can benefit from using a liability-driven investment (LDI) framework that takes into account correlations between assets and liabilities. Three factors—the financial strength of the fund's sponsor, the fund's investment horizon, and the funding status of the fund—affect the risk tolerance of a pension fund, and these same factors affect the relevance of using an LDI framework. Compared with a traditional asset-only approach, an LDI approach can significantly reduce risk while improving performance.

Experience from the two financial storms over the past decade supports the use of liability-driven investing

Within the past decade, two financial storms—the collapse of the technology bubble in 2000–02 and the global financial crisis in 2008–09—resulted in significant declines in U.S. equity prices and interest rates. Both events severely affected pension funds worldwide. During these crisis periods, the equity risk premium, defined as the premium of equity returns over long-term U.S. Treasuries, was –7.75 percent. Yields on 10-year U.S. Treasury bonds fell from 6.44 percent at the end of December 1999 to about 3.46 percent at the end of May 2009 (figure 4.31). Over the same time period, the funded ratio of U.S. pension funds dropped from an average of 135 percent in 1999 to 80 percent at the end of 2008 (figure 4.32).

Experience from the two crises suggests that the most appropriate investment framework for public pension funds is liability-driven investment (LDI). LDI has two main objectives: to effectively hedge unrewarded risks and to provide a framework for taking rewarded risks. Given the importance of correlations between

---

* The author would like to thank Gabriel Petre of the World Bank Treasury for assistance with data analysis, financial modeling, and preparation of graphs.

Figure 4.31 **Evolution of Value of U.S. Equities and Interest Rates**

Index value   Interest rate (%)

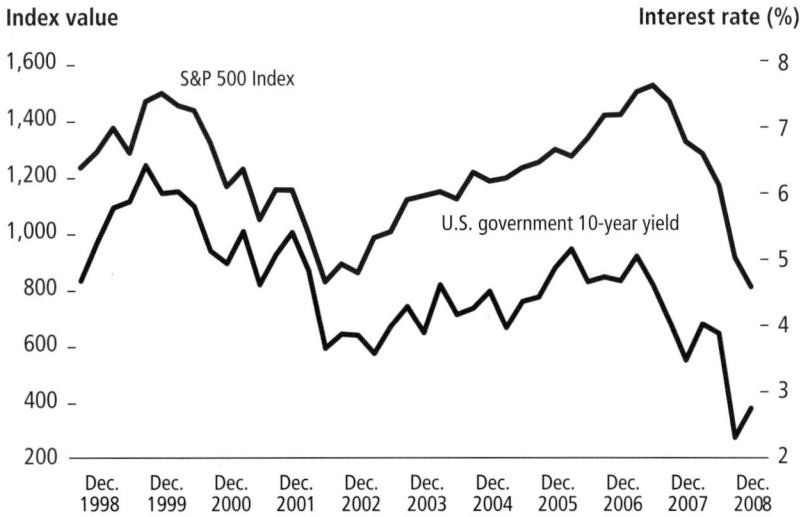

Source: Bloomberg.

Figure 4.32 **Evolution of Funded Ratio and Equity Returns for U.S. Pension Funds**

Funded ratio (%)   S&P total return (%)

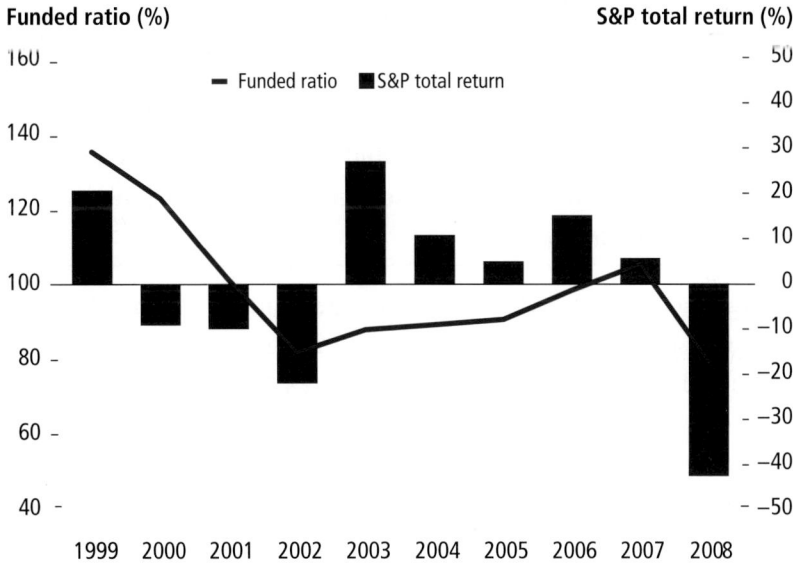

Source: Ehrhardt and Morgan 2009.

assets and liabilities, pension portfolios should be constructed on an asset-liability basis. This is illustrated in figure 4.33, where expected surplus returns and surplus standard deviations vary substantially between the asset-only efficient frontier and the asset-liability efficient frontier.

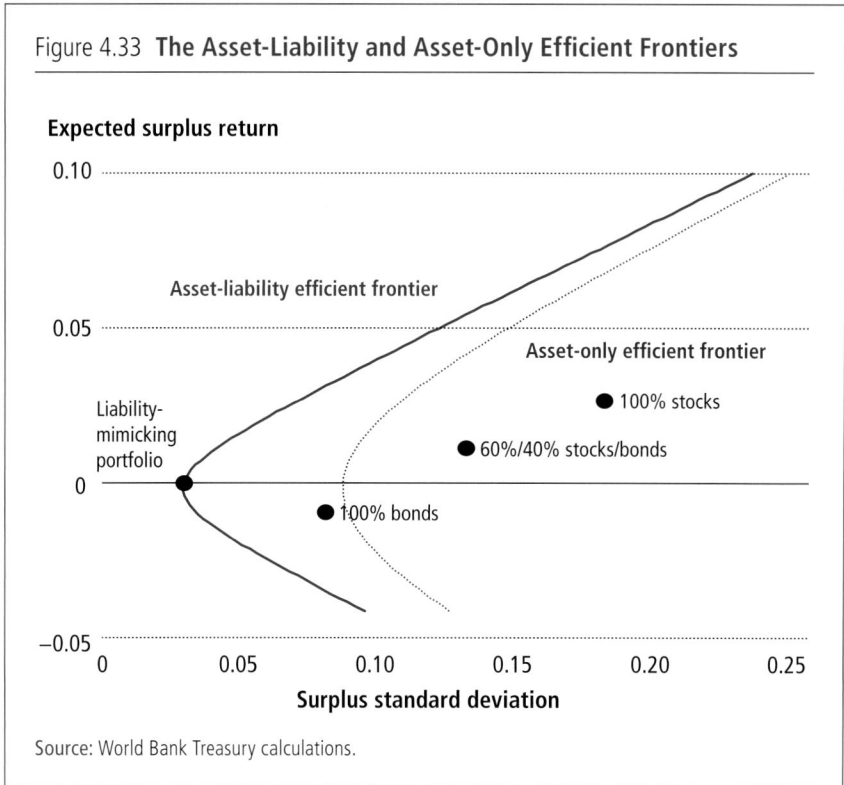

Figure 4.33 **The Asset-Liability and Asset-Only Efficient Frontiers**

Source: World Bank Treasury calculations.

Pension funds' tolerance for risk should broadly determine the extent to which they take into account asset-liability considerations in making investment decisions

Three main factors affect risk tolerance within a pension fund: the financial strength of the fund's sponsor, the fund's investment horizon (measured by the maturity of the plan), and the funding status of the fund (figure 4.34). Overall tolerance for risk should broadly determine the extent to which a pension fund takes asset-liability considerations into account in its investment decisions, including investing in assets with liability-hedging characteristics.

As figure 4.35 indicates, asset allocations of defined-benefit pension funds in the United States are unrelated to their funded status and maturity (as shown by low R^2 values), suggesting that U.S. pension funds are not adopting LDI as a guiding performance approach. According to a recent survey by Bank of America/Merrill

Figure 4.34 **Factors Determining Pension Funds' Risk Tolerance**

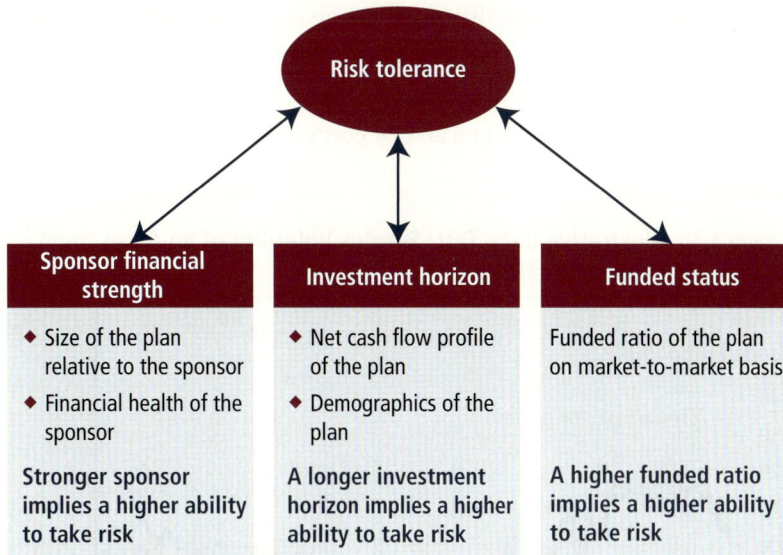

Sponsor financial strength	Investment horizon	Funded status
◆ Size of the plan relative to the sponsor ◆ Financial health of the sponsor	◆ Net cash flow profile of the plan ◆ Demographics of the plan	Funded ratio of the plan on market-to-market basis
Stronger sponsor implies a higher ability to take risk	**A longer investment horizon implies a higher ability to take risk**	**A higher funded ratio implies a higher ability to take risk**

Source: World Bank staff.

Figure 4.35 **Asset Allocation of U.S. Pension Funds**

a. Equity & alternatives allocation versus plan funded status: 100 largest U.S. corporate plans

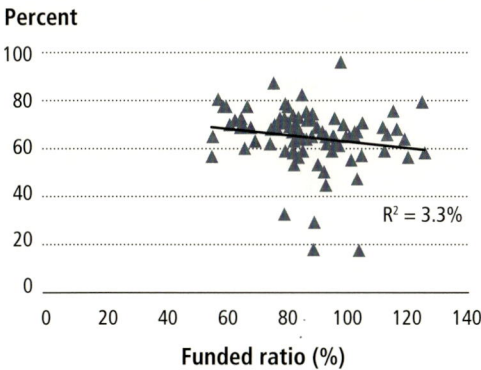

Percent

$R^2 = 3.3\%$

Funded ratio (%)

b. Bond allocation versus plan maturity: U.S. public plans

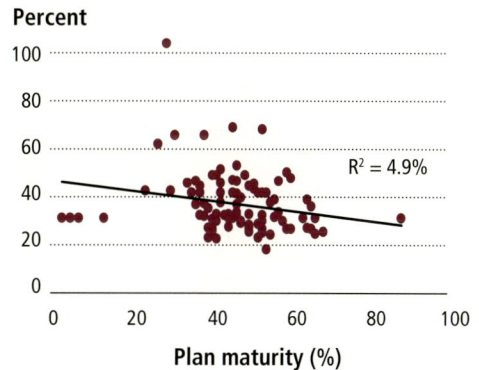

Percent

$R^2 = 4.9\%$

Plan maturity (%)

Source: Wilshire Associates and Milliman; World Bank Treasury calculations.

Note: Plan maturity is measured as the ratio of the number of retirees to the total number of plan members.

Lynch, 26 percent of U.S. pension funds have implemented an LDI approach, while 34 percent say they will not adopt an LDI framework in the foreseeable future.

Tolerance for risk also affects pension funds' decisions about desired amounts of surplus volatility and return

Illustrative back tests suggest that decisions about desired amounts of surplus volatility and surplus return are driven by the risk tolerance of each specific pension fund. Figure 4.36 compares the back-tested outcomes of two portfolios, an asset-only pension portfolio and an LDI portfolio that does not include deriva-

Figure 4.36 **Illustrative Back Test: Surplus Volatility of an Asset-only versus LDI Pension Portfolio**

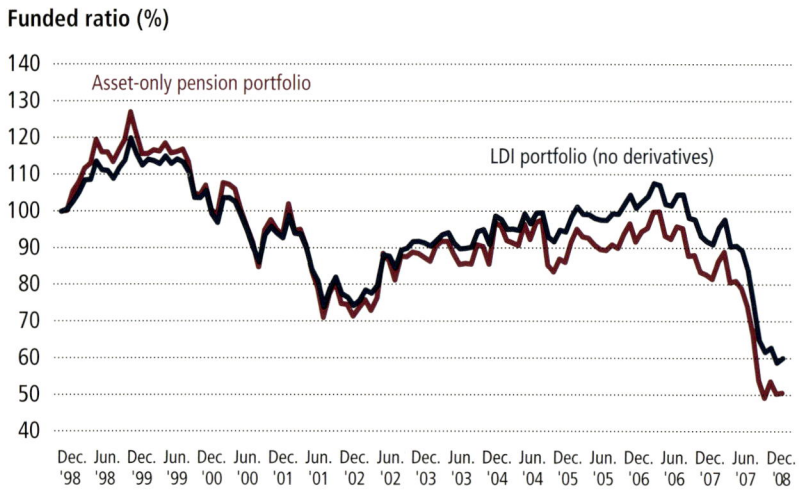

Parameter	Asset-only pension portfolio	LDI portfolio
Allocation		
U.S. equity	35%	35%
International equity	15%	15%
Lehman Global agg. (hedged)	40%	
Long-maturity Treasury bonds		40%
Real estate	10%	10%
Surplus return	−7.1%	−5.3%
Surplus volatility	17.8%	13.1%
Asset-only volatility	9.5%	10.6%

Sources: Ryan Labs Liabilities Index, Bloomberg, and World Bank Treasury calculations.

tives. Between December 1998 and December 2008, shifting the 40 percent allocation to the Lehman Global Aggregate Index (now Barclays Global) under the asset-only portfolio to long-maturity U.S. Treasury bonds under the LDI portfolio would have resulted in a decline in surplus volatility from 17.8 percent to 13.1 percent. Though it is not shown in the figure, using derivatives (such as swaps) instead of cash instruments (such as bonds) would have further decreased volatility while improving overall portfolio performance.

Options for how to hedge liabilities are typically considered during implementation of an LDI portfolio

During the implementation stage of a desired LDI portfolio, pension funds must make decisions with respect to assets to be considered for the purpose of hedging liabilities. A typical U.S. pension fund is exposed to long-term interest rate risks: as interest rates decrease, the fund's liabilities increase. In general, the most effective hedging options for long-term interest rates are long-maturity U.S. Treasury bonds, long-maturity corporate bonds, TIPS (Treasury Inflation-Protected Securities), and derivatives. While other asset classes may also have hedging properties, typically their correlation coefficients are too unstable over time to make them useful in terms of hedging (figure 4.37).

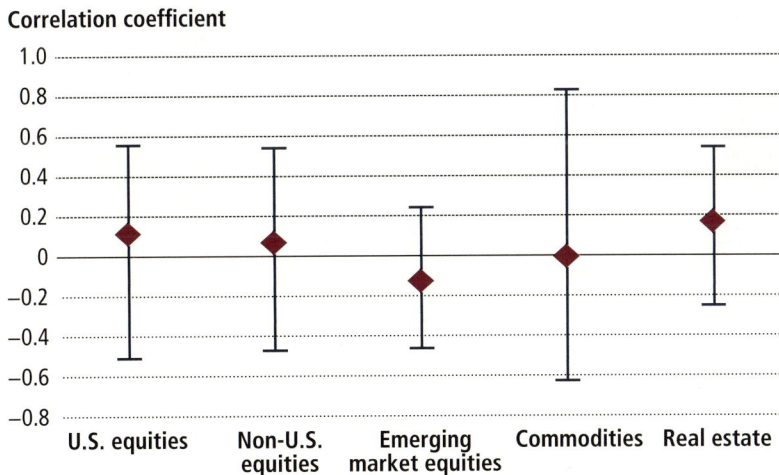

Figure 4.37 **Correlation of Various Asset Classes with Long-Duration Government Bonds, 1980–2009**

Sources: Bloomberg and World Bank Treasury calculations. Calculations presented above assume a five-year rolling investment window.

Note: For each asset class, diamonds indicate average correlation and the upper and lower bars indicate minimum and maximum correlation.

233

Within a liability-driven investing framework, the liability-hedging portfolio represents risk-free assets in the asset-liability space. A pension fund can think of its overall portfolio as being on a spectrum between a portfolio of risk-free assets and a market portfolio representing the asset-only efficient portfolio. In the absence of derivatives, a pension fund would need to allocate some of its assets to the liability-hedging portfolio, thereby limiting the assets available for the return-generating portfolio. This would require it to make a trade-off between hedging liabilities and generating returns (figure 4.38). Derivatives, however, would allow for a more flexible implementation of this framework.

For pension funds, the objectives of hedging liabilities and generating returns are sufficiently disparate that they are best served by separate subportfolios with distinct objectives and assets. At the overall fund level, separate subportfolios also offer advantages in terms of governance, management, and reporting. In a commingled structure of separate subportfolios, a pension fund's asset managers might undo some of the liability hedge in their implementation stage in the search for alpha.

Figure 4.38 **LDI: Liability Hedging and Return Generation**

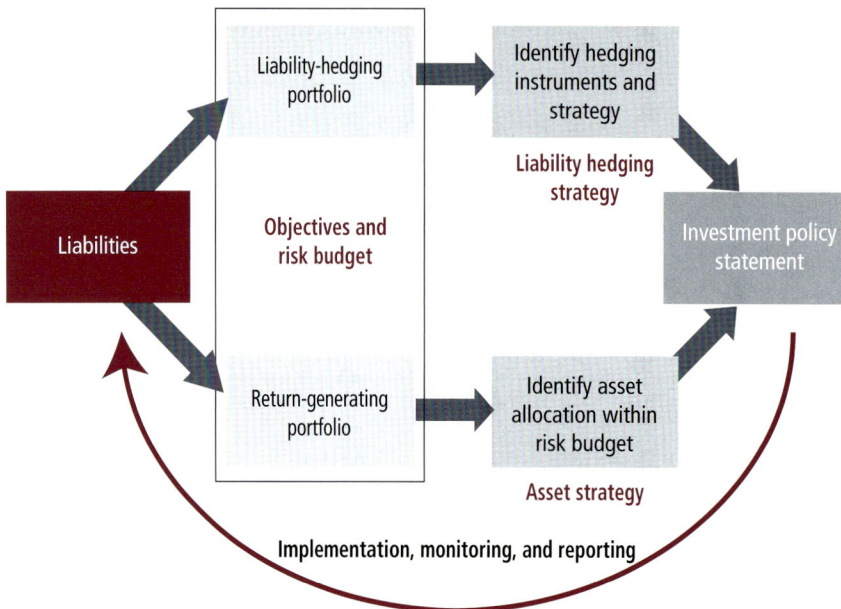

Source: World Bank Treasury.

Though the use of derivatives for liability hedging can increase a pension fund's surplus return, it also increases exposure to counterparty credit risk and requires a strong back office for management of cash collateral

As suggested in figure 4.39, allowing liability hedging through derivatives improves the efficient frontier of expected surplus returns in the asset-liability framework. Though derivatives have the potential to increase a pension fund's surplus return, they have other significant implications for pension funds, such as increasing exposure to counterparty credit risk and requiring a strong back-office operation for management of cash collateral. Derivatives can also increase leverage and thus the overall volatility of portfolio returns when viewed from an asset-only perspective (figure 4.40). Finally, the use of derivatives is limited by the size of the overall market for instruments such as TIPS with which to hedge real interest rate risks.

Figure 4.39 **Impact of Derivatives on the Surplus Efficient Frontier**

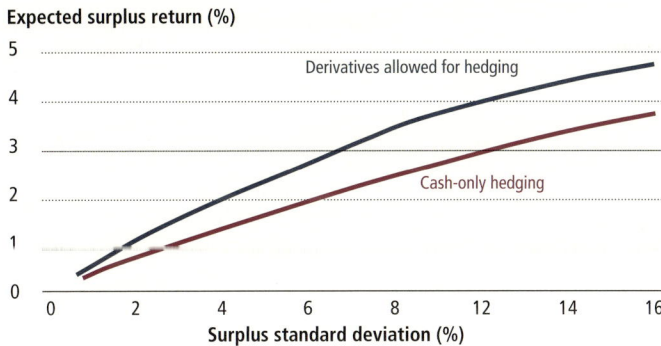

Sources: Bloomberg and World Bank Treasury calculations.

Conclusion

For pension funds, an LDI framework offers effective ways of dynamically managing surplus volatility. Separation between a liability-hedging portfolio and a return-generating portfolio can be used to achieve the desired risk profile of the plan and to allocate the overall risk budget. Though derivatives are the most efficient tool for hedging interest rate risk in the liabilities, they need to be appropriately understood and the challenges resulting from using them adequately managed.

Figure 4.40   **Illustrative Back Test: Surplus Volatility of an Asset-Only versus LDI (with Derivatives Overlay) Pension Portfolio**

Funded ratio (%)

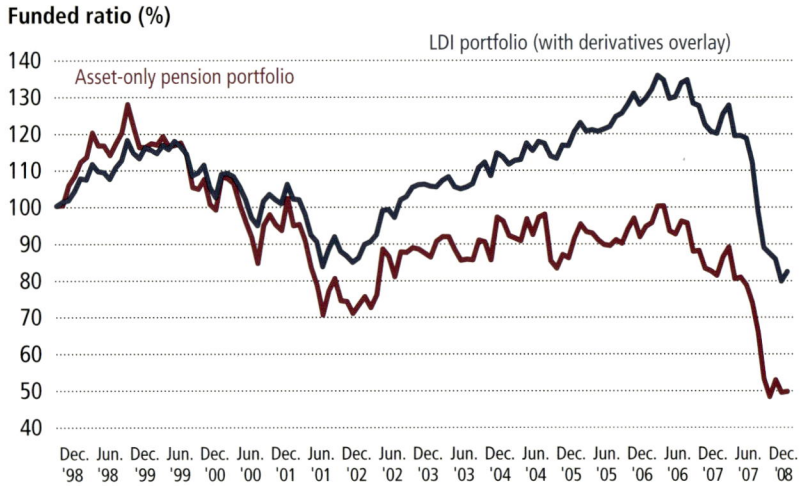

Parameter	Asset-only pension portfolio	LDI portfolio (with derivatives overlay)
Allocation		
U.S. equity	35%	35%
International equity	15%	15%
Long-maturity Treasury bonds	40%	40%
Real estate	10%	10%
Derivatives overlay		25%
Surplus return	−7.1%	−2.0%
Surplus volatility	17.8%	10.9%
Asset-only volatility	9.5%	12.8%

Sources: Ryan Labs Liabilities Index, Bloomberg, and World Bank Treasury calculations.

Reference

Ehrhardt, J., and P. Morgan. 2009. "Five Years of Pension Gains Wiped out in 2008." Milliman 2009 Pension Funding Study. Seattle: Milliman.

Strategic Asset Allocation as a Risk Management Exercise: A Perspective from the QIC

Adriaan Ryder, Managing Director, Queensland Investment Corporation, Australia

For the Queensland Investment Corporation (QIC), risk is defined not as a statistical measure, but as a failure to meet the multiple and often conflicting portfolio objectives set by QIC's governing body. In general, these objectives are driven by the liabilities of its pension schemes, asset performance, peer performance, risk metrics, and cost-benefit considerations. Several approaches can be taken as part of the strategic asset allocation exercise with respect to assessing the link between assets and liabilities. Optimization can be measured from an asset-liability management or a liability-driven investment perspective.

The Queensland Investment Corporation perceives risk as a failure to meet its multiple portfolio objectives

For pension funds, the process of strategic asset allocation (SAA) can be viewed as a risk management exercise. Within the Queensland Investment Corporation (QIC), which has more than $53 billion of assets under management, risk is not perceived as simply volatility, tracking error, value at risk (VaR), conditional value at risk (CVaR), or any other statistical measure. Rather, QIC recognizes risk as a failure to meet multiple portfolio objectives set by QIC's governing body.

For QIC, determining portfolio objectives involves assessment of five often conflicting goals:

- *Asset-driven objectives* typically deal with absolute performance hurdles (for example, wage inflation of 4 percent) and limiting the probability of negative return.

- *Liability-driven objectives* (for example, within defined-benefit pension plans or insurance funds) typically set surplus/deficit objectives for a fund (such as a deficit of no more than 5 percent over a 10-year time horizon) and contribution rate stability. Meeting these objectives is crucial, as assets and liabilities of all state defined-benefit pension plans are usually reported on the country's balance sheet and any deficit resulting from a fund's performance can directly affect the country's credit rating.

◆ *Peer-driven objectives* typically assign performance benchmarks against peers within the public pension funds industry.

◆ *Risk metrics objectives* typically relate to benchmarks such as tracking error, VaR, or CVaR.

◆ *Cost-benefit-driven objectives* focus on managing the pension schemes in an efficient manner.

The Queensland Investment Corporation targets a stable risk portfolio that results in a dynamic strategic asset allocation

In determining its SAA, QIC weighed two main options: a stable (targeted) risk portfolio with resultant dynamic SAA, or a stable SAA with resultant risk volatility. In conjunction with QIC's governing body, QIC decided to pursue the first option. Following the decision, QIC crafted a portfolio with asset allocation ranges for each asset class and took into account the risk premiums embedded in each class.

In general, key drivers of *asset risk* are

◆ level of exposure to various risk premiums within the asset allocation parameters,

◆ time-varying levels of various risk premiums: asset class/sub-asset class exposures,

◆ the level and nature of alpha,

◆ risk appetite compared to objectives.

Key drivers of *liability risk*, on the other hand, are

◆ level of exposure to interest rate risk (distribution and duration),

◆ level of exposure to wage inflation risk (distribution and duration),

◆ experience risk (retirement, withdrawal, death, and other areas),

◆ policy risk (approach to funding and employment),

◆ open versus closed schemes.

The Queensland Investment Corporation applies a consistent decision-making process for each of three core risk areas

QIC addresses three core risk themes: portfolio objective risk, liability risk, and asset risk (figure 4.41). For each of these themes, QIC's trustee committee applies a consistent decision-making process, one that involves defining the unambiguous

Figure 4.41 **Risk Themes for Pension Funds**

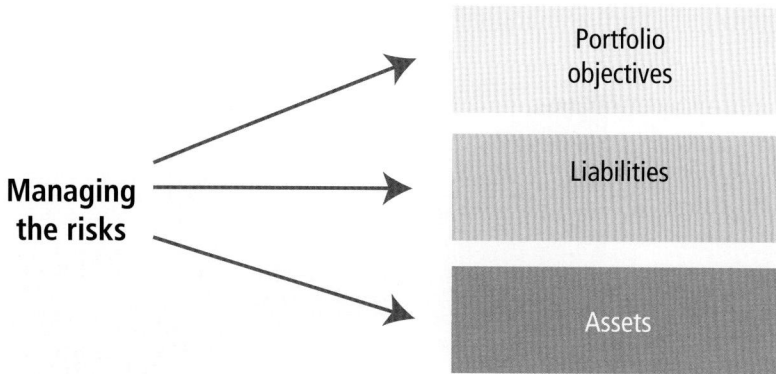

Source: QIC.

objectives of the portfolio and ranking those objectives by scale and importance. This set of objectives then determine the decision-making framework for investment decisions.

In an asset-only world with unmanaged liability risk, investment processes generally allocate funds to asset classes, with a focus on meeting only assets-related objectives. An example is a fund with exposures to equities, fixed income, and property as shown in figure 4.42. An unmanaged liability portfolio, however, typically results in inadequate hedges against movements in interest rates and inflation and overreliance on the equity risk premium, as equities do not provide a stable hedge against interest rates or inflation (Fama and Schwert 1977; Aakko and Litterman 2005). In short, the true risk exposure of a fund with an SAA drawn from an asset-only perspective remains masked. An asset-only managed portfolio backing a defined-benefit plan would result in a risk distribution as shown in figure 4.42: interest rates (40–50 percent), wage inflation (15–20 percent), equities (10–20 percent), alpha (10–15 percent), and credit (0–5 percent).

In a risk-managed asset and liability world, one investment approach would be to design an investment portfolio composed of equities (40 percent), bonds (40 percent), and alternative assets (20 percent), and to overlay this asset allocation with inflation and interest rate swaps (figure 4.43) customized to the liability profile of the fund. In general, QIC's strategy is to manage overlay exposures relative to liabilities in a separate hedge portfolio customized to the liability profile of the fund. Risk distribution in a risk-managed asset and liability portfolio would be significantly different (figure 4.43): equities (40–50 percent), alternatives (20–40 percent), alpha (20–30 percent), interest (10–15 percent), and credit (0–5 percent).

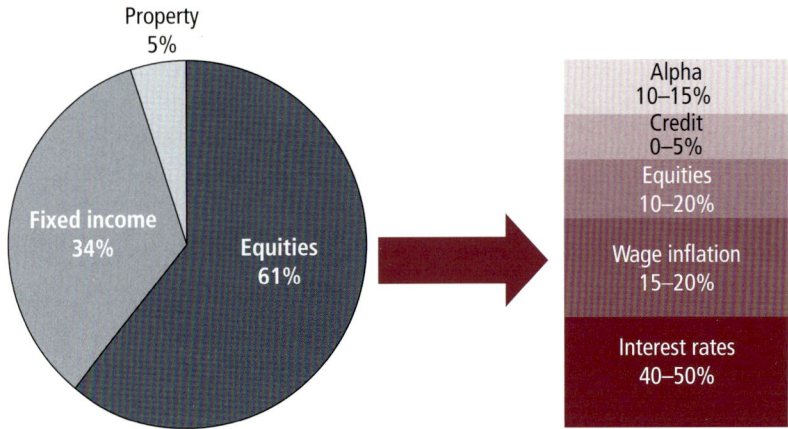

Figure 4.42 **An Illustrative Asset-Only Portfolio with Unmanaged Liability Risks**

Property
5%

Fixed income
34%

Equities
61%

Alpha
10–15%

Credit
0–5%

Equities
10–20%

Wage inflation
15–20%

Interest rates
40–50%

◆ Inadequate hedges against movements in interest rates and inflation
◆ Overreliance on the equity risk premium
◆ Typical strategic asset allocation masks the true risk exposures of the fund

Source: QIC.

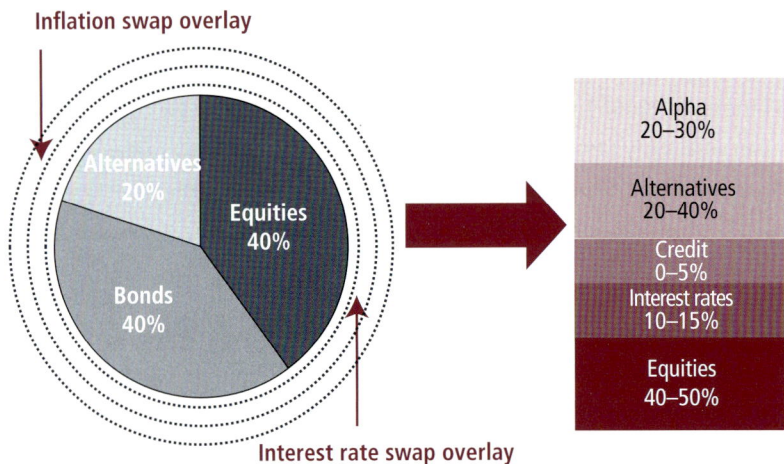

Figure 4.43 **An Illustrative Risk-Managed Asset and Liability Portfolio**

Inflation swap overlay

Alternatives
20%

Equities
40%

Bonds
40%

Alpha
20–30%

Alternatives
20–40%

Credit
0–5%

Interest rates
10–15%

Equities
40–50%

Interest rate swap overlay

Source: QIC.

Note: Overlay references should be to liabilities and then converted to the asset exposures.

Several key measures can help mitigate risks in strategic asset allocation, though the exercise remains challenging

Successful risk mitigation in the SAA exercise can be accomplished by periodically rebalancing a portfolio in order to maintain the long-term objectives. This can be done through several actions: (1) moving from a static SAA framework to a dynamic SAA framework within broad ranges; (2) understanding each asset class and its relationship to key economic drivers and other asset classes; (3) incorporating liability risks into an integrated model with the assets, and managing them holistically; (4) using a wide range of tools (synthetic and physical) to manage risks (for example, inflation or interest rate instruments alongside the other asset classes); (5) managing the instability, and often unpredictability, of alpha risk; and (6) contemplating future prospective outcomes rather than extrapolating from past experience (future paths versus equilibrium levels).

In general, the following are the main challenges involved in an SAA exercise:

◆ Measuring risk—defining the assets and liabilities in a market context

◆ Using synthetic/derivative exposure and instruments at levels that are appropriate for the portfolio or a particular market

◆ Managing liquidity—stress testing risks such as foreign exchange and interest rate exposure

◆ Understanding asset classes in terms of their ability to mitigate wage inflation and interest rate risks

◆ Stress testing objectives: surplus/deficit versus absolute return

References

Aakko, M., and B. Litterman. 2005. "The Active Alpha Framework and Inflation-Protected Securities." In B. Benaben, ed., *Inflation-Linked Products: A Guide for Investors and Asset and Liability Managers*, pp. 247–65.

Fama, E., and G. W. Schwert. 1977. "Asset Return and Inflation." *Journal of Financial Economics* 5: 115–46.

Using Asset-Liability Analysis to Make Consistent Policy Choices: The Approach in the Netherlands

Peter Vlaar, Head of Corporate Asset-Liability Management and Risk Policy, All Pensions Group, the Netherlands

The All Pensions Group of the Netherlands uses asset-liability management analysis to establish an optimal strategic asset allocation and to assist its board of trustees in making appropriate, consistent policy choices. In general, for pension plans, a complicating factor of the investment policy process is that the multiple objectives of pension funds are potentially conflicting, partly because of supervisory rules. Moreover, the fact that future economic developments relating to inflation and interest rates are highly uncertain means that pension funds should gravitate toward policies that perform reasonably well under more than one scenario.

The All Pensions Group, Europe's largest pension provider, has to take the Dutch pension system's indexation and solvency policies into account when formulating its financial strategies

The All Pensions Group (APG) provides asset management, administration, and communication services for several defined-benefit pension funds in the Netherlands. As of mid-2010, APG services pension funds covering 2.7 million active participants. With $325 billion in assets under management, APG is the largest pension provider in Europe and the third largest pension provider in the world.

Within the Dutch pension system, benefits are calculated based on average wages during the course of pensioners' careers. Generally, only a nominal pension is guaranteed, whereas the goal of the system is to provide indexation in line with either average wage or average price increases. Indexation is provided, however, only if the financial position of the pension fund allows it. A pension fund's contribution policy should be consistent with its communicated objectives, including those related to conditional indexation. As indexation cuts affect all vested pension holders, including active workers, they act as the most important recovery mechanism during financial crises.

Solvency requirements established by the regulator of the Dutch pension system are applied only to the guaranteed pension. For all pension funds in the Netherlands, the minimal level of wealth should at all times be at least 105 percent of nominal liabilities (liabilities are measured using the nominal swap curve). If the nominal funded ratio drops below this value, the fund must notify the regulator and show how it will regain solvency within three years. Besides this minimal level of wealth, each pension fund is required to hold a solvency buffer (typically, about 25 percent of nominal liabilities) high enough to prevent insolvency in the one year ahead with 97.5 percent probability. If this buffer is insufficient, the fund has 15 years to recover. The contribution policy of each fund should be consistent with these solvency objectives and policies.

Development of a pension fund's financial strategy covering contribution policy, indexation targets, and investment strategy involves six steps

In general, the process behind development of a pension fund's financial strategy can be decomposed into six steps. A fund must determine

- the pension deal (what results the fund wants to deliver to its members),
- resulting expected cash flows (liabilities),
- the utility function of the board of trustees,
- its policies regarding contribution and indexation,
- its strategic investment plan,
- its current asset mix.

In theory, asset-liability management (ALM) analysis is used by pension funds primarily to determine their policies regarding contribution and indexation and their strategic investment plan, taking the first three steps in the development of a financial strategy as given. In practice, ALM is also used to determine the utility function of the board or even to redesign the pension deal.

Boards of trustees of Dutch pension funds face a trade-off between fulfilling their indexation targets and avoiding binding solvency requirements

While it may be used in only part of the financial strategy process of Dutch pension funds, ALM analysis is an essential step in achieving the multiple and potentially conflicting indexation and solvency objectives established by funds' boards of trustees. The core objective of most Dutch pension funds is to have a high probability of fulfilling their indexation target. To meet this goal, assets providing inflation protection in the long run are favored. At the same time, the boards of trustees seek to avoid binding solvency requirements that apply only to the nominal guarantees. Moreover, as these solvency requirements should always be adhered to, short-term interest rate movements and investment returns also become important. Besides, boards seek a stable contribution rate, thereby allowing for only limited mismatch risk between assets and liabilities. Seeking a stable contribution rate, however, sometimes conflicts with the objective of achieving a low contribution rate. Taking investment risk is necessary to achieve a high probability of meeting indexation targets, and the investment policy must exhibit a long-run perspective.

Objectives of the Board of Trustees of Pension Funds
in the Netherlands

◆ Fulfill indexation objective   ◆ Maintain a stable contribution rate

◆ Avoid binding solvency requirements   ◆ Strive for a low contribution rate

---

Asset-liability management analysis allows APG to manage conflicting objectives and measure risk using forward-looking economic scenarios

ALM analysis reflects the impact of a fund's policy in managing conflicting objectives by taking into account three main areas:

◆ Investment policy—equity versus fixed income, duration of fixed-income investments, and impact of currency and inflation hedges

◆ Indexation policy and its correlation to the funded ratio

◆ Contribution policy

The main indicators APG uses to show the outcomes of its ALM analysis are the pension result (actual pension relative to the objective) over a 15-year horizon, the nominal funded ratio, and the contribution rate. The pension result gives a good indication of whether the goal is realistic, whereas the nominal funded ratio, which is the main indicator for supervisors, helps determine whether the guarantees are at risk. Mean and median results are shown for bad outcomes (for instance, the 5 percent or 10 percent of the worst results) and good outcomes. Moreover, sensitivity analyses are performed in order to take account of the uncertainty regarding long-run returns. Apart from examining the most likely economic environment, ALM analysis also studies scenarios under unfavorable circumstances emerging from factors such as low mean equity premiums, high mean inflation, or low mean interest rates. All economic environments are forward looking, meaning that expected future rates or returns may deviate from historical values.

APG has analyzed the impact of using interest rate versus inflation swaps and found that using a combination of the two is optimal

Figure 4.44 shows an example of the impact of ALM analysis on interest rate and inflation swaps over a 15-year time horizon. The left column illustrates the impact of incremental interest rate swaps: from a no-interest-rate swaps scenario on the left to 100 percent hedging of remaining interest rate risk of the funded ratio on the right. The center column shows the impact of hedging inflation risk, from no hedge to 80 percent hedging. The right column combines the two: 20 percent of the inflation risk is always hedged, while the figures show the consequences of hedging the remaining interest rate risk, from 0 to 100 percent. The top row shows the probability that the pension result after 15 years is at least 90 percent. The center row depicts the median nominal funded ratio after 15 years. The bottom row plots the probability that the funded ratio will be below 100 percent in any of the first 15 years. The contribution rate was held constant for all scenarios in this exercise and therefore it is not depicted.

As the column on the left indicates, closing about 50 percent of the interest rate gap provides better outcomes in the expected economic environment, resulting in a somewhat higher probability of an indexed pension, a higher median funded ratio, and a much lower probability of underfunding than if no interest rate swaps were used. If inflation picks up, however, the interest rate swap will cost money and the pension fund will be able to provide less indexation, especially if the inflation rise is permanent.

As shown in the second column of figure 4.44, these trends are more or less the other way around when a pension fund uses inflation swaps. In the expected economic environment, the swap will cost money and it will not improve the indexation quality, whereas the impact on the funded ratio is negative. If the average inflation rates are higher than expected, however, the protection bought with the inflation swaps improves the results. Since investment managers cannot accurately forecast long-term inflation and interest rates, they are advised to opt for a combined hedging strategy, as illustrated in the third column of figure 4.44. Indeed, the combined strategy seems to perform reasonably well in all inflation scenarios.

To further illustrate the effectiveness of the combined swap strategy, figure 4.45 compares the probability of a pension result higher than 90 percent over the 15-year

Figure 4.44 Illustrative Results for Dutch Pension Funds' Swap Strategies over a 15-Year Horizon

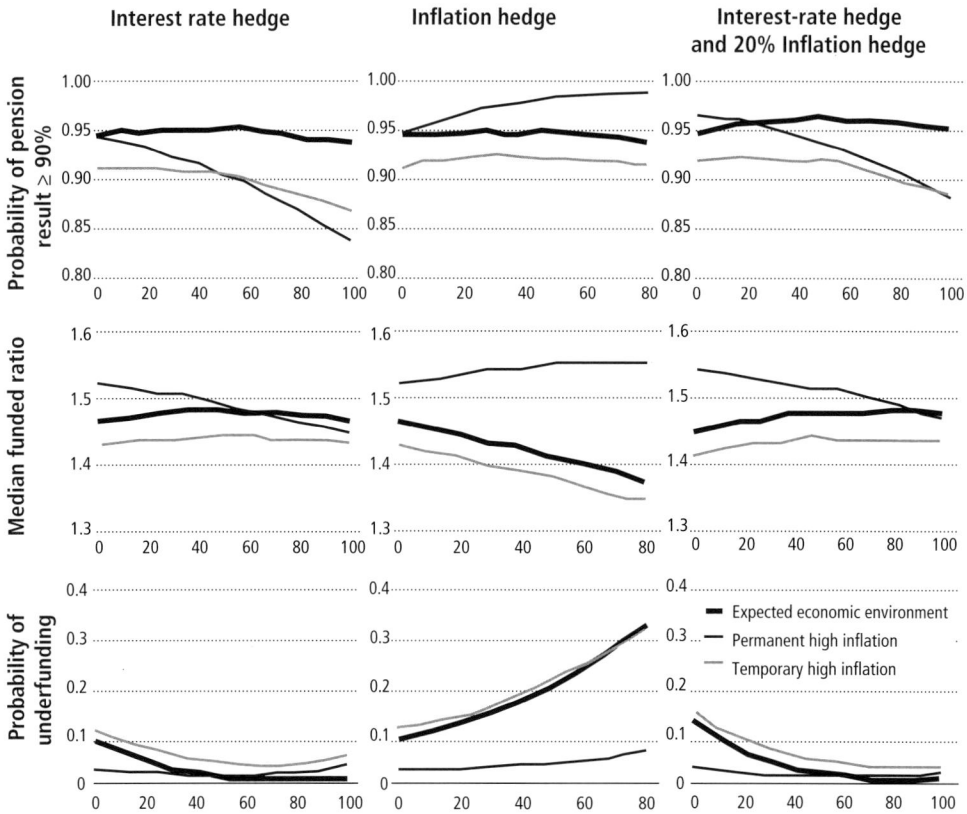

Source: APG.

simulation horizon using the original portfolio with no swaps and a portfolio with 25 percent interest rate swaps and 20 percent inflation swaps. In every year and under all three economic environments, the swap-augmented portfolio provides a higher probability of meeting indexation targets. ALM simulations such as these facilitate pension funds' cost-benefit analysis and decision-making process in applying appropriate swap strategies.

Conclusion

For pension funds, ALM can provide insights into potential outcomes under different expected future economic environments resulting from various investment strategies. This helps boards choose the appropriate investment strategy in a consistent manner. The choice of investment strategy reflects both a board's utility

Figure 4.45 **Impact of Swap Strategies on Pension Result over Time: Probability of Pension Result ≥ 90%**

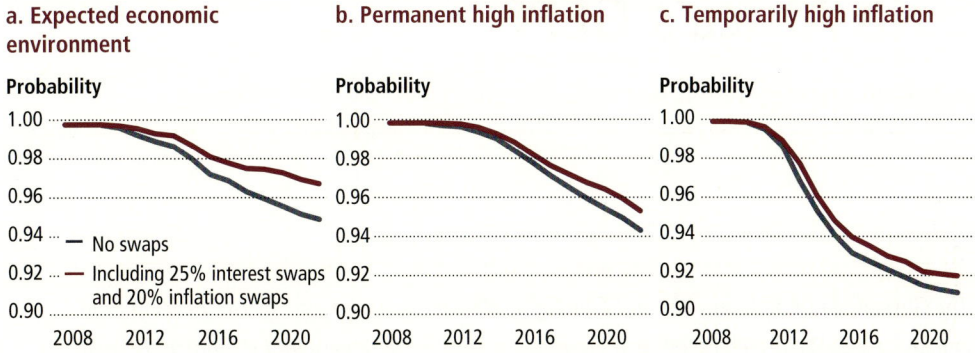

a. Expected economic environment

Probability

1.00	
0.98	
0.96	
0.94	— No swaps
0.92	— Including 25% interest swaps
0.90	and 20% inflation swaps

2008   2012   2016   2020

b. Permanent high inflation

Probability

1.00
0.98
0.96
0.94
0.92
0.90

2008   2012   2016   2020

c. Temporarily high inflation

Probability

1.00
0.98
0.96
0.94
0.92
0.90

2008   2012   2016   2020

Source: APG.

function (as defined by its contribution and indexation policies) and the weight the board assigns to different expected future economic environments. In the Netherlands, APG uses ALM analysis to help establish its investment strategy (embodied in its strategic asset allocation) and to help its board make appropriate policy choices relating to contribution and indexation.

Determining Investment Strategy from the Liability Structure: South Africa's GEPF

John Oliphant, Head of Investments, Government Employees Pension Fund, South Africa*

The Government Employees Pension Fund of South Africa, the largest African pension fund, employs a liability-driven investment approach to maximize returns and minimize risk relative to liabilities, a strategy that worked successfully even during the 2008–09 global financial crisis. The key to successful implementation of the liability-driven investment approach, which focuses on pension fund assets in the context of promises made to members and pensioners, lies in understanding pension funds' current and long-term obligations achieved by setting liability portfolio cash flows as the benchmark and accounting for all decrements that can potentially affect such cash flows. To accurately forecast its future cash flows, the Government Employees Pension Fund has calculated separate projections for active members, pensioners, and active members and pensioners combined. Cash flow projections combined with asset class return assumptions have then been used to derive optimal portfolios for each level of risk relative to liabilities.

Investment strategies for pension funds—both in South Africa and globally—have evolved and become more sophisticated in recent years

The Government Employees Pension Fund (GEPF) of South Africa is the largest pension fund in Africa in terms of both assets under management ($100 billion) and membership (1.2 million active members and 320,000 pensioners). It is one of the few defined-benefit schemes in South Africa with the government as its main sponsor. GEPF is managed by a 16-member board of trustees that includes 8 employer representatives, 7 employee representatives, and 1 pensioner representative. Under law, GEPF's investment strategy is developed in consultation with South Africa's minister of finance.

* The author would like to thank the research team of RisCura for assistance with data analysis, financial modeling, and preparation of graphs.

248

Significant developments in the management of pension assets and creation of new and complex financial instruments have taken place in South Africa and globally over the past several decades. In the past, the focus in South Africa was on using pension contributions to buy insurance products, while today the liability structure of the GEPF scheme is central in determining an appropriate investment strategy for the fund. Figure 4.46 traces the evolutionary process for pension funds, beginning with the development of insurance products; continuing with the development of techniques such as strategic asset allocation, risk budgeting, and manager modeling; and ending in the creation of more sophisticated investment strategies (such as liability-driven investment, or LDI) and measurements.

Figure 4.46 **Evolution of Pension Products and Strategies**

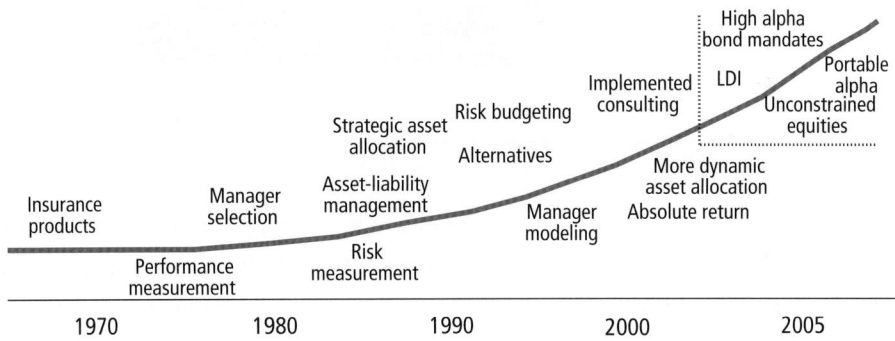

Source: Watson Wyatt Worldwide.

Liability-driven investment differs from other investment strategies in that it focuses on both assets and liabilities

LDI is an investment strategy intended to maximize returns while minimizing risk relative to liabilities. In an LDI framework, a focus on assets is replaced by a focus on both assets and liabilities, meaning that a pension fund's managers need to gain an understanding of both the portfolio's objectives and the universe of investable assets. At the individual pension fund level, understanding the structure of liabilities and how liabilities are affected under different economic scenarios is critical to determining an appropriate investment strategy. Figure 4.47 reviews an LDI investment strategy exercise performed by GEPF.

As a general rule, pension funds must ensure that they have adequate assets to meet their pension payment commitments. Fund managers should thus have a good understanding of the extent of their current liabilities to pensioners and of their future liabilities to active and contributing members. Figure 4.48 presents

Figure 4.47 **GEPF's LDI Exercise: Strategy Overview**

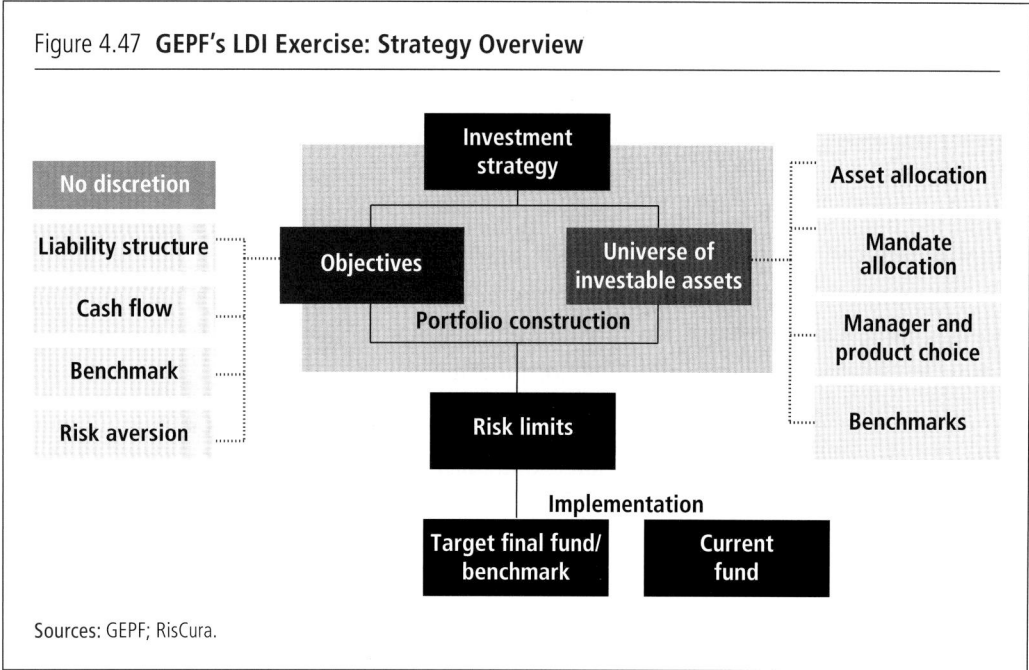

Sources: GEPF; RisCura.

GEPF's estimation of such liabilities. After setting liability portfolio cash flows as a benchmark, pension fund managers typically build a portfolio that matches those cash flows. Deviations from this optimal portfolio are supported only if the potential rewards outweigh the additional risk. A second step in the process of pension fund managers fully understanding a fund's liabilities includes recognizing and modeling all decrements that will lead to a reduction in future payment obligations (such as members' death, health issues, withdrawals, or retirement). All of these decrements may affect the fund's asset composition and cash flow projections.

Pension funds can use a combination of cash flow projections and assumptions for various asset classes to derive optimal portfolios

In order to more fully understand their obligations and the factors affecting those obligations, pension funds should produce projections of future cash flows for each group of members separately. Figure 4.49 provides a summary of GEPF's cash flow projections for active members, pensioners, and active members and pensioners combined, giving an overall liability profile of the fund.

Using a combination of cash flow projections and return assumptions for various asset classes, pension funds can derive optimal portfolios for each level of risk relative to liabilities. A comparison of the current GEPF portfolio with seven alter-

Figure 4.48 **GEPF's Liability Estimations**

ACTIVE MEMBERS

a. Types

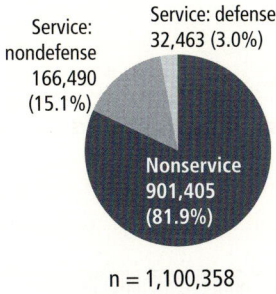

Service: nondefense 166,490 (15.1%)

Service: defense 32,463 (3.0%)

Nonservice 901,405 (81.9%)

n = 1,100,358

PENSIONERS

d. Types

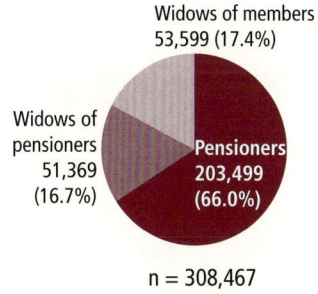

Widows of members 53,599 (17.4%)

Widows of pensioners 51,369 (16.7%)

Pensioners 203,499 (66.0%)

n = 308,467

b. Total salaries versus age

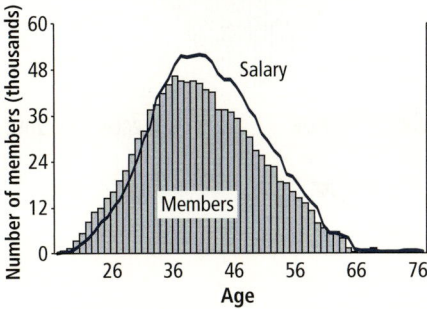

e. Total pensions versus age

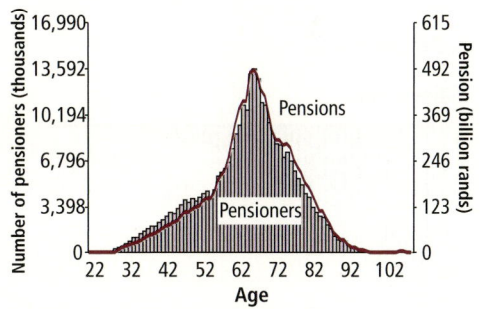

c. Range of salaries versus age

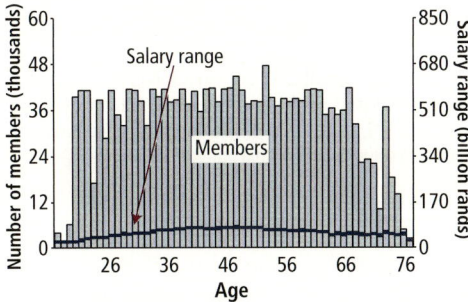

f. Range of pensions versus age

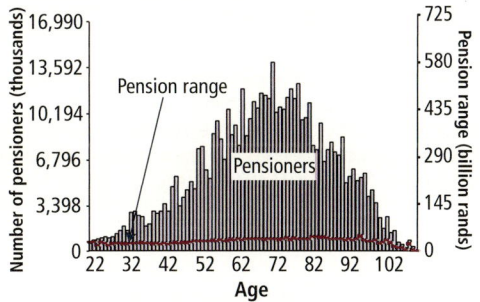

Sources: GEPF; RisCura.

native optimal scenarios is illustrated in figure 4.50. It is important to note that all seven scenario portfolios are below the efficient frontier; this is the case because the efficient frontier is built without taking into account the regulatory constraints, whereas the seven scenarios have been constructed incorporating these constraints. However, all the scenarios, which are at different risk levels, appear to be closer to the unconstrained efficient frontier than GEPF's current portfolio, with the

Figure 4.49 **GEPF's Projected Cash Flows, 2007–82**

a. Active members

Billion rands

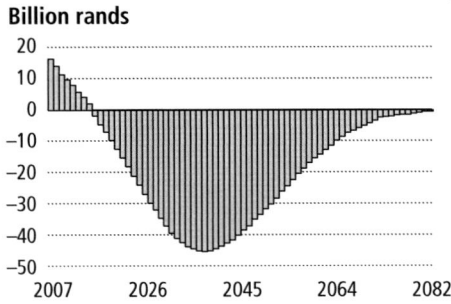

c. Active members and pensioners

Billion rands

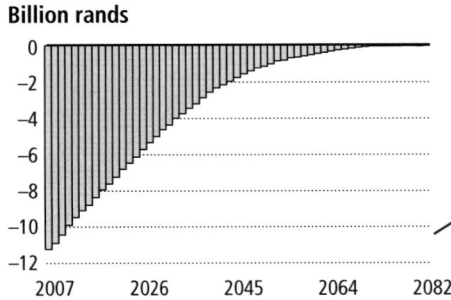

b. Pensioners

Billion rands

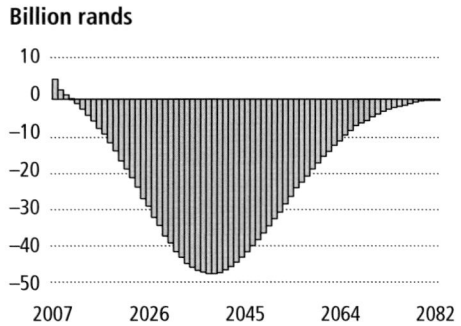

Sources: GEPF; RisCura.

Note: Fixed-income assets used to meet total future cash flows for active members of GEPF are estimated to have a duration of 33 years, convexity of 1,016, and yield to maturity (YTM) of 3.9 percent. Assets used to meet projected future cash flows for pensioners are estimated to have a duration of 8.7 years, convexity of 139, and YTM of 4.3 percent. Combined future cash flows for active members and pensioners require fixed-income asset compositions with a duration of 26.4 years, convexity of 779, and YTM of 3.9 percent.

portfolio of the fourth scenario being the closest. It is also notable that all seven scenarios result in higher risk along with the expectation of higher returns.

Because they generate cash flows similar to the liability structure of the GEPF, inflation-linked bonds appear to be appropriate investments for low-risk portfolios. However, if a pension fund's objective is for its assets to outperform its liabilities (as is the case for GEPF), it should combine inflation-linked bonds with an appropriate level of growth-oriented assets, such as equities, to maximize the return per unit of additional risk. Asset allocations for portfolios with different levels of risk relative to liabilities are summarized in figure 4.51.

Figure 4.50 **GEPF's Current Portfolio Allocation versus Alternative Allocations**

Efficient frontier (total)

Real surplus return (%)

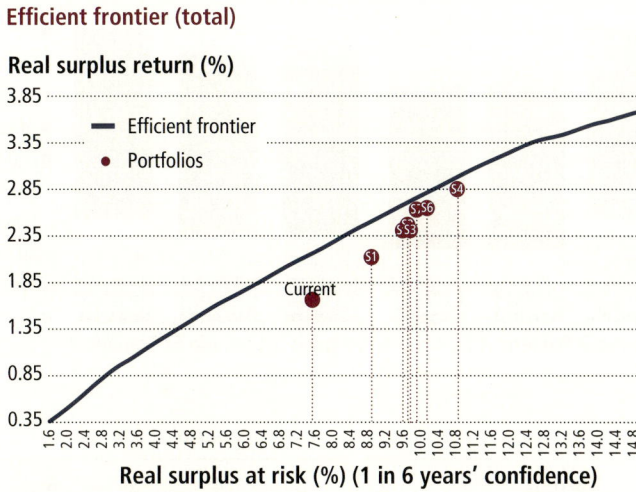

Real surplus at risk (%) (1 in 6 years' confidence)

Optimal asset allocation

Asset allocation (%)

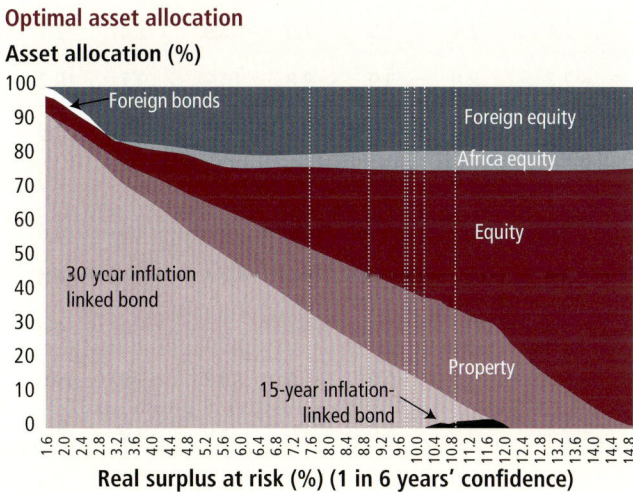

Real surplus at risk (%) (1 in 6 years' confidence)

Sources: GEPF; RisCura.

As of mid-2010, about 50 percent of GEPF's assets ($47 billion) were invested in equities, making GEPF the largest investor in most of the companies listed on the Johannesburg Stock Exchange. On average, GEPF owns 10 percent of issued shares in each publicly traded South African company. GEPF's equity portfolio is passively managed, because adding value through active management is almost impossible. Active trading in shares of companies in which the fund is so heavily invested would result in significant price movements of such shares, and thus can be self-defeating. Restrictions on offshore investing further limit GEPF's investment strategy. Going

Figure 4.51 **Recommended Asset Allocations for GEPF under Different Scenarios**

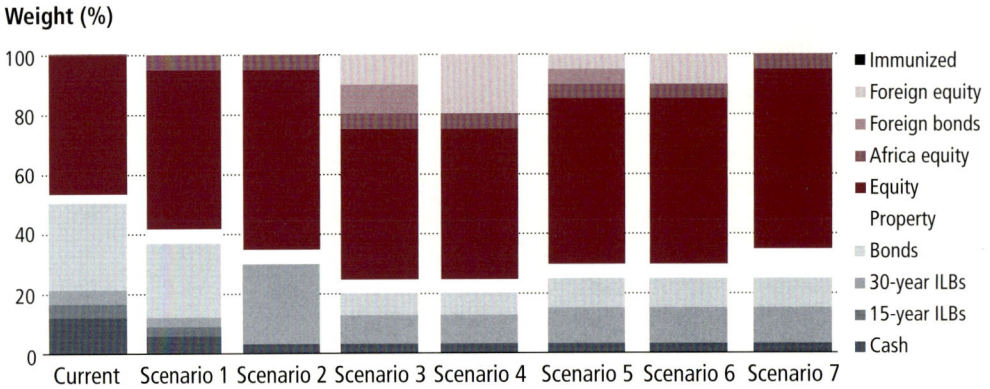

	Current	Scenario						
		1	2	3	4	5	6	7
Real surplus return	1.6	2.1	2.5	2.5	2.9	2.4	2.7	2.6
Real surplus risk	7.7	8.9	9.9	9.8	10.9	9.7	10.2	10.1
Cash	12.1	6.0	3.0	3.0	3.0	3.0	3.0	3.0
15-year inflation-linked bonds	4.7	3.0	0.0	0.0	0.0	0.0	0.0	0.0
30-year inflation-linked bonds	4.7	3.0	27.0	10.0	10.0	12.0	12.0	12.0
Bonds	28.9	25.0	0.0	7.0	7.0	10.0	10.0	10.0
Property	3.1	5.0	5.0	5.0	5.0	5.0	5.0	10.0
Equity	46.5	53.0	60.0	50.0	50.0	55.0	55.0	60.0
Africa equity	0.1	5.0	5.0	5.0	5.0	5.0	5.0	5.0
Foreign bonds	0.0	0.0	0.0	10.0	0.0	5.0	0.0	0.0
Foreign equity	0.0	0.0	0.0	10.0	20.0	5.0	10.0	0.0
Immunized	0.0	0.0	0.0	0.0	0.0	0.0	0.0	0.0

Sources: GEPF; RisCura.

forward, GEPF needs to diversify away from domestic equities and toward other asset classes with similar risk and return characteristics. Without such adjustment, the size of the domestic equity market relative to GEPF's equity portfolio will lead to undue market concentration risks and result in distortions in pricing.

Conclusion

Because they are dealing with a defined-benefit pension fund, GEPF's managers prefer an LDI approach, which ensures that contribution rates remain relatively stable and that liabilities and assets move in a synchronized manner in the same direction. Over time, the strategy has worked well for GEPF, even during the 2008–09 global financial crisis. GEPF has been able to honor its commitment to members by granting inflation-related increases while maintaining a healthy financial position.

4. In-House Investment versus Outsourcing to External Investment Managers

◆ Evaluating Internal and External Management of Assets: New Trends among Pension Funds

◆ In-House Investment Management by Public Pension Funds: Risks and Risk Mitigation Strategies

Evaluating Internal and External Management of Assets: New Trends among Pension Funds

Jolanta Wysocka, Chief Executive Officer, Mountain Pacific Group, United States

Though using in-house investment management is usually more cost-effective and essential to strengthening other aspects of investment activities than using external management, it is often difficult for the public sector to attract and retain appropriate staff, or to provide the incentive structure needed to engage in high-risk/high-return investment strategies. Overall, certain investment strategies lend themselves naturally to internal management, while others usually are better managed by external managers. That said, the importance of appropriate governance structures in effectively managing both internal and external managers cannot be overemphasized. Among large pension funds, there is a growing trend for bringing more investment activities in house, and for close collaboration with external investment managers in crafting tailored investment solutions that meet the specific needs of the fund rather than handing out standard investment mandates.

The trade-offs involved in choosing between internal and external investment management are significant—particularly in terms of costs, monitoring infrastructure, confidentiality, and investment discipline

There are significant trade-offs involved in using external managers to invest a pension fund's assets versus managing these investments in house. Governance and implementation aspects need to be carefully considered when employing external experts. For pension funds and other large institutional investors, the greatest impact on investment returns comes from fund-level asset allocation, both strategic and tactical. The pension sponsor determines the fund's risk tolerance and investment horizon decisions, and while external experts can be retained to assist with these decisions, the responsibility for and governance of same cannot be outsourced.

The world is moving toward specialization and outsourcing, and managing pension assets is no exception. The decision about whether to in-source or outsource a particular investment area is a function of fund size, objectives, and availability of staff with appropriate skills sets. Success in asset management depends on managing and developing human capital. The chief factor here is the ability to identify, attract, inspire, and retain key professionals.

There are considerable cost trade-offs when assessing internal investment managers against external. Though external managers, in many cases, offer stronger and more specialized investment expertise than internal managers, they also typically come at a higher cost. On the other hand, it is not uncommon for large public pension funds' internal staff costs for investment management to be less than 10 percent of total management costs.[1] This provides a strong incentive for bringing investment management in house. Using internal investment managers, however, comes with its own set of challenges. The remuneration policies of many public funds simply do not allow them to attract and retain top staff. If internal investment managers develop an attractive track record, they can be lured away by the private sector. If they do not perform well, the fund faces higher headline risk or the equally difficult issue of layoffs and restaffing.

In addition to low cost, there are other major advantages in building up internal expertise within public pension funds. Such expertise includes the ability to adequately monitor and evaluate the investment performance of external managers, and to ensure better alignment of their mandates and investment guidelines with the pension fund's overall investment objectives. Another advantage of having an in-house investment team is the ability to better maintain the confidentiality of investment decisions.

At the same time, internal investment managers may be more vulnerable to making investments that are justified by noneconomic arguments. These pressures, even if well intended, may shift the fund's objectives from maximizing returns for all plan members to benefiting specific groups.

Initial strategies for internal investment management typically involve liquid fixed-income instruments

When pension funds begin managing assets internally, they usually start with allocations to the most liquid and high-quality asset classes. To minimize invest-

---

[1] Mountain Pacific Group's estimate based on discussions with various pension funds including those of IBM and General Motors, and the California Public Employees' Retirement System.

ment risk, internal investment managers typically establish an index or quasi-index with low risk and institute core mandates. These same aspects can be extended to undertaking rule-based investment internally. In many cases, public pension funds manage domestic fixed-income and domestic equity investments in house. The low-risk, index-like strategies used for such investments are generally easier to manage than specialized or high-risk strategies in the context of public funds.

It is especially important that internal investment management does not result in large losses, as internal failures are disruptive to a fund's larger management process

For all pension funds, it is especially important to avoid large losses when using internally managed investment programs. If external managers cause large losses, their services can be easily terminated. If internally managed investments result in large losses, however, their replacement or termination can be highly disruptive to the entire management process, as internal politics within the fund become difficult to manage.

It can also be extremely difficult to maintain an internal investment team's long-term focus if there has been a highly visible investment loss, even if the loss amounts to a small percentage of the overall portfolio value. One Australian fund, for example, lost a tiny percentage of its portfolio value (equivalent to less than one week's normal fluctuation in the value of the overall fund) by investing in a failed infrastructure deal. However, media attention to the event caused the fund's senior management to spend a significant amount of time handling criticism of the investment. In another case, a Japanese pension fund lost money on a small investment in securitized structures, resulting in massively disproportionate media attention. Such examples create an enormous disincentive for internal investment managers to invest in high-risk/high-return assets, even though such high-risk investments may be particularly suitable for long-term funds.

Internal investment management is more likely to be successful if the fund

◆ has little headline risk and low external pressure,

◆ is not subject to major political agendas for the use of its assets,

◆ can put in place competitive remuneration programs to attract and retain quality staff,

◆ has empowered its senior staff with broad discretion to take risks (subject to proper due diligence and reporting),

◆ has knowledgeable senior staff and governing body members—either an empowered chief investment officer (CIO) or board member(s) who can approve new investments initiatives quickly.

External managers are generally engaged to design strategies related to derivatives, currency overlay and hedging, and to structure international equity, venture capital, private equity, and hedge fund investments (figure 4.52).

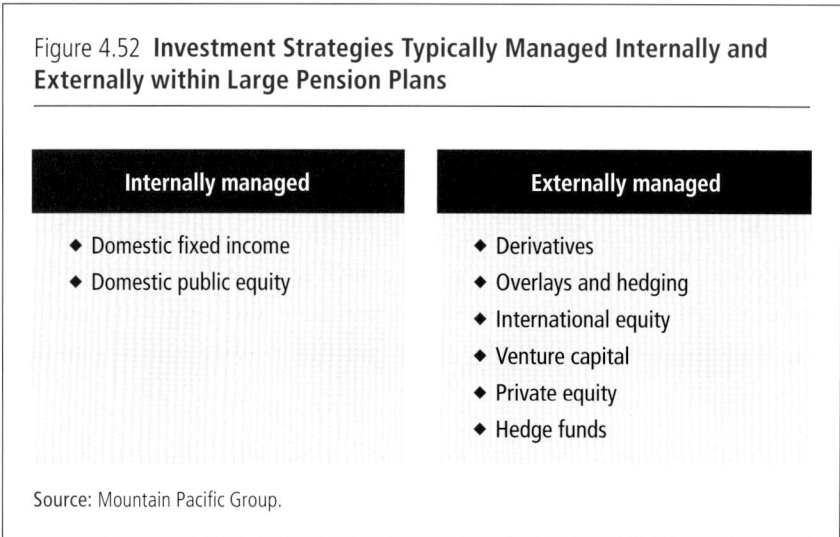

Figure 4.52 **Investment Strategies Typically Managed Internally and Externally within Large Pension Plans**

Internally managed	Externally managed
◆ Domestic fixed income	◆ Derivatives
◆ Domestic public equity	◆ Overlays and hedging
	◆ International equity
	◆ Venture capital
	◆ Private equity
	◆ Hedge funds

Source: Mountain Pacific Group.

A pension fund's investment governance framework should clearly delineate the responsibilities, accountabilities, and reporting structure of all parties involved

Clearly delineated responsibilities, accountabilities, and reporting relationships are imperative in the implementation of a pension fund's investment governance strategy. The board's responsibilities should include setting investment objectives, conducting independent oversight, and ensuring that its members have adequate investment experience upon appointment. Consultants to the board need to regularly report to the board, educate the board, and design and perform independent checks on the CIO. The CIO and his or her staff report to the board, implement objectives set by the board, supervise internal management, and select and oversee performance of external managers. Consultants to the CIO report to the CIO, assist in investment strategy implementation, and perform manager research. Table 4.5 summarizes the accountabilities of the various parties involved in this process.

Table 4.5 **Roles and Accountabilities of Pension Funds' Governing Body, Staff, and Consultants**

Entity	Roles and responsibilities
Board	◆ Set objectives ◆ Independent oversight ◆ Board members with investment experience
Consultant to the board	◆ Reports to the board ◆ Educate the board ◆ Independent check on the CIO
CIO and staff	◆ Report to the board ◆ Implement objectives set by the board ◆ Internal management ◆ Selection and oversight of external managers
Consultant to the CIO	◆ Reports to the CIO ◆ Assists in strategy ◆ Manager research

Source: Mountain Pacific Group.

Practical guidelines for the effective management of internal investment managers are similar to those for external managers

Several practical management issues arise in the process of employing both external and internal investment managers, including the role of consultants, avoiding conflicts of interest, headline risk, using a fund of hedge funds versus selection of individual hedge fund managers, internal management of private equity, and encouraging pension funds to work together.

A key question is the role of the board in such organizations. Noninvestment boards set broad policy themes, while investment boards have vast investment expertise and in some cases may override the CIO in making direct investment decisions. Operational challenges for governing bodies include overseeing internal and external investment mandates in a manner that ensures sound risk management at a reasonable cost, and with expectations of positive excess return. As figure 4.53 indicates, effective management of internal and external managers requires having the right governance structure, the right incentives, and the right people.

Figure 4.53 **Requirements for Effective Management of Internal and External Managers**

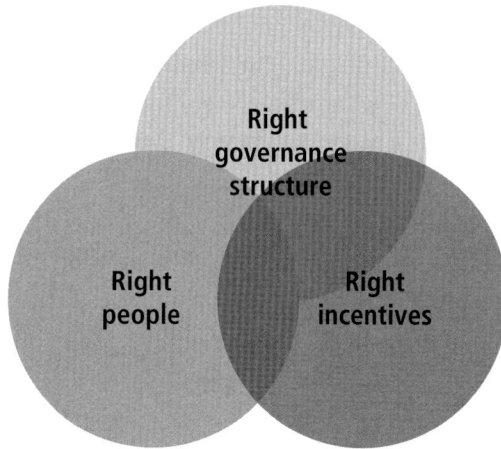

Right governance structure

Right people

Right incentives

Source: Mountain Pacific Group.

Selecting an appropriate number of external managers is crucial to the overall performance of the fund

There is a growing tendency among large pension funds, particularly those in the United States, toward internal management of assets. One obvious reason for this trend is the need to reduce costs, but the desire to enhance a fund's human capital by challenging internal staff to manage assets is also a factor. Another factor is the difficulty in effectively monitoring the large number of external managers typically used by the big pension funds. While hiring, monitoring, evaluating, and terminating external managers may take a lot of staff time and effort, the contribution of a single external manager to the overall portfolio return of a large pension fund is relatively small. On the other hand, small pension funds (those with assets less than $2 billion) may not have sufficient capacity for efficient monitoring of external managers and as a result use too few managers. Individual manager selection decisions may, as a result, have a disproportionate impact on the overall investment performance of a small pension fund.

As a result of these factors, leading large pension funds are migrating to a new model in which they work closely with managers to meet the fund's specific investment needs. At a minimum, this constitutes better reporting and better information gathering, the latter of which can be used to support the fund's overall investment activities. At the maximum, this represents closer collaboration with the manager to create a tailored solution to the particular issues facing the fund.

A key catalyst behind the use of this new model is the observation that innovations in finance over the past 30 years were driven by sell-side institutions. Developed by the sell side in order to accomplish its goals, these structures generally were not optimal for investors. Examples of such structures are bond indexes, which have duration characteristics far too short for most institutional investors.

Conclusion

Going forward, there is expected to be a trend among pension funds (representing, as they do, the buy side) to demand and create tailored solutions for their needs and goals. To do this, funds must have skilled, knowledgeable staff, and funds' boards should focus as much time on the development of their internal human capital as they do on reviewing external managers. Starting internal management programs can be a useful step in developing this human capital, though they require appropriate governance and oversight structures. Many leading pension funds around the world have already experienced the long-term benefits of implementing human capital development programs.

In-House Investment Management by Public Pension Funds: Risks and Risk Mitigation Strategies

Adriaan Ryder, Managing Director, Queensland Investment Corporation, Australia

For public pension funds, the choice between internal and external investment management is an important one that involves not only selection of an investment manager but also consideration of a range of investment strategies and principles. In general, pension funds seek high-performance managers capable of generating alpha at reasonable costs to the fund. Often, external managers have an advantage over internal managers in terms of investment expertise, though there are circumstances in which internal investment management is more advantageous. Because they are subject to less governance rigor than external managers, internal investment managers should be subject to continuous performance evaluation, and steps to mitigate the risk of their poor performance should be taken.

Many factors, including managers' specific expertise, level of costs, unique investment processes, motivations, and direct market access should be considered in selecting internal investment managers

Several key strategies and principles need to be considered when pension funds are deciding between internal and external investment management, not least of which are methods for reviewing management performance and minimizing poor performance. As the number of experts with specialized knowledge has increased significantly in recent decades, access to "best of breed" managers and enhanced investment processes has never been easier. Given this, the key rationale to consider when choosing pension fund investment managers includes the managers' specific expertise, level of costs, unique investment processes, motivations, and direct market access. Additionally, it is important to recognize that investment managers' strategies have different degrees of effectiveness in different economic or market cycles. For internal pension fund investment managers, it is essential to be able to develop and maintain a leading edge and a meaningful investment culture and

264

operational strategy over an extended period of time. Pension funds must also have the ability to meet remuneration objectives and to attract and retain capable staff.

Given the wealth of management expertise available externally and the benefits that external investment managers can bring, it is necessary, in some sense, for public pension funds to justify development and selection of an internal investment management team. Prior to deciding to make in-house investments, it is advisable that pension funds' decision makers focus and agree on the strategies they want such internal investment managers to employ. Strategies can include strategic asset allocation, beta strategies (with a distinction between listed and unlisted securities), and alpha strategies (figure 4.54).

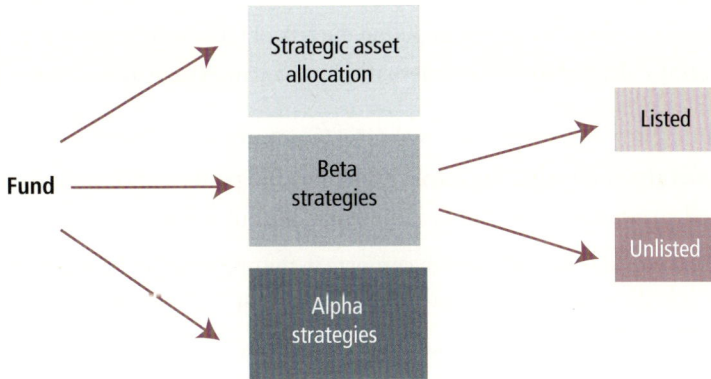

Figure 4.54 **Internal Investment Management in the Face of a Wealth of Global Expertise**

Draw some distinctions…

Fund → Strategic asset allocation

Fund → Beta strategies → Listed / Unlisted

Fund → Alpha strategies

Source: QIC.

Though it is difficult to identify strategies that will consistently generate pure alpha, some unlisted asset classes and alternative assets may provide such opportunities. Alpha strategies frequently require long investment horizons to prove that they can add value, particularly those involving unlisted markets. The ability to craft and implement investment strategies, without their becoming public information, is also key in the alpha generation process. Internal investment managers may be able to implement such strategies at a lower cost than external managers, especially those involving unlisted asset classes. In addition, an in-depth understanding of asset classes by the internal teams provides the value added of a direct "market feel" from within the pension fund. Full, continuous insight into all internal portfolio holdings is also essential to minimizing costs and managing risks.

Setting up appropriate measures and monitoring tools can mitigate many risks involved with using internal investment managers, especially the risk of poor investment performance

With respect to long-term sustainability, some investment strategies are relevant only in certain parts of the growth, interest rate, inflation, and market cycles. Similarly, some strategies are required only when risk premiums are high, and should be eliminated when risk premiums are too narrow. Internal investment teams typically are not subject to the same level of governance rigor as external managers (who usually are subject to ongoing review and evaluation by several independent consultants, as standard industry practice). Sometimes resulting pension funds' senior management has insufficient independence of judgment and objectivity when evaluating internal investment managers. Further, it is often difficult for many organizations to remove individuals or teams in the event of poor performance. Motivating individuals and internal teams over extended periods can be challenging for large funds, which build exposures over a long time.

Numerous methods exist for mitigating the risk of these sorts of poor performance. In general, risks related to poor internal investment management can be mitigated by

- third-party assessment and overview (for example, by investment consultants assessing and evaluating team capabilities and performance, and management and governance committees acting upon the outcomes);
- allowing internal managers to compete in the open market for mandates, which results in a virtuous circle of review, assessment, and growth;
- de-risking underperforming strategies, with consequent outcomes;
- eliminating underperforming strategies, individuals, and teams within a strong governance framework;
- developing a strong investment culture, with a commitment to excellence;
- ensuring that remuneration and compensation are competitive;
- establishing very tightly defined mandates and benchmarks, with continuous review.

Conclusion

Among the numerous challenges that public pension fund managers face in the current economic environment are decisions regarding allocation of their investment portfolios to internal versus external managers, strategic asset allocation strategies, alpha and beta strategies, identification of high-alpha managers (in a "zero sum game" universe), and ensuring persistence of above-average performance. While there may be sound reasons to embark on internal management for certain investment strategies, a careful evaluation of the risks and implementation of several suggested risk mitigation strategies can help ensure successful outcomes.

5. International Investments and Managing the Resulting Currency Risk

- A Framework for Evaluating International Diversification and Optimal Currency Exposure

- International Investments: Developing a Strategy to Manage Currency Risk

- Managing the International Investments of Pension Funds in Latin America

- International Diversification and Hedging: The Netherlands' All Pensions Group

A Framework for Evaluating International Diversification and Optimal Currency Exposure

Tørres Trovik, Assistant Director of Risk Management, Storebrand, Norway

Expanding investments into foreign markets carries both benefits and risks for public pension funds. Currency risk is an important consideration in such investments and needs to be analyzed and managed separately. Analysis suggests that pension funds should focus on a global hedge ratio for their overall portfolio (domestic and international) rather than hedge individual asset classes separately. Due to potential diversification benefits from currencies—in particular if the allocation to foreign markets is low—a 100 percent hedge ratio is rarely optimal. Optimal hedging policy is strongly dependent on the strategic asset allocation of each particular fund, and conclusions are hard to generalize.

Diversifying equity investments internationally can reduce a portfolio's volatility

Though the traditional reason for diversifying investments internationally is to reach a broader economic base in a globalized economy, increasing correlation of equity returns in different countries suggests that gains from diversification may not be as strong as they once were. Levels of equity market and currency correlations, as well as underlying volatilities, influence the effect of diversification. As shown in table 4.6, volatility in various equity markets has varied substantially over the past three decades.

And as suggested in figure 4.55, though the reduction in volatility achieved from diversifying equity investments to multiple countries has varied over different time periods, it is still substantial in the most recent period. Analysis of a broader data set indicates that the benefit of international diversification is particularly acute for an investor based outside the United States. This is due to the generally higher level of risk in equity markets that are less diversified than the larger U.S. market. Even though correlations of equity returns in different countries have increased, there is

---

Table 4.6 **Annualized Equity Market Volatility, 1975–2009 (Local Currency)**

Country	Percentage
United States	16.0
Switzerland	17.0
Canada	17.7
Japan	18.7
Netherlands	19.0
Australia	19.3
United Kingdom	19.4
Hong Kong, China	19.7
New Zealand	20.7
Germany	20.9
France	21.8
Spain	23.8
Sweden	24.0
Italy	30.3
Finland	33.7

Sources: Datastream and World Bank.

---

still a wide dispersion in volatility across countries. That said, the marginal benefit of international diversification to the overall portfolio performance decreases with an increase of the number of international equity markets diversified into and appears to be exhausted after a portfolio is invested in six to seven different equity markets.

Currency risk/return trade-off and embeddedness of currency risk in international asset returns are important considerations when diversifying a portfolio internationally

Figure 4.56 depicts the value of various currencies over the past 108 years compared to returns from U.S. equities and fixed-income instruments. The risk premium for equities and fixed income is evident in their upward-trending graphs. Currency returns, on the other hand, do not exhibit a similar long-term

Figure 4.55 **Effect of Investment Diversification over Different Time Periods and in Different Equity Markets (Local Currency)**

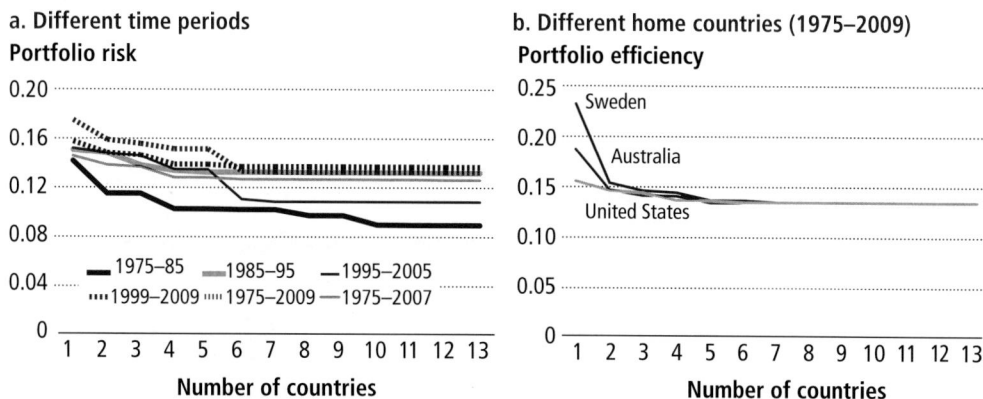

a. Different time periods
Portfolio risk

b. Different home countries (1975–2009)
Portfolio efficiency

Sources: Datastream and World Bank.

risk premium; rather, currencies are mainly characterized by long periods of no trending followed by large, sudden changes in their levels. Often, these changes are due to major events such as international conflicts or adjustments to the global exchange rate system. In the sample of currencies examined in figure 4.56, it is possible to identify somewhat different patterns for emerging market currencies such as the Chinese renminbi, South African rand, and Korean won—which have been prone to trending and regime shifts in recent years—than for developed market currencies.

All in all, it is difficult to defend taking on currency risk for the sake of long-term investment returns, as the risks may be substantial. When diversifying internationally, currency risk comes bundled with the local return from a particular market. The key to unbundling this risk is currency hedging. However, as currency risk may have a diversifying effect as well, a 100 percent currency hedge will not always be optimal.

Simultaneous optimization can assist investors in optimizing exposure to various asset classes, countries, and currencies

Simultaneous optimization allows the risks involved in international diversification of investments to be examined more holistically by attempting to concurrently optimize exposure to asset class, countries, and currencies. The goal of the exercise is to construct a mixed portfolio of domestic and international equities and fixed income with an optimal hedge ratio for each currency.

Figure 4.56 **Long-Term Trends in Currency Values and Equity and Fixed-Income Returns**

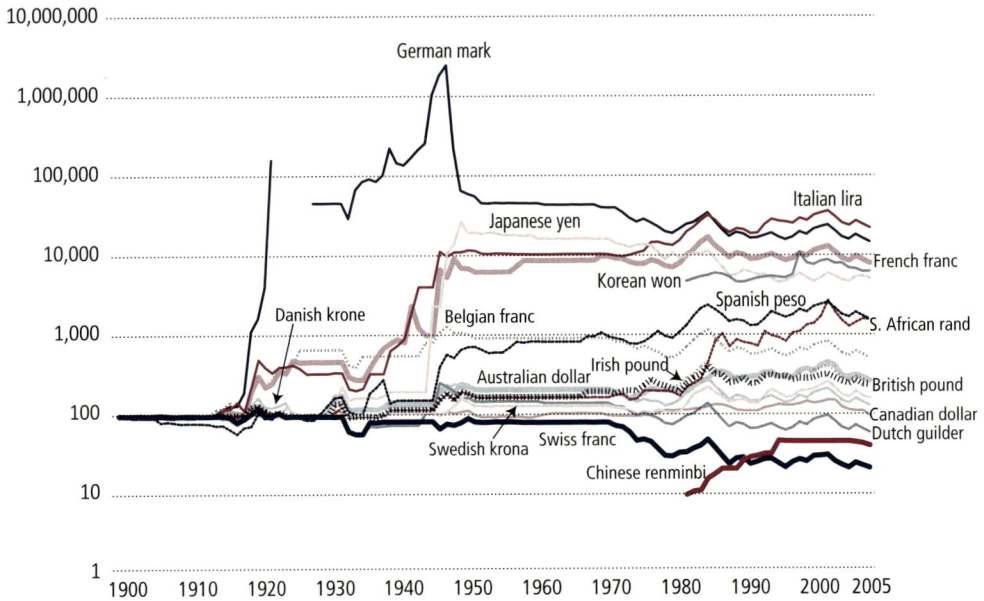

Currency/U.S. dollar (index: 1900 = 100)

Sources: World Bank and Ibbotson.

Table 4.7 shows the results of simultaneous optimization with the goal of minimizing a portfolio's risk; a full efficient frontier could have been constructed using the same approach. Five optimizations are presented, each assuming that a portfolio is invested in a different number of countries. When a portfolio has no foreign markets in its potential investment universe (the first row in the table), the risk-minimizing portfolio contains 2 percent equities and 98 percent fixed-income instruments, resulting in volatility of 3.6 percent. Similar analysis is presented for portfolios invested in 1, 2, 3, 5, and 12 foreign markets.

As shown in the second column of table 4.7, the number of foreign markets in an optimal portfolio depends on how many foreign markets are in the potential investment universe. Generally, the allocation to equities and the allocation to foreign markets increase as the number of foreign markets in the potential investment universe increases. Moreover, the optimal hedge ratio (percentage of currency exposure that is hedged) varies across currencies. In the exercise below, the markets in the potential investment universe expand in the following order:

◆ The United States
◆ Euro area
◆ Japan

Table 4.7 **Simultaneous Optimization Results for Portfolios Assuming Varying Numbers of Foreign Markets in the Investment Universe**

In potential investment universe	In optimal portfolio	Equities (domestic and foreign)	Foreign bonds and equities	Hedge ratio	Portfolio volatility (%)
0	0	2	0	No hedge	3.60
1	1	8	59	$0.85	2.35
2	2	8	66	$0.03, €1	2.05
3	3	7	84	$0.38, €1, ¥0.97	1.51
5	3	7	82	$0.38, €1, ¥0.97	1.47
12	6	8	83	€1, ¥0.97, Can$1, others 0	1.46

Number of foreign markets / Allocation to

Source: World Bank.

Note: The hedge ratio shows what percentage of the entire portfolio is exposed to investment risk by comparing the value of a position protected via a hedge with the size of the entire position.

◆ The United Kingdom
◆ Canada
◆ Switzerland
◆ Hong Kong, China
◆ Brazil
◆ China
◆ Taiwan, China
◆ Australia
◆ the Russian Federation

As shown in this optimization exercise, the diversification effects between asset classes, domestic and foreign exposures, and different currencies all interact with each other.

A pension fund's investment committee should determine its hedging policy and whether to use a single global hedge ratio for the entire foreign currency exposure or to hedge individually for each asset class

Though it results in important conclusions for investors, the approach illustrated in table 4.7 is rarely used in practice. One reason for this is that determination of the overall strategic asset allocation (SAA) under simultaneous optimization would be

Ideally, a pension fund's investment committee should decide whether to

◆ use a single global hedge ratio (for each currency) for the foreign part of the portfolio and, if so, determine how much currency exposure the fund should have in its total return; or

◆ hedge according to asset class.

largely left to the optimizer program. This tends to make investors uncomfortable, since they have varying convictions about the assumptions that go into an elaborate analysis such as simultaneous optimization. In practice, pension funds more often make SAA and hedging policy decisions in sequence rather than concurrently.

The latter approach—hedging according to asset class—is often used by pension funds when the asset class is managed as an isolated profit center. However, if the objective is to reduce total portfolio volatility through currency hedging, a global approach should be used because the interaction between the domestic and foreign parts of the portfolio and between asset classes is then allowed to have an impact on the hedging ratio. In particular, the percentage allocation to foreign markets versus the home currency market is an important input in hedging policy decisions.

A hedging policy should specify not only the size but also the impact of the hedge ratio

Figure 4.57 presents the results of a case study illustrating the importance of total allocation to the home currency market in determining the optimal hedging ratio. The case study uses the example of a Republic of Korea–based investor who is investing in Korean won and U.S. dollars and has a balanced fixed-income and equity portfolio. As suggested in the figure, when allocations to foreign markets are low (less than 20 percent), the optimal hedge ratio is also low. Moreover, as the optimal hedge ratio increases when the foreign allocation increases, the risk reduction due to that optimal hedge ratio is negligible until the foreign allocation is more than 40 percent (home market allocation less than 60 percent). All of this points to the conclusion that decisions about hedging policy should involve not only the size of the hedge ratio but also evaluate the impact of the hedge ratio in reducing total portfolio risk or volatility.

The main driver behind the low hedge ratio in the case of a low allocation to foreign markets is the correlation between domestic equity market return and home currency return, which is seemingly lower than the correlation among foreign equity indexes. In the case of Korea, there is a very low correlation between domestic equity returns and the Korean won (table 4.8). This low correlation

Figure 4.57 **Hedge Ratio versus Home Allocation**

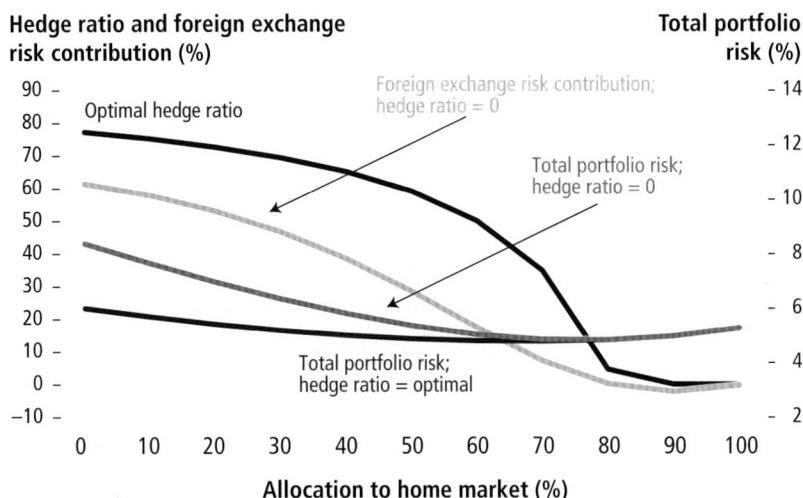

Source: World Bank.

Note: The data presented here assumes a diversified portfolio in U.S. dollars and base currency Korean won. Data considered here are for the period September 2000 through July 2008.

Table 4.8 **Currency and Equity Index Correlations**

	UKX	SXXP	NKY	AS51	KOSPI
SXXP Index	0.90				
NKY Index	0.59	0.60			
AS51 Index	0.74	0.77	0.67		
KOSPI Index	0.58	0.59	0.61	0.63	
£/$	0.05	−0.03	−0.09	−0.14	−0.06
€/$	−0.10	0.08	−0.11	−0.11	−0.06
¥/$	0.05	0.17	0.13	0.15	0.00
$A/$	−0.43	−0.34	−0.47	−0.44	−0.45
Won/$	−0.37	−0.35	−0.41	−0.44	−0.32

Sources: World Bank and Bloomberg.

Note: Calculations are based on monthly data from 1999 to 2009. Correlations are between equities in the United Kingdom (UKX), the United States (SXXP), Japan (NKY), Australia (AS51), and the Republic of Korea (KOSPI), and between the respective currency rates to U.S. dollars.

between any local market index and that market's currency is also quite common in other countries.

Conclusion

International diversification is a useful approach for pension funds seeking to maximize the total returns and reduce the overall risk of their investments. Although currency return represents an unrewarded risk—that is, a risk not associated with any benefit for the party accepting the risk—there are often diversification benefits. Therefore, hedging 100 percent of currency exposure is not recommended in many cases. An optimal hedging policy is heavily dependent on the fund's SAA. Investment committees of pension funds wishing to reduce volatility due to currency risk should use the following framework:

◆ International diversification has the potential to improve the risk/return trade-off.

◆ Separate hedge ratios for each asset class should be avoided. Instead, the strategy should be to hedge the aggregate currency exposure of the overall portfolio; this should take into account the percentage of overall portfolio allocated to foreign markets.

◆ The size of the optimal hedge ratio should be evaluated by reviewing the marginal reduction in risk resulting from an increase in the hedge ratio. If the marginal risk reduction is not significant, a smaller hedge ratio might be equally appropriate.

International Investments: Developing a Strategy to Manage Currency Risk

Jolanta Wysocka, Chief Executive Officer, Mountain Pacific Group, United States*

Several factors contribute to public pension funds' decisions about the level of their international investments: the risks and rewards of investing in foreign capital markets, thresholds for active management of currency exposure, types of currency hedging programs, and the trade-offs involved with each investment strategy. For all pension funds with international investments, a sound and comprehensive currency policy is necessary. Diversifying internationally is particularly critical for public pension funds based in countries in which domestic capital markets are not fully developed.

Maximization of returns and reduction of portfolio volatility are two main benefits of diversifying internationally, but there are risks as well

The two main rewards of investing in international markets are maximization of returns and reduction of risks (figure 4.58). One of the biggest risks any pension fund faces is headline risk. When a pension fund posts poor results due to under-performance in international markets or inadequate foreign currency hedging, it tends to get a lot of negative media coverage. Other international investment risks include currency risk, peer pressure, transparency issues, expropriation risk, and poor governance.

As global investing has increased the impact of currency movements on portfolio returns, managing currency risk has become essential

International investing has substantially increased the impact of currency movements on pension funds' total portfolio returns. Managing currency risk has

---

* The author is grateful for discussions with colleague Ron Liesching at Mountain Pacific Group and the staff of funds who participated in discussions about the development of currency policies.

Figure 4.58 **Rewards and Risks of International Investments**

Rewards	Risks
◆ Maximize return – Increase the opportunity set – Select the most globally competitive sectors/companies ◆ Risk reduction – Hedge home country/currency risk – Currency diversification benefit – Reduction of sponsor risk	◆ Currency risk ◆ Peer pressure ◆ Headline risk ◆ Transparency ◆ Expropriation ◆ Governance

Source: Mountain Pacific Group.

therefore become a fundamental consideration in management of pension portfolios. Though public pension funds are advised to include international investments in order to maximize returns and maintain an acceptable level of volatility, their portfolios often have an extreme home country bias. In many cases, this is due to the local currency composition of liabilities and regulations restricting or prohibiting foreign investments. Managing currency risk may not be easy, but it is critical. Further, limited liquidity in most currency markets makes it challenging to manage large currency exposures outside of the six most prominent currencies. Many large public pension funds have sufficiently high levels of currency exposure that active currency management programs can materially affect the local exchange rate.

Currency risk should be hedged when international asset holdings reach a certain percentage of a pension fund's total portfolio

Financial theory suggests that managing or hedging currency risk is recommended when foreign currency–denominated assets exceed 10 percent of a portfolio. In the experience of the Mountain Pacific Group, however, currency fluctuations have a significant impact on total fund returns, and a formal currency hedging policy becomes necessary when international equity assets exceed 20 percent of a total portfolio. That said, the policy may be to simply remain unhedged—to not manage currency at all. But given the potential impact of currency movements, it is important for a fund to issue a clear policy statement with regard to management of currency risk.

Fully hedging foreign currency undiversifies exposure to the global value of the home currency and unhedges a fund's cash flows

It is useful to note that many early academic analyses argued that foreign currency risk should be fully hedged. The argument was that full hedging would eliminate unrewarded currency risk. Though fully hedging currency risk appears attractive because liabilities are generally denominated in local currency, it does not eliminate the risk. Rather, it simply changes the nature of the risk. In 2008, for example, several funds in Australia, Canada, and the Republic of Korea with fully hedged foreign currency exposures were forced to pay out massive amounts to settle losses on forward currency contracts as currencies in those countries plunged. Worse, these cash calls came at a time of extremely tight liquidity in the markets. In short, the experience highlights the fact that hedging foreign currencies can unhedge a fund's cash flow. That said, fully hedging foreign currency exposure means that the fund then has completely undiversified exposure to the global value of the domestic currency. At the same time, the local currency is more likely to plunge when the domestic economy is not doing well. So there are several powerful arguments for the diversification benefit of having some foreign currency exposure.

A primary concern for institutions investing overseas is the foreign currency risk relative to their home, or base, currency. Consider a pension fund based in Europe, Japan, Australia, or Switzerland (with liabilities denominated in its home currency) that invests in U.S. equities. Even when U.S. share prices rise, the dollar may fall by more against the fund's home currency, causing the institution to incur a net loss. The currency impact on the reported home currency returns on international investing is called *currency translation risk*. Figure 4.59 illustrates how the dollar has moved in recent years compared to five other major currencies. Between 2000 and 2008, the value of the dollar fell relative to four of the five currencies shown here (with the exception of the British pound). As a result, European, Japanese, Australian, and Swiss holders of U.S. dollar assets would find their returns on these assets (translated into home currency) reduced by the extent of such dollar depreciation vis-à-vis their home currency.

At times, foreign currency volatility can be so great it dwarfs the underlying asset's return. Furthermore, currency exposure adds volatility to an international portfolio. Table 4.9 shows annualized volatility for each of the currencies shown in figure 4.59 relative to the dollar over the same time period.

Assuming that an investor had an equally weighted exposure to these five currencies, the average annualized standard deviation of daily log returns relative to the dollar was 10.09 percent between January 1998 and September 2008. With a

Figure 4.59 **Cumulative Returns Relative to U.S. Dollars, 1997–2009**

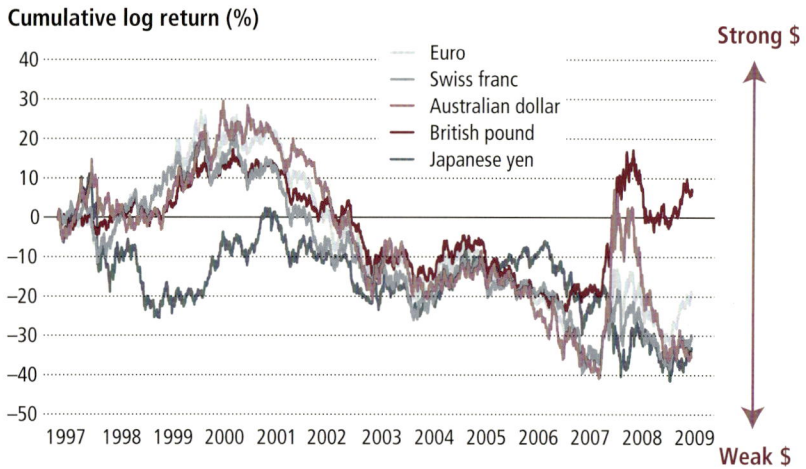

Cumulative log return (%)

Strong $

Weak $

Source: Mountain Pacific Group.

Table 4.9 **Annualized Volatility for Selected Currencies Relative to the U.S. Dollar, January 1998–September 2008 (%)**

Euro	Japanese yen	British pound	Swiss franc	Australian dollar
9.60	10.88	8.01	10.54	11.41

Source: Mountain Pacific Group.

17 percent allocation to international equity, an additional 1.7 percent of incremental volatility at the total fund level with no incremental expected return would be incurred.[1] An international currency depreciation (versus the home currency) of 3 standard deviations thus would have resulted in a 5.1 percent loss of asset value. Again, this risk arises as a peripheral exposure embedded in the international equity investment. Theoretically, it is possible for a positive correlation to exist between currency returns and returns on portfolio assets, but any such relationship is unstable and certainly not a dependable method of passive risk reduction.

_____

[1] An asset cannot provide ex ante expected compensation for currency risk to foreign and domestic holders of the same asset simultaneously. Foreign exchange rates are merely exposures. They are relative prices and as such cannot generate a global expected return.

Recently, many pension funds in countries with currencies that are not exceptionally liquid are starting to consider how to manage their home currency risk.[2] This is a topic of great importance for funds domiciled in small, open economies such as Australia, Korea, and New Zealand, as massive swings in the value of the domestic currency may not only lead to large swings in the value of assets held by the fund but may adversely affect the purchasing power of retirees in the future. Increasingly, even funds domiciled in the United States are addressing the need to hedge their home currency risk.

Pension funds need to consider a range of factors when determining a currency policy

Once a fund invests more than 20 percent of its assets in instruments denominated in currencies other than the home currency, currency fluctuations will have a major impact on total fund return. Instituting a currency policy then becomes vital. While different factors for establishing a currency policy will prevail for different public pension funds, in general, the following aspects should be considered when determining such policy:

◆ *International exposure.* If the proportion is greater than 20 percent, a currency policy is crucial.

◆ *Types of international assets.* Bonds and other absolute return assets should be fully hedged. Equities should be hedged according to specifications in the firm's investment policy. Private equity and real estate are often significantly invested overseas, but adequately hedging these assets may pose operational challenges due to information time lags and market illiquidity.

◆ *Fund risk appetite.* The level of hedging depends upon the risk appetite of the fund; low risk tolerance requires greater hedging.

◆ *Funding status.* A weak funding position generally requires greater hedging.

◆ *Cash flow concerns.* The level of hedging should reflect the cash flow needs of the fund; greater cash flow requirements may require more active hedging.

◆ *Sponsor currency exposure.* The sponsor's currency exposure will influence the fund's exposure and need for hedging—any offset will reduce the need for hedging.

◆ *Political/headline or peer risks.* The investment policy statement should provide clear guidance on addressing political or peer risks and specify review processes

---

[2] Home currency is the currency used to measure the performance of a fund or portfolio with holdings across several international markets.

on how to mitigate these risks (for example, precluding the fund from investments in particular asset classes, institutions, or countries).

◆ *Hedging in illiquid markets.* A fund may need to invest in a basket of proxy
securities with the same risk/reward characteristics as the characteristics of the
securities it seeks to invest in order to avoid limitations imposed by illiquid
markets.

◆ *Currency view.* A strong view on specific currencies by a fund's management
needs to be documented and stop-loss points need to be established to manage
risk.

The first step for a pension fund in developing a currency policy is to establish
what a neutral currency position means. Under a policy of active management,
the fund's currency exposure is varied in order to add value. The benchmark is the
currency position that the fund would maintain if no active currency management
were employed or the currency position would be neutral.

Historically, mean variance analysis was used to identify an "optimal" currency
benchmark. Such analysis, however, provides very unstable hedging recommendations because the "optimal" currency hedge depends on the time period analyzed.
In the late 1990s, for example, this instability led to many analysts recommending
a 50 percent hedged currency position. Active currency managers preferred this
benchmark because it gave them the opportunity to add value over the benchmark
in both strong and weak home currency environments.

Appropriate currency policy differs significantly according to a pension fund's individual circumstances

Currency policy must be developed for each pension fund's individual needs. These
needs vary enormously based on the environment in which the institution operates,
the currency composition of its overall portfolio, and the currency composition
of its liabilities. As the needs and environment evolve, optimal currency policy
also changes. Typically, a fund changes its currency policy every four or five years.
While a fund may be very cautious when initially investing internationally and
want to hedge most of the foreign currency exposure, it is not unusual for a less
strict hedging policy to be adopted as the fund gains experience and a more global
view of investments, particularly if it has a strong funding position.

Because currency is an unrewarded risk, an explicit currency policy is needed for
any portfolio with significant currency exposure. When currency risk is significant, it can materially affect total fund return. For an Australian fund investing
in global equity markets, for example, fully hedged global equities have a volatility

of approximately 14 percent per year. When capital is invested in international equities, the investment risk has an associated expected return. However, the additional currency volatility against the Australian dollar by itself is about 10 percent per year. This foreign currency risk has no associated expected return. So, if 25 percent of the Australian fund's portfolio is invested in international investments, its portfolio would have 2.5 percent unrewarded volatility from unmanaged currency swings.

All large and changing currency risks should be actively managed

At the fund level, currency impact is much larger for funds in small economies, which have less liquid markets and more volatile currencies. Often, large funds in these countries have high international allocations in order to diversify away from small, sector-concentrated, local equity markets. For example, some Canadian pension funds have 40 percent of their assets invested outside of Canada. In a situation in which the Canadian dollar appreciated by 20 percent against the U.S. dollar, this international allocation, if not hedged, would have resulted in a negative impact of 8 percent on total home currency returns for such funds. The decision to hedge currency risk would therefore avoid this negative impact. Though international investments are indisputably justified, particularly in countries with small capital markets, high levels of currency volatility require that currency risks be actively managed to fully capture the diversification benefits, just as all large and changing risks should be actively managed.

Mean variance analysis does not offer useful assistance in the development of currency policy beyond the commonsense conclusion that the higher the international allocation, the wiser it is to have some currency hedging in place and that an explicit currency policy must be developed for funds with significant foreign exposure. The best way for a pension fund to develop such a policy is to lay out the list of potential factors that may affect its currency policy and to assign an appropriate weight to each of those factors. An important aspect of this discussion is developing an internal consensus within the fund's management and its governing board on the goals for currency management. The process of explicit policy discussion means that the goals of currency management are clearly specified and agreed upon. If this is not done in advance, future disappointment is highly likely.

The best way to develop a currency policy is to lay out the list of potential factors that can affect the currency policy and assign an appropriate weight to each of those factors.

Suitable currency policy also differs according to type of investor, country of domicile, nature of liabilities, and other factors

Appropriate currency policy also differs significantly depending on the type of investor (pension fund, foundation, family office, or sovereign wealth fund, for example), the country in which the investor is domiciled, nature of future payments/liabilities, funding status, nature of the fund sponsor, the size of the exposure relative to foreign exchange market liquidity, and liquidity of the home currency.

Questions All Investors Should Address When Considering a Currency Policy

- ◆ How large is the foreign currency exposure?
- ◆ What are the assets to be hedged?
- ◆ How much of the currency risk is already hedged by individual asset managers managing the fund's assets?
- ◆ Is there concern about the outlook for the home currency?
- ◆ Is there concern about the outlook for specific international currencies?
- ◆ How knowledgeable about global investing are the fund's investment staff and governing board?
- ◆ What is the expected profit and loss from explicit currency management programs?
- ◆ How sensitive is the fund and the fund's governing board to the cash flow implications of currency hedges?
- ◆ What is the risk appetite of the fund?

When developing a currency policy, pension funds should define their neutral currency position and determine how the currency policy will evolve over the next three to five years

When drafting a currency policy, decision makers within a pension fund need to agree on the objectives and have a good understanding of the risks associated with the policy. In general, they should consider how to define the neutral currency position, whether developed-economy currencies should be treated differently from emerging market currencies, whether exposure should be limited to under-lying foreign exposures, what are the appropriate currency exposure ranges and currency risk stance, and whether home currency risk should be addressed.

Currency policies typically evolve based on a three- to five-year horizon and should be established and revised through a systematic review process. Reasons to change a fund's currency policy include the home currency reaching an extreme high or low, a rise in international allocation, changes in funding status, and changes in senior investment staff or governing board members.

Reasons for Changes to Currency Policy

◆ Home currency reaching an extreme valuation

◆ Rise in international allocation

◆ Change in funding status

◆ Senior staff or governing board member changes

Currency exposure to developed markets can be managed using only six major currencies

Currency exposure in a diversified portfolio of the world's developed equity markets can be managed using only six major trading currencies, as shown in table 4.10: the U.S. dollar, euro, Japanese yen, British pound, Swiss franc, and Australian dollar. Using these six major currencies reduces transaction costs because these currencies are generally liquid and trading costs are relatively low. More importantly, limiting exposure to only six currencies means that currency exposure can almost always be hedged in extreme market conditions, as the market for trading in the smaller currencies disappears during a major currency crisis.

When a fund undertakes currency management, it will need to regularly make cash settlements of gains and losses on currency positions. For this, it is best to use forward currency contracts. A fund typically has between 2 and 12 settlement dates per year (that is, the term of currency forward contracts typically ranges between one and six months), allowing monitoring of the fund's foreign currency exposure either electronically by the custodian or directly by the fund managers. Based on the active signals, the currency positions can be altered as the risk changes.

Managing currency positions in illiquid markets requires customized actions

Within an investment fund, decision makers must have a strong understanding of which currency risks can and should be managed and the means by which to manage such risks. In some cases, passive currency management (for example, a fixed currency hedging ratio) may be preferable to active management. But in all cases, the currency management strategies should focus on:

Table 4.10 **Percentage of Foreign Exchange Trading Volume**

Currency	2001	2004	2007
U.S. dollar	90.3	88.7	86.3
Euro	37.6	36.9	37.0
Japanese yen	22.7	20.2	16.5
British pound	13.2	16.9	15.0
Swiss franc	6.1	6.0	6.8
Australian dollar	4.2	5.9	6.7
Other currencies	25.9	25.4	31.7

Source: Bank for International Settlements 2007.

Note: The sum of the percentage shares of all currencies totals 200 percent rather than 100 percent because two currencies are involved in each transaction.

◆ long-term market liquidity, availability, and cost of hedging instruments;

◆ the currency composition of assets and liabilities;

◆ whether the potential value created by medium-term shifts in exchange rates based on changing fundamentals justifies a move to active currency management.

Active management of currency is only possible once the currency starts to float freely. Figure 4.60 lists various currency regimes from the least liquid to a free-float system.

Figure 4.60 **The Spectrum of Currency Regimes**

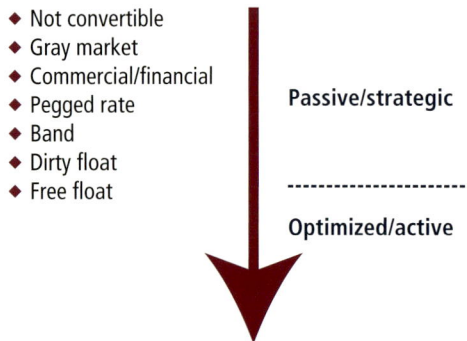

◆ Not convertible
◆ Gray market
◆ Commercial/financial
◆ Pegged rate
◆ Band
◆ Dirty float
◆ Free float

Passive/strategic

Optimized/active

Source: Mountain Pacific Group.

If a fund's home currency is illiquid relative to the exposure size, only a passive currency hedge may be possible. A fund with an illiquid home currency that nevertheless wishes to undertake active currency management may be able to do so by getting exposure to a basket of foreign currencies and/or other instruments which serves as a proxy for the home currency. This proxy basket exposure would partly hedge the home currency risk. As the proxy basket would be placed in liquid currencies or other instruments, the pension fund would then be able to actively manage its currency risk profile, if desired.

Active foreign currency management works best for some pension funds, while passive currency hedging works better for others

Because it is extremely difficult to maintain a fixed currency policy, some pension funds prefer to fully hedge all foreign currency exposure.[3] Other funds leave foreign currency exposure completely unhedged in order to benefit from the diversification of foreign currency returns. That said, currencies move in large and often unforecastable ranges, and invariably, there will be a time when any fixed currency policy causes unacceptably large losses, even when a fund's investment techniques are sophisticated and its board is investment savvy.

In an active currency overlay program, a fund manager alters the amount of currency that is hedged based on changing risks. Having an expert continually monitor currency exposures reduces the risk of unacceptably large losses due to unforeseen market movements. Though policy analysis might conclude that the fund should fully hedge, if the home currency then loses value, it is preferable to have an expert in place to reduce the amount of hedging and partially offset the loss to the fund's global purchasing power from the home currency losing value. That expert can then be measured against the policy benchmark—in this case, a fully hedged position.

There are three forms of active currency mandate: pure alpha, currency overlay hedging, and hedging of both home and foreign currencies, as described in table 4.11. Pure currency alpha programs simply speculate in currencies to make money; this is a specialized "global macro" activity. In home and foreign currency hedging, the policy hedges both the fund's foreign currency and home currency exposures on an opportunistic basis. For any given fund, the appropriate currency

---

[3] A fixed currency policy directs the fund to hedge a specific, predetermined amount of currency risk and may designate a particular percentage of the foreign exchange risk exposure to be hedged, from no hedge to full hedge.

Table 4.11 **Construction of Active Currency Mandates**

Mandate	Goal	Characteristics
Pure alpha	Generate return by creating new currency risk	◆ Active positions are identical for all funds globally ◆ Active positions are not tied to existing foreign currency exposures ◆ All currencies and cross rates can be traded
Overlay hedging	Hedge the existing fund foreign currency risk	◆ Active positions differ for each fund ◆ Active positions are tied to existing foreign currency exposures ◆ Foreign currency is only sold against the home currency
Hedging of home and foreign currencies	Generate return by hedging both home and foreign currency risk	◆ Active positions taken are different for each fund ◆ Both foreign currencies and the home currency are traded to manage existing currency risk, converting it into return

Source: Muntain Pacific Group.

---

management mandate usually becomes clear following discussion of the goals of currency policy.

Historically, investors in major economies have not recognized the risk inherent in their home currencies. In emerging economies, on the other hand, home currency risk has always been evident to investors, who hedge that risk by holding assets in other currencies. But as G4 currencies (the U.S. dollar, euro, Japanese yen, and British pound) have become increasingly unstable in recent years, home currency risk has become a major issue for all global investors. As a result, more pension funds are employing home and foreign currency hedging mandates that permit hedging of both their home currency risk and the foreign currency risk created by international investment, with the goal of maintaining the overall purchasing power of the fund's assets. Dollar-based investors, for example, can hedge their dollar risk by partly hedging their dollar-based assets into other global currencies. In case of a significant decline in the value of the dollar during a currency crisis, the global value of such investors' assets will decline by less than it would have without the hedge.

A crisis that causes the home currency to fall by 30 percent against all other currencies, for example, would lead to huge losses on all the domestic assets in the portfolio. Because the U.S. dollar, euro, and Japanese yen are quite volatile at the moment, investors with these home currencies are now actively managing their home currency risk.

Pros and Cons of Hedging Home and Foreign Currencies

◆ **Pro:** Home and foreign currency hedging preserves a pension fund's global value. When the home currency declines substantially against other currencies, value is added by buying foreign currencies to hedge this loss of value.

◆ **Con:** Home and foreign currency hedging may deprive a pension fund of the benefit of diversification.

Appropriately addressing foreign currency risk is particularly important for funds investing internationally whose home currency is susceptible to illiquidity during financial crises

Korean financial markets represent a small proportion of global capital markets, and demand for Korean won in foreign exchange markets is small relative to the real size of the Korean economy, Korean participation in world trade, foreign exchange reserves, and domestic institutional savings. Korean pension funds must therefore be careful about exchange rate risk when investing internationally. During the 2008–09 global financial crisis, the market for won became illiquid: deal size dropped to $5 million and the value of the won fell 61 percent versus the U.S. dollar (figure 4.61), making active currency management, which would have altered the currency hedge ratio from foreign currencies back to won, impossible.

Figure 4.61 **Korean Won versus U.S. Dollar**

Source: U.S. Federal Reserve.

Educating a governing board is essential to successful implementation of a currency mandate

Educating a pension fund's board about currency mandates is an important step in putting a currency mandate in place. Three main points are worth noting to board members. The first is how to proceed when the fund has large preexisting currency risk. In this case, monthly reports showing the currency impact on a fund's total return should be introduced. This separates the movement of currency from movements in, for example, equity markets. The second point is that currency hedging is not currency speculation. In currency hedging, the goal is always to reduce preexisting fund currency risk. Currency hedging also means there will be periods of cash losses on the hedges, which are offset by larger paper translation gains on the value of the international assets and vice versa. This can have important cash flow implications which a fund's governing board needs to be aware of and accept. The third point is that currency returns are episodic. Major currencies move sideways more than 80 percent of the time. Therefore, active currency programs may result in many periods of small positive and negative return, and brief periods of large payouts.

Conclusion

For institutional investors, the best way to improve return relative to risk is to diversify internationally. Diversification of international returns may be enhanced by the accompanying foreign exchange risk, up to a point. A Korean institution, for example, faces two currency risks: the risk specific to home currency (financial, economic, or political) and the risk that a major foreign currency will depreciate vis-à-vis its home currency. In response to these risks, one option is to diversify internationally into an optimal currency basket to hedge won-specific risk (that is, stabilize the fund's wealth in terms of its global purchasing power). The fund can then actively manage risk within the basket—for example, if the U.S. dollar starts a major downtrend, the dollar weight in the basket can be reduced.

When a pension fund's international investments reach more than 20 percent of its total assets, a currency policy should be developed, and the foreign currency should be at least partially hedged. Factors determining a fund's currency policy include level of currency exposure; the profile, risk characteristics, and market liquidity of the international assets in which it is invested; and the funding status, cash flow, and overall risk tolerance of the fund. Managing currency positions in illiquid markets requires both expertise and an explicit currency policy. One option to achieve an appropriate risk-return profile in countries with insufficient currency liquidity is to invest in a proxy basket of liquid foreign currency and/or other instruments.

Though active currency hedging reduces risk and adds value for a fund, exchange rate volatility will remain and may even increase. Continuing large global trade and debt imbalances, and the fact that growth in the major economic blocs is not always synchronized, contribute to this exchange rate volatility. This creates a large amount of currency risk, but it also creates a major opportunity for generating additional value from active currency programs.

As investors continue to globalize their assets, currency swings will have an increasing impact on a fund's total performance. The fact that there is no evidence that currency returns wash out over time, however, makes active currency management an inevitable consequence of global investing (Goodhart 1988). Discussions about currency policy often consume a disproportionate amount of time of a fund's management and governing board. Active currency hedging programs can add value and help manage the currency risk to which all funds are exposed as a result of global investing.

References

Bank for International Settlements. 2007. "Triennial Foreign Exchange Survey of Foreign Exchange and Derivatives Market Activity." Basel, Switzerland: Bank for International Settlements.

Goodhart, Charles. 1988. "The Foreign Exchange Market: A Random Walk with a Dragging Anchor." *Economica* 55 (220): 437–60.

Managing the International Investments of Pension Funds in Latin America

Augusto Iglesias, Vice Minister for Social Security, Chile

The overall premise for investing in international markets is the benefit of diversification, which may result in increasing returns and/or reducing risk within a pension fund's investment portfolio. In several Latin American countries, diversification into international investments has assisted public pension fund affiliates in mitigating country-specific economic and political risks. Nevertheless, investment outside the home country remains constrained by pension fund regulators in numerous developing countries.

Pension funds face several major constraints in achieving their objective of maximizing accumulated returns for members at retirement age

The overall investment objective of a funded, mandatory pension system is to maximize accumulated returns for its members at retirement age. That objective is constrained by several factors, including contribution rate, members' income, and the length of time investments are held. Volatility of returns—another essential determinant of the long-term, risk-adjusted rate of return on retirement assets—can be affected by external factors such as political decisions and the reaction of future pensioners to unexpected erosion of the value of their pension benefits. Mitigating volatility risk, which increases the chance that a pension fund will not reach its desired income replacement rate, is particularly essential for cohorts of members close to retirement age. For pension funds that invest internationally, designing and implementing appropriate currency hedging policies is also important in ensuring that adequate funds are available to members upon retirement. Assessments regarding currency policy should focus on a fund's objectives of maximizing accumulated returns while minimizing the volatility of accumulated returns.

Because public pension funds are key actors in local capital markets in Latin American countries, regulators use macroeconomic considerations to justify restrictions on international investments

In various countries, policy makers who oversee public pension funds have argued that suitable regulation of funds' foreign investments is crucial for achieving funds' long-term investment objective of maximizing accumulated returns for a given level of volatility. In Latin American countries, though, mandatory pension funds are key actors in local capital markets. Moreover, currency controls and restrictions on international capital flows prevail in most of the region's economies. Thus, macroeconomic considerations have been used to justify additional restrictions on pension funds' international investments.

In this context, levels of foreign investments and currency hedging policies by Latin American pension funds are heavily influenced by the particular characteristics of domestic regulation and are not necessarily a result of unconstrained optimal portfolio allocation rules. Regulators have used several arguments in order to limit or prohibit pension funds' international investments:

◆ The need for financing public deficits, which raises concern that such investments would adversely affect government debt and foreign exchange markets

◆ Retaining capital at home as an incentive for the development of local capital markets

◆ The fact that currency controls are applied to other types of investors

◆ Political opposition

◆ Limited capacity by pension funds' supervisors to control events outside their jurisdiction and lack of experience investing in foreign markets

Limits on pension funds' international investments in various countries—many of them significant—are summarized in table 4.12.

Foreign investments of pension funds are not limited by regulations alone. Pension fund managers in various emerging markets also argue against investment in foreign assets for the following reasons:

◆ Expected returns are often higher in emerging markets than in developed markets

◆ Investment managers have more expertise assessing domestic risk than they do international risk

◆ Cost considerations

◆ Political pressures

Table 4.12 Foreign Investment Limits for Pension Funds in Selected Countries

Country	Global investment limit in foreign assets
Australia	No limit
Brazil	Limited to 2–3% through retail investment funds and restricted to Brazilian depositary receipts and stocks listed in the Mercosur capital markets
Chile	Joint limit for all funds: 60%[a]
Colombia	20%[b]
Costa Rica	25%
Czech Republic	Foreign investment permitted only for securities traded in regulated Organisation for Economic Co-operation and Development markets
Dominican Republic	Foreign investment not allowed
El Salvador	Foreign investment not allowed
Mexico	20%
Peru	30%
Poland	Open Pension Fund: 5%; Employee Pension Fund: at least 70% of assets denominated in Polish zloty
Slovak Republic	70%[c]
Uruguay	Foreign investment not allowed

Sources: International Federation of Pension Funds Administrators; OECD 2008; individual pension fund superintendent Web sites.

Note: — = not available.

a. The limit for all funds increased to 80 percent in October 2009.

b. Joint limit for fixed-interest securities issued, backed, or guaranteed by foreign governments, foreign central banks, international organizations, or foreign banks and participation in mutual funds that invest exclusively in international investments.

c. At least 30 percent of pension asset management funds must be invested in Slovak securities. There are no specific limits for different asset categories.

As a result, public pension funds in various emerging markets still opt primarily for domestic investments and often have only insignificant exposure to international markets (table 4.13).

Table 4.13 **Levels of Local and Foreign Investment of Pension Funds in Selected Countries**

Mandatory second pillars	Local investment		Foreign investment	
	2007	2008	2007	2008
Latin America				
Bolivia	97.76	100.00	2.24	0.00
Chile	64.43	71.47	35.57	28.53
Colombia	88.04	90.62	11.96	9.38
Costa Rica	86.63	91.02	13.37	8.98
Dominican Republic	n.a.	100.00	n.a.	0.00
El Salvador	95.83	96.37	4.17	3.63
Mexico	91.10	90.01	8.90	9.99
Peru	86.81	87.59	13.19	12.41
Uruguay[a]	n.a.	95.83	n.a.	4.17
Europe & Asia				
Bulgaria	81.29	71.96	18.71	28.04
Kazakhstan	—	88.28	—	11.72
Poland	98.98	99.36	1.02	0.64

Source: International Federation of Pension Funds Administrators.

Note: — = not available; n.a. = not authorized.

a. Since May 2008, the maximum foreign investment limit is 15 percent (all of which must be invested in fixed-income instruments issued by international institutions).

Though expansion into foreign investments can mitigate country-specific economic and political risks, overcoming political impediments to diversifying internationally requires a gradual approach developed in tandem with supportive regulators

In emerging economies, factors such as underdeveloped local capital markets and lack of investment opportunities are incorporated into pension funds' investment risk profiles. In such cases, international diversification offers a unique opportunity to mitigate country-specific economic and political risks. In order to overcome domestic political pressures and adopt international diversification, pension funds can develop a gradual approach to the liberalization of international investments. In the best-case scenario, public pensions' expansion into foreign capital markets is implemented in coordination with home country monetary authorities. Initially, pension funds' international investments may include transactions in authorized and preselected markets (those with high levels of liquidity, strong corporate governance standards, and efficient settlement and transfer mechanisms) along with the requirement of additional rigorous reporting on such investments.

Regulatory Approach Supporting International Diversification for Public Pension Funds

◆ Develop a gradual strategy to liberalize international investments.

◆ Authorize transactions in preselected markets.

◆ Establish rigorous reporting requirements on foreign investments.

◆ Coordinate with domestic monetary authorities.

Mutual funds are the most popular and cost-efficient way for pension funds in Latin American countries to invest internationally

For pension fund managers in Latin America, mutual funds are the most popular and cost-efficient way to diversify their portfolios internationally, providing a generally liquid investment vehicle even for overseas markets that are relatively illiquid. To guarantee liquidity, pension funds generally do not take a significant position in a single mutual fund; rather, they invest in several funds. A separate investment advisor is often used to assist in the selection of mutual funds and in monitoring the performance of investment in such funds. Selection of mutual funds is based on

◆ a long track record,

◆ consistency of results,

◆ comparison with similar funds,

◆ ability to capture bull markets and ability to withdraw rapidly from bear markets,

◆ personal knowledge of mutual fund managers and their teams,

◆ alignment with a pension fund's investment style.

Direct investments and separately managed mandates to investment managers are seldom used by pension funds in Latin American countries. Such instruments tend to be expensive (as a result of back-office, trading, and custodial costs), tend to require local knowledge of specific assets and sizable research teams, and may pose substantial governance risks.

Currency hedging by pension funds in Latin America is heavily regulated

As is the case for foreign investments, currency hedging by pension funds is heavily regulated in Latin American countries. In Chile, pension funds may use only authorized hedging instruments (options, futures, forward contracts, and swaps). "Overcoverage" of currency positions—that is, short selling of the foreign currency on which one may have a negative view vis-à-vis the home currency—is not permitted.

The traditional argument in favor of currency hedging is that while foreign investments help to improve the risk-return profile of a pension fund, they may also invite additional volatility in returns as a result of the risk of currency movements vis-à-vis the home currency of the pension fund, and that hedging foreign currency exposure could reduce such risk. This assertion, however, has been challenged (see Campbell, Serfaty-de Medeiros, and Viceira 2007; Walker 2006). While the major reserve currencies tend to be negatively correlated with global stock markets, commodity-based currencies tend to be positively correlated with global stock markets.

In Chile, the market for currency hedging instruments has developed rapidly in response to increasing demand

Currently, many pension funds in Chile hedge a higher proportion of their foreign currency positions (mostly using forward contracts[1]) than is required by national regulations. As the demand for currency hedging instruments in Chile has grown, the local market for such instruments has also developed quickly. Underlying reasons for the growth in the local market for currency hedging in Chile may be the result of robust growth in per capita gross domestic product, a flexible exchange rate system, open capital markets, and a strong banking sector (banks are the main providers of hedging instruments).

References

Campbell, J., K. Serfaty-de Medeiros, and L. Viceira. 2007. "Global Currency Hedging." NBER Working Paper 13088, National Bureau of Economic Research, C

OECD (Organisation for Economic Co-operation and Development). 2008. "Survey of Investment Regulations of Pension Funds." Paris: OECD.

Walker, E. 2006. "Currency Hedging And International Portfolio Investments: A Local Perspective." *Journal Economía Chilena* (The Chilean Economy) 9 (2): 41–59.

---

[1] Hedging using forward contracts is equivalent to selling foreign currency deposits and buying local currency deposits with the proceeds.

International Diversification and Hedging: The Netherlands' All Pensions Group

Peter Vlaar, Head of Corporate Asset-Liability Management and Risk Policy, All Pensions Group, the Netherlands

The All Pensions Group of the Netherlands employs various methods to maximize its portfolio returns and reduce its overall risk and volatility, including allocations to international investments. When making international investments, public pension funds should employ an active currency hedging strategy. Cost-benefit analysis of the currency hedge, however, should not be neglected, since the optimal hedge ratio is not easily determined due to the complexity of currency movements on the one hand and inflation (indexation demand) and interest rates (liability risk) on the other.

For pension funds, the interest in taking advantage of global financial market opportunities sometimes clashes with regulatory constraints on such investments and creates tension

Pension fund regulators, particularly those in developed countries, are striving to adapt their policies to the increasing burden of population aging. On the other hand, pension fund practitioners perceive dynamically developing global financial markets as an opportunity to manage their exposure in domestic markets. In the process, tensions sometimes arise with domestic regulators, who seek to limit international investments in order to sustain the development of domestic capital markets. As a result of such restrictions, the investments of many pension plans have a home bias not only in equities but also in other asset classes.

International investments can reduce the volatility of investment returns or overcome the constraints of small domestic financial markets, but a home country bias is evident in pension fund investments for a variety of reasons

For pension funds, international diversification reduces the overall volatility of returns as long as the correlation of domestic assets with international assets and the volatility of international assets is not too high. This is especially important if the local economy or the domestic financial market is small relative to a fund's size. Further, international investments reduce home country risk. Indeed, the worst time to be underfunded is when the premium base is small—that is, when domestic economic conditions are weak.

In some cases, pension funds may impose a home country bias in their portfolios as a hedge against liabilities, in particular by increasing their holdings of local currency government bonds. Further, local investments are typically more correlated with local inflation (direct real estate or infrastructure) than are international investments, thereby serving to hedge inflation risks for the fund. There are legal constraints to foreign investments in many cases, even if expansion into other markets would not necessarily result in substantial exchange rate effects. A fund's sponsor may also impose a home country bias so that resources can be diverted from pension funds to the domestic economy and local firms. Such misuse of pension assets clearly comes at the expense of a plan's participants, as poor performance or even bankruptcies of domestic companies may affect not only the future labor income of plan participants but also the value of pension assets and future pension benefits.

Given the size of the home capital markets and other domestic investment opportunities vis-à-vis the size of APG, only 13 percent of the fund's assets are allocated domestically

Geographically, the investment exposure of APG is global in equity markets, skewed toward euro area exposure in government bonds, and skewed toward the Netherlands in real estate investments. APG's most significant portfolio exposure (43 percent) is to U.S.-based assets, including equities, hedge funds, and debt instruments (figure 4.62). The second largest allocation is to the euro area (excluding the Netherlands), in equities and government bonds (26 percent). The Netherlands represents 13 percent of APG's total exposure, primarily in real estate and mortgage markets. Remaining asset class allocations include other European markets (7 percent), other developed markets (7 percent), and emerging markets (4 percent).

Currency risk should be hedged, although costs and liquidity implications should be taken into account

In general, pension funds should hedge currency risk when they invest internationally, since currency exposure increases the volatility of returns. They need to

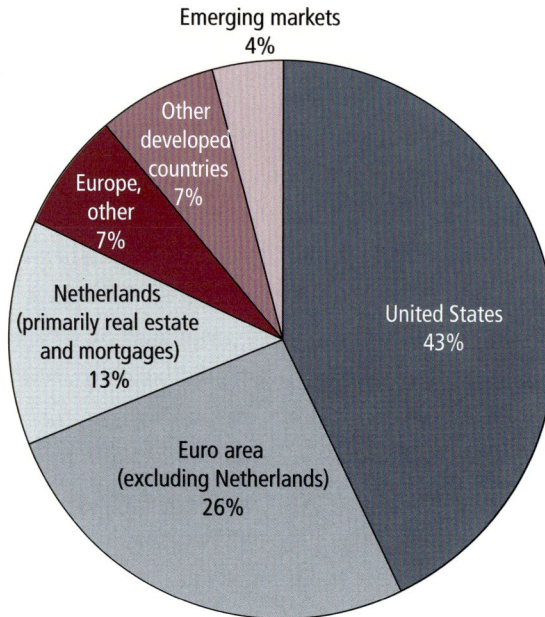

Figure 4.62 **APG Portfolio's Regional Asset Mix**

Emerging markets 4%

Other developed countries 7%

Europe, other 7%

Netherlands (primarily real estate and mortgages) 13%

United States 43%

Euro area (excluding Netherlands) 26%

Source: APG.

be aware, however, of the liquidity risk to which full currency hedging may expose them. At times, it is possible that the liquidity requirement resulting from the collateral obligations may lead pension funds to reduce their currency hedge in order to allocate a larger proportion of their portfolio to less liquid assets. The cost of currency hedging is generally higher for funds based in countries with pegged or weak currencies than for funds in countries with strong currencies. Neverthe-less, it is usually still worthwhile for funds domiciled in countries with weak or relatively illiquid currencies to undertake currency hedging due to the asymmetric risk involved in a scenario such as the breakdown of a currency peg. If domestic foreign exchange markets are not well developed, though, hedging is likely to be very expensive or inadequate. In such cases, it is useful to diversify investments across a broad range of emerging market investments.

Asset-liability management analysis can be used to determine the optimal level of currency hedging needed on a fund's investments

APG applies asset-liability management (ALM) analysis to estimate the impact of currency hedging on its investments. Figure 4.63a presents the indexation results that follow from ALM analysis. According to the analysis, a hedge of about

Figure 4.63 **ALM Analysis: Impact of U.S. Dollar Exposure**

a. Impact on indexation result after 15 years

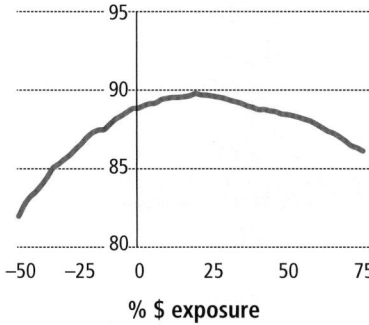

b. Impact on shortfall probability in first 15 years

75 percent of exposure to the U.S.-dollar-based assets yields optimal indexation results for the APG (inflation indexation is given to members only if the funding status is sufficient). Such outcomes, however, may be the result of a positive correlation between the U.S. dollar and inflation in the Netherlands. Figure 4.63b illustrates the probability of APG being underfunded in any of the next 15 years, with the lowest probability occurring when the pension fund is slightly overhedged. One rationale for this result may be that the liabilities of Dutch pension funds are calculated using the actual nominal-term structure. Consequently, a decline in European interest rates increases liabilities. If this decline also induces the euro to weaken, then being overhedged reduces the probability of being underfunded.

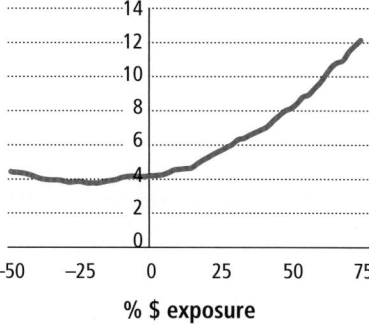

Conclusion

Diversification into international markets has helped pension funds achieve superior investment performance in terms of reduced risk and volatility and, in general, higher returns. Foreign exchange risks should be hedged if an appropriate currency market is available, though the level of hedging may vary from case to case. ALM analysis can be useful in this process, helping pension funds determine the optimal level of currency hedging needed and its impact on key factors. If no proper market exists for hedging foreign exchange risks, it is recommended that exposure to an individual currency be limited through diversification across several markets.

6. Alternative Asset Classes and New Investment Themes

◆ Characteristics, Risks, and Risk Mitigation Approaches for Alternative Asset Classes

◆ A Framework for Evaluating Alternative Asset Classes and New Investment Themes

Characteristics, Risks, and Risk Mitigation Approaches for Alternative Asset Classes

Jai Parihar, retired Chief Investment Officer, Alberta Investment Management Corporation, Canada

The investment characteristics of and risks associated with various alternative asset classes, including private equity, real estate, infrastructure, absolute return strategies, commodities, and timber, are quite distinctive from those of traditional securities and as such should be considered differently by the institutions investing in them. Alternative assets are regarded as attractive investments mainly because their returns have low correlation with those of standard asset classes. Nevertheless, alternative assets have unique features—relative illiquidity, difficult-to-determine market values, and sometimes limited risk and return historical data—that require investors to understand both the potential risks associated with investing in them and the methods for mitigating those risks.

Because they have low correlation with traditional investment classes, alternative assets are often used as a tool to reduce investment risk within a portfolio

Alternative assets complement the realm of the traditional asset types—stocks, bonds, and other instruments traded on international financial markets. They encompass a wide range of categories, including private equity, real estate, infrastructure investments, absolute return strategies, commodities, and timber, among others. Due to their low correlation with traditional financial instruments, alternative investments are often used as a tool to reduce overall investment risk through diversification (table 4.14).

In many cases, alternative investments provide opportunities for greater returns than are likely to be found in liquid or efficient markets. Many large institutional funds, such as pension funds and private endowments, have begun to allocate some portion (typically less than 10 percent) of their portfolios to alternative invest-

Table 4.14 **Correlations among Various Asset Classes**

Asset class	Fixed income	U.S. equities	Non-U.S. equities	Emerging markets equities	Private equity	Hedge funds	Global TIPS	Real estate	Infrastructure	Commodities	Timber
Fixed income	1										
U.S. equities	0.01	1									
Non-U.S. equities	−0.06	0.70	1								
Emerging markets equities	−0.21	0.62	0.56	1							
Private equity	−0.09	0.68	0.50	0.52	1						
Hedge funds	0.13	0.59	0.38	0.40	0.30	1					
Global TIPS	0.30	−0.13	0.02	−0.22	−0.03	−0.07	1				
Real estate	−0.20	0.04	0.04	0.05	0.26	−0.13	−0.05	1			
Infrastructure	0.26	0.50	0.54	0.21	0.12	0.37	0.20	0.03	1		
Commodities	−0.31	0	0.13	0.09	0.27	−0.07	0.02	0.16	−0.06	1	
Timber	−0.07	0.36	0.27	0.17	0.34	0.28	−0.06	0.23	0.28	0.07	1

Source: World Bank Treasury.

Note: TIPS = Treasury Inflation-Protected Securities

ments. The characteristics and investment risks of each alternative asset class vary, as do methods for mitigating such investment risks.

Common Characteristics of Alternative Investments

◆ Low correlation with traditional asset classes
◆ Relative illiquidity
◆ Difficult in determining current market values
◆ Limited historical risk and return data
◆ Extensive investment analysis required prior to buying
◆ Relatively high transaction costs

Private equity investments usually produce negative returns in early years and positive returns as the portfolio of companies matures

Private equity refers to an equity investment in an entity or asset not publicly traded on organized stock exchanges. The three most common investment strategies are as follows (figure 4.64):

◆ *Leveraged buyouts:* acquisitions of another company using a significant amount of borrowed money (bonds or loans)—usually a 90 percent debt to 10 percent equity ratio—to meet the cost of acquisition

◆ *Venture capital:* funds pooled from various investors with a goal of acquiring a diversified portfolio of private emerging companies with perceived long-term growth potential

◆ *Distressed investing:* acquisition of equity or debt of operationally sound companies in financial distress

Figure 4.64 **Share of Private Equity Market by Fund Type**

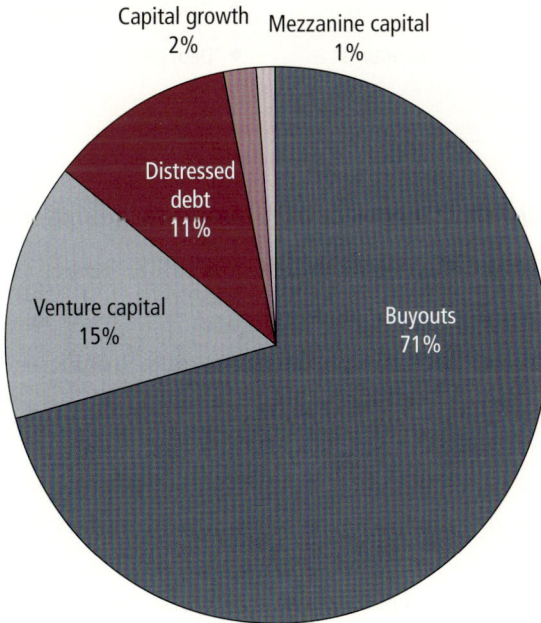

Source: Russell Investments.

Mechanisms used to invest in private equity include funds, funds of funds, and principal investments. Private equity investments represent a large universe of investable assets and provide diversification to a traditional stock and bond portfolio. They also give investors the ability to obtain control and influence operations, and have the advantage of allowing investors to focus on the business without allocating additional resources to reporting and disclosure requirements of publicly listed companies. Private equity investments tend to be illiquid in the short term. They require high-quality information, extensive analysis, and due diligence prior to entry and typically involve a long-term commitment in order to generate superior returns. Private equity investments also offer the option to leverage in order to increase returns. They tend to deliver negative returns in early years, as fees are paid to the general partners to cover their expenses without corresponding investment returns (the "J-curve effect").

The investment risks of private equity include illiquidity, a long cycle of investments and realization of returns, risks associated with selecting a general partner (management company), potential debt refinancing risks, and "vintage year" risk (the uncertainty of the future economic environment in the year a private equity fund makes its first investment).

Investment Risks: Private Equity

◆ Liquidity risk

◆ Long cycle for investment returns

◆ Vintage year risk

◆ General partner risk

◆ Debt refinancing risk

Real estate investments may deliver strong cash flows and offer a hedge against unexpected inflation

Real estate investments come in several forms, including ownership in individual assets, public real estate structures such as real estate investment trusts, public and private commercial real estate debt, and fund investments. Compared to other types of alternative investments, real estate tends to deliver strong cash flows and can be a current income provider. As an asset class, real estate is an effective portfolio diversifier, as its correlation with other assets is low or even negative and its volatility of returns is lower than that of stocks but higher than that of bonds. Real estate typically offers investors a hedge against unexpected inflation.

Several unique characteristics of real estate should not be disregarded by investors. As a tangible asset, real estate is immovable and indivisible, and despite some similarities, every property is unique. This lack of uniformity and comparability makes it difficult to assess market value and to trade in homogenous markets, which further escalates transaction costs and management fees. Because of its immobility and indivisibility features, real estate is an asset class with limited liquidity relative to other investments. It is also cash flow dependent, especially if initial capital has been deployed using leverage. Other real estate investment risks that need to be well understood and accounted for include significant cyclical variation in returns, regulatory and environmental risks, partner risk, and tax regime risk.

Investment Risks: Real Estate

◆ Market risk	◆ Regulatory risk	◆ Liquidity risk
◆ Cyclicality of returns	◆ Partner risk	◆ Leverage risk
	◆ Tax regime risk	

Infrastructure investments have high barriers to entry, but they offer stable and predictable cash flows and long-term income streams

Infrastructure investments cover a wide spectrum of tangible, long-life assets, including the following:

◆ *Transportation:* bridges, railways, roadways, transit systems, and tunnels

◆ *Ports:* airports, barges, seaports, and container terminals

◆ *Energy resources:* clean energy, hydrocarbons, gas, geothermal, wind, water, and transmission and distribution systems

◆ *Utilities:* electricity, gas, pipelines, storage and distribution, power transmission

◆ *Water:* distribution, treatment, storage, desalination, and other water-related investments

◆ *Communications:* broadcast and wireless towers and cable systems

◆ *Social infrastructure:* educational facilities, health care facilities, and judicial buildings

A number of favorable characteristics that attract pension funds to this asset class include stable and predictable cash flows and long-term income streams; attractive, risk-adjusted returns; duration matching versus pension funds' liabilities; and inflation-sensitive real returns. Infrastructure investments are capital intense and have high barriers to entry.

Infrastructure investment risks that should be avoided (since they are uncompensated) include commodity price risk, contracting risk, merchant power risk, interest rate risk, and early stage development risk. Risks that are compensated and therefore worth taking include manager selection, regulatory risks, demand risk or traffic risk, later-stage development or expansion with proven partners, and capital expenditure plans (figure 4.65).

Figure 4.65 **Investment Risks: Infrastructure**

Risks to avoid	Risks to take and get paid for
◆ Commodity price ◆ Contracting risk ◆ Merchant power risk ◆ Interest rate risk ◆ Early-stage development	◆ Manager selection ◆ Regulatory risk ◆ Demand risk/traffic risk ◆ Later-stage development/ expansion with proven partners ◆ Capital expenditure plans

Source: Author.

Risks related to infrastructure investments can be mitigated through

◆ selection of the right deals by performing extensive investment analysis and ensuring proper due diligence;

◆ diversification by country, regulator, and industry sector;

◆ foreign currency hedging;

◆ alignment of interests between investors and development/operating management;

◆ prudent leverage and refinancing.

Absolute return strategies seek positive returns regardless of market conditions and access risk premiums that cannot easily be captured in traditional investments

Absolute return strategies are a collection of investment strategies intended to generate consistent, positive absolute returns regardless of the direction of financial markets. These strategies consistently balance investment opportunities with the risk of financial loss and access risk premiums that cannot easily be captured in traditional portfolios. Absolute return strategies are highly diverse and their classification is somewhat arbitrary. The most common are these:

◆ *Long/short strategies* take both long and short positions in equities based on manager expectations of individual stocks' future performance.

- *Market-neutral equity strategies* employ long and short strategies to eliminate overall market risk by betting on valuation differences of individual closely related securities and by aiming for a zero net exposure to the market itself.

- *Global macro funds* bet on the direction of various macroeconomic variables such as currency, interest rate, commodities, or emerging market securities.

- *Event-driven strategies* exploit event-specific investment opportunities such as merger arbitrage (buying and selling simultaneously the stock of two merging companies in order to create a "riskless" profit) or distressed securities (investing at deeply discounted prices in the debt and/or equity of companies having financial difficulty).

Although they offer low correlation to equity and other asset classes, attractive long-term risk-adjusted returns, and creative and unique approaches, absolute return strategies have lower transparency than many other investments, high fees, and liquidity risk due to the prevalence of lock-up periods.

Investment Risks: Absolute Return Strategies

◆ Market risk	◆ Coinvestor risk
◆ Illiquidity risk	◆ Fraud
◆ Lock-up periods	◆ Reputation/headline risk
◆ Leverage/financing risk	◆ Short investment history

Commodity investments are more volatile than global equities but tend to have low negative correlation with stock and bond returns and positive correlation with inflation

Commodity investments offer an opportunity to directly participate in the real economy. They can be grouped into three major categories:

- *Agricultural products:* grain, food, livestock, fibers, lumber, and ethanol

- *Energy:* crude oil, heating oil, Brent crude, natural gas, and uranium

- *Metals:* gold, silver, copper, aluminum, platinum, and palladium

Commodities do not generate cash flows, and the return to the investor is through price increases. Long-term commodity investments offer the benefit of low correlation with other investable asset classes, thereby reducing the overall risk of a portfolio. Commodity investments also serve as a hedge against inflation and political or economic uncertainty. Since commodities do not generate a stream of cash flows, they are difficult to evaluate using financial models.

Timber is endowed with several unique characteristics that are attractive to pension funds

Timber investments are equity investments, primarily in private timberlands. Examples include freehold land with timber, private and public leases with timber, and plantations with fast-growing species. For pension funds and private endowments, timber has become a particularly attractive asset class due to its unique characteristics such as inflation-sensitive real returns (biological growth and timber price increases have matched inflation), duration matching with pension funds' liabilities, attractive risk-adjusted returns, and the ability to diversify portfolios. As illustrated in figure 4.66, timber investments have increased exponentially over the past two and a half decades. Between 1982 and 2009, timber investments increased by an annual average of almost 32 percent, from a negligible amount to $41 billion.

Figure 4.66 **Timberland: Assets under Management**

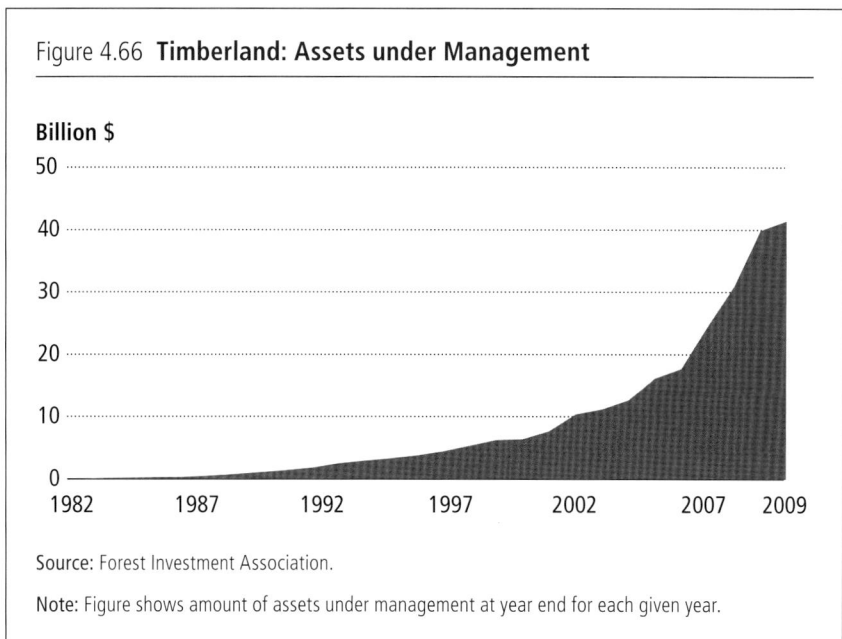

Billion $

Source: Forest Investment Association.

Note: Figure shows amount of assets under management at year end for each given year.

Sources of timber's continued annual accretion of value include volumetric growth (3–6 percent), grade change (1–2 percent), intensive management (1–3 percent), and real price increase (1–2 percent).

Investors in timber face a variety of risks that do not affect more traditional asset classes. Timber generally is exposed to long investment horizons and consequent liquidity risks. Since timber does not generally provide continuous income streams, it requires investors to be particularly careful about leverage, refinancing, and interest rate risks. Natural hazards such as adverse weather (namely drought and flooding), fire, insects, and diseases pose additional risks for timber investments.

Investment Risks: Timber

- ◆ Manager selection
- ◆ Regulatory/policy risk
- ◆ Environmental and social risks
- ◆ Market cycle risk
- ◆ Natural hazards (for example, disease, fire, insects, drought)
- ◆ Leverage/refinancing/interest rate risks
- ◆ Time horizon and liquidity risks

Pension funds need to take into account the risk of changing regulatory, policy, environmental, and social circumstances when deciding to invest in timber. Decisions on forestry investments also should take into consideration various means of managing timber-specific risks by selecting the right investments; performing proper due diligence; hedging foreign currency risk; and diversifying by species, end-market user, country, and regulator.

Conclusion

Alternative asset classes often provide attractive investment opportunities for pension funds in addition to public equities and public or private bonds. The improvement to overall portfolio performance may be due to higher returns as well as risk reduction from low correlation with traditional asset classes. Such investments can include private equity, real estate, infrastructure, absolute return strategies, commodities, and timber. Each asset class has distinctive characteristics and risks and therefore needs distinctive management and risk mitigation approaches.

A Framework for Evaluating Alternative Asset Classes and New Investment Themes

Adriaan Ryder, Managing Director, Queensland Investment Corporation, Australia

The Queensland Investment Corporation (QIC) of Australia employs a disciplined approach to investing in alternative assets, using a framework to determine the relationship of each alternative asset class to both key economic variables and traditional asset classes. QIC analyzes the nature of the risk premiums within each asset class, including the illiquidity premium. Further, it examines asset classes/themes for evidence of long-term structural breaks, and thematic, structural, or strategic trends. QIC primarily seeks to invest in assets that provide high risk premiums that will persist for extended periods of time. Challenges involved in this approach include deconstructing the asset classes (or themes) and their drivers and determining the current level of risk premium for each asset class.

A disciplined approach to investment in alternative assets requires assessment of the nature and the level of risk premiums and their relationship to economic measures

For any institutional investor, a disciplined approach to investment in alternative investments requires a framework incorporating each asset class and its relationship to key economic variables and other asset classes. In this process, it is important to assess both the nature of risk premiums embedded in each asset class—for example, credit and term structure—and the current level of those risk premiums. The Queensland Investment Corporation (QIC), one of Australia's largest institutional fund managers, applies a stochastic, future-focused approach to investing in alternative assets that incorporates three main areas (figure 4.67).

For investors, risk premiums need to be assessed at both the asset class level and the portfolio level. At the asset class level, analysis of three crucial areas should be performed: (1) the nature of the risk premiums within each asset class, including the illiquidity premium; (2) the relationships of asset classes to key economic variables

---

Figure 4.67 **Framework for Analysis of Investment in Alternative Assets**

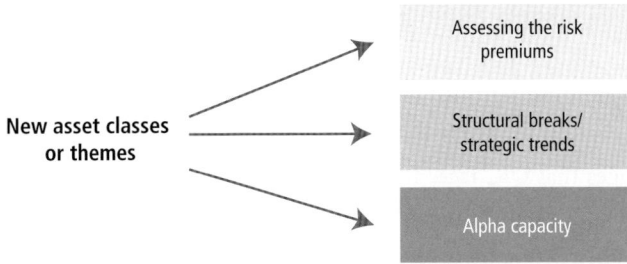

New asset classes or themes → Assessing the risk premiums

New asset classes or themes → Structural breaks/ strategic trends

New asset classes or themes → Alpha capacity

Source: QIC.

---

and to other asset classes; and (3) the current level of risk premiums in the asset class and the expected future (stochastic) paths. At the portfolio level, managers should ascertain that adding any asset class into the portfolio will help meet the fund objectives (that is, improve the probability of outcomes such as return, risk, and surplus stability).

An institutional investor should not add a new asset class if

◆ it replicates either an existing asset class (in terms of risk premiums, for example), or

◆ it does not improve the probability of the investor meeting its investment objectives.

Capacity to select managers who generate alpha and ability to recognize long-term structural or other breaks are also key to successful alternative asset investment

Selection of managers who can generate superior, higher-than-market returns (alpha) is key in successful investment in alternative assets. Typically, alternative asset classes have a deeper pool of talented investment managers than traditional assets. Though it is often difficult to separate what is considered alpha from what is considered beta in relation to alternative assets, alpha-generation skill is discernible. In general, that skill is also highly specialized. There are typically only a handful of investment managers in the world who exhibit persistent alpha-generating capabilities in each alternative asset class.

Investment in alternative assets also involves examination of those asset classes for evidence of long-term structural breaks or thematic, structural, or strategic trends. In this regard, investment managers must fully understand and be able to justify the long-term risk premiums involved with a new asset class. Examples of such investments include assets related to climate change, water, peak oil, energy, and the shift from developing to developed economies in driving global economic growth.

Conclusion

The challenges that QIC faces in the course of investing in alternative assets are common among all institutions investing in this asset class. Specific challenges include deconstructing the asset classes (or themes) and their drivers, ruthlessness in managing any duplications and overlaps, sourcing the beta exposures, sourcing the best alpha available, and incorporating new customized and targeted mandates into the asset allocation framework in order to assess the appropriate level of risk premiums.

Glossary

Accrual rate. The rate at which pension benefits build up as a member's professional service is completed in a defined-benefit plan.

Accrued benefits. The amount of accumulated pension benefits of a pension plan member based on the pension accrual formula for a particular plan.

Accumulated assets/accumulated contributions. The total value of assets accumulated in a pension fund.

Active member. A pension plan member who is making contributions (and/or on behalf of whom contributions are being made).

Active strategy. An investment strategy characterized by monitoring and attempting to capitalize on short-term market conditions to optimize the risk and return of a portfolio.

Actuarial surplus. A situation in which the actuarial value of a pension fund's assets exceed the actuarial value of the fund's liabilities.

Actuarial valuation. A valuation carried out by an actuary on a regular basis to estimate the present value of a pension fund's future liabilities.

Agency problem. A situation in which agents of an organization (for example, the management) use their authority for their own benefit rather than for the benefit of the principals (for example, the pension beneficiaries).

Alpha. A measure of performance. The excess return of the fund/portfolio relative to the return of the benchmark index is a fund's/portfolio's alpha.

Alternative asset. Any nontraditional asset with potential economic value that would not be found in a standard investment portfolio (for example, private equity, hedge funds, commodities, and infrastructure).

Asset-liability management (ALM). Risk management techniques designed to manage a pension fund's assets by explicitly taking into account the nature and size of the fund's liabilities.

Annuity. A form of financial contract that guarantees a fixed or variable payment of income benefit (monthly, quarterly, half-yearly, or yearly) for the life of a person (the annuitant) or for a specified period of time.

Asset allocation. The spread of fund investments among different asset classes.

Asset class. A group of securities that exhibit similar characteristics, behave similarly in the marketplace, and are subject to the same laws and regulations. The three traditional asset classes are equities (stocks), fixed-income (bonds) and cash.

Asset manager. The individual(s) or entity(ies) endowed with the responsibility to physically invest any particular assets.

Basic pension. A nonearning related pension paid by the state to individuals with a minimum number of service years, and/or to individuals over the retirement age and below a certain income level.

Beneficiary. An individual who is entitled to a benefit, including the plan member and dependants.

Benefit. Payment made to a pension fund member or dependants after retirement.

Beta. A measure of the volatility, or systematic risk, of a security or a portfolio in comparison to the market as a whole. Beta is also, separately, often used to refer to returns generated from passively investing in a particular asset class, as distinct from the incremental returns generated from pursuing an active investment strategy in that asset class (which is called 'alpha').

Competitive advantage. An advantage that a firm has over its competitors that allows it to generate greater sales or margins and/or retain more customers than its competition. Cost structure, product offerings, distribution network, and customer support are all types of competitive advantage.

Contribution. A payment made to a pension plan by a plan sponsor or a plan member.

Contribution rate. The amount that must be paid into the pension fund over a certain period of time, typically expressed as a percentage of the contribution base.

Contributory pension scheme. A pension scheme in which both the employer and the members must pay into the scheme.

Correlation. A standardized measure of the relationship between two securities, portfolios, or asset classes (the degree to which the two variable's movements are associated) that ranges from -1 to +1.

Covariance. A measure of the degree to which returns on two securities, portfolios, or asset classes move in tandem. Covariance and correlation are similar terms.

Custodian. The entity responsible, at a minimum, for holding the pension fund's assets and for ensuring their safekeeping.

Defined-benefit plan. A retirement plan in which benefits are linked through a formula to the members' wages or salaries, length of employment, or other factors.

Defined-contribution plan. A retirement plan under which the plan sponsor pays fixed contributions and has no legal or constructive obligation to pay further contributions to an ongoing plan in the event of unfavorable plan experience.

Distressed investing. Acquisition of equity or debt of operationally sound companies in financial distress.

Downside risk. Estimation of a portfolio's potential to suffer a decline in value if market conditions become worse than expected.

Efficient frontier. The graphic presentation of the set of optimal portfolios offering the maximum expected return for a given amount of risk (often defined as the variance or volatility of that portfolio).

Expected rate of return (expected return). The rate of return an investor anticipates earning from a specific investment over a particular future holding period.

Fair value. The price at which an asset would change hands between a willing buyer and a willing seller when neither party is under compulsion to buy or to sell and both parties have reasonable knowledge of relevant facts.

Funding level. The relative value of a pension scheme's assets to its liabilities, usually expressed as a percentage.

Funded ratio. A pension scheme's ratio of assets to liabilities, expressed as a fraction.

Governing body (of a pension fund). The person(s) ultimately responsible for managing a pension fund with the overriding objective of providing a secure source of retirement income to the fund's beneficiaries. In cases in which operational and oversight responsibilities are split between different committees within a fund, the governing body is the executive board with overall responsibility for the entity. Where the pension fund is not a legal entity, but managed directly by a financial institution, that institution's board of directors is also the governing body of the pension fund.

Hedge ratio. The proportion of a particular asset or risk that is being hedged.

Hedging. A general strategy usually aimed at reducing, if not eliminating, a particular kind of risk.

Indexation. The method with which pension benefits are adjusted to take into account changes in the cost of living (for example, by indexation to consumer price inflation) and/or to target a particular level of replacement income during retirement (for example, by linking to average wages or increases in average wages).

Inflation-linked bond (ILB). A bond that provides protection against inflation. Most inflation-linked bonds are principal indexed to inflation. This means their principal is increased by the change in inflation over a given period.

Investment horizon. The total length of time an investor expects to hold a security or an asset portfolio. The investment horizon can be viewed as the minimum length of time or periodicity over which portfolio returns and/or changes in market value of the portfolio have meaningful significance for the institution and its governing board.

Investment strategy. A decision regarding how to invest an asset portfolio to meet the goals and objectives for which the assets are being held.

319

J-curve. A graph in which a curve falls at the outset and eventually rises to a point higher than the starting point, suggesting the letter J.

Leveraged buyout. A transaction whereby the target company's management team converts the target to a privately held company by using heavy borrowing to finance purchase of the target company's outstanding shares.

Liability-driven investment (LDI). A form of investing in which the main goal is to gain sufficient assets to meet all liabilities, both current and future.

Mark to market. The accounting method of recording the price or value of a security, portfolio, or account to reflect its current market value rather than its book value.

Mean. The sum of all values in a distribution or data set, divided by the number of values; a synonym of arithmetic mean.

Minimum pension. The minimum level of pension benefits the plan pays out in all circumstances.

Nominal rate. A rate of interest yielded by a security based on the security's face value.

Noncontributory pension scheme. A pension scheme in which members do not have to pay into the scheme.

Normal distribution. A continuous, symmetric probability distribution which is completely described by its mean and its variance.

Optimal portfolio. The portfolio on the efficient frontier that has the highest possible potential return at a given level of risk.

Pay-as-you-go plan/unfunded pension plan. Benefits are paid directly from contributions from the plan sponsor and/or the plan participant, with no reserves or assets set aside for this purpose.

Pension fund. The pool of assets forming an independent legal entity that are bought with the contributions to a pension plan for the exclusive purpose of financing pension plan benefits. The plan/fund members have a legal or beneficial right or some other contractual claim against the assets of the pension fund. Pension funds take the form of either a special-purpose entity with legal personality (such as a trust, foundation, or corporate entity) or a legally separated fund without legal personality managed by a dedicated provider (pension fund management company) or other financial institution on behalf of the plan/fund members.

Pension fund governance. The operation and oversight of a pension fund. The governing body is responsible for administration, but may employ other specialists, such as actuaries, custodians, consultants, asset managers, or advisers, to carry out specific operational tasks or to advise the plan administration or governing body.

Pension plan sponsor. An institution (for example, a company or an industry/ employment association) that designs, negotiates, and normally helps to administer an occupational pension plan for its employees or members.

Portfolio rebalancing. The process of realigning the weightings of one's portfolio of assets. Rebalancing involves periodically buying or selling assets in the portfolio to maintain the desired level of asset allocation.

Price discovery. A method of determining the price of a specific security or commodity through basic supply and demand factors related to the market.

Private equity. Equity capital that is not quoted on a public exchange and consists of investors and funds that make investments directly into private companies or conduct buyouts of public companies that result in a delisting of public equity. Private equity investments often demand long holding periods to allow for a turnaround of a distressed company or a liquidity event such as an initial public offering or sale to a public company.

Rate of return. The income earned by holding an asset over a specified period.

Replacement rate. The ratio of an individual's (average) pension in a given time period to that person's (average) income over a given time period.

Required rate of return. The rate of return needed to induce investors or companies to invest in a particular asset.

Risk averse. The assumption that investors will choose the least risky alternative, all else being equal.

Risk budgeting. The establishment of objectives for individuals, groups, or divisions of an organization that takes into account the allocation of an acceptable level of risk.

Risk management. The process of identifying the level of risk an entity wants, measuring the level of risk the entity currently has, taking actions that bring the actual level of risk to the desired level of risk, and monitoring the new actual level of risk so that it continues to be aligned with the desired level of risk.

Risk premium. The expected return on an investment minus the risk-free rate.

Risk tolerance. The degree of uncertainty an investor is comfortable with in regard to a negative change in the value of his or her portfolio.

Risk-free asset. An asset with returns that exhibit zero variance.

Risk-free rate of return. The theoretical rate of return of an investment with zero risk. The risk-free rate represents the interest an investor would expect from an absolutely risk-free investment over a specified period of time.

Risky asset. An asset with uncertain future returns.

Sharpe ratio. The portfolio return minus the risk-free rate of return and divided by the standard deviation of the portfolio returns. The Sharpe ratio is a measure of a portfolio's returns adjusted for the amount of risk taken.

Sortino ratio. A ratio that differentiates between good and bad volatility in the Sharpe ratio. This differentiation of upward and downward volatility allows the calculation to provide a risk-adjusted measure of a security or fund's performance without penalizing it for upward price changes.

Standard deviation. A measure of the dispersion of a set of data from its mean, calculated as the square root of variance. The more spread apart the data, the higher the standard deviation.

Strategic asset allocation (SAA). A portfolio strategy that involves making long-term allocations to different asset classes which are not influenced by short-term movements in the returns of these asset classes.

Tail risk. A form of portfolio risk that arises when the value of an investment moves more than 3 standard deviations from the mean.

Tactical asset allocation. An active management portfolio strategy that periodically changes the percentage of assets held in various asset classes in order to take advantage of short-term movements in the returns of these asset classes.

Tracking error. The standard deviation of the difference in returns between an active investment portfolio and its benchmark portfolio; it is also called tracking error volatility, tracking risk, or active risk.

Underfunding. A situation in which the value of a plan's assets is less than its liabilities (that is, there is an actuarial deficiency).

Value at risk (VaR). A money measure of the minimum value of losses expected during a specified time period at a given level of probability.

Variance. A measure of the dispersion of a set of data points around their mean value. Variance is a mathematical expectation of the average squared deviations from the mean.

Variance-covariance matrix. The variance-covariance matrix computes the covariance between each of the columns of a data matrix. That is, row i and column j of the variance-covariance matrix is the covariance between column i and column j of the original matrix. The diagonal elements (for example, i = j) are the variances of the columns. The variance-covariance matrix is symmetric (since the variance-covariance of column i with column j is the same as the variance-covariance of column j with column i).

Venture capital. Money provided by investors to start-up firms and small businesses with perceived long-term growth potential. Venture capital typically entails high risk for the investor, but it has the potential for above-average returns.

Voluntary contribution. A pension contribution in addition to the mandatory contribution that a member may pay to the pension fund in order to increase his or her future pension benefits.

References

CFA Program Curriculum, 2010.

OECD (Organisation for Economic Co-operation and Development). 2005. *Private Pensions: OECD Classification and Glossary.* Paris: OECD.

Contributors

Keith Ambachtsheer is director of the Rotman International Centre for Pension Management and an adjunct professor of finance at The Joseph L. Rotman School of Management at the University of Toronto. A respected author, researcher, and commentator on pension and investment topics, he is the recipient of numerous awards and recognitions on those topics. Mr. Ambachtsheer has authored three critically acclaimed books: *Pension Revolution: A Solution to the Pensions Crisis* (2007), *Pension Fund Excellence – Creating Value for Stakeholders* (with Don Ezra in 1998), and *Pension Funds and the Bottom Line* (1986). Through his firm, KPA Advisory Services, and a monthly publication, Mr. Ambachtsheer advises clients in the private and public sectors around the world. He is a graduate of the Royal Military College of Canada and received a master of economics from the University of Western Ontario and McGill University.

Sergio B. Arvizu is the deputy chief executive officer and deputy secretary to the pension board of the United Nations Joint Staff Pension Fund (UNJSPF). Mr. Arvizu chaired the UNJSPF's Steering Committee in its first ever formal comprehensive asset-liability management (ALM) study, which provided independent confirmation of the Fund's sound actuarial valuation process, favorable funded status, and solid asset allocation. Mr. Arvizu also chaired the Steering Committee for the modernization of its operational platform, which is expected to improve the UNJSPF's entire processing infrastructure and provide new and enhanced services to clients. Before joining the UNJSPF, Mr. Arvizu was the chief investment officer and treasurer general of the Mexican Social Security Institute, where he worked for 10 years. In the past, Mr. Arvizu held senior positions at JP Morgan, Citibank, Chase Manhattan Bank, and Interacciones.

Arjan Berkelaar is head of investment strategy and risk management at KAUST Investment Management Company. He is a recognized expert in asset allocation strategies and risk management for multi-asset class investors such as pension funds, sovereign wealth funds, and central banks. Prior to joining KAUST, Mr. Berkelaar was a lead investment strategist for the World Bank's pension funds. He led the Quantitative Strategies team's multi-asset class initiatives in the World Bank Treasury. He also advised central banks, sovereign wealth funds, and pension funds on asset allocation, investment strategy, risk budgeting, and related policy matters. Mr. Berkelaar holds a PhD in finance from Erasmus University Rotterdam and an MS in mathematics (summa cum laude) from the Delft University of Technology. He is both a CFA and a Chartered Alternative Investment Analyst charter holder.

Mercedes Bourquin is director for the coordination and control of social security schemes in the Ministry of Labor, Employment, and Social Security in Argentina, and is a member of the Permanent Commission for Mercosur Agreement. She intervenes on social security policy design and coordinates more than 130 national, provincial, and municipal schemes. In her earlier positions with the Ministry of Labor, Employment, and Social Security, Ms. Bourquin served as the advisor of the Argentina Social Security Secretary of State, assessing results and impact of the implementation of social security policies. Prior to joining the ministry, she was in charge of the actuarial valuation of the Argentina National Pension Scheme for the International Labour Organization in Geneva, Switzerland. Ms. Bourquin holds a diploma in actuarial techniques from the Institute of Actuaries, London and the actuary diploma from the University of Buenos Aires, Argentina.

John Carpendale is a board member of the Queensland Superannuation Fund of Australia, a director of QSuper Limited, and a former superannuation fund executive. He is also a member of several board subcommittees, including the recently enhanced Investment Committee. In 2005, he retired from full-time work, after more than 45 years of employment in the Australian superannuation industry. John holds a BA and a graduate diploma in applied finance and investment and a graduate diploma in financial planning. He is also a graduate of the Australian Institute of Company Directors.

Krishnan Chandrasekhar is a senior manager within the World Bank Treasury. Mr. Chandrasekhar heads the group that is responsible for formulating investment policy, strategic asset allocation, and the development of quantitative strategies and techniques for various internal and external client portfolios managed by World Bank Treasury. Prior to assuming these responsibilities in 2002, he was the head of asset-liability management. Mr. Chandrasekhar joined the World Bank Treasury in 1986, and has since had diverse experience in areas including investment management, derivatives and structured finance, capital markets, and risk management. He holds a BS in electrical engineering from the Indian Institute of Technology, Madras, and an MBA from the Indian Institute of Management, Ahmedabad.

Arporn Chewakrengkrai is chief economist of Thailand's Government Pension Fund. Prior to joining the Government Pension Fund in 2001, she was an economic advisor to the prime minister, Chuan Leekpai, from 1997 to 2000. Earlier in her career, Ms. Chewakrengkrai served as a chief economist in Deutsche Morgan Grenfell Securities and held various positions in the Economic Analysis and Planning Divisions of the National Economic and Social Development Board in Thailand. Ms. Chewakrengkrai has published extensively on economic development, infrastructure, and macroeconomic issues in Thailand. She holds a PhD in economics from Boston University; a postgraduate diploma in development planning technique from the Institute of Social Studies, the Hague, the Netherlands; and a BA in economics from Chulalongkorn University, Bangkok, Thailand.

Mark C. Dorfman is a senior economist with the Pensions Team in the Social Protection Group of the World Bank, where he works on pensions and contractual savings reform in developing countries. Prior to assuming this position in 2004, he worked on debt sustainability, debt relief, and risk management in low-income countries. During his 22 years with the World Bank, Mr. Dorfman has worked on several areas of financial market reform, including contractual savings, debt management, banking, and capital markets. He has worked in three regions—East Asia and the Pacific, Latin America and the Caribbean, and Sub-Saharan Africa. Mr. Dorfman holds an MBA in finance from The Wharton School.

Andrew Fung is vice president, actuarial services, of the Ontario Municipal Employees Retirement System, where he is responsible for developing and managing actuarial capabilities and services and liaising with the external actuarial consultants. He has more than 20 years of experience in the pension consulting field. Prior to joining OMERS in early 2009, Mr. Fung was a client manager and senior consulting actuary in the Toronto office of Watson Wyatt. He has extensive experience providing advice to a wide range of clients regarding pension plan design, governance, financing, accounting, and operation. Mr. Fung has served as a member of the Industry Advisory Group on Prudent Investment and Funding, established by the Canadian Association of Pension Supervisory Authorities. He graduated on the Dean's Honor List from University of Waterloo with a B. Math in Computer Science and Combinatorics and Optimization. He is a fellow of both the Canadian Institute of Actuaries (FCIA) and the Society of Actuaries (FSA) and holds a CFA designation.

John Gandolfo is the director and chief investment officer of the Pension and Endowments Department of the World Bank. The department manages about $14 billion of pension and other retirement benefit portfolios invested across a range of asset classes, including fixed income, public and private equity, real estate, and hedge funds. Prior to assuming these responsibilities, Mr. Gandolfo was the director of the Quantitative Strategies, Risk and Analytics Department, where he was responsible for the development of strategic and tactical asset allocations, risk management, and financial modeling for the asset management, capital markets, and banking businesses. Previously, Mr. Gandolfo was the director of investments. He holds a BA from the University of Pennsylvania and an MBA from the George Washington University.

Samuel W. Halpern, president of Independent Fiduciary Services (IFS), has specialized for 30 years in the financial and fiduciary aspects of employee benefit plan investment programs. As president, he is responsible for guiding development and delivery of the firm's services overall and personally works with select retainer and project clients across the full range of IFS' services. Prior to helping establish IFS, Mr. Halpern was a partner in a Washington, DC labor law firm, where he specialized in investment matters representing pension and welfare funds, trustees, labor unions, and participants in litigation and administrative matters involving the U.S. Department of Labor. Before private practice, Mr. Halpern litigated fiduciary responsibility cases under the Employment Retirement Income Security Act (ERISA) for five years at the U.S. Department of Labor. Mr. Halpern received his law degree with honors from the George Washington University Law

Center. He attended the London School of Economics and is a magna cum laude and Phi Beta Kappa graduate of Brown University.

Richard Hinz is a pension policy adviser and the team leader of the Pensions Team in the Social Protection Group of the Human Development Network at the World Bank. His work is focused on the reform of social security systems and the development, regulation, and supervision of funded pension arrangements in a broad range of settings around the world. Prior to joining the World Bank in 2003, he was the director of the Office of Policy and Research at what is now Employee Benefits Security Administration (EBSA) of the U.S. Department of Labor. In this capacity, he was responsible for managing research and economic and legislative analysis for the agency responsible for the regulation and supervision of private employer sponsored health insurance and pension programs. He has contributed to pension reforms in many countries since 1991 through policy development and technical assistance programs of the U.S. government, the World Bank, the OECD and the International Organization of Pension Supervisors (IOPS). He is the coauthor of the recent World Bank book *Old Age Income Support in the 21st Century*.

Robert Holzmann is a senior policy adviser and former sector director of the Social Protection Group of the Human Development Network at the World Bank. This unit is the Bank's focal point for labor market interventions, including child labor and youth employment; social insurance, in particular pensions; targeted interventions, such as social safety nets and social funds; and the disability and development program of the Bank. Before joining the World Bank, Mr. Holzmann was the managing director of the European Institute and full professor of international economics and European economy, both at the University of Saarbrucken (Germany). He also frequently acted as consultant to the International Monetary Fund, the Commission of the European Union, International Labour Organization (ILO), International Social Security Association, German Technical Cooperation Agency (GTZ), and the Council of Europe. In this capacity, he has been involved in the reform of budgets and pensions and other social programs in Eastern Europe and Latin America. Mr. Holzmann holds a master's degree in economics from the University of Graz, and a PhD and "habilitation" in economics from the University of Vienna.

Augusto Iglesias has been vice minister for social security in Chile since March 2010. Prior to his nomination, he was a senior partner of PrimAmérica Consultores, specializing in social security and welfare, private pensions, insurance, and pension fund regulations. His areas of expertise include industrial organization and labor economics, pension systems, pension reforms, pension fund management, and capital market regulations and development. During his career, Mr. Iglesias has participated in pension reform projects in 17 countries in Latin America and Central and Eastern Europe. He is a member of the Technical Council for Pension Funds Investments and of the Academic Council of the Institute for Banking Studies in Chile. In 2006–07, he was a member of the Presidential Advisory Council for Pension Reform in Chile. Mr. Iglesias holds a degree in economics from Catholic University (Chile) and an MS from the University of California, Los Angeles.

Ross Jones is deputy chairman and member of Australian Prudential Regulation Authority (APRA). Within APRA, he takes principal responsibility for superannuation/private pensions and chairs APRA's Enforcement Committee. He is also president of the International Organization of Pension Supervisors, a group whose members include pension supervisors and regulators from more than 70 countries, and vice chairman of the OECD Working Party on Private Pensions and a member of the Singapore Central Provident Fund Advisory Panel. Prior to joining APRA, Mr. Jones was a commissioner of the Australian Competition and Consumer Commission and chairman of the International Air Services Commission. He was also an associate professor in the School of Finance and Economics at the University of Technology, Sydney for a number of years.

Seuran Lee is the chief of the National Pension Finance Division in the Ministry of Health, Welfare, and Family Affairs in the Republic of Korea, where she is responsible for pension fund investment and management, establishment and implementation of investment policies and strategies, and supervision of institutions involved with pension fund investments. Prior to assuming these responsibilities in March 2008, Ms. Lee held various positions in the Ministry of Health, Welfare, and Family Affairs, which she joined in 1997. She holds an MA from Carnegie Mellon University.

Liew Heng San is the chief executive officer of Central Provident Fund Board of Singapore. Prior to this appointment, he was the permanent secretary of the Ministry of Law. Mr. Liew joined the Administrative Service in 1979 and held several appointments including: chief executive officer of the Land Transport Authority, deputy secretary of the then Ministry of Communications, principal private secretary to deputy prime minister Lee Hsien Loong and director (industry) in the Ministry of Trade and Industry. He also headed the Economic Development Board as managing director, served as the chairman of Singapore Land Authority, and as deputy chairman of the Intellectual Property Office of Singapore. Mr. Liew graduated from Cambridge University with a BA (Honors) on an Overseas Merit Scholarship and subsequently obtained a master's degree in public administration from Harvard University.

Anne Maher is a nonexecutive director of Allied Irish Banks p.l.c., chairman of the Irish Medical Council Performance Committee, and a board member of the Professional Oversight Board of the United Kingdom and the Retirement Planning Council of Ireland. She is also a member of the FTSE Policy Group, a Governor of The Pensions Policy Institute (United Kingdom), and a member of the Actuarial Stakeholder Interest Working Group (United Kingdom). Ms. Maher was formerly chief executive officer of the Irish Pensions Board, chairman of the Irish Association of Pension Funds, and a member of the Commission on Public Service Pensions and several other public service boards. She also has represented Ireland at the European Federation for Retirement Provision and on the Committee for European Insurance and Occupational Pensions Supervisors. She holds a law degree from University College, Dublin.

Tim Mitchell is general manager, corporate strategy at the New Zealand Superannuation Fund. He is responsible for the Guardians' overall strategy in best-practice activities, including best-practice portfolio management, responsible investment, legal, and communications. Before joining the Guardians in 2003, Mr. Mitchell was a consultant to the board in charge of establishing the Guardians' infrastructure and policies. Formerly, he was a principal advisor at The New Zealand Treasury. Prior to moving into the public sector, he spent seven years with Colonial First State Investment Managers, most recently as chief investment officer.

John Oliphant is the head of investments and actuarial for the Government Employees Pension Fund of South Africa, where he is the main driver behind the investment strategies and performance. Mr. Oliphant also sits on the Investment Committee of the Pan African Infrastructure Development Fund, which invests in infrastructure projects throughout Africa. Mr. Oliphant is an esteemed leader in the field of quantitative methodologies, and was head of quantitative strategies at STANLIB Asset Management—the third largest asset manager in South Africa in terms of assets under management. He has managed both long-only and market-neutral hedge funds using different quantitative methodologies. Mr. Oliphant holds a BS in actuarial science and a BS (Honors) in advanced mathematics of finance, both from the University of the Witwatersrand, Johannesburg.

Jai Parihar is the retired chief investment officer of the Alberta Investment Management Corporation in Canada. During his 35-year career with the Province of Alberta, he held a number of senior positions, including head of investment administration and systems, senior bond trader and manager of the Province of Alberta's debt program. He is also a member of the Investment Committee of the Alberta Teachers Retirement Fund, and a director on the board of the University of British Columbia Investment Management Trust. Mr. Parihar holds an MBA and an MS in engineering from the University of Alberta, and a BS in Engineering from the University of Udaipur, India. He also holds an ICD.D designation from the Institute of Corporate Directors in Canada, a CFA charter, and has completed an investment management workshop, sponsored by the CFA Institute, at Harvard University.

Sudhir Rajkumar is head of pension advisory at the World Bank Treasury. He leads advisory activities for public pension funds and other multi-asset class investors seeking to build global investment operations, and has served as a senior advisor to several such funds and institutions. During 22 years in global investments, Mr. Rajkumar has managed various World Bank, external client, and pension asset portfolios; been responsible for investment strategy formulation and management of external investment managers; and led teams originating and executing private debt and equity transactions, as well as corporate finance and privatization mandates, in emerging markets in Asia and Europe (with the International Finance Corporation). Mr. Rajkumar holds an MBA from University of Chicago, an MS in economics from the London School of Economics, a BS in engineering from University of Delhi, and a CFA charter. He serves on the Advisory Committee on Investments of the Food and Agriculture Organization of the United Nations, and served on the Investment Committee of the UN World Food Programme during 2004–10.

Lars Rohde is the chief executive officer of ATP, a Danish pension scheme, which he joined in 1998. Earlier in his career, Lars held various positions, including chief executive officer of Realkredit Denmark, one of the leading Danish mortgage banks, and deputy chief executive officer of Lægernes Pensionskasse respectively. Prior to joining Lægernes Pensionskasse (Medical Doctors' Pension Fund) as head of asset management, Mr. Rohde worked as an economist at the Danish central bank. From 2003 to 2005, he was a member of the Copenhagen Stock Exchange Committee on Corporate Governance and from 1993 to 1996 he served as a member of the board of the Copenhagen Stock Exchange. He holds an MS in economics from School of Economics and Management, University of Aarhus. He has also been a part-time associate professor in financial planning at Copenhagen Business School.

Adriaan Ryder is the managing director of Queensland Investment Corporation (QIC). He is responsible for formulating and implementing strategic asset allocation policies for major clients, risk management, portfolio construction, capital market and asset class research, and beta portfolio management across all asset classes. Mr. Ryder has extensive experience in developing and implementing investment strategies and solutions for institutional clients, from both asset and liability perspectives, across a wide range of funds and regions. Prior to joining QIC, he was a director at Old Mutual in the United Kingdom, where he was responsible for advising and managing institutional clients' portfolios. He also served as senior vice president of United Asset Management in the United States. Mr. Ryder is an actuary, holding an Honors degree in Actuarial Science, and holds membership in several professional associations.

Yvonne Sin is the head of investment consulting (China) at Towers Watson and the former head of the global pensions practice in the Social Protection Group at the World Bank. Ms. Sin specializes in social insurance and employee benefit issues and conducts research on pensions and investments. She is an expert with more than 30 years of experience in the development and application of financial models on funding alternatives for pension systems around the world. She has provided technical assistance in policy development for social security and civil service reform for some 20 countries. As a key member of the World Bank task force to reform human resource policies, Ms. Sin was instrumental in changing the Bank's own pension plan. Ms. Sin has been appointed adjunct professor of finance and economics at Nanjing University, where she lectures on pensions and insurance and on human resource topics. She received a BS in mathematics from the University of Toronto and graduated from the World Bank's Pensions Fellowship Program.

Tørres Trovik, assistant director of risk management of Storebrand, in Norway, joined the company in 2010 and is responsible for risk management and allocation of economic capital. He previously worked on strategic asset allocation for internal portfolios and external clients for the World Bank. Prior to joining the World Bank in 2008, Mr. Trovik was a senior portfolio manager within Norges Bank Investment Management since 1998. In 2002, he was appointed special adviser in the staff of the governor of Norges Bank, where he worked on strategic asset allocation and governance issues. He also has participated in several technical assistance missions for the International Monetary Fund on sovereign wealth funds, and has been a member of the Investment Advisory Board of the Petroleum Fund on East Timor since 2005. Mr. Trovik holds a PhD in finance from the Norwegian School of Economics and Business Administration.

Roger Urwin is global head of investment content at Towers Watson, where he is responsible for a number of the firm's major investment clients in the United Kingdom and elsewhere, advising them on all investment issues. He joined the company (formerly Watson Wyatt) in 1995 to start the firm's investment consulting practice, which grew to a global team of 500 staff under his leadership. He was also head of the firm's thought leadership group (TAG). His prior career involved investment consulting for Hewitt, heading the Mercer investment practice, and leading the business development and quantitative investment functions at Gartmore Investment Management. He is the author of a number of papers on asset allocation policy, manager selection and governance. He is on the board of the CFA Institute and INQUIRE (the institute for quantitative investment research) and the editorial board of MSCI. Mr. Urwin has a degree in mathematics and a master's degree in applied statistics from Oxford University. He qualified as a fellow of the Institute of Actuaries in 1983.

Masaharu Usuki is a member of the investment committee of Government Pension Investment Fund of Japan and senior pension economist at NLI Research Institute, a research affiliate of Nippon Life Insurance Company. He has also served as a member of several other public advisory councils and private research panels, and on several investment committees. Mr. Usuki has conducted extensive research in areas of corporate finance, macroeconomic forecasting, banking, and social security. His recent research has focused on pensions, retirement benefits, and pension management. He has worked on issues such as liability-driven investments, long-term risk control within defined-benefit plans, the influence of accounting rules on pension fund investment, and investor behavior in defined-contribution plans. He has authored several books and published numerous articles on pension-related topics. Mr. Usuki graduated from the University of Tokyo, has studied at Harvard Business School, and received a PhD in commercial economics from Senshu University.

Peter Vlaar is the head of corporate asset-liability management and risk policy modeling at All Pensions Group (APG) in the Netherlands, where he is actively involved in the strategic asset allocation choices and in the further development of APG's ALM model. Prior to joining the APG, he worked as a researcher at the Dutch Central Bank (DNB), where he investigated a broad spectrum of topics including monetary transmission in Europe, inflation forecasting, exchange rate economics, and several financial subjects. Since 2003, the main focus of his research has been pension economics. For this purpose, a pension asset and liability model was developed, focusing on the impact of market valuation on optimal pension fund policy. Mr. Vlaar holds a PhD in econometrics from Maastricht University and a master's degree in economics from Vrije Universiteit, Amsterdam.

Jolanta Wysocka is a founding principal and the chief executive officer of Mountain Pacific Group. She is also an active speaker on issues concerning investment, corporate governance, and developments in emerging markets. Ms. Wysocka has more than 20 years of investment experience in portfolio management and research. She served as a portfolio strategist focusing on product structuring and risk management at Russell Investments and as the director of global quantitative equities at Deutsche Asset Management. Formerly, she was a lead emerging markets portfolio manager and member of the Investment Committee of Federated Investors in New York and Parametric Portfolio Associates in Seattle. She managed a top-performing emerging market equity fund between 1993 and 1999. She holds an MS in computer science from Zielona Gora Institute of Technology, Poland.

Juan Yermo has been the head of the Private Pensions Unit in the OECD's Financial Affairs Division since 1999. He manages the research and policy program of the Working Party on Private Pensions, a body that brings together policy makers and the private sector from 37 countries around the world. His work covers issues related to the operation and regulation of privately managed retirement income systems. He has acted as a trustee of the OECD staff pension fund and as an advisor on governance issues to pension funds of other international organizations. Previously, he worked at the World Bank as a consultant on capital markets and pension reform and as an analyst in the Risk Management Department at Bankers Trust. Mr. Yermo has a master's degree in economics from Cambridge University and an MPhil in economics from Oxford University.

Institutional Profiles

The **Alberta Investment Management Corporation (AIMCo)** is one of Canada's largest institutional investment fund managers. It manages $67 billion for Alberta pensions, endowments, and government funds. AIMCo is governed by its board of directors, with the sole objective of inspiring the confidence of Albertans by achieving superior risk-adjusted investment returns. It was established as a crown corporation to continue providing investment management services to various Alberta provincial public sector bodies through a corporate structure. AIMCo manages the funds of only those clients designated by Alberta's minister of finance and enterprise.

All Pensions Group (APG), the Netherlands, is one of the world's largest pension administration organizations, specializing in the administration of collective pensions. APG was incorporated in 2008 to administer the collective pension scheme for the government and educational sectors in the Netherlands. With 2,500 staff, APG administers the pensions of 2.7 million Dutch citizens. Through its subsidiaries, APG Algemene Pensioen Groep N.V. and Cordares N.V., APG provides products and services for pension funds in the areas of pension administration, communication, asset management, management support, and in the field of additional income security. As of mid-2010, APG had $325 billion of assets under management, representing more than 30 percent of all collective pensions in the Netherlands.

The **Australian Prudential Regulation Authority (APRA)** is the prudential regulator of the Australian financial services industry. It oversees banks, credit unions, building societies, general insurance, and reinsurance companies, life insurance, friendly societies, and most members of the superannuation industry. APRA is funded largely by the industries that it supervises. Established in 1998, APRA currently supervises institutions holding approximately $3.6 trillion in assets for 22 million Australian depositors, policy holders, and superannuation fund members.

ATP is Denmark's largest pension scheme, with more than 30 years of experience in administering labor market schemes. The scheme covers almost the entire Danish population and has approximately $76 billion in assets under management. ATP pays pensions to more than 675,000 pensioners and administers contributions for approximately 4.6 million members and clients. The group's responsibilities fall into several categories: hedging activities (managing the hedging portfolio and ensuring optimal hedging of the interest rate risk on the pension liabilities, thereby protecting the bonus potential), investment activities (generating a return high enough to preserve the long-term purchasing power of pensions), and pension activities (setting the terms for pension savings [guarantees], and advising ATP's board on bonus allowances).

The **Central Provident Fund (CPF)**, established in 1955, is a compulsory comprehensive social security savings plan that aims to provide working Singaporeans with a sense of security and confidence in their old age. As of December 2008, the CPF had 3.23 million active members. The CPF is administered by the Central Provident Fund Board, a statutory board under the Ministry of Manpower. The overall scope and benefits of the CPF encompass retirement, health care, home ownership, family protection, and asset enhancement. Total member assets as of March 2010 were $122.5 billion.

The **Government Pension Investment Fund (GPIF), Japan**, is a pension fund established in 2006 as an independent administrative institution to manage the reserve fund of the Government Pension Plan entrusted by the minister of health, labor, and welfare. The size of its portfolio is well above $1 trillion, making the GPIF the world's largest pension fund. The GPIF has defined and appropriately managed the portfolio in order to secure a real investment yield which takes into account various pension financing preconditions and controls the variation risk (on variations in rate of return) within a certain range with the objective of stabilizing pension financing. Its long-term strategic asset allocation includes market investments, fiscal investment and loan program bonds, domestic stocks, international bonds and stocks, and short-term assets.

The **Government Employees Pension Fund (GEPF), South Africa**, established in 1996 through the consolidation of various funds, including the Government Service Pension Fund, is the largest pension fund administrator in Africa, with approximately 1.2 million contributing members and 320,000 pension recipients. On a global level, the GEPF is acknowledged as the 21st largest pension fund in the world, with approximately $100 billion in assets under management. It is a self-administered, defined-benefit pension fund committed to effectively and efficiently providing benefits to members, pensioners, and beneficiaries. The GEPF is the largest asset portfolio of the Public Investment Corporation (PIC), which acts as its investment portfolio manager. The PIC invests in five asset classes: fixed-interest instruments, equities, money market, property (commercial and residential), and other investment instruments.

Government Pension Fund (GPF), Thailand, is the first public sector defined-contribution fund in Thailand, established in 1997. The objectives of the GPF include ensuring member benefits upon retirement, encouraging member savings, and providing members with other benefits. The GPF investment philosophy emphasizes the safety of the principal fund, good returns that outperform the long-term inflation rate, appropriate asset allocation, diversified investment choices that survive changes in global markets, and an efficient investment control and supervision process. As of the end of 2008, the GPF had $11.2 billion in assets under management.

Independent Fiduciary Services (IFS) is a highly specialized investment advisory firm based in Washington, D.C. IFS advises public (domestic and international) and private institutional investment funds and their fiduciaries. The firm is independent and fully aligned with its clients. IFS provides three lines of service: operational reviews and "fiduciary audits;" ongoing investment consulting to defined-benefit, defined-contribution, and welfare plans advising on investment policy, asset allocation, manager search, custody, and performance evaluation; and fiduciary decision-making assignments.

King Abdullah University of Science and Technology Investment Management Company (KAUST IMC) is a wholly owned subsidiary of the university and is responsible for the investment strategy of its endowment fund. It is governed by an independent board of directors that includes some of the most accomplished and respected leaders of the global investment community. This educational endowment, one of the largest in the world with over $10 billion in assets under management, is essential to KAUST's core mission: to enable advances in science and technology that positively transform the lives of people in Saudi Arabia, the Middle East, and the world.

The **Ministry of Labor, Employment, and Social Security of Argentina** has an objective of serving the governmental administration in the elaboration and execution of public policies. Nevertheless, its primary purpose is to serve citizens by acting as a nexus between the state, government, and society. Its functions are to elaborate, design, administer, govern, and control policies for all areas of labor and labor relations, employment, vocational training, and social security. The Ministry of Labor, Employment, and Social Security also assists the president of Argentina in all issues related to labor conditions and relations, promotion of employment, social security, and the legal regime of worker associations and employer associations.

Ministry of Social Security and Welfare, Chile, regulates and supervises the enforcement of social security benefits and guarantees that the rights of workers, retirees, and their families are respected. The Office of the Superintendent of Social Security, a branch within the Ministry of Social Security and Welfare, addresses inquiries, complaints, and appeals, and proposes measures for the improvement of the Chilean Social Security System. It regulates compensation funds, workers compensation, and occupational diseases insurance, and welfare services for public sector employees, and oversees the committees for health and safety.

Mountain Pacific Group (MPG) is an independent investment management company focused on assisting large, sophisticated institutions in attaining their investment goals and objectives. By leveraging sophisticated quantitative techniques, it manages a mix of highly scalable, alpha-seeking strategies to create customized, liability-focused, adaptive solutions. MPG's core competency is the ability to measure and manage financial risks. It adds value by forecasting risk, as opposed to the more traditional approach of forecasting return. This investment theme manifests itself in the portfolio construction process, which aids in enhancing returns and managing tail risk. MPG offers a highly differentiated, low-risk, and complementary approach to traditional active investment management styles.

The **National Pension Service (NPS)** of the Republic of Korea is the third largest pension fund in the world in terms of assets under management. Since its introduction in 1988, NPS has experienced phenomenal growth, reaching $312 billion of assets under management as of September 2010. NPS is charged with administering a contributory, partially funded, defined-benefit social security scheme covering all residents in Korea. Currently, 18 million people, or nearly 40 percent of the nation's total population, are insured under the national pension scheme, while the number of beneficiaries is expected to exceed 3 million. Korea's minister for health has supervisory responsibility for NPS.

The **New Zealand Superannuation Fund (NZSF)** is a crown-owned fund created by an act of the New Zealand Parliament in 2001 in order to partially provide for the future costs of New Zealand superannuation payments. The investment program, financed by capital contributions from the government, commenced with $2.4 billion in cash. The government plans to allocate, on average, $1.5 billion a year to the NZSF over the next 20 years. In 2010, NZSF's assets under management reached $11 billion.

Ontario Municipal Employees Retirement System (OMERS) is one of Canada's leading pension funds, with more than $48 billion in net investment assets as of December 31, 2009. OMERS was established in 1962 to serve local government employees across Ontario. Today, it represents approximately 900 employers and 400,000 members, retirees, and survivors. As one of the largest institutional investors in Canada, it manages a diversified global portfolio of more than 2,800 stocks and bonds as well as real estate, infrastructure, and private equity investments. Through highly skilled investment professionals, its innovative asset mix consistently yields superior returns, which fund about 70 percent of the plan over the long term, while the remaining 30 percent comes from employee and employer contributions.

The **Organisation for Economic Co-operation and Development (OECD)**, established in 1961, is an international organization that brings together the governments of 31 (mostly high-income) countries committed to democracy and the market economy from around the world to support sustainable economic growth, boost employment, raise living standards, maintain financial stability, assist other countries' economic development, and contribute to growth in world trade. The OECD provides a setting where governments compare policy experiences, seek answers to common problems, identify good practice, and coordinate domestic and international policies.

The **Pensions Board of Ireland** is a statutory body set up under the Pensions Act, 1990, to regulate occupational pension schemes, trust retirement annuity contracts, and personal retirement savings accounts in Ireland. Part of the Pensions Board's statutory role is to monitor and supervise operation of the Pensions Act. It also serves as an advisory body to the minister for social and family affairs on pension matters. The Pensions Board's duties fall into four general areas: (1) to promote the security and protection of members of occupational pension schemes and contributors to personal retirement savings accounts, in accordance with the Pensions Act, 1990; (2) to promote the development of efficient national pension structures;

(3) to promote a level of participation in the national pension system that enables all citizens to acquire an adequate retirement income; and (4) to provide information and authoritative guidance to relevant parties in support of pension security, structures, and participation.

Queensland Investment Corporation (QIC) is the leading provider of dynamic investment solutions for super funds and other institutional investors in Australia. QIC excels at developing an intimate knowledge of its clients' investment goals and creating and adapting tailored investment solutions that continue to perform well over time. The company offers extensive experience, global capability, and a strong track record of innovation for clients, offering a broad range of solutions across equities, fixed interest, international property, infrastructure, absolute return strategies, and capital and exposure management. QIC commenced operations in 1989 and was formally established in 1991. Since then, it has grown to be one of the largest institutional investment managers in Australia, with more than 70 institutional clients and $53 billion in funds under management as of April 30, 2010.

The **Queensland Superannuation Fund (QSuper)** is a leading fund within the Australian superannuation industry. QSuper has more than 530,000 members and more than $25.3 billion in funds under management. QSuper offers nine investment options to suit its members' needs and cooperates with other industry leaders on various investment issues. Its strategic partners include the Queensland Investment Corporation in the investment management area, QInvest Limited in financial planning, and Watson Wyatt Australia Pty Ltd in investment consultancy.

The **Rotman International Centre for Pension Management (ICPM)** is a research center at the Joseph L. Rotman School of Management, University of Toronto, supported by an international consortium of 15 major pension organizations. The ICPM is recognized as a global catalyst for improving pension management. Through its research funding, discussion forums, and publications, the ICPM produces a steady stream of innovative insights into optimal pension system design and the effective management of pension delivery organizations. Using "Integrative Investment Theory" as its guide, research and discussion topics focus on agency costs, governance and organization design, investment beliefs, risk measurement and management, and strategy implementation. Through these activities, the ICPM also creates opportunities to raise pension-related content in regular and executive courses at the Rotman School of Management and other education-oriented institutions and forums around the world.

The **Storebrand Group**, with roots back to 1767, is a leading player in the Nordic markets for pensions, life and health insurance, banking, and asset management. Based in Norway, Storebrand has also established life insurance, asset management, and health insurance activities in Sweden. Following the acquisition of the Swedish life insurance and pension provider SPP in December 2007, Storebrand is now the Nordic region's leading provider of life insurance and pensions. Its activities are carried out through four main business areas: life insurance, property and casualty insurance, asset management, and banking.

Towers Watson is a leading global professional services company that helps organizations improve performance through effective people, risk, and financial management. With 14,000 associates around the world, Towers Watson offers solutions in the areas of employee benefits, talent management, rewards, and risk and capital management.

The **United Nations Joint Staff Pension Fund (UNJSPF)** was established by the United Nations General Assembly in 1949 to provide retirement, death, disability, and related benefits for staff of the United Nations and other select international organizations. As of 2010, UNJSPF has $32 billion in assets and serves 23 member organizations, with 106,600 active participants and 58,100 beneficiaries. UNJSPF continues to outperform the policy benchmark using effective stock selection and periodic rebalancing of assets to maintain its long-term investment objective. UNJSPF holds equity, bonds, real estate, and short-term investments in 41 countries and 7 international/regional institutions, and 27 currencies.

The **World Bank Treasury** embodies over 60 years of experience as financial manager for the World Bank Group and other official sector institutions. The Treasury manages about $115 billion in assets for the World Bank Group and external clients, including pension assets. These assets are invested in global markets across a broad spectrum of asset classes, including high-grade global fixed income, global equities, emerging market bonds and equities, private equity, real estate, hedge funds, timber, commodities, and infrastructure. About 80 percent of the assets are managed in house (primarily high-grade global fixed income), while the other assets are managed by external investment managers. The Treasury also manages more than a $100 billion debt portfolio for the International Bank for Reconstruction and Development (IBRD) and executes more than $20 billion in derivatives transactions annually for IBRD's balance sheet and on behalf of clients. In addition to managing assets, arranging bond market financings, and promoting innovative and cost-effective financing and risk management, the Treasury provides advisory services and training to official sector investment managers (central banks, pension funds, sovereign wealth funds) to help countries efficiently manage foreign currency reserves and other long-term, multi-asset class investment portfolios. The focus is on building a governance and risk management framework that balances return objectives with prudent risk management and controls. The World Bank Treasury has over 20 years of experience in consulting and capacity building with official sector asset managers and manages assets for over 40 World Bank Group and other official sector institutions.

Index

V